ORDERING WISDOM
The Hierarchy of Philosophical Discourses in Aquinas

"Multitudinis usus, quem in rebus nominandis sequendum Philosophus censet, communiter obtinuit, ut sapientes dicantur qui res directe ordinant et eas bene gubernant. Unde, inter alia quae homines de sapiente concipiunt, a Philosopho ponitur, quod sapientis est ordinare."

Summa Contra Gentiles
I, c.1, n.2

PUBLICATIONS IN MEDIEVAL STUDIES
THE MEDIEVAL INSTITUTE
THE UNIVERSITY OF NOTRE DAME
EDITED BY
RALPH MCINERNY

*A Series Founded by Philip S. Moore, C.S.C.†,
Joseph N. Garvin, C.S.C.†,
and A. L. Gabriel*

XXIV

ORDERING WISDOM
*The Hierarchy
of Philosophical
Discourses in Aquinas*

MARK D. JORDAN

UNIVERSITY OF NOTRE DAME PRESS
NOTRE DAME 1986

Library of Congress Cataloging-in-Publication Data

Jordan, Mark D.
    Ordering wisdom.

    (Publications in medieval studies; 24)
    Bibliography: p.
    Includes index.
    1. Thomas, Aquinas, Saint, 1225?–1274.
2. Languages—Philosophy—History. I. Title.
II. Series.
B765.T54J56   1986   189'.4   86-40335
ISBN 0-268-01500-7

Manufactured in the United States of America

ACKNOWLEDGMENTS

Cardinal Cajetan, they say, began his study of the *Summa* as a boy. I came to the text at least ten years older and much poorer in gifts. But I have not been poorer in teachers, colleagues, or patrons. The distant origins of this study lie in conversations with Jacob Klein, Robert Neidorf, and Louis Mackey, who would be surprised to see their names together. Outlines and early drafts were written during a National Endowment for the Humanities summer seminar directed by John Murdoch. The final writing was supported in part by a grant from the De Rancé Foundation, through the American Catholic Philosophical Association, which allowed me to spend the best part of a summer with the late Fr. James Weisheipl. The final draft of the book was read by Fr. Weisheipl and by two of my colleagues, Kent Emery, Jr. and Francis R. Swietek. Each provided careful criticism and correction. If I have not been able to see my way through to agreeing with them in all cases, let it be attributed to my contumacy and not to their learning.

During the five years of reading and writing, I have been struck by the remarkable courtesy with which great libraries welcome perfect strangers. I am particularly grateful to the staffs of the Perry-Castañeda Library in the University of Texas, to the Widener Library in Harvard University, and to the superb working collection of the Pontifical Institute of Medieval Studies.

Earlier versions of parts of Chapter 2 appeared in *The New Scholasticism*. An earlier French version of parts of Chapter 3 was published by the *Revue Thomiste*. I thank the editors, Ralph McInerny and Fr. Marie-Vincent Leroy, for their encouragement and for their kind permission to incorporate revised forms of some of that material into this book.

The manuscript was typed and retyped by Susan Martin and Alice Osberger. Jean Oesterle served both as a rigorous copy editor and as a philosophic reader. Brendan Kelly and Gregory Froelich checked the final version with great care. My thanks to all.

To Sofia Bozhidarovna, who is both wise and God-given, I dedicate whatever there is here of a book.

A NOTE ON CITATIONS TO AQUINAS

There is no single best edition for the works of Thomas Aquinas. When finished, the Leonine *Opera omnia* (Rome, 1882-) will be a superb edition of the complete works. But the Leonine is now unfinished in two senses. First, not all of Thomas's works have been edited in the series. Second, those works published before 1950 need to be revised in varying degrees. The best complete edition now available is that compiled by Roberto Busa, which appeared as a supplement to the *Index Thomisticus: Sancti Thomae Aquinatis Opera omnia* (Stuttgart — Bad Canstatt, 1980). This edition contains the texts used as the basis for the *Index*, the best available as of December, 1971. Busa used as many of the Leonine texts as he could, both the printed editions of the 'old' and 'new' series and the typescripts of then unpublished volumes. He also sought out a number of unpublished emendations for other printed versions. Thus, although Busa's text does not have the apparatus of a critical edition, it is certainly based on several types of critical editions.

Faced with an unhappy choice, I have adopted a split system of citation. I will cite first according to the medieval textual divisions, that is by Books and *lectiones*, by Questions and Articles, as these are marked in Busa's edition. I will add to these in all cases a reference to the volume, page, and column numbers in Busa (abbreviated as EB). Where there are significant discrepancies in a Leonine text published since Busa's versions were gathered, I will add a citation to the Leonine edition (abbreviated as EL), citing volume, page, and line numbers. I will also note discrepancies for the *Scriptum* on the *Sentences*, for which cases I will add to the citation in Busa (who uses the Parma text) a second citation to the edition of Mandonnet and Moos (1929-1947).

The citations to Thomas will use the following abbreviations, for which I give short titles and a reference to the number in Weisheipl's "Brief Catalogue," as in his *Friar Thomas*:

Catena   *Catena aurea* (Weisheipl, #31)

Contra err.	*Contra errores graecorum* (#63)
Contra gent.	*Summa contra gentiles* (#2)
Contra impugn.	*Contra impugnantes Dei cultum* (#52)
De ente	*De ente et essentia* (#58)
De fall.	*De fallaciis* (#57)
De mixt.	*De mixtione elementorum* (#74)
De motu	*De motu cordis* (#73)
De subst. sep.	*De substantiis separatis* (#61)
In Job	*Expositio in Job* (#25)
Post. Isaiam	*Postilla super Isaiam* (#28)
Post. Jeremiam	*Postillla super Jeremiam* (#29)
Post. Threnos	*Postilla super Threnos* (#30)
Q.D. De anima	*Quaestiones de anima* (#8)
Q.D. De malo	*Quaestiones de malo* (#6)
Q.D. De pot.	*Quaestiones de potentia* (#5)
Q.D. De verit.	*Quaestiones de veritate* (#4)
Q.D. De virt. comm.	*Quaestiones de virtutibus in commune* (#9)
Quodl.	*Quaestiones quodlibetales* (#12-24)
Resp. art. 36	*Responsio de articulis 36* (#76)
Resp. art. 42	*Responsio de articulis 42* (#65)
Resp. art. 108	*Responsio de articulis 108* (#64)
Sent. De caelo	*Sententia De caelo et mundo* (#39)
Sent. Ethic.	*Sententia libri Ethicorum* (#46)
Sent. Pol.	*Sententia libri Politicorum* (#47)
Summa theol.	*Summa theologiae* (#3)
Super Ave	*Super Ave Maria* (#88)
Super Coloss.	*Super ad Colossenses* (#34)
Super Credo	*Super Credo in Deum* (#86)
Super De anima	*Super De anima* (#42)
Super De caus.	*Super librum De causis* (#51)
Super De gen.	*Super De generatione et corruptione* (#40)
Super De hebd.	*Super librum Boethii De hebdomadibus* (#49)
Super De Trin.	*Super librum Boethii De Trinitate* (#48)
Super Galat.	*Super ad Galatas* (#34)
Super Hebreos	*Super ad Hebreos* (#34)
Super I Cor.	*Super I ad Corinthios* (#34)

Super II Tim.	*Super II ad Timotheum* (#34)
Super Joh.	*Lectura super Johannem* (#33)
Super Matt.	*Lectura super Mattaeum* (#32)
Super Meta.	*Super Metaphysicam* (#44)
Super Meteor.	*Super Meteora* (#41)
Super Peri	*Super Peri hermeneias* (#36)
Super Phys.	*Super Physicam* (#38)
Super Post. An.	*Super Posteriora Analytica* (#37)
Super Sent.	*Super libros Sententiarum* (#1)

TABLE OF CONTENTS

INTRODUCTION

Aquinas had not been dead five years when concerted disputes began over what he had said. These were indeed disputes about his correctness, but they were also and persistently disputes about how he ought to be read. It was sometimes the question of how to read an argument, sometimes the question of how to place the whole of his inquiry. Such disputes persisted because Aquinas's works made many hidden demands on diligence in reading. Not the least of these was the demand that the reader recognize the limit to the inquiry in particular texts. The limit seemed to blur as changes in thinking effaced the conventions according to which Thomas had written. It is almost invisible today, when the reader is accustomed to the enormous claims of both post-Cartesian philosophy and an established 'neo-Thomism'.

In Aquinas, the limit to philosophy is set explicitly by theological doctrine. Theology uses sources and procedures which cannot be used by philosophy, since philosophy cannot assume the Christian's faith in a revelation mediated by tradition. The same limit is traced implicitly but no less strictly by Aquinas's holding that the human soul has the weakest intellectual powers. It is an intelligence confined through the body to the 'shadows' of abstractive knowledge. In Aquinas's writing, then, the discourses of philosophy must be both limited and preparatory. What is more interesting, Aquinas seems to think that philosophical discourse can know its own limitation without losing confidence in its being philosophy. He offers philosophical discourses as sufficient, speculative accounts which cannot in principle be complete. Philosophy is denied finality by human failing, both natural and sinful, but it remains philosophy nonetheless.

What conception of philosophical discourses is it which allows Aquinas to teach coherently both their incompleteness and their sufficiency? It is not, I think, simply one of the modern conceptions of philosophy. Thomas learned from his predecessors not only a set of doctrines or premises, but also an example of inquiry on the way to wisdom. He took to himself particularly the Aristotelian care in teaching philosophy. Thomas traces this care in his commentaries on Aristotle; he practices it in his own composition. The *ordo disciplinae*, the forms of dispute, the expositor's attention to grammar — these are samples in Thomas's own works of the pedagogical view of philosophy. The features of the pedagogy will be studied below. I can suggest now that the pedagogical emphasis allows philosophy to be both adequate and incomplete, to be a certain sort of wisdom which is nonetheless itself open to the perfecting wisdom promised in revelation.

I will want to argue below that philosophy's pedagogical ordering to revelation is seen not only in certain philosophical doctrines, but also in the character of philosophical discourses at various steps in the hierarchy of speculative sciences. The pedagogy of philosophy is embodied in the different ways that philosophical discourses mean what they teach. Exegetically, this assertion points to the rule that Thomas's works ought to be read as wholes, as just the sorts of integral works they are. Substantively, it amounts to the claim that the manner of Thomas's teaching is as significant as the final formulations to which he concludes. The order of discourses which undergirds the corpus is meant to embody a philosophic *disciplina* which leads the best reader not only upwards through a series of truths to be apprehended, but also upwards through modes of discourse which correspond to types of knowing.

It is not new to claim that the question of philosophic language is somehow decisive for a correct reading of Thomas. There is a small group of earlier works that makes or presupposes the argument.[1] Yet the claim is still fresh enough to be worth rehearsing again and misleading enough to need more rigorous examination. Nor is it new to insist upon the general importance of language in medieval philosophy, though there is an opposite failing here. In the recent emphasis on terminist logic, on the literature of *insolubilia, sophismata*, and infinitessimal sequences, one risks forgetting the more substantial connections between logico-grammatical speculation and metaphysics. However one judges them in the authors of the fourteenth century, such connections are paramount for Aquinas.

Ernest Moody said some years ago that contemporary logic had most to learn from the medievals about the semantics of natural language.[2] Many Latin writers of the twelfth and thirteenth centuries saw clearly those uses of natural language which are of greatest metaphysical interest. It is by relying on such a tradition of speculation in philosophical grammar that Aquinas was able to write as he did. He is not, of course, explicitly or chiefly a logician, except in that sense in which a thirteenth-century Master of Theology at Paris was perforce a logician. On the contrary, it is just because the semantic insights are applied implicitly and concretely in his writings that Aquinas becomes a useful guide in understanding philosophical language as pedagogical.

The embodiment of philosophic pedagogy in a hierarchy of discourses can be studied only through a close rereading of typical texts drawn from the several steps of the hierarchy. Since my intention is to concentrate on the rereading, I will not pretend to give a general account of what was said about philosophy by Aquinas's predecessors, whether remote or immediate. It will not be possible to read Aquinas well, of course, without seeing that the details of his arguments are frequently intelligible only as gestures towards or against certain other positions and certain other texts. I will therefore include from his sources what seems essential for the rereading. Given the conservatism of medieval teaching, this rule will cover much. Still, I will exclude what is not essential and shall reject altogether causal inferences in the intellectual order that rely on historical reductions.

A similar principle of exclusion will be invoked with regard to the question of Thomas's development. I will note, of course, those apparent discrepancies within the Thomist corpus that are pertinent to the discussion. But I will not try to locate these discrepancies within a narrative hypothesis about doctrinal development. Although there are many signs of Thomas's having learned as he continued to study, there is no *prima facie* evidence of some grand revolution in his thought. The 'late' Aquinas is distinguished from the 'early' not by a chronology of reversed opinions but by a maturity in speculative virtue. It will be the case, not coincidentally, that most of the texts with which I work will be those of Thomas's later years.

A third principle of exclusion must apply to the mass of existing commentary. The history of Thomism is counted a separate field; Thomistic bibliography fills its own yearbooks. Those who are interested by the advances and retreats in the reading of Aquinas can begin by consulting the extensive standard bibliographies.³ I will cite below only those secondary works that enter into the argument as interlocutors.

A fourth principle of exclusion will be invoked with regard to neo-Thomism and its controversies. It is a difficult question, how far the neo-Thomism established in the nineteenth century understood itself as an exegesis of Aquinas and how far as a supplement to him. De Wulf, for example, insists upon the distinction between neo-Scholasticism and paleo-Scholasticism, the second of which he regards as an impossible nostalgia for times best past.⁴ My intention is to interpret the texts of Aquinas, faithfully and philosophically, without attempting to make instant capital of them for contemporary polemics. I must, then, set aside the many monographs that attempt to construct a philosophical grammar or method *ad mentem sancti Thomae*. It is not possible to discover the *mens*, in any case, without having mastered the *littera*.

Beyond these four exclusions, it remains to be said that I do not imagine that a definitive or comprehensive 'solution' can be found for the question about the nature of philosophical discourse in Aquinas. Thus I do not pretend to discuss every pertinent passage, nor even to exhaust the main ones. I do intend to provide a set of local readings which, taken together, ought to trace the whole hierarchy of philosophical discourses with which Thomas is concerned. The following chapters fall, then, somewhere between an anthology of case studies and the comprehensive treatise; they are offered as limited inquiries into the main structures of the corpus so far as they can be considered to be philosophical. The passages described are only examples of the shapes of those structures. Thus, the book is not a summary of Thomas's philosophical discourse. It intends only to be a typology of the sorts of philosophical discourse in his writings.

The division of the work will be straightforward. I will begin with a chapter on Aquinas's theory of discourse in its most general aspect, that is, the treatment of the elements in a philosophical account of linguistic meaning. The second chapter will then take up the more detailed and prescriptive representation of language given by the three liberal arts of the *trivium*. This will complete the consideration of the elements and materials for philosophic discourse. There will follow three chapters which consider, in ascending order of semantic complexity, the discourses comprised by the first and third of the speculative 'sciences'. The double discourse of physics considers both matter and soul; the discourse of metaphysics reaches further, by a kind of negation, to separate being. From the consideration of metaphysics, it is no real step to the question of the divine names, which is the highest point of philosophical thought and the lowest of theological. With the names, the typology of speculative discourses is complete. The last chapter considers the consequences of their ambiguous closure for Aquinas's 'authorship'.

PART ONE
ELEMENTS OF
PHILOSOPHICAL DISCOURSE

CHAPTER 1

Words and Signs

Aquinas wrote no treatise on philosophical language. Even of logical treatises loosely construed, he left few by the standards of his successors. There may be two works in his own voice on logical matters, but both would seem to have been written before Thomas had turned twenty.[1] The *De fallaciis ad quosdam nobiles artistas* and an epistolary extract *De propositionibus modalibus* are, if by Thomas, the works of an exceptional student who is mastering the received logical teaching. Later, near the end of his life, Aquinas wrote two expositions of treatises from the Aristotelian Organon, the *Sententia super Posteriora Analytica* and the *Sententia super Peri Hermeneias*.[2] These expositions are accomplished acts of the mature teacher, but they elude easy interpretation for that very reason. Besides these early and late works, there are several treatises with logical content which are dubiously ascribed to Aquinas; together they make up a few dozen pages.[3] Even if all of the *dubia* were to be proved authentic, the explicitly logical and linguistic writings by Aquinas would remain few in number. They would also remain opaque: the original works are imitative and the commentaries pose persistent exegetical difficulties.

The lack of a synthetic treatment of questions about philosophic language is not entirely regrettable. It can serve as a reminder, from the very start, of the circumstances surrounding Thomas's writing. It recalls the fact that Thomas was a Master of Theology very much at the service of his order. He does not seem to have taught as a Master of Arts, despite the strong injunctions binding new Masters to do so.[4] Moreover, Aquinas wrote relatively little in the genres of the arts faculty; the literary shapes of his greatest works are taken from the patterns of academic theology. So it would have been odd, even improper, for Aquinas to dwell on the arts as such. One remembers the admonition, *non est consenescendum in artibus*, and the frequent disruptions caused during Aquinas's life by those at Paris who tried to make the arts sovereign in the hierarchy of learning.[5]

The most interesting exception to the rule that Aquinas writes in the genres and with the voice of an academic theologian would seem to be found in the Aristotelian commentaries. The exception is ambiguous because of several peculiarities in the commentaries' composition. Except for the commentary on the *Metaphysics*, the expositions were written within the last five years of Aquinas's life.[6] The commentary on the *Metaphysics* was finished in these same years.[7] Together the commentaries are usually taken as showing Aquinas's final desire to recover the original sense of Aristotle — hence the many hagiographic stories of his collaboration with the translator William of Moerbeke. Aquinas employs the new translations, which he cites as if they were the Greek itself,[8] to free the reading of Aristotle from the distortions of the Islamic exegetes, especially Averroes. What is not so often said is that Aquinas is dependent, in varying degrees and combinations, on the newly translated late Greek commentators.[9] Written at a great pace in a pressed time, Aquinas's commentaries are not chiefly a private meditation on Aristotle. They are the public attempt to balance the distortions of a faddish academic exegesis against a more authentic one.[10] The attempt requires detailed textual division and specific clarification; it makes heuristic networks for the dialectically dispersed and aphoristic Aristotelian texts.

The attention to detail leaves three large questions without explicit answers. The first question concerns Aquinas's intention in writing the Aristotelian commentaries: How did he understand his role as commentator? It is possible to imagine plausible motives for Aquinas by considering the controversies then troubling the University of Paris as well as his probable role in them.[11] But such motives remain conjectural and must be tested against the considerable ambivalence in the Latin tradition of commenting on Aristotle. Albert's disclaimers in his commentaries, for instance, must complicate the reading of those by Thomas.[12]

The second large question which is not answered explicitly in the commentaries asks how far what is said in them can be used as evidence of Aquinas's own thought. All of the writings of Aquinas are fugues in which dissonant technical vocabularies are brought into some truthfully harmonious relation, which is not a synthesis. Aquinas will frequently adjust his vocabulary from one counter-argument to the next, from an *ad primum* to an *ad secundum*. This does not mean that the result is a pastiche in which there is no philosophy.[13] The whole thrust of Aquinas's work is, rather, a creative thinking in and through the tradition. Such complexities are only compounded in the commentaries on Aristotle. There is no simple rule for separating exposition from doctrine; there is no way to state a single, univocal intention. On the contrary, Aquinas embodies the complexity of the ancient genre of the commentary just as he reflects the varied history of the reception of Aristotle by the Latin West.

The third question follows: What is the exact character of Aquinas's 'Aristotelianism'?[14] After the period in which Boethius's versions of the logical works held sway, there are two receptions in the West of the Aristotelian corpus. To speak simply, the first is seen most clearly in the twelfth century and comes through Arabic sources and with Arabic commentary. Its protagonists are such translators as Gundissalinus, Hermann of Carinthia, and Gerard of Cremona. The second reception is seen more clearly in the latter half of the thirteenth century and is made from the Greek. Its famous protagonist is William of Moerbeke, but there are also forerunners like James of Venice in the twelfth century.[15] The difference between the two entries, Arabic and Greek, is not only chronological or philological. It is specifically philosophical. Aquinas seems himself to have moved in part from the Arabic to the Greek reception in the course of his reading of Aristotle. One might view this as a foreshadowing of the historical purism of the Renaissance Peripatetics. It is, at least, a third difficulty in using the Aristotelian commentaries as univocal sources for Aquinas's own philosophical doctrine in logic or in any other matter. The three questions together show how important it is that one understand the circumstances of Thomas's academic writing.

If the absence of substantial works in the arts of the *trivium* recalls Thomas's service as a Dominican Master of Theology, it also recalls the confusing circumstances of his early education. It is not known what curriculum Thomas followed at Naples.[16] His early biographers have preserved the names of two of his Arts masters: an unknown Martin, who taught him grammar and

Peter of Ireland, who taught him natural philosophy.[17] The sources disagree over whether it was Martin or Peter who taught logic.[18] There have been unsuccessful attempts to identify writings by this Martin.[19] There are at least three extant works by Peter of Ireland.[20] Portions of two of them have been edited, but they are unsteady guides in reconstructing Thomas's curriculum. The public determination by Peter of a question in physics dates from the 1260's and could be used only with great caution in characterizing his teaching at Naples some thirty years earlier.[21] More promising is the division of philosophy which introduces Peter's exposition of the *Peri Hermeneias*, a work dating from around mid-century.[22]

The division is indebted to similar schemes in Avicenna's *Logica* and the *De divisione philosophiae* of Gundissalinus.[23] The text divides philosophy into practical and theoretical; theoretical philosophy is divided into the Aristotelian triplet of physics, mathematics, and metaphysics by reference to the 'mixture' with matter in the objects of theory.[24] More pertinent to an arts curriculum would be Peter's treatment of the claim that logic is a part of philosophy. It is not part of theory or practice, he reasons, but it is the "instrumentum philosophiae" so far as it makes the unknown to be known.[25] The subject-matter of logic is thus divided between the knowledge of apprehension and the knowledge of judgment. The first is produced from premises already known, such as definition, description, sign, and example. The second knowledge, that of judgment, is called *ratio* and comprises induction, syllogism, enthymeme, and other, weaker ways towards conviction.[26] So far the doctrine on logic. As regards it *auctoritates*, there are, in the portion edited so far, explicit references to the logical writings of Avicenna, Boethius, Porphyry, and Aristotle. The *libri naturales* of Aristotle and Avicenna also appear, as does Priscian's *Institutiones*. There are no citations to Averroes.

It is difficult to draw any strong conclusion about what Thomas may have studied with Peter of Ireland. Certainly Peter knew the Aristotle recently received from the Arabs and used that knowledge in teaching the *trivium*. Indeed, Thomas may have received an education at Naples which was informed by the *libri naturales* of the Aristotelian corpus to a greater extent than would have been true at the same time in northern Europe.

It may also be that the education was more technical. With regard to the *trivium*, Father Weisheipl writes that the studies at Naples seem to have taught Thomas "a great deal about grammar and rhetoric" if one can judge from his "beautiful use of the *cursus*" and "his remarkable poetry."[27] Weisheipl might also have added that there was a strong tradition of applied rhetoric at the Italian universities, which included a broad training in letters.[28] There are, then, two impressions of the *trivium* at Naples. The first is that it was colored by the Arabic Aristotle, whose *libri naturales* appear perhaps especially as construed by Avicenna. The second impression is that the *trivium* was connected to the rhetorical and literary ferment also evident in the northern Italian universities. The two impressions may be seen as the axes of the cultural confluence in Naples. They may also be seen as putting an emphasis on the concrete character of pedagogical or persuasive discourse.

Before Naples, Thomas was an oblate at Monte Cassino. It was at the abbey that he learned his letters. He doubtless also learned something of the Benedictine literary tradition, though he would have been rather young for anything beyond a technical relation to poetry.[29] Monte Cassino itself, moreover, was not without several centuries of concern for preserving the physical learning of antiquity. In the eleventh century, the abbey had provided a home for Constantine the African and had probably helped secure for him Byzantine and Arabic exemplars of the medical works which he translated so quickly.[30] Both Monte Cassino and Naples continued to benefit in the twelfth and early thirteenth centuries from the proximity of the medical school at Salerno.[31] Thomas's education at Monte Cassino could have encouraged in him too that interest in physical and medical knowledge which marks the intellectual circles of the Norman kingdom of Sicily during his youth. Whether at Monte Cassino or at Naples, Thomas was not taught by the poet grammarians of Orléans or by the dialecticians of Paris. His approach to discourse would remain that of an induction from the actual discourses of the speculative sciences and especially of physics. The matter for his *trivium* was the matter of Aristotle's treatises about the world. It is in them that Thomas sees philosophical language working and not in cosmological poetry or artificial analyses of syntax.

   The biographical account would be complicated by Thomas's early studies as a Dominican, especially because of the difficulty of getting any detailed view on Albert's teaching of Thomas. During Thomas's first years in Paris, Albert had in hand the project of commenting on the Dionysian corpus.[32] Albert lectured on the *Celestial Hierarchy* before leaving for Cologne, Thomas with him. Thomas would hear Albert on each of the Dionysian works before returning to Paris in 1252. Indeed, he kept his own copies of Albert's expositions until his death.[33] What could be further from the concrete and particular Neapolitan Aristotle than Pseudo-Dionysius? Yet the first few pages of Albert's exposition of the *Celestial Hierarchy* contain, besides the grammarian's pattern of the *accessus*,[34] four substantive references to Aristotle, two to Boethius, and one to Averroes.[35] Even Albert's explanation of Scriptural or theological meaning stresses its multiple, concrete appearance.[36] Too little is known of Thomas's other work at Paris during these years to allow large conclusions, but one can say at least that the passage from Naples to Paris need not have required a denial of the multiplicity and specificity of language. What the passage meant positively for Thomas's grasp of language will be better known, of course, when Albert is better read.

   Thus, the absence of a synthetic treatment of logical and linguistic matters recalls the circumstances of Thomas's teaching and his own early learning. He taught language and learned it by induction from concrete discourses, especially those of Aristotelian science. But the absence of a synthetic treatment does not imply that there is no evidence in Thomas's corpus for a satisfactory account of language in general along the lines of the *trivium*. Rather, the evidence comes in unexpected places and unusual forms. Thomas presents one of his most lucid recapitulations of semantic doctrine, for example, in a reply to a list of theological points given him by the Dominican Master General.[37] Within the structure of Aquinas's writings, in their ubiquitous use of logical and grammatical devices, in the diversity of their modes of discourse, there is much to consider. Too much, indeed, to be synthesized. The most that can be done compendiously is to describe the starting-points of Aquinas's thought about language and then to suggest a few of their consequences. It is safest to begin with the surface of language; for Aquinas, this is to begin with the expressive nature of words as signs.

1.1 WORDS

The great occasion on which the medieval Aristotelians could discuss questions of linguistic meaning came while expounding Aristotle's *Peri Hermeneias*. Aquinas takes the occasion as readily as his predecessors and contemporaries. Before him, the Aristotelian treatise had a long history in ancient thought,[1] then acquired a solitary importance for that early medieval period which was dominated by Boethius as translator and annotator.[2] Thomas's own commentary on the *Peri Hermeneias* appropriates both the ancient and the Boethian traditions. He writes largely in dependence on the eclectic commentary of Ammonius, with its avowed debt to Proclus, but continues to use Boethius's second commentary, the staple of Latin exposition after the eleventh century.

If there is an explanation for linguistic meaning in the original Aristotelian text, it is presupposed rather than constructed. One result of the lengthy tradition of commentary is to give a weight to each of Aristotle's words which a first reading of the text would not discover. Thomas comes to the text knowing what he is looking for and how carefully he must read. A second result is perhaps more important. The constant rereading of Aristotle after the 'recovery' of his pedagogical treatises by Andronicus was a rereading of a *corpus* of writings. The more obscure treatises, among which the *Peri Hermeneias* would surely be included, begin to gather sense from the more discursive treatises. Thus the doctrine on signs in the *Peri Hermeneias* is supplemented not only by the context of the augmented Organon, which includes the *Poetics* and the *Rhetoric*, but also by the context of such works as the *De Anima*, the *Politics* and the *Ethics*. This second result of the commentary tradition can be seen in Aquinas's readiness to read the concerns of the human community into Aristotle's elliptical discussion of word-types.

The treatment of linguistic meaning comes in the very first

chapters of the *Peri Hermeneias*, where Aristotle seems to take up the great issues of Plato's *Cratylus* and of sophistic nominalism. Before turning to those chapters, Aquinas provides a proemium which is a short *accessus ad auctorem*. For him, such an *accessus* is more than a rhetorical orientation. It is a way of connecting any limited exegesis with fundamental philosophical issues. Aquinas follows Ammonius in regarding the treatise as a systematically conceived element in a comprehensive curriculum. So he starts from the division of the operations of the intellect and proceeds to the division of logic. There is more pertinently in the proemium some explanation of Aristotle's title. Aquinas takes the Latin title *De interpretatione* as prefiguring the analysis of linguistic meaning which follows. Boethius holds, according to Thomas, that *interpretatio* means "vox significativa quae per se aliquid significat"; it does not refer to syncategorematic terms or to naturally significant sounds such as cries of pain.[3] Thomas wants to correct Boethius by adding a stricter criterion, which he also finds in Ammonius: "Ille enim interpretari videtur, qui exponit aliquid vel esse verum vel falsum. Et ideo sola oratio enunciativa, in qua verum vel falsum invenitur, interpretatio vocatur.... Non autem hic agitur de nomine et verbo, nisi in quantum sunt partes enunciationis."[4] From the beginning, then, the study of language is set within the limit of the *interpretatio*, a logical entity which seems to have no exact rendering in modern philosophic debate.[5] The distinguishing mark of the *interpretatio* is that it has to do with truth and falsity. Aristotle's treatise will attend just to that mark in order to understand language. So Thomas's whole disposition is to begin from the observation that language is ordinarily used to tell truths. His *interpretatio* is not a logical posit so much as it is the intentional instrument for arriving at that linguistic end.

Some clarification of what it is to be an intentional instrument is offered as Aquinas begins to explain the first chapter of Aristotle's treatise. To the first sentence, a rough list of topics, Aquinas adds a long justification, which treats the list as exhaustive and its members as the principles of knowledge about language as an intentional instrument. The first topics mentioned are "quid sit nomen et quid verbum."[6] Why, Aquinas asks, is it necessary to consider these two again, once they have been

treated in the *Categories*? Following Ammonius, he answers
with a threefold division of the ways of considering simple
locutions (*dictiones*).7 The first division considers those simple
locutions "secundum quod absolute significant simplices intellectus." This consideration informed the *Categories*. The second division considers the simple locutions "secundum rationem, prout sunt partes enunciationis," which perspective
will inform the *Peri Hermeneias* itself. The third division treats
the locutions "secundum quod ex eis constituitur ordo
syllogisticus," a treatment forthcoming in the *Prior Analytics*.
The syllogistic consideration of the locutions may be clear; the
distinction between the other two treatments needs reflection.
It is tempting to identify the study of locutions as signifying absolutely with semantics; the study of locutions as parts of an
enunciatio would then become syntactics. But these identifica-
tions would not be just. The second consideration, which sees a
locution as linguistically modifiable, does stand closer to the
grammatical surface of the language, but it is still a consideration "secundum rationem" of a part of what already possesses
both semantic and syntactic features — the *enunciatio*. A locution can only be understood within that prior unity of the
noetic and linguistic which is truth-telling language. Thus, for
the consideration of speech which corresponds to the *Peri
Hermeneias*, simple locutions "traduntur sub ratione nominis et
verbi: de quorum ratione est quod significent aliquid cum tempore vel sine tempore, et alia hujusmodi, quae pertinent ad rationem dictionum, secundum quod constituunt enuncia-
tionem."8

In the *Peri Hermeneias, nomen* and *verbum* are the elements
out of which it is possible to construct a simple enunciation.
This is reason enough for treating them as subordinating other
parts of speech to themselves (granted that the noun includes
the pronoun, the verb the participle).9 Another reason is that
they sustain the truth-bearing role of the enunciation. The noun
and the verb point to the greater context within which the
enunciation finds its place, that of argument or teaching by
demonstration. The study of enunciations is not a study of
statement-patterns constructed out of *suppositiones* and filled
with nominal possibilities.10 Nor is the study of enunciation the
study of the *vox*, a catalogue of phonemic clusters.11 It is,

rather, a compound of the elements which constitute truth-
bearing discourse, especially in the eminent form of
demonstrative argument. Thomas's treatment of enunciations is
thus neither simply logical nor simply linguistic; it views the
enunciation and its elements as always tending toward the end
of speech in teaching and thinking.

With this prologue, Aquinas can turn to the main Aristotelian
discussion of significant speech. His second *lectio* describes
Aristotle's famous correlation of words, understandings, and
things, arguing from this correlation and the fact of common
understandings to an isomorphism behind linguistic diversity.
The Latin Aristotle begins with three terms — *scriptura, voces,
passiones animae* — to which Aquinas adds a fourth, *res*.
These four are held together in a pattern of communication
which Aquinas explains by describing the genesis of language.
Language is crafted in view of man's political nature, which requires communication. Since man is not only communal but
also intellectual, his communication must go beyond the sense-
bound cries of animals to refer to things distant from sense in
time and space.[12] The genesis of writing can be described on the
same principles, as resulting from the desire to communicate
with hearers distant in either of the two ways. Since writing is
derivative, it does not fall within the scope of philosophical investigation, which turns rather to the exemplars, to the
"significatio vocum, quam est immediata ipsis conceptionibus
intellectus."[13] The order of four terms is then reduced to three:
voces, passiones animae, res. This is the Boethian triplet which
establishes the *triplex ordo* of speech, thought, and reality.[14]

One ought to note two nuances in the text. First Thomas is here
using *vox* differently than he did in the first *lectio*. There it meant
only physical sound. Here it means the type or class of 'physical'
words of some one sort. Aquinas is not thinking only of a particular speaking of the sound "dog"; he has in mind the word-
type 'dog'. His usage shifts, I think, because he is wrestling with a
circumlocution in the Latin Aristotle, who writes not *vox* but "ea
quae sunt in voce."[15] The second thing to be noted is that
Boethius and Moerbeke use *'res'* for Aristotle's *'pragmata'*.[16] Yet
neither of the Latin translators renders Aristotle's looser use of the
cognate *'pragmateias'* just two lines below. Aristotle writes that
the epistemological ground of language belongs to another in-

quiry, "allês gar pragmateias." Boethius and Moerbeke translate as "alterius est enim negotii."[17] By omitting the looser use, the translators foster a tendency, which Thomas inherits, to treat *res* very literally as physical object. Aristotle's authentic sense of *'pragmata'* is perhaps closer to the English 'affairs' or 'matters'. The thoroughgoing transformation of the Greek Aristotle which the various Latin translators achieved is, of course, a question which Aquinas could not address. He will often use Moerbeke to correct other translators. But where the Latin versions do not disagree, Aquinas has no access to the concealed features of the underlying Greek. It is to his credit that he will, nonetheless, escape from any gross literalization of the notion of *res*.

Voces signify by convention the *passiones animae*, which signify by nature *res*. There is no direct passage from word to thing. The logical properties of the word establish it in a mediate relation to reality.[18] The differences among words in distinct languages show further that they are not simply natural. By contrast, the *passiones animae* are the same for all men and have a certain natural similarity to the things of which they are the thoughts. Thomas notices two objections to this claim. The first is that men do not agree on the things in the world. The second is that equivocal terms confusedly signify different things and so men do not understand the same things by them. The second objection is handled easily. Boethius resolves it by pointing to the single intention in the mind of the speaker. More cautious even here, Aquinas reiterates that Aristotle is not trying to assert a one-to-one correspondence of words and concepts among men, but rather a correspondence of conceptions to things.[19]

The first objection to the sameness of the *passiones animae* in all human speakers remains, and it deserves a longer reply. Boethius has said that Aristotle is talking about those infallible conceptions of the mind which, as infallible, would be the same for all. Aquinas's reply is subtler. It begins with a distinction between complex and simple conceptions. The former are fallible, the latter not. It is at the level of the simple conceptions of the intellect that there is uniformity: "Huiusmodi autem simplices conceptiones intellectus sunt, quas primo voces significant."[20] Thus, "si quis vere intelligit quid est homo, quodcunque aliud aliquid, quam hominem apprehendat, non intelligit hominem."[21] Thomas then follows Aristotle in postponing the fuller explanation of cognitive activities to *De Anima*.

It is not clear that Aristotle had in mind a particular passage of the *De Anima,* which may well not have been in any final textual form when this part of the *Peri Hermeneias* was composed. He may have meant only that an account of cognition capable of explaining the natural likeness between the mind's conceptions and the world could be given only in a full-scale discussion of the soul. I am not sure that Aquinas's reference is any more exact, despite Ammonius's citation of *De Anima* III, 8.[22] On the other hand, an independent argument is already implicit in the terminology. By calling the mind's conceptions "passiones," one has implied that they are from being acted upon from outside the mind. The mind being a recipient of the world, two minds ought presumably to receive the same world in the same way. Yet the objection argues that men disagree about the world. How then can the reception theory hold? It is tempting to think that Thomas answers with an argument for the discreteness and clarity of notions, for the transparency of introspection with regard to one's own meaning. But I think that his argument is rather different. If someone truly grasps what a man is, it is just the case that he will not understand man when he apprehends something which is not man. Aquinas is arguing, in short, from the operation of the mind as it is actualized by the world. If men disagree more than nominally, their disagreement must be attributed to a confusion of names or to a lack of experience with the world.

On Aquinas's reading, Boethius has said that all error must be due to a confusion, since there can be no mindful error. Aquinas refines the argument not only in distinguishing the two operations of the mind, but in tacitly recalling that understanding is contingent: "si quis vero intelligit quid est homo...." The contingency arises from the variety of experience. Aquinas reads Aristotle's argument not as a tautology or as a reliance on the intuition of concepts, but as a remark about the possibilities of experience given the receptivity of similar minds for the one world. The logical circularity of the argument, which seems to assume the unity which it will prove, can be taken as a sign that a correct grasp of cognition will have to wait on another inquiry and, indeed, a richer experience of human dealings with the world.

Aristotle turns next to the distinction between simple and composite conceptions, which is reflected in a distinction between simple and composite verbal constructions. The simple conceptions do not fall under the consideration of truth and falsity; the complex do. Thomas justifies the parallelism between the intellectual and the verbal in a striking phrase: "conceptiones intellectus preambulae sunt ordine naturae vocibus, quae ad eas exprimendas proferuntur."[23] Again, "quia voces significativae formantur ad exprimendas conceptiones intellectus, ideo ad hoc quod signum conformetur signato, necesse est quod etiam vocum significativarum similiter quaedam significent sine vero et falso, quaedam autem cum vero et falso."[24] There follows a reconsideration of the operations of the intellect, which I set aside except to notice two things. The first is that Aquinas repeats the subordination of word to concept throughout as a subordination of sign to signified.[25] The second is that Aquinas introduces God as the ground of intelligibility and of truth in things by means of a very Aristotelian comparison with craft: "omnia etiam naturalia comparantur ad intellectum divinum, sicut artificiata ad artem."[26] Even that causal analogy contains the view of signification as intended and as communal.

This discussion concludes the general treatment of the relations among *voces, intellectus,* and *res* which make significant discourse possible. Aristotle's text now brings forward the specific elements of that discourse, beginning with the *nomen.* The discussion of these elements, which might seem merely grammatical, also enables Thomas to show the relation of human speaking to politics, to communicative intention, and to artifice.

The Latin Aristotle defines '*nomen*' as "vox significativa secundum placitum sine tempore, cuius nulla pars est significativa, separata."[27] Aquinas regards it as a definition with five parts, a genus and four differences. The genus is *vox,* the differences are *significativa, secundum placitum, sine tempore,* and *cujus nulla pars est significativa separata.*[28] An objection is raised with regard to putting *vox* as the genus, since the genus of a word ought rather to be 'sign'. Aquinas's reply shows his insistence on the conventional nature of verbal signs.[29] Because words are made by the imposition of an artificial and thus accidental form on a naturally existing thing, sound, the signification of words must be regarded as something inhering in material substance, sound, as an accident in a subject. Words are made and their significations are imposed by the makers. They can, then, be counted in the genus 'sign' only artificially.

The model of artistry also figures in Thomas's explication of why the parts of names cannot signify separately. "Cuius ratio est quod unum nomen imponitur ad significandum..., ab eo quod nomen significat; sicut hoc nomen lapis imponitur a laesione pedis, quam non significat; quod tamen imponitur ad significandum conceptum cuiusdam rei."[30] The intention of the word maker is sufficient not only to direct the word away from its etymological genesis, but also to insure its unity as a signifying whole. The emphasis on *impositio* derives from the view of language as determined by the social necessity of expressing the *passiones animae*. Words are tools for speaking within a community. Their divisions and their properties are to be explained by going back to their having been crafted. The genesis of language lies in the intentions of social craftsmen.

The same argument is made more connectedly in Aquinas's writings on the natural basis for political foundings. In the *De Regno*, written some five years before the commentary on the *Peri Hermeneias*, Aquinas deduces man's political nature immediately from the fact of his possessing language.[31] He writes: "est proprium hominis locutione uti, per quam unus homo aliis suum conceptum totaliter potest exprimere.... Magis igitur homo est communicativus alteri quam quodcumque aliud animal, quod gregale videtur."[32] The same argument is repeated at greater length in the commentary on Aristotle's *Politics*, where language is described not only as generally communicative, but also as signifying the fundamental political virtues and vices.[33] The genesis of language is coeval with the city — because it is convertible with man's political nature.

Pushed to details, Aquinas's analysis of a particular term's genesis produces variously· an onomatopoetic etymology, a postulated original intention, or a sketch of the epistemological conditions of human language-making.[34] The interest in original imposition or original intentions finds support in earlier grammatical theory. Its Latin sources go back at least to Boethius's commmentary on the *Categories*,[35] though its technical development took place in the century before Aquinas' birth. Under the heading '*causa inventionis*', the eleventh- and twelfth-century commentators on Priscian used the notion of origin or imposition to explain such grammatical features as the distinction of the parts of speech.[36] Their postulation of an original choice to explain grammatical features was greatly expanded by Peter Helias[37] and by the glossators from the 'school' of Ralph of Beauvais.[38] It also serves the dialectical tradition from Abelard[39] to Peter of Spain.[40] Of course, the philosophical use of the origin of language extends beyond the traditions within which Aquinas worked. It goes back to the etymological puns of the *Cratylus*[41] and forward to Vico and the Enlightenment's interest in general grammar and the speech of Adam.[42]

I have already said that one effect of Aquinas's postulation of an inventor or impositor is to stress that language is conventional. This stress also leads Aquinas to explain the plurality of existing languages. It serves to turn his attention from particular conventions to the frames for convention itself — from the features of language to the acts of understanding for which language is the artificial instrument. Aquinas's point is, then, that the end of language in regard to man's intellectual community must always be kept in view. The modern triplet semantics, syntactics, pragmatics, does not serve this end, though Aquinas will make remarks which can be assigned to one of these three divisions.

It would be more helpful to grasp the connections among the organizing notions in Thomas's exposition on their own terms. There was, first, the political character of human life. This character required, second, that human language be communicative. Moreover, third, the means of communication, while dependent on natural sounds and natural understandings, were seen to be artificial. The three features come together when one considers the ambivalences of the founding of the city in the Aristotelian account. The city comes to be naturally,

but its specific institutions and many of its later decadences are
decidedly artificial. So it is with language. The origin of
language lies in the political nature of man, and its matter is
equally natural. But the founding of language is an imposition of
artifice on natural needs and natural matter. To found language
is to make an artifact as complex as the city and coextensive
with it. It is also to form and then to embody an intention. Such
an intention animates the founding of language, on Thomas's
view, as well as the construction of particular linguistic acts.

I skip over the treatment of the verb, though the interesting
remarks on consignification will appear below, in order to consider the Aristotelian definitions of '*oratio*' and '*enunciatio*',
with Thomas's comments on them in *lectiones* 6 through 8. In
these three *lectiones*, the hypothesis of the importance of the
social basis can be put to the test. The first of the readings treats
of *oratio*, the second two, of *enunciatio*. Moerbeke's Aristotle
defines '*oratio*' as "vox significativa, cuius partium
significativum est separata (ut dictio, sed non ut affirmatio)."[43]
An *oratio* signifies a complex *intellectus*, as opposed to the
simple *intellectus* which are signified by the parts of *orationes*,
namely nouns and verbs. To this it can easily be objected that
there are many sentences the parts of which signify by way of affirmation. The Porphyrian and Ammonian solutions, which
Aquinas adopts, read Aristotle as speaking generally to cover both
simple and compound sentences.[44] In any case, the main point is
reiterated, that *orationes* are significant by convention, not by
nature. Aquinas explicitly cites the doctrine which he takes to be
that of Cratylus in order to contradict it.[45] He makes the point
graphically: "instrumenta naturalia virtutis interpretativae sunt
guttur et pulmo, quibus formatur vox, et lingua et dentes et labia,
quibus litterati ac articulati soni distinguuntur; oratio autem et
partes ejus sunt sicut effectus virtutis interpretativae per instrumenta praedicta.... Unde oratio et partes eius non sunt res
naturales, sed quidam artificiales effectus."[46]

Aristotle now turns — Aquinas with him — from the general
class of *orationes* to the particular subclass of *enunciationes*,
which are *orationes* capable of being true or false. Thomas fills
up Aristotle's silence by giving the other four forms of complete *oratio* as *deprecativa, imperativa, interrogativa,* and

creation, which hierarchy is itself a communicating order established by the creator. As soon as one admits the conventional character of sign-systems in human speech, one also must recall that the distinction between convention and nature is transformed by virtue of the doctrine of creation.

In the intersection between conventionally expressed intention and ontologically expressed creative will, Aquinas finds the notion of disclosive likeness, of manifestation, which serves him as a constant principle for understanding discourse. This principle appears in the account of language to explain both the immediate reference of words to thought and the origin of communication in a universal pedagogy of human souls. It will be possible to see the principle at work in these two places without tracking its whole range.

1.3 OUTER WORDS AND INNER WORDS

Words are signs. They signify because they are used intentionally. They signify mediately *res* and immediately what so far have been called the *passiones animae*, the *conceptiones animae*, and the *intellectus*. In Thomas's technical vocabulary, the immediate referents of spoken words are themselves also called words — 'inner words' as against the outer words which are their signs. Aquinas writes in the first Part of the *Summa Theologiae*: "Verbum tripliciter quidem in nobis proprie dicitur, quarto autem modo, dicitur improprie sive figurative.... Ex hoc ergo dicitur verbum vox exterior, quia significat interiorem mentis conceptum. Sic igitur primo et principaliter interior mentis conceptus verbum dicitur, secundario vero ipsa vox interioris conceptus significativa, tertio vero, ipsa imaginatio vocis verbum dicitur.... Dicitur autem figurative quarto modo verbum, id quod verbo significatur vel efficitur."[1] Of the four senses of '*verbum*', then, the first is that which refers to the inner *verbum* of the understanding. The other three — the spoken word, the *imaginatio vocis*, and the effects of speech synechdochically named '*verbum*' — depend upon this inner word. In it, one finds the word in its purest form.

It is, of course, Bernard Lonergan who has discussed the Thomist doctrine of the inner word most extensively.[2] His interest in it was, it seems, ancillary to his interest in cognitional theory and transcendental methodology.3 But the immediate context of the doctrine for both Aquinas and Lonergan is Trinitarian. The text quoted above is taken from an article in the *Summa* on the Son. Elsewhere, Aquinas usually discusses the inner *verbum* in Trinitarian passages and it is not surprising that the culminating section of Lonergan's study is entitled "Imago Dei." Lonergan attaches the study of the *verbum* to questions not only of subjectivity generally, but to the study of divine procession particularly. My own intention at present is different. I want to suggest how the contrast between inner and outer words, and the claim that outer words signify inner words, serve together to emphasize the tenets of expression and intentionality already found in Aquinas's remarks on linguistic words and signs.

The strongest source of both the doctrine and its ramifications is, again, Augustine. Lonergan quotes a famous passage from *De Trinitate*, which describes the genesis of the "verbum verum, quando quod scimus loquimur, sed verbum ante omnem sonum, ante omnem cognitionem."4 It is a "verbum linguae nullius, verbum verum de re vera, nihil de suo habens sed totum de illa scientia de qua nascitur."5 There is another passage in which Augustine makes the Trinitarian analogy more strikingly, though the linguistic lessons remain as fruitful.6 Lonergan takes such passages as triumphs of introspection;7 this aids his own program of a transcendentally derived cognitional theory. What is perhaps more obvious in such passages is that the mind reflecting on itself encounters an outward thrust which seeks expression. The inner *verbum* can be called '*verbum*' because it is the mind communicating with itself, because it is the mind already enacting the intelligible expression which grounds physical speech.

Aquinas works from these materials. Lonergan finds in Aquinas's completed doctrine of the inner *verbum* seven related points. Let me rehearse Lonergan's summary treatment of these points before disagreeing with him on their application to the analysis of language. The seven points are these: (1) Outer words signify directly inner words. (2) This relation of signification does not imply any literal, one-to-one correspondence between outer words and inner words as regards type. (3) Inner words are divided into definitions and judgments. (4) The inner word, which is a product of the mind, "supplies the object of thought." (5) In and through the inner word, "intellect comes to knowledge of things." (6) An inner word is necessary for the act which Thomas calls *intelligere*, which Lonergan renders as 'understanding'. (7) The "inner word of the human mind emerges at the end of a process of thoughtful understanding" which terminates with an act of understanding, from which the *verbum* is distinguished, but which the *verbum* expresses.[8] The cognitional intention of Lonergan's summary is clear enough. It is not so clear that he has done justice to the reasons for which Aquinas chooses to appropriate the tradition in calling this product of cognitional activity a '*verbum*', a 'word'.

The treatment of the *verbum* in the *Sentences*-commentary is repeatedly set aside by Lonergan as immature and unrepresentative of Aquinas's developed thought.[9] This judgment may be justified with regard to the difficult emphasis which the early work places on the efficient causality behind the *verbum*. But it is not justified when it treats the early emphasis on manifestation or expression as the result of a youthful confusion in Aquinas. Aquinas begins his reply to the question, "utrum verbum dicatur proprie in divinis," with a citation to the prologue of John's gospel.[10] It is in that scriptural text, of course, besides Augustine, that one has the authoritative warrant for using the audacious metaphor of the *verbum* in Trinitarian theology. Aquinas adds to the citation a distinction among the three proper senses of '*verbum*' — those three proper senses that appear in the text already cited from the *Summa*. Here one reads of the "verbum cordis," the "verbum vocis," and the "verbum quod habet imaginem vocis."[11] Aquinas gives as his authority for this triplet the *glossa ordinaria* on *John*.[12] The *imaginem vocis* is explained abstractly as "quandam virtutem particularem quae apprehendit intentionem particularem rei, circa quam est operatio." It is likened to a particular minor in a syllogism the conclusion of which is the spoken word, the *verbum vocis*: "in parte intellectiva habeatur major universalis, et in parte sensitiva habeatur minor particularis, et demum sequatur conclusio

operationis particularis, per virtutem motivam imperatam."
This *verbum* which is like a particular minor premise is found in
the imagination, "quando scilicet quis imaginatur voces quibus
intellectus conceptum proferre valeat." The imagined word is
the link between the inner word and the physical production of
speech, the pattern for the production of the word-sound. Thus
it takes on in Thomas a number of names associated with formal
causality; it is called the "verbum speciei vocis," the "verbum
in corde enuntiatum" (after John Damascene), and the "verbum
animi sinu cogitatum" (after Augustine). The analogy to art,
which played so large a role in stressing the conventional nature
of language, now appears even in the internal description of the
processes of speech.

The role of the major in the productive syllogism is filled by
the *verbum cordis* itself, which is also called "verbum rei."
Aquinas finds this innermost *verbum* described by John
Damascene as "naturalis intellectus motus"[13] and by Augustine
as "verbum animae impressum."[14] Only this *verbum cordis* can
be attributed analogously to God. Indeed, it is attributed to God
most properly inasmuch as God is the eminent intellect.
Aquinas describes three steps in intellectual operation by way of
arriving at the nature of the *verbum*. The first step is that of
"simplex intuitus intellectus," which — he says here — does
not have the character of *verbum*. The second step is the "ordinatio illius intelligibilis ad manifestationem vel alterius,
secundum quod aliquis alteri loquitur, vel sui ipsius, secundum
quod contingit aliquem etiam sibi ipsi loqui, et haec primo accipit rationem verbi, unde verbum nihil alius dicit quam quamdam emanationem ab intellectu per modum manifestantis."[15]
The relation to the '*modus manifestantis*' is what constitutes a
verbum as such. Without it, there is no *verbum*, either interior
or exterior, because there is no "ratio verbi."

Lonergan explains this emphasis on communication, even of
self to self, by dividing the two senses in which one speaks of
the 'Word' of God. The 'Word' can be either the Son or the
revelation. Lonergan would wish to derive the emphasis on expression as constitutive of a *verbum* only from the second
sense, that is, from the theological notion of revealed word.[16]
But rather than set the passage from Thomas aside because it
denies the status of *verbum* to simple intuition, one ought

perhaps to retain the connection between *verbum* and *manifestatio* and hold that Thomas changed his mind about intuition as manifestation. The change in Thomas's thinking after the *Sentences* is not an abandonment of the criterion of communication; it is, rather, the realization that intuitions too communicate. Lonergan is right to say that Aquinas will later call the intuition a '*verbum*'; he is wrong to conclude that this is due to an abandonment of the principle of manifestation. Other texts, in the *Sentences* commentary and after it, can show as much.

There is another passage in the *Sentences* where Thomas offers the same teaching. It is a discussion of the speech of angels, a topic already considered in establishing the primacy of language (see 1.2, above). Starting from an analogy to human affairs, Thomas writes: "species ergo conceptae interius, secundum quod manent in simplici conceptione intellectus, habent rationem intelligibilis tantum: secundum autem quod ordinantur ab intelligente ut manifestandae alteri, habent rationem verbi, quod dicitur verbum cordis."[17] The *verbum cordis* can be expressed corporeally, in visual or aural signs. "Similiter in angelis interior conceptus mentis libero arbitrio subjacens ad alio videri non potest. Quando ergo speciem conceptam ordinat ut manifestandum alteri, dicitur verbum cordis."[18] So ordered, the species can be displayed to another angel by means of intellectual signs. It will be seen that this explanation is much like those later treatments of angelic speech in the *De Veritate* and the first Part of the *Summa* that were treated above. I adduce it now as a piece of evidence for retaining expression as constitutive of *verbum* and for refusing to set aside the discussion of *verbum* in the commentary on the *Sentences*.

In *De Veritate*, which Lonergan takes as recording Thomas's mastery over the problem of the inner word, the link between manifestation and words or speech is as clear as it was in the *Sentences*-commentary. At issue again is "utrum verbum proprie dicatur in divinis."[19] Many of the objections from the treatment in the *Sentences* text are repeated here with only slight modification.[20] So are the connections between word and manifestation. Aquinas begins to determine the *quaestio* by recalling that words are named from human experience and then applied to God, even though the order of intelligibility descends from God to men. So it is that men call '*verbum*' chiefly that exterior word of speech, even though the interior word is naturally prior to the exterior as its efficient and final cause. It is the final cause, "quia verbum vocale ad hoc a nobis exprimitur, ut interius verbum manifestetur: unde oportet quod verbum interius sit illud quod significatur per exterius verbum."[21] Note here the close alignment of the final cause of manifestation and the constitution of the signifying relation. The former *implies* the latter ("unde oportet"). Aquinas underscores the implication when it comes to the inner word as efficient cause: "verbum prolatum exterius, cum sit significativum ad placitum, eius principium est voluntas, sicut et ceterorum artificiatorum."[22] The will of the speaker constitutes external words. On the analogy to artistry, then, the word is found in the speaker in three ways: as "id quod per intellectum concipitur, ad quod significandum verbum exterius profertur"; as "exemplar exterioris verbi"; and as "verbum exterius expressum." These are named the "verbum cordis," the "verbum interius quod habet imaginem vocis," and the "verbum vocis," just as they were in the commentary on the *Sentences*.

Aquinas goes on in the replies to the objections in *De Veritate* to emphasize the finality of manifestation. To the fifth objection, he replies: "quamvis apud nos manifestatio, quae est ad alterum, non fiat nisi per verbum vocale, tamen manifestatio ad seipsum fit etiam per verbum cordis; et haec manifestatio aliam praecedit; et ideo etiam verbum interius verbum per prius dicitur. Similiter etiam per Verbum incarnatum Pater omnibus manifestatus est; sed per Verbum ab aeterno genitum eum manifestavit sibi ipsi; et ideo non convenit sibi nomen Verbi secundum hoc tantum quod incarnatus est."[23] Here again Thomas seems to transform the earlier distinction between intuition and manifestation by holding that even within the intellect there is a manifestation to oneself, an interior discourse. The inward manifestation is found in both God and creatures. In the reply to the sixth objection, Aquinas repeats that manifestation is the basis of similarity between created words and uncreated Word. Their dissimilarity comes only on the score of the unity of sign and signified in the Word. Similar arguments can be found in other texts from *De Veritate*.[24]

If one moves from *De Veritate* to later works, one finds the

principle of manifestation used quite explicitly. In the seventh
Quodlibet, the issue is the existence of senses in Scripture
beyond the literal. Thomas argues in his determination of the
question that the "[m]anifestatio autem vel expressio alicuius
veritatis potest fieri de aliquo rebus et verbis; in quantum
scilicet verba significant res, et una res potest esse figura
alterius."[25] '*Manifestatio*' seems here to be a synonym for '*expressio*'; both are linked with the order of signification. In a different context, Aquinas defends in the first *Quodlibet* the practice of auricular confession with this argument: "in manifesta-
tione peccatorum convenit uti verbis, quibus homines com-
munius et expressius suos conceptus significare consueverunt."[26] Similar passages appear in a number of the other
works, in articles dealing with quite other problems.[27]

If these references should seem somewhat arcane, let me
close the series with instances of the principle of manifestation
from the *Contra Gentiles* and the *Summa Theologiae*. In the
Contra Gentiles, there are passages corresponding to the questions on the mutual understanding of angels. These do not
consider explicitly, however, the question of speech among
angels. More interesting are those passages in the fourth Book
which explicate and justify with probable arguments the or-
thodox position on the begetting of the Son and his character as
the wisdom of God.[28] Of these, Chapter 12 is full of the imagery
of light and manifestation. It contains an explicit statement of
the connection between manifestation and the *verbum*: "Ipsum
autem sapientiae Verbum mente conceptum est quaedam
manifestatio sapientiae intelligentis: sicut et in nobis omnes
habitus per actus manifestantur. Quia ergo divina sapientia lux
dicitur, prout in puro actu cognitionis consistit; lucis autem
manifestatio splendor Ipsius est, ab ea procedens."[29] In the ar-
chetypal case, the inner act of understanding has been interpreted as a kind of discourse which preeminently constitutes
the *verbum*.

The same principle appears in many places in the *Summa*.
There are, as I have already mentioned, questions on the speech
of angels, on whether '*verbum*' can be predicated with proprie-
ty of God, and on the use of words in the sacraments. Still, the
principle appears in other pedagogical contexts where communication is paramount. For example, "ille qui addiscit ab

homine non accipit immediate scientiam a speciebus in-
telligibilibus, quae sunt in mente ipsius, sed mediantibus sensibilibus vocibus, tamquam signis intellectualium concep-
tionum."[30] Words are used not only to teach, but to praise: "Ad
hominem enim utimur verbis ut conceptum nostri cordis, quem
non potest cognoscere, verbis nostris ei exprimamus."[31] The
plurality of motives for which expression can be used is treated
by Aquinas explicitly in a question on the liceity of malediction.
The motive for expression can be the indicative expression of
enunciation, or the imperative volition of command, or the op-
tative "quasi expressio" of desire.[32]

Let me add to these scattered texts one final passage in which
the various strands are recalled and gathered. The context for it
is an article on the eternal law which asks "utrum lex aeterna sit
summa ratio in Deo existens." In reply to the second objection,
Aquinas writes that any word can be considered for what it is or
for what it expresses. "Verbum enim vocale est quiddam ab ore
hominis prolatum; sed hoc verbo exprimuntur quae verbis
humanis significantur. Et eadem ratio est de verbo hominis men-
tali, quod nihil est aliud quam quiddam mente conceptum, quo
homo exprimit mentaliter ea de quibus cogitat."[33] "Quo homo
exprimit mentaliter" — the inner verbum can now truly be called *verbum* because of the principle of manifestation. It has now
been seen as an internal expression, an inner discourse.

The ultimate ground of signification in language is the intention of an agent to express, to speak, to communicate. The intention is not only the conscious intention which reaches out to
produce an outer word. It is also the spiritual 'intention' of the
human soul which speaks to itself even in the basic act of
intuition. The *verbum cordis* is the primary and proper utterance from which all others derive. It grounds the others by
being first and always expressive, communicative, manifesting.

Still, it might seem that Thomas's account of language rests
merely on the positing of an interior speech, as if he had wanted
to explain language by creating a small speaker within the mind.
That his account is not merely a transposition of the problem
can be seen in recognizing that the principle of manifestation is
not a principle of literal representation. On the contrary, it contains within it a hierarchy of different modes of manifestness.

The inner *verbum* has a type of manifestness which is different both from that of outer words and from that of signified things. The inner *verbum* is made manifest naturally while outer words are made manifest conventionally. Thus, as compared to inner words, all outer words must seem refracted and less than exact, less than literal. The inner *verbum* itself is, as Aristotle taught, something like an expression of the intuition of things. But that expression is also modally different from the things which are intuited. The inner *verbum* is an intelligible 'likeness' of things, the outer *verbum* is a conventional sign of the inner. So it is that the outer word, the language spoken and received, is doubly removed from things — once by the modality of intelligence itself, a second time by its own conventional construction.

The communicative intention is thus seen to be teleologically rather than actually present. An utterance typically desires to communicate, to teach, some truth about things. But its proper reception depends both on an understanding of the conventions of the particular language and the natural mode of understanding itself. The conventions of a particular language specify it, shape it, in order to make it more useful for teaching. Beyond the social conventions which establish speech, there are the conventions of art which amplify meaning by creating a richer context of choices for its expression. These artful conventions are embodied for Thomas in the *trivium*. Without the *trivium*, linguistic meaning would remain almost entirely in potency, kept to the barest minimum of communication. With the *trivium*, language is opened to the possibility of philosophic teaching and speculative science.

CHAPTER 2

The Arts of the *Trivium*

Medieval doctrine about language was embodied not only or even chiefly in explicit speculations on the semantics of linguistic signs. It was taught most often and during a longer period as embodied in the three arts of the *trivium*. These arts Thomas learned in rudimentary form at Monte Cassino and then, more technically, at Naples. In learning them, he learned authoritative texts in which the liberal arts of antiquity had been preserved and cultivated among the medieval Latins. But not all is continuity. If Thomas is in some measure the heir of traditions of the *trivium*, he also comes after movements which reinterpret traditions and partially reject them. Earlier Thomists were eager to see in Thomas the synthesis or at least the apex of medieval thought. With regard to the *trivium*, he is neither apex nor synthesis.[1] He could not be, given the conflict of traditions within the arts themselves.

In order to read Thomas exhaustively, it would be necessary to recognize the traces of the competing traditions, particularly since Thomas writes by means of a clarifying reconstruction of his academic inheritance. Recognizing every trace of earlier materials would be impossible. There is, first, the fact of collective ignorance about many of the lines of tradition for the *trivium*. The lines are hidden in part because of the medieval practice of citation without reference, usually at second hand. In Thomas's texts, the citations become more opaque as they become more recent. Nor does he indulge in the reportorial digressions of such writers as John of Salisbury or Roger Bacon. There is, as the second general difficulty, the fact that Thomas does not belabor the obvious. No skillful writer cites a textbook authority, even an ancient one, when his readers share his education. To take one example: There are in Thomas two explicit citations of Priscian and one of Donatus.[2] It does not follow, however, that Thomas had not studied the imperial grammarians or that he neglected to use them. It is rather the case, I think, that he would not have bothered to cite texts which his readers had learned by rote.

The second difficulty looms even larger when one sees how little Thomas says explicitly about the liberal arts. He has an objector refer to them as a group in the exposition of Boethius's *De Trinitate*. The objection has it that "communiter dividitur philosophia in septem artes liberales."[3] Thomas replies that the arts are not comprised in philosophy because they are preparatory to it: "praetermissi quibusdam aliis connumerantur, quia his primum erudiebantur, qui philosophiam discere volebant, et ideo distinguuntur in trivium et quadrivium."[4] The reply rests on an explicit quotation from Hugh of St-Victor's *Didascalicon*.[5] Thomas adds, after further references to Aristotle and Averroes, "Et sic datur intelligi quod post logicam consequenter debet mathematica addisci, ad quam pertinet quadrivium; et ita his quasi quibusdam viis praeparatur animus ad alias philosophicas disciplinas."[6] But there is no enumeration of the arts here, much less any discussion of their interconnections. The *quadrivium* is enumerated in another text.[7] The *trivium* is enumerated nowhere and seems regularly to collapse into logic.[8] So the second difficulty persists: Thomas will not rehearse the obvious, the rudimentary, for his readers.

These two are the stubborn obstacles to any cataloguing of the use by Aquinas of materials from the *trivium*. They cannot be overcome by shifting to a study of Thomas's relation to particular authors in the arts. Of course, some of Aquinas's texts can still be read as palimpsests within which layers of the authorities for the *trivium* can be uncovered. At times, indeed, Aquinas will judge the authors in those layers explicitly and very differently. There is much more of the Academic and Arabic Aristotle, for example, than of the Chartrian poetical grammar. Boethius, again, remains as an interpreter of Aristotle, but he no longer occupies the privileged position of sole mediator which had once been almost his. Still, it is not precise enough to speak of judgments on authors in the arts as if Thomas conceived his sources in terms of authors or even of whole works. It is much more the case that Thomas thinks of passages or particular doctrines. Isidore may serve as an example. He is the only one of the Latin encyclopaedists who figures directly as an authority in arts for Thomas.

The *Etymologiae* are cited frequently in Thomas's writings from early to late. But even here the explicit influence is selective. For example, citations in the *Summa* to the second Book of the *Etymologiae*, which concerns rhetoric and dialectic, refer only to a single chapter, the tenth. That chapter, "De lege," is used for the properties that it ascribes to law as such. All citations to this chapter fall within Questions 90-101 of the *prima secundae*.[9] The part of the *Etymologiae* next in frequency of citation is Book X, "De vocabulis," which is used throughout the *secunda secundae* for more than two dozen of its fanciful etymologies. Curiously enough, such citations appear only in the *secunda secundae*. Next in frequency is Book V of the *Etymologiae*, "De legibus et temporibus," which is used in the *secunda pars* chiefly for its doctrine on the public finality and annexed properties of law.[10]

If an exhaustive contextual study is not possible, and if the analysis of individual authors in the arts is too imprecise, there remains the possibility of tracing particular materials and particular doctrines. But even these pieces of evidence must be treated carefully because of the historical tensions surrounding them. Thomas is content in one text to repeat the mythical version of the origin of the arts which he receives from Aristotle.[11] But his texts show just how far the history of the *trivium* is in one sense the history of disagreement about the unity and hierarchy of the arts within it. There is much rivalry among the arts from the encyclopaedists onward.[12] Indeed, Thomas's own handling of the *trivium* from the perspective of logic is only another in the series of attempts by one art to encompass or at least to subordinate the others. Layers or clusters in the arts tradition can be distinguished by the different sorts of unity and of hierarchy which they achieve within the *trivium*. Some seem to be dominated by the forms and content of grammar, others by that collaboration of grammar and logic which is called dialectic, still others by the splitting of the three arts into technical isolation. Each of these characterizations, however, would have to be multiplied according to the varied local histories of instruction in the arts.[13] What can be seen or guessed of the variety is enormous. It remains to be shown where Aquinas stands in it.

2.1 MATERIALS FROM THE ART OF GRAMMAR

When Martianus Capella brings Grammar forward at his wedding feast, she appears as a woman of many years, "sed comitate blandissima," who carries a polished box.[1] From it, she produces the instruments of her therapy: a pruning knife for correcting childish pronunciation, stronger medicine for the barbarous speech of adults, balms for harsh voices, stimulants to attention, and a golden file for smoothing solecisms.[2] Daughter of Mercury, she claims the antiquity of an Egyptian origin and speaks first among the arts as propaedeutic of all, whom even the gods liken to a birth-giver ("Genethliace") and a physician ("Iatrice").[3] Yet Grammar is allowed to complete only a portion of her speech. She is interrupted by Minerva, who taxes her with boring the gods by a recital of lessons for beginners ("ab scholaribus inchoamentis").[4] Minerva also warns Grammar not to trespass into the fields of other arts; Music, for example, will defend its right to analyze poetic speech. Interrupted, chided, Grammar is compelled to retire.

The allegory captures many of the ambivalences which attended the study of grammar in medieval curricula. On the one hand, it was regularly asserted that grammar was the foundation for the other arts and, thus, for the higher bodies of knowledge. On the other hand, grammar was the elementary study which was repeatedly subordinated to more advanced learning and more proficient techniques. Moreover, its ancient connection with poetry was challenged on the technical side by music and on the side of substance by ethics.[5] While grammar could claim a sovereignty as the first art without which the others would not be possible, it could not presume to claim a place as a perfective study. So it is that Conrad of Hirsau feels the need to defend Donatus. His '*Magister*' says: "Donatus quidem tibi inter minorus auctores numerandus videtur quia rudimentis parvulorum aptus cognoscitur, sed ... inter maximos ponendos est et quasi quoddam singulare fundamentum in ceteris auctoribus habendus."[6]

The ambivalent status of grammar is reflected in the materials for reconstructing its teaching in the Latin West. There are two poles around which the extant grammatical materials cluster. The first is that of the teaching grammars, those textbooks used in grammatical instruction. These would differ, of course, according to the academic level, but their didactic character is clear. The second pole is that of speculative grammars loosely conceived, texts in which the end is reflection on the philosophical or other properties of the grammatical features of the language. These are two poles rather than two categories because it would be very difficult to find works which were purely one or the other. Even a rudimentary textbook will employ some notions from semantics; conversely, the most elaborate works of *grammatica speculativa* must rely on a normative description of the language.

Grammatical texts near both poles have been edited recently at an increasing pace, though much of medieval grammar remains hidden.[7] Despite the gaps, there have been various attempts to retell the history of medieval grammar at the second or speculative pole, chiefly with regard to the transformations of the twelfth and thirteenth centuries. R.W. Hunt has written a series of detailed essays on the grammatical tradition of the twelfth century.[8] If one looks to the glossators on Priscian, one finds at the beginning of the century what Hunt considers a fusion of logical and grammatical concerns.[9] The untwining of grammar and logic, their separation, was the work of Peter Helias at the mid-century. Helias "has made a determined effort to free himself from questions that do not belong to grammar,"[10] such that his *Summa* "marks a great advance in effecting this separation."[11] Indeed, Helias's work soon achieved among grammarians a "commanding position — comparable to that of Peter Lombard in the theological schools."[12] On the basis of this *Summa*, a group of glossators identified by Hunt as the "school of Ralph of Beauvais" began after the mid-century the twofold extension of grammar into syntax and into the classical authors.[13] But the dual project was not carried out in the later development of grammar, which tried to push syntax along "rigorously logical lines."[14]

Bursill-Hall clarifies this philosophical change in one place by concentrating on the philosophical texts which would lead to the *grammatica speculativa*.[15] From the beginning of the twelfth to the middle of the thirteenth centuries, Bursill-Hall traces two large stages. The first stage, which included William of Conches, Peter Helias, and Ralph of Beauvais, saw the mixture of grammar and dialectic separated out into treatments of syntax and systematic grammar.[16] The second stage, comprising Robert Kilwardby, Jordan of Saxony, Nicholas of Paris, and Roger Bacon, was one of consolidation and refinement.[17] Both stages go beyond the earlier grammarians in speculation; both tend towards the construction of a systematic syntax, though in different modes and with different materials. Of course, there is a striking material and didactic continuity across these stages. The continuity is particularly important in understanding Thomas, who relies on it in collating materials from the different layers.

Aquinas comes, of course, at the end of these developments. How much he learned of them at Monte Cassino or Naples can only be inferred. Weisheipl writes that Aquinas was "most probably" tutored in the *Priscianus minor* and the *Barbarismus* by the Benedictines.[18] Nothing more certain is known about the grammatical curriculum at Naples. Aquinas does refer in the *Sentences* to Priscian. In an objection about the suitability of predicating '*verbum*' of God, Aquinas's objector argues: "Omne enim nomen quod significat corporalem operationem, non potest Deo convenire nisi metaphorice. Sed verbum est hujusmodi: dicitur enim a verberatione aeris, ut dicit Priscianus, lib. I, cap. 'De verbo'."[19]

The reference is not difficult to pin down, though the citation in the printed texts seems to be corrupt. The first Book of the *Institutiones* concerns the '*vox*'; it is only in the eighth Book that one gets the discussion "de Verbo." The etymology which the objector has in mind comes in fact from that later book. Priscian writes, "verbum autem quamvis a verberatu aeris dicatur."[20] The etymology also appears in Servius's commentary on the *Ars maior*.[21] One finds it again in the *Explanationum in Artem Donati*, assigned by Keil to Sergius but known in the manuscripts as another work by Servius himself.[22] Servius is widely read as a commentator on Virgil and as a grammarian; the *Explanationum* appears in several eighth, ninth, and tenth-century manuscripts.[23] Their etymology of '*verbum*' is repeated by Isidore and so enters the mainstream.[24] Can the citation of this etymology be used then as evidence of Aquinas's having read into the *Institutiones* as far as the eighth Book? On the contrary, it is much easier to imagine that he receives the etymology and its authoritative source from an intermediate digest.

The same is true of the other explicit mentions of Priscian and Donatus. Earlier in the first Book of the *Scriptum* on the *Sentences*, an objector had bolstered a point about the meaning of '*alius*' by the reference, "secundum Priscianum, lib. II, cap. 'De pronomine.' "[25] Pronouns are discussed in Book II of the *Institutiones*, but in neither case is there a mention of '*alius*'.[26] The reference to a chapter on pronouns, if textually correct, might point to the discussion of the supposition in pronouns in *Priscianus minor*, i.e., *Institutiones* XVII, ix, which was the source of much comment in the thirteenth and fourteenth centuries.[27] Still, the reference is not entirely clear. The sole reference to Donatus seems to be a conflation as well. Thomas replies to an argument about Adam's vision of God with an explanation of the meaning of '*aenigma*' drawn, as he says, from Donatus: "aenigma est, secundum Donatum, quaestio verborum obscuritate involuta."[28] This definition seems in fact to combine a definition given by Donatus with one in Isidore.[29]

One is left with very little by way of direct evidence for Thomas's acquaintance with the tradition of grammar. This does not mean that there is no evidence. Indeed, the evidence is of the kind one would expect with regard to sources learned in boyhood. Aquinas uses certain traditional phrases without citation precisely because they formed part of his earliest training and part of the most common learned tradition. Let me take as an example the definition of grammar and its parts. There is in the sources at Aquinas's hand considerable continuity in the definition of grammar. Martianus Capella has Grammar explain herself in these terms: "Officium vero meum tunc fuerat docte scribere legereque; nunc etiam illud accessit, ut meum sit erudire intelligere probareque."[30] Capella here echoes a tradition going back through Marius Victorinus, Servius, Cassiodorus, and Augustine, to Varro and the Greeks.[31] Martianus's definition is taken up by Isidore in the *Etymologiae*, where it becomes: "Grammatica est scientia recte loquendi, et origo et fundamentum liberalium litterarum."[32] The formula is repeated verbatim by Gundissalinus[33] and Peter Helias;[34] a formula somewhat like it appears in Hugh of St-Victor.[35]

Thomas himself offers very similar formulations throughout his works, although he usually does so parenthetically. At times, he recalls the definition itself: "sicut grammatica per hoc quod dicitur esse scientia recte loquendi...."[36] Again, "per habitum grammaticae habet homo facultatem recte loquendi,"[37] and "grammaticus potest secundum grammaticam recte loqui."[38] The same point is said with slight verbal variation in the claim that grammar considers the "congruum" and the "incongruum" in speech.[39] In many places, of course, Aquinas uses "grammatica" and "grammaticus" as nothing more than examples of the *habitus* of knowledge, in this respect following Aristotelian custom.

The tradition with regard to the parts of grammar is much less unanimous, as are the remarks in Aquinas. Part of the difficulty is the plurality of divisions found in the authoritative texts — different distinctions are made in Donatus's *Ars minor*, the *Ars major*, and Priscian.[40] Martianus attempts to draw these together, but his eclecticism is more confusing than helpful; it leads his Grammar into the disordered loquacity for which she is faulted by Minerva.[41] Isidore is, if anything, more luxuriant in his schemata, repeating without explicit attribution a division of grammar into thirty parts.[42] His list forms the basis of the lengthy analyses of Book I of the *Etymologiae*. It combines items of very different linguistic standing, including some that would now be classed under descriptive linguistics, under the study of literary tropes, and under historiography. This variety should make clear again the ambivalent nature of medieval grammar, which was at once the study engaged in by the young and by masters in interpretation.

For Gundissalinus, there is a stricter economy which yields the division of grammar into seven parts, which he claims have been recognized "apud omnes gentes."[43] The division is taken over from al-Farabi's *De Scientiis*.[44] In his *De Grammatica*, Hugh of St-Victor admits the confusion of sources and offers a list of twenty-parts of grammar; he counts only the first four as the principal ones, namely "littera, sillaba, dictio, oratio."[45] This division is repeated by Peter Helias on the basis of the texts of Priscian.[46]

Writing in the thirteenth century, after the 'shift' towards logic, Eberhard of Bethune offers a threefold division: "Or-

thographia, prosodia, dyasintastica species tres grammatice
sunt.''[47] An augmented version of this triplet is frequently
repeated in the thirteenth century with a citation to Priscian:
"Secundum ... Priscianum dividitur gramatica in quatuor partes,
scilicet orthographiam, ethimologiam, prosodiam, et diasin-
tasticum; et hec divisio sumitur a parte subiecti.''[48] A com-
plementary division is based on *Donatus minor*: "Dividitur
autem gramatica a Donato in tres partes, scilicet in preceptivam,
permissivam, et prohibitivam.... Et ista divisio a parte passionis
sumitur.''[49] The preceptive part of grammar considers what is
simply "congruum" and corresponds to the *Ars minor*. The
prohibitive part considers the "incongruum" and the
"congruum" *secundum quid*, i.e., considers the figurative uses
of the poets.[50] The last two divisions correspond to *Donatus
major*.

Alexander of Villa-Dei is less meticulous when it comes to
stating the division of the subject in the *Doctrinale*'s Proemium.[51] But the division of the work itself into topics provides
something like the fourfold division of names (cc.1-7), constructions (cc.8-9), syllables and accents (cc.10-11), and figures
(c.12). This appears to be a conflation of the *littera, sillaba, dictio, oratio* of Helias and the *orthographia, ethimologia,
prosodia, diasintastica* division of the *Graecismus* and other
thirteenth-century texts cited by Thurot.

The commentary on *Priscianus minor* attributed to Robert
Kilwardby, after considering the division of subject-matter into
"litteris, syllabis, dictionibus, et orationibus," as well as the
division of ends into "recte scribere, recte pronuntiare," rejects
the conclusion that grammar is not one science.[52] The author
insists that the whole of grammar is gathered under one end,
which is "eloquentia vel humanae voluntatis significatio.''[53] He
defends against the various traditional alternatives the claim
that the subject-matter of grammar is "oratio congrua et perfecta ... quia est illud in quo est status et complementum grammaticae.''[54] The commentary goes on to give as one division of
grammar the fourfold schema of the new grammarians: "de
litteris quae dicitur orthographia," "de syllabis quae dicitur prosodia," "de dictione quae dicitur ethimologia," and "de oratione quae dicitur diasinthetica.''[55]

Aquinas offers no such exhaustive division of subject-matter in grammatical studies. He does mention, however, a number of components in grammar, drawing from various of the competing traditional divisions. The "elementa" which are taught by grammar are the "litterae";[56] their consideration is explicitly reserved to grammar.[57] Letters are the "subiectum" which grammar first considers, just as natural science first considers matter and form.[58] Aquinas elsewhere writes that "grammatica considerat omnes voces."[59] Moreover Aquinas recalls that grammar ought to correct solecisms and barbarisms. He quite frequently adduces the example of the faulty grammarian in analyzing cases of cognitional or volitional failure.[60] It is in connection with solecisms that Aquinas introduces what was meant among his predecessors by the term 'dyasintastica'. He writes: "Soloecismus est vitium in contextu partium orationis contra regulae artis grammaticae factum, ut vir alba."[61] In these various fragments, one sees Thomas appropriating some among the medieval uses of grammar. Despite the absence of a formal division of grammar, then, Aquinas inherits and uses the bewildering range of grammar's sub-divisions.

Aquinas also shares with the tradition the ambiguity about the role of grammar as both propaedeutic and authoritative. Grammar seems to be subsumed under logic at the beginning of his ideal plan of studies.[62] His definitions of grammar also give it a preparatory role. On the other hand, grammatical distinctions must be considered whenever one tries to rise from the human level to that of the separated substances, especially the divine Trinity. There are, then, numerous passages where Aquinas says that something holds only "grammatice loquendo."[63] This latter use is anything but rudimentary, since it touches on the fundamental limit of human understanding.

With this in mind, one can answer the question posed above: What is the philosophical import of grammatical studies? What grammar gives that cannot be gotten elsewhere and cannot be overlooked is the analysis of the *modi significandi* which mark human speech. Thomas reiterates the connection between grammar and the concern with the modes of human speech precisely so far as these differ from the modes of the real. Consider these phrases: "grammaticus non considerat substantiam actionis, sed modum significandi"; "grammaticus accipit substantiam quantum ad modum significandi, et similiter qualitatum"; "quantum ad modum significandi, prout grammaticus considerat."[64] Less technically, Aquinas often remarks on the difference between what language would suggest about God and what reason, or reasoned faith, knows to be the case. He proposes, in short, an ongoing correction of the language. Grammar is not ontology; the grammarian is not directly concerned with anything but the modes of signifying. The very need for grammar is an admission of the question about human knowing. The mind would not need to learn conventional rules if it could speak the intelligible without words. A man needs grammar and the rest of the *trivium* because he is not endowed by nature with angelic insight. So the need for an *ars* of grammar is already of significance to philosophic discourse.

2.2 THE MODES OF SIGNIFICATION

One of the inspirations for reflection on the modes of signification is a term which Aristotle uses in *On Interpretation*. The term is by no means the only inspiration for what becomes a number of mixed doctrines, but it is a starting-point. In the third chapter, on predicates (*rêma*), Aristotle introduces the notion of what the Latins will come to call consignification. Aristotle writes: "A predicate is what consignifies time."[1] The operative term in the Greek is *prossêmainon*. It suggests that a predicate signifies something beyond its specific reference to the world. It has another axis of signification than mere naming.[2]

Of course, Aristotle has immediately in mind the predicate's tense. But he adds that the predicate is always a sign of things said about something else (*kath' heteron*).[3] What is clearly implied is that there is a possible plurality of significations in a single word which will qualify its referring. To speak metaphorically, there is a field of types of signification which is held together in a word's ordinary use. This plurality is not the one analyzed in the study of equivocals. It concerns, not diverse objects uniformly denoted, but a complex simultaneously signified on different planes by the same word. The focus has moved from what is signified to the modes of signification, to the particular province of the grammarian. That shift, made here by Aristotle in a limited context, will gather momentum in his commentators and issue in the doctrine of the modes of signification elaborated by medieval grammar.

Among the later appearances of Aristotelian consignification, the treatments by Anselm and Abelard are striking.[4] But a history of the *modi significandi* through Aquinas would dwell on the emergence of the 'Dacian' school of speculative grammarians, as well as on the progress of speculative grammar as a whole. The school's flowering in Paris falls during and after Thomas's two regencies there. It was prepared by the works of the 'generation' of Robert Kilwardby and Roger Bacon, including the *Compendium Modorum Significandi* of Vincent Heremita and the *Questiones super Modos Significandi* of Matthew of Bologna.[5] The first of the Dacians, Simon, seems to have written his own *Questiones super Priscianum* between 1260 and 1270.[6] A grammatical treatise by the well-known Boethius of Dacia, entitled precisely *De Modi Significandi*, appeared in 1270. It was followed by the works of Martin and John of Dacia after Thomas's death.[7]

Was Aquinas familiar with this contemporary line of inquiry? Manthey, O'Mahony, and Pinborg agree that Thomas did not know the technical elaboration of the *modistae*.[8] But the sort of semantic speculation evident in the *modistae* did not escape his notice. His writings give testimony to it. If Thomas's relations with the *modistae* were indirect, the issues of signification and its modes were present in his academic community and attracted his philosophic attention. Aquinas is aware of the issues, first of all, in their Aristotelian context. His remarks about *On Interpretation* are based on the translation of Moerbeke, who retains *consignificat* precisely to render the Aristotelian *prossêmainon* of I,3. Aquinas adopts this word and discusses the problem of verbal temporality and the plurality of verbal forms in his commentary.[9]

But the force of the Aristotelian text reaches far beyond this single exposition. Aquinas employs the notion of the *modi significandi* in a variety of contexts. It occurs as early as the *De Ente et Essentia*, both in parsing technical terms and in the doc-

trine of the various *considerationes* of essence. As an example
of the first, one should note that even the familiar distinctions
between genus and difference are explicated as differences in
the ways of signifying the whole of what is in a species.[10] In
each such case, the distinctions are not stated as differences of
extension, but as differences of signification.

If the use of the modes of signification is common in *De Ente*,
it is more explicitly applied in the slightly later commentary on
Boethius's *De Hebdomadibus*. Here the task is in part a careful
analysis of terms having to do with beings and being. Thomas
begins the second *lectio* with an example familiar from
Abelard:[11] "aliud significamus cum dicimus currere, et aliud per
hoc quod dicitur currens."[12] Thomas draws from this a cardinal
distinction for his analysis of *esse* and *id quod est*: "Nam currere
et esse significantur in abstracto, sicut et albedo; sed quod est,
idest ens et currens, significantur sicut in concreto, velut
album."[13] He continues: "esse non significatur sicut ipsum
subiectum essendi, sicut nec currere significatur sicut subiectum
cursus: unde, sicut non possumus dicere quod ipsum currere
currat, ita non possumus dicere quod ipsum esse sit: sed sicut id
ipsum quod est, significatur sicut subiectum essendi, sic id quod
currit significatur sicut subiectum currendi."[14]

The passage is interesting for many reasons. Its chief per-
tinence at present is that it brings out the difference in the
signification of what is referentially the same. *Esse* signifies
abstractly; *quod est* signifies concretely. Whatever difference in
the referent might emerge, it does not do so as a result of the
distinctions in the object, but as a result of the ways in which
this must be signified by the human understanding. Similar
arguments might be found in *De Ente*'s handling of the two
sorts of *consideratio* of essence.[15]

The same point is also made at some length in a late
quodlibet.[16] At issue is "utrum enuntiabile, quod semel est
verum, semper sit verum."[17] Thomas remarks that "huius
dubitationis vis in hoc consistit, ut sciatur utrum sit idem enuntiabile, quod et de praesenti, praeterito et futuro." It is a doubt
about the semantic effects of tense. Aquinas attacks this question — precisely with the authority of Aristotle — by positing
the triple order of words, understandings, and things: "tria

quaedam per ordinem inveniuntur: nam voces sunt signa in-
tellectuum, intellectus autem sunt rerum similitudines."

Thomas insists that the unity or diversity of signifying words
is not taken from that of the thing signified. The varieties of
word depend, rather, on the order of signs or the order of
understandings. "Dependet ergo unitas vel diversitas vocis
significativae, sive complexae, sive incomplexae, ex unitate vel
diversitate vocis vel intellectus." Thus, words can be
differentiated either by a difference in the words alone (as with
synonymy), or by a difference in the understanding. There are
two cases of the latter. One is that of a difference in the thing
understood; the other is a difference in the way of understanding some one thing. This second occurs, Thomas notes,
whenever there is a case of consignification. Consignification
follows upon a "diversum modum intelligendi unam et eamdem
rem." This happens particularly in the case of time in so far as
the human soul adds a temporal marker in all its judgments.
Thus, 'Socrates sits,' 'Socrates was sitting,' and 'Socrates will sit'
are *not* the same *enuntiabile*; rather, each one of them is a simple *enuntiabile* because each is one set of words and one mode
of signification: " 'Socratem sedere' est idem enuntiabile, quia
est eadem vox, et idem modus significandi." Let me underscore
the importance of this. It shows that Thomas makes his own the
doctrine of the modes of signification as reflections of the ways
of human understanding.[18]

Thomas's appropriation of this doctrine is felt even more in
the analysis of language which secures his remarks on analogy.
He treats the limited mode of all language in each of his
works.[19] The treatments show variations which are worth
studying. But I will now take up only one of them; that from the
Contra Gentiles is most suitable because least elliptical.

The issue of the modes of signification arises in the *Contra
Gentiles* as part of the attempt to provide underpinnings for the
description of God.[20] Aquinas begins by distinguishing three
sorts of words: those which express a pure perfection which
can be predicated of God (e.g., 'wise'); those which express
rather a created species (e.g., 'stone'); and those which express
what can be said only of God (e.g., 'highest good'). The first and
third sorts signify something appropriately said of God. The second sort signifies something which could only be applied to

God metaphorically. All three sorts of words, whatever the degree of suitability as regards what is signified, suffer a radical limitation in their mode of signification. This is true even of the third sort of eminent names which apply only to God. Even these must be taken as literally inapplicable.

The limitation of all names results from their implicit consignification of inherence. Human knowledge has its origin from sensible things. In them, it finds a distinction between *forma* and *habens formam*, between the simplified abstract and the unsimplified subsistent. This distinction cuts across the threefold order of being, intellect, and sign. It is an ontological distinction between subsisting individual and the facets which its creaturehood produces within it. It is a distinction between the source and the terminus of abstractive knowledge. It is, finally, a semantic distinction between modes of signification. The three distinctions are brought together in a summary statement: "intellectus noster quidquid significat ut subsistens, significat in concretione; quod vero ut simplex significat, non ut quod est, sed ut quo est; et sic in omni nomine a nobis dicto, quantum ad modum significandi, imperfectio invenitur, quae Deo non competit."[21] The only way of reaching up to God through human language is by the artifice of apophatic negation.

Yet Thomas will qualify his adoption of the Dionysian stance by transposing it into the doctrine of analogy. That doctrine, with its many branches, extends considerably the basic notion of signifying modes. It begins, nonetheless, with the familiar thesis that no name can be applied univocally to God and creature.[22] The passage is worth recalling as a summary of the arguments for the signifying modes as inherent limitations. The most interesting arguments are those which move from modes of being to differences in predication and the final one, which reiterates the modes of predication itself.[23] The first arguments bring to mind the recurrent comparison between the modes of being and the modes of meaning. The former modes, which rest on a participational hierarchy, are reflected in the latter, in which the hierarchical bond seems to be a kind of participated intelligibility tied to the possibility of the *signum* itself.

The *ars* of grammar culminates, then, in a number of suggestions which are of great importance for philosophical discourse.

The doctrine of the modes of signification becomes the means by which to analyze the use of language in metaphysics and theology. It frees the language for metaphysical use. But the doctrine of the modes is still a study directed to the elements of discourse and not to its structures. It does not describe how language is concatenated — or how it teaches. These topics are left to the other arts and, beyond them, to the sciences of speculation.

2.3 MATERIALS FROM RHETORIC

Aquinas does judge the art of rhetoric rather harshly, even if he uses its lessons.[1] He is aware, first, of the ancient tension between the Gospel and pagan rhetoric. He resolves it in favor of Christian writers who best the rhetors in their own field: "sancti viri elegantius loquuntur quam etiam rhetores mundi, sicut Ambrosius, Hieronymus, et Leo Papa."[2] An objection puts the contrast between the two rhetorics more strongly in the *Contra Impugnantes Dei Cultum*: "excommunicandi sunt qui verbis sacrae scripturae eloquentiam rhetoricam vel sapientiam philosophicam immiscent."[3] In the same passage, however, Thomas rejects the complete divorce of Christian wisdom and pagan rhetoric, citing Jerome on the scriptural use of the books of the Gentiles. His general conclusion is this: "commendabile est quod aliquis eloquentiam et sapientiam saecularem ab obsequium divinae sapientiae trahat; et quod hoc reprehendentes sunt sicut caeci invidentes videntibus, quaecumque ignorant blasphemantes."[4] But there is a critical distinction to be drawn, Thomas thinks, between those who seek secular wisdom vainly as an end and those who use it justly for the propagation of the faith. "Commendatur autem quando non ad se ostentandum, sed ad utilitatem audientium ... utitur aliquis sapientia et eloquentia saeculari: et iterum quando aliquis non principaliter eis intendit, sed eis utitur in obsequium sacrae doctrinae, cui principaliter inhaeret, ut sic omnia alia in obsequium eius assumat."[5] Rhetoric can be saved by being radically subordinated not only to the practice of preaching, but to the higher rhetoric of theology.

There are other dangers in rhetoric, however, beyond the vanity of skill. Among these are the alignment of rhetoric with political and civic contention, as well as with the public (if not forensic) desire for persuasion. The political character of rhetorical persuasion is recognized several times during Aquinas's consideration of prudence in the *secunda secundae*. At issue in one context is the number and names of the parts of prudence. After giving the strict answer, Aquinas adds: "si vero prudentia sumatur large, secundum quod includit etiam scientiam speculativam ... tunc etiam partes eius ponuntur dialectica, rhetorica, et physica, secundum tres modos procedendi in scientiis.... [T]ertius modus est ex quibusdam conjecturis ad suspicionem inducendam, vel ad aliqualiter persuadendum, quod pertinet ad rhetoricam."[6] This same issue arises negatively in the next Question, when it is asked whether quickness of wit (*solertia*) is a part of prudence. The third objection argues that it is not because it belongs most properly to rhetoric and not to prudence generally. It argues, "[S]olertia ... est quaedam bona conjecturatio. Sed conjecturis uti est proprium rhetorum."[7] Aquinas replies that "rhetorica etiam ratiocinatur circa operabilia. Unde nihil prohibet idem ad rhetoricam et prudentiam pertinere. Et tamen conjecturatio hic non sumitur solum secundum quod pertinet ad conjecturas quibus utuntur rhetores, sed secundum quod in quibuscunque dicitur homo coniicere veritatem."[8]

These two passages recall quite distinctly the definitions of rhetoric in the arts sources available to Thomas. Indeed, Thomas echoes the definitions more formulaically in several other texts: "rhetorica ... negotiatur circa materiam civilem,"[9] or "rhetorica ... sit scientia bene dicendi ad persuadendum,"[10] or "[rhetorica], quae docet ornate loqui."[11] On the traditional divisions of rhetorical doctrine, Aquinas has less to say. He recognizes in an objection its three 'offices': "[E]x naturali ratione adinventa est ars rhetorica, per quam aliquis potest sic dicere ut doceat, ut delectet, ut flectat, sicut Augustinus dicit."[12] But Thomas replies to this very objection, in defense of the divine gift of eloquence *gratis data*, that the Holy Spirit "excellentius operatur per gratiam sermonis id quod potest ars operari inferiori modo."[13] Thomas elsewhere makes his own the three "genera causarum" of classical rhetoric, the demonstrative, the deliberative, and the judicial.[14] Of technical rhetorical styles and devices, he mentions exhortation, enthymeme, example, praise, and vituperation, as well as that use of conjecture which seems to him to be the special mark of rhetoric.[15] His favorite technical allusion is to the rhetorical requirement for an exordium to win the hearer's benevolence, a requirement which he applies even to prayer.[16] In the *Summa*, Thomas analyzes the Annunciation according to rhetorical headings. Gabriel is discovered to have had three intentions in speaking to Mary: "rederre mentem eius attentam," "eam instruere," "animam eius inducere ad consensum."[17] These three correspond to the main divisions of Ciceronian argument.[18] Rhetoric makes one last technical appearance in the discussion of whether the faith ought to be articulated in a creed divided into 'articles'. Thomas's answer contains a careful explication of what 'article' means in Roman rhetoric, buttressing his remarks with a quotation from Book IV of the *Ad Herennium*, which he takes to be a work by Cicero.[19]

Beyond the definitions and the devices, there is a thoroughgoing subordination of rhetoric, here connected with dialectic, to philosophy and its logic. This denigration of rhetoric is not only motivated by Aristotle's arguments in the Organon; it is also fueled, I think, by that ancient Christian disquiet over the pretensions of forensic rhetoric. Thus the attack comes in two stages. Thomas insists that rhetoric be subordinated, in first place, to theology. He asks at one point in the *prima secundae* whether theology ought to treat of the circumstances of human action. An objection argues that the consideration of circumstances belongs properly to rhetoric, which is not a part of theology.[20] Aquinas replies that the consideration of the circumstances of human actions belongs equally to the moralist, the politician, and the rhetor — to the first with regard to the investigation of the virtues, to the second as part of judgment, to the third as ordered to persuasion. But such consideration belongs equally and more properly to the theologian in all of the previous modes, since all the arts serve him — "cui omnes aliae artes derserviunt."[21] This principle, taken together with Aquinas's earlier remarks on the superiority of inspired speaking over the speech crafted by rhetoric, makes clear that there is no room for an autonomous rhetoric.

The second stage comes in defining rhetoric's subordination to the best of arts and sciences. Rhetoric must be subjected to logical demonstration. Here Thomas links rhetoric to dialectic, now in its pejorative sense, in order to contrast the probabilism of both with the rigorous necessity of demonstration. (The rarer couplings of rhetoric and poetry have roughly the same sense.)[22] The charges against the linked arts are many. Rhetoric and dialectic both use motley opinion.[23] They prey upon the freedom of the human will.[24] Rhetorical argument is disputatious, as is dialectic.[25] Rhetoric, then, falls far short of philosophical reasoning and cannot be expected to provide certain demonstrations.[26]

One finds the same points made against dialectic itself. I will consider the critique of dialectic below, in tracing the genesis of notions about logic. But let me simply recall this much of the Aristotelian attack, which Thomas makes largely his own. Dialectic has pretensions to universality and tries in this to mimic the philosopher, a mimicry which it shares with sophistry.[27] When this pretension cannot be fulfilled, the dialetician resorts to probabilities and common opinions. Unable to reason demonstratively about what is, he reasons by heaping together whatever is said by the many, whatever is usually thought.[28] Of course, the dialectician can from such foundations and with such a procedure produce in fact no more than opinion.[29] When dialectical arguments pretend or appear to be demonstrative, they become plainly sophistical.[30] Thomas's agreement with Aristotle is clear, as is his sympathy with the wider reorganization of the trivium which makes dialectic and rhetoric, both, distant reflections of demonstrative logic.

Yet the explicit doctrine ought not to blind one to an abiding presence of rhetorical structures in Thomas's work. If Thomas has little use for the claims of rhetoric, he nonetheless finds himself constantly trying to do what he has said is the office of the rhetorician. I mean, he tries to persuade. This is not only true in the general, if forgotten, sense that all philosophy must offer itself as an act of persuasion. It is also true in the specific and technical sense that Thomas's favorite literary form, the *quaestio disputata*, is a public act of dialectic and of *inventio* which is completed in an act of persuasion. I will consider the general rhetorical stance of Aquinas before turning to the specific persuasion of the *quaestio*.

A great part of Aquinas's corpus consists of commentaries. It ought not to be surprising that rhetorical considerations arise in writing those commentaries. It is perhaps more surprising that Aquinas applies the classical analysis of the *exordium* to the opening of Aristotle's *De Anima*. He construes the opening paragraphs of the treatise as a *proemium* with a specific rhetorical purpose — or, rather, three purposes. "Primo ut auditorem reddat benevolum. Secundo ut reddat docilem. Tertio ut reddat attentum. Benevolum quidem reddit, ostendendo utilitatem scientiae; docilem, praemittendo ordinem et distinctionem tractatus; attentum attestando difficultatem tractatus. Quae quidem tria Aristoteles facit in proemio huius tractatus."[31] Aquinas goes on to read the rest of the opening under this threefold division, just as if he were analyzing a speech in court.

Now it might seem that the most obvious source for such a reading would be Aristotle himself. If the *Rhetoric* could be applied to the *De Anima*, this would be a perfect case of reading *Aristoteles ex Aristotele*. But there are only slight resemblances between what Aquinas says here and what Aristotle writes about "introductions" in the *Rhetoric*, II,14. They disagree strongly, in fact, both with regard to the need for an introduction and with regard to its aims. Aristotle finds the introduction dispensable and variable. Aquinas finds it indispensable and fixed — because he is thinking of the classic source in Cicero's *De Inventione*: "Exordium est oratio animum auditoris idonee comparans ad reliquam dictionem; quod eveniet si eum benivolum, attentum, docilem conficerit."[32] A similar list occurs in the *Rhetorica ad Herennium*.[33] The same list of three attributes, with different orders, recurs in Martianus,[34] in Isidore,[35] and in Thomas's contemporary Guido Faba,[36] to mention only three names. Thomas also applies such classical patterns in commenting on Isaiah, Jeremiah, and *Lamentations,* for each of which he supplies a short *accessus*.[37]

Aquinas sees in many places, then, good examples of a rhetorically constructed *exordium*. Other have found in the structures of Aquinas's works the rhetorical schemes of Greek and Latin rhetoric. Guy Allard, for example, has argued that the entire *Summa Contra Gentiles* must be read as a deliberative discourse, on Aristotelian lines, aimed at convincing its readers about the best way to happiness.[38] Allard finds more interesting than Aquinas's use of Aristotelian models of deliberative speech the political character of the resulting argument, which he calls a "response to a social menace."[39] Here Allard seems to be misled, though in an interesting way. For Thomas to take the model of deliberative speech as civil, as still part of that forensic rhetoric which died with democratic antiquity, would again entail the issue of rhetoric's subordination to theology and philosophy. It would be much more appropriate not to think of civil deliberation, but of theological deliberation — that is, of preaching or disputation. It may be that preaching is the Christian political activity in the widest sense, since it is a public speaking which constitutes the true community. But the community is not civic. Indeed, it stands over against the civic. Preaching is the most obvious theological embodiment of medieval rhetoric and may be the immediate source for many of Aquinas's rhetorical patterns.[40] Still, he finds a more technical practice in the formal persuasion or disputation of the Christian academic community.

2.4 THE DISPUTED QUESTION

If there are rhetorical schemata imbedded in Aquinas's works, there are also rhetorical facets in his arguments. He takes the *quaestio disputata* as his preferred literary form; it has any number of rhetorical aspects. Indeed, the specific form of the *quaestio* was first tested in the rhetorical ambience of the law schools and the exegetical practice of theologians, passing then into the arts and philosophy. The history of its popularity has been retold elsewhere; there is no need to paraphrase it here. Nor is there any need to reiterate the arguments of de Ghellinck which link the emergence of the *quaestio* and the *summa* to developments in jurisprudential exegesis and codification.[1] One ought to notice, however, the re-emergences of the forensic character of rhetoric in the *quaestio disputata*. Indeed, '*quaestio*' is a technical term in rhetoric which denotes something at issue, whether a particular case or a general principle.[2]

The dialectic of opposing positions is, of course, the characteristic of litigation and is specifically described in the rhetorical tradition as the means of finding the issues in a case. Martianus, for instance, writes: "Ex his [scil. intentio, depulsio] inter se concurrentibus vocibus nascitur quaestio, quae dicitur status, quod ibi quasi ad pugnandum actionum acies ordinata consistant."[3] In the great wealth of analysis devoted to the types of *status*, one finds further the use of complex exegetical stratagems for shifting the case one way or the other. Martianus, again, provides in his discussion of *to krinomenon* a list of exegetical and logical difficulties which can arise in the use of evidence, including amphiboly, textual criticism, or the conflict between 'letter' and 'spirit'.[4] Similar cases occur in the consideration of the conflict of laws.[5] There is much more detail in the analysis of the types of argument, which Martianus defines quite interestingly as "ratio, quae rei dubiae fidem facit," where "res dubia est intentio et dupulsio, vel ratio et infirmatio rationis," thus recalling the definition of *quaestio*.[6]

The forensic turn can also be seen in the appearance of such works as the *Ecclesiastica Rhetorica* during the latter half of the twelfth century; the book is, according to Caplan, "virtually a forensic rhetoric for canon law, and professedly developed in accordance with rhetorical doctrine."[7] There was also a much broader use of question-and-answer in arts contexts, such as in the medical and naturalistic *quaestio*-literature derived from numerous classical models.[8] Perhaps these forms lie on the border between the catechetical questioning of Alcuin and the forensic, disputed question of the canonists.[9]

Even if the historical connections were better known, the importance of the *quaestio* as a device for philosophic investigation would not have been settled. It would still be necessary to understand the peculiarities of the *quaestio* as a rhetorical form. These peculiarities are the best clues to exegesis, because they foreshadow the short of truth which is sought and offered in *quaestiones*. The rhetorical form of the *quaestio* is a sign of the motion of philosophic inquiry which is tacitly presupposed by its users, including Aquinas. It is the expression of Aquinas's daily rhetorical practice.[10]

If it can be assumed that philosophical texts do have rhetorical forms of interest for philosophy itself, there are still three specific points to be made about the rhetorical character of the *quaestio* as Thomas uses it. First, it is an imitation of public procedures for oral inquiry and instruction. Chenu is right in quoting Mandonnet's insistence that a disputed question is not simply a transcript of the festal debates in the universities.[11] It is equally true that an Article in the *Summa* is a stylized version of an actual disputed question. Both the written disputed question and the Article are 'imitations' (to use the Platonic word) of the form of public inquiry. Of course, the forms of that inquiry themselves go back to earlier literary and verbal forms, among which would be the Platonic dialogues and courtroom debates. Then, too, the influences in academic communities between written work and formal speech go in both directions. The Aristotelian treatises record school *logoi*; the school *logoi* are written texts used to control oral inquiry. So, for Aquinas, the disputed questions are ideal versions of public debate, and public debate is a debate built on *sententiae* from authoritative texts.

To be an imitation of public inquiry, to be a dialogue, has certain consequences. The first is that any given discourse admits of the continuing possibility of conversation. More concretely, there is the assumption of a community of *auditores*, of listeners, which can supply what is not stated and aptly qualify what is. The assumption of *auditores* is not a license to posit 'unwritten doctrines'; it is a reminder of the temporal character of Aquinas's inquiry. The answer of the *magister* is given as the answer on a particular day, to a particularly phrased question, on the basis of the adduced authorities and arguments. To say this is not to imply, of course, that the answer can be discarded as unimportant, or that it was given in haste, or that all answers are equal. But it does suggest that the solution of a *quaestio*, much as the opinion on a case in common law, is an utterance which recognizes itself as subject to further reasoning and interpretation. Such an utterance is read differently than a monograph written in the false eternity of the 'light of reason'.

A *quaestio* is an imitation of public dialogue — that is its first feature. The second feature is related, but concerns not so much the dialogue in the present as the dialogue with an authoritative past. The evolution of the *quaestio* accelerated with the work of legal harmonization and codification. Abelard himself remarks that it is the "dissonance" of magisterial texts which gives rise to questions.[12] As the heir of the *florilegia*, the *compendia* of laws, the various compilations of *sententiae* (which culminate in Peter Lombard), and Abelard's own works of dialectic, the *quaestio* is a device for digesting apparently insoluble conflicts among authoritative statements. It is well to remember that the conflicts are real. If Clarembald of Arras thought that the zeal for questioning had been carried to ridiculous heights,[13] it would nonetheless be wrong to overlook the posing of real questions in Aquinas and to assume that the *quaestiones* are only handy section headings. The *quaestiones* arise at least in part because of conflicts among the statements of the tradition. The hope for a resolution implicit in the *quaestio* is the hope of reconciling these fragments of discourse, these *sententiae*.

Here enters the discovery of hierarchies in discourse for which Abelard's Prologue to *Sic et Non* can serve as a summary example.[14] Far from being a skeptic's gleeful dismantling of the tradition, that book is concerned to assemble the various *sententiae* into a hierarchy which would save the particular authority of each.[15] This can be done, Abelard sees, by admitting the possibility of semantic variability. On its simplest level, this admission recognizes equivocity. "Facilis autem plerumque controversiarum solutio reperietur si eadem verba in diversis significationibus a diversis auctoribus posita defendere poterimus."[16] The second step is to see that these different meanings can be ordered in a coherent pattern — can constitute an analogy.

What Abelard sees is something more than the rudimentary exegetical rule that one must interpret according to context. He sees that there is nothing impossible in having languages operate at different levels of signification. The levels can be put extrinsically as a hierarchy of the authorities themselves. "Quod si forte adeo manifesta sit controversia ut nulla possit absolvi ratione, conferendae sunt auctoritates, et quae potioris est testimonii et maioris confirmationis potissimum retinenda."[17] But levels are also put intrinsically as a plurality of meanings which witness to the distances separating author, text, and reader. Perhaps the author misspoke himself; perhaps the text has been corrupted; perhaps the reader has not understood. In all cases, Abelard insists, the exegete must carefully consider what *sort* of text it is, and how meaning is to be found in it, and what sort of authority it has.[18]

Abelard's ordering of contexts is crucial to the work of the *quaestio*. The *quaestio* is a symphony of competing *sententiae*, competing voices, each sounding a different instrument differently. The fact that one brings these together to make sense and not mere cacophony, suggests already that there must be some possibility of ordering them harmoniously. One can already see in this the third feature of the *quaestio*, what developed after Abelard in the new theories of syntax. The refinement of Abelard's dialectical manipulations issued in an emphasis on the determination of disputed questions. A determination is nothing but the bringing together of the various levels of *sententiae*. Having put the fragments in their proper constellation, the determination is an act of judgment on their truth, which judgment entails a judgment of their signifying relations. In short, the very form of the *quaestio* must raise questions about the possibilities of establishing a hierarchy in discourse.

The possibilities for hierarchy in the authorities could be seen directly in a passage where Thomas reflects on the determining act of the Master in theology. The issue is "utrum magister determinando quaestiones theologicas magis debeat uti ratione, vel auctoritate."[19] Thomas distinguishes two sorts of dispute. The first of these is a dispute ordered to removing some doubt about whether a certain thing is or is not the case. In this sort of dispute, one ought to use authorities which are accepted by one's interlocutor. If he accepts no authorities — if he does not stand somewhere in the hierarchy — then one must descend to natural reason ("ad rationes naturales confugere").[20] The second sort of dispute, however, is the one most associated with academic situations — that is, with Aquinas's own theological work. Here the dispute is not for the purpose of removing doubt, "sed ad instruendum auditores ut inducantur ad intellectum veritatis quam intendit." In this second case, the master ought to use reasons to seek out the "veritatis radicem," leading the hearers to understand *in what way* the statements are true. Otherwise, they leave empty-handed. The master gives arguments to show in what way the proposition is true — arguments which interpret and organize the authorities adduced in the first moment of dispute.[21]

A much more extended consideration of the nature of dispute is found in Aquinas's commentary on *Job*. He is simply following Jerome and Gregory in viewing *Job* as that book of Scripture that embodies the art of dialectic.[22] It is not surprising that Thomas should be tempted to describe Job's conversations with his interlocutors on the analogy to formal disputes. It may not even be surprising that he extends the analogy to treating God as the master of disputation.[23] What is striking, however, is the detail with which the analogy is worked out. There are meticulous analyses of the logic of each speech; there are also explicit reflections on the practice of disputation. The reflections can be as simple as the remark that in proceeding "more disputationis" one speaks according to the opinions of one's adversaries before speaking the plain truth.[24] The reflections can also be assembled into something like a model for disputation.

The aim or purpose of disputation is to make some truth clear. There are various obstacles to that purpose. Two such obstacles are physical or passionate: a disputant may be prevented from defending truth by bodily ailment or by an overweaning passion.[25] Three more serious obstacles block the way to *finding* truth.[26] The first is a failure to listen to one's adversary. The second is a choice to respond to him "clamose et contumeliose." The third obstacle is a perversion of pedagogical motive; it is the desire, not for truth, but for victory and glory, as in litigious and sophistical disputes.

The solution to these three obstacles is to be found in the character of those disputing. Two characters appear in a dispute, the "opponens" and the "respondens."[27] The "opponens" must have a sharp mind by which to construct arguments for the point to be shown; the "respondens" must have wisdom so that he may judge what he hears.[28] Both must be able to listen "attente," "graviter et cum stupore [i.e., with wonder]," even "silenter et sine mussitatione."[29] Moreover, and this is the great difficulty, both disputants must act according to the proper motive. Even interlocutors of great skill must enter into dispute only in order to bring about a mutual disclosure of truth.[30] When Thomas defends Job against the charge of sinfulness, he captures the problem of motive in a pedagogical distinction: one may seek to dispute with God "sicut ad contradicendum de pari" or, rather, "quasi ad addiscendum sicut discipulus cum magistro."[31] The first is sinful, the second not. The second, more generally, expresses that subordination to the learning of truth which is required by any disputation. That is why every disputant must be willing to answer as well as to ask, to listen as well as to assert.[32]

The disputed question is heir to this long rhetorical tradition, which it appropriates with varying self-consciousness. One can argue as to how far Aquinas was concerned with the rhetorical underpinnings of his most common literary form. But two things he surely took over from the tradition with full awareness. The first was the conviction that a dispute was intended to settle some doubt by means of rational persuasion — that philosophical argument was fundamentally rhetorical according to the old definition of 'rhetoric'. The second conviction was that one of the best means of persuasion was that taught by logic. Argument is, as Martianus says, a means of producing credence. Credence comes, Aquinas remarks, by the reading of authorities and by reliance on 'natural' reasoning. This reasoning is studied in the logical forms of demonstration.

2.5 MATERIALS FROM LOGIC

Logic, Thomas writes, is the art of arts and the key to the sciences; it is the study of the general way of all knowledge. "[H]aec ars est logica, idest rationalis scientia. Quae non solum rationalis est ex hoc, quod est secundum rationem (quod est omnibus artibus commune); sed etiam ex hoc quod est circa ipsum actum rationis sicut circa propriam materiam. Et ideo videtur esse ars artium, quia in actu rationis nos dirigit, a quo omnes artes procedunt."[1] He writes of *logica* rather than *dialectica*. He will make clear shortly in the same text that the aspirations of *dialectica* to rational universality are impotent. Slightly more than a century earlier, in another attempt to free logic from calumnies and to give it the "principatum" which it deserved, Abelard had equated logic with dialectic.[2] Indeed, the title of his work was simply *Dialectica*. Is the change from Abelard to Aquinas merely nominal?

There had been another change of terminology with the arrival, during the 1120s if not before, of the Aristotelian texts which constituted the *'logica nova'*. The *'logica vetus'* had been dialectical and disputative, interested in terms and strings of terms chiefly for their usefulness in controversial reading. Its three central texts were Aristotle's *Categories* and *On Interpretation* and Porphyry's *Isagoge*, as these were translated and interpreted by Boethius.[3] Less central were four other Boethian treatises, including his *Liber de Divisione* and the unfinished commentary on Cicero's *Topica*, as well as his studies of categorical syllogisms and topics.[4] The *'logica nova'* added to these works the rest of Aristotle's Organon, as well as a *Liber Sex Principiorum* later attributed to Gilbert Porretanus.[5] Of these, the most startling was the *Posterior Analytics*. The paradigm of demonstrative *scientia* offered there by Aristotle was the difficult but appealing alternative to the practice of dialectic. When dialectic itself was subjected to the dissection of Aristotle in the *Topics* and the *Sophistical Refutations*, the effect on the conception of logic was bound to be thoroughgoing.

It was not sudden. Abelard himself, the embodiment of dialectical logic, seems to have had some knowledge of the *Analytics*, the *Topics*, and the *Sophistical Refutations*, the latter two of which were clearly in circulation by the time Adam Balsamiensis wrote his *Ars Disserendi*.[6] The Abelardian texts are ambiguous as to the extent and source of the knowledge of the new Aristotelian logic, however, and it seems that Abelard had by no means fully appropriated it.[7] Abelard also sometimes distinguishes and sometimes conflates *'logica'* and *'dialectica'*, a vacillation which may be attributable to the conflation of traditions in the Boethian texts with which Abelard worked.[8] With Adam Balsamiensis and the other members of the generation which spans Abelard's death, the presence of the new texts is more pronounced, but their appropriation is still local, piecemeal.[9] Their first impact was on those areas which were already central in the late dialectical tradition.

The introduction and gradual assimilation of the *'logica nova'* accounts at least in part for the shift from Abelardian *'dialectica'* to Thomist *'logica'*. Yet the shift from Abelard to Aquinas also sees the development of a *'logica moderna'* as

against a *'logica nova'*. This distinction is not made in order to
mark the influx of still another body of ancient texts. On the
contrary, the *'logica moderna'* is a specifically medieval contribution to the study of logic, which is especially associated
with the analysis of the *proprietates terminorum*.[10] The *'logica
moderna'* was triumphant in the fourteenth century, but its
roots reach back to the twelfth. I have already indicated some
misgivings about any sharp division between *'logica moderna'*
and *'logica nova'* in the twelfth and thirteenth centuries; to emphasize the distinction too much is to project the victory of the
fourteenth century back into the twelfth. It is also possible to interpret the study of terms in the earlier authors not as a
foreshadowing of the later terminists, but as the antecedent to
the thirteenth-century *modistae*.[11] Whatever the resolution of
these difficulties, Aquinas is separated from Abelard in logic not
only by the new texts, but by the growth of a new doctrine
about the syntactic study of terms.

The new doctrine reinforced the more ancient predominance
of logic over the other arts of the trivium and within
philosophy. When Aquinas describes logic as the art of arts, he
is merely echoing a tradition that goes back to the boasting of
Dialectic at Martianus's wedding feast. There the woman, pale
from study, claims that "meique prorsus iuris esse, quicquid
Artes ceterae proloquuntur,"[12] since each of the arts must use
reasoning. In Rabanus, the superlative phrase appears: "Haec
ergo [scil. dialectica] disciplina disciplinarum est."[13] Eriugena's
glosses on Martianus show the same tendency to exalt logic; he
devotes by far the greatest time and interest to the glosses on the
speech of Dialectic.[14] In Abelard, the excellence of logic is
argued precisely on the grounds that it is not an *'ars'* but a
'scientia'.[15] In Adam Balsamiensis, however, the *'ars disserendi'* or dialectic is once again an art, though it is distinguished as
'scientia', *'ars'* and *'facultas'*.[16] It is, Adam Balsamiensis notes,
one of the last arts to develop, in part because of the fact that its
expositors assume much in the way of prior preparation.[17] By
the time of Shyreswood's *Introductiones in Logicam*, there is
not only the exaltation of logic as a part of the *scientia ser-
monicalis* centered on truth, but also a subsuming within logic
of the treatment of terms which might have seemed the province of grammar.[18]

Aquinas learns of the exaltation of logic in being a student of
the *'logica antiqua'* and the *'logica nova'*, if not of the *'logica
moderna'*. Indeed, he conflates several different definitions,
which themselves show the progress of logic from dialectic to
demonstration. In the passage already quoted, Thomas calls
logic "rationalis scientia," the "ars artium" which "in actu rationis nos dirigit." The language comprehends both old and
new. The Isidorean definition of *'dialectica'* saw it as
"disciplina ad disserendas rerum causas inventa. Ipsa est
philosophiae species, quae Logica dicitur, id est rationalis
definiendi, quaerendi et disserendi potens. Docet enim in
pluribus generibus quaestionum quemadmodum disputando
vera et falsa diiudicentur."[19] This is also one of the definitions
in Boethius.[20] It is echoed in Alcuin[21] and Rabanus.[22] It
reemerges in the twelfth-century texts which define dialectic or
logic as *'ars'* or *'ratio disserendi'*.[23] That is the old. The same
definition is repeated with a new sense by Gundissalinus.[24]
Gundassilinus teaches that there are eight parts to logic —
named according to the books of the Organon together with the
Rhetoric and the *Poetics* — and that the chief among them is the
fourth part, the *Posterior Analytics*.[25] He relies here explicitly
on the authority of al-Farabi.[26] It is Farabi who gives Gundissalinus a view of logic already reworked around the *'logica
nova'*, already reordered away from dialectic and towards
demonstrative science. So Gundissalinus explicitly subordinates
dialectic to demonstration.[27] Again, in describing the arrangement of the Organon, Gundissalinus sharply distinguishes the
demonstrative science taught by the second *Analytics* from the
(dialectical) teaching of the *Topics*.[28] Indeed, the second reason
which Gundissalinus can find for the inclusion of the *Topics* and
the *Sophistical Refutations* within the Organon is that they
serve to warn the unwary that these arts cannot produce certitude, but merely *'fides'* or *'opinio'*.[29] His first reason is that
these lesser books might serve as propaedeutics for those who
are not yet able to be moved by the necessity of demonstration.[30]

The assimilation of the Aristotelian model for science which
is asserted by Gundissalinus in an abstract way is accomplished
in practice by Aquinas's immediate predecessors in the early
thirteenth century. It is seen in logic with writers such as

Shyreswood and Lambert of Auxerre.[31] It is seen in the theological use of logical materials among the first mendicant writers. In Thomas himself, the appropriation of the new logic is complete both as program and as practice. The program which he sets forth in his commentaries on Aristotle and elsewhere is an elaboration of that proposed by Gundissalinus. The practice is that of the ubiquitous use of demonstration on the model of the *Analytics*.

Thomas offers a coherent description of his programmatic view of logic in the preface to his commentary on the *Posterior Analytics*. Schmidt argues that this can be taken as a doctrine given in Aquinas's own voice, since it is placed before the point at which he actually turns to the Aristotelian text.[32] I think that Schmidt misconstrues the rules of the commentary genre in the thirteenth century; there is no reason why Aquinas cannot be speaking *aristotelice* in the proemium as much as in the exposition. But the passage will serve, in either case, to show both the dominance of the second *Analytics* and Thomas's ease in handling those once strange materials.

Thomas begins his introduction by recalling Aristotle's remark that human life is to be distinguished from animal because of its use of art and reasoning. Art orders human actions to their various ends, since an art is "certa ordinatio rationis quomodo per determinata media ad debitum finem actus humani perveniat."[33] Reason, as self-reflective, is capable of directing the actions both of itself and of other powers. So logic is nothing other than the art which reason discovers by reflecting on its own acts. It is in this way that logic becomes the 'art' of arts.

Any division of logic would then most appropriately be made according to the division of reason's activity.[34] Thomas finds three acts in reason. The first two pertain to reason in so far as it is "intellectus quidam," whether simple or complex. To simple "intellectus" there corresponds the work, called by some "informatio intellectus" or "imaginatio per intellectum," of grasping what a thing is.[35] This activity, Thomas writes, is analyzed in the Aristotelian *Categories*. To the complex "intellectus," which produces by composition or division the true and the false, there corresponds the teaching of the *Peri Hermeneias* (cf. 1.1, above). The third act is the one that per-

tains to reason *per se*. This is the discursive activity: "discurrere
ab uno in aliud, ut per id quod est notum deveniat in cognitionem ignoti." It is delineated in the remaining books of the
Organon — or, as Thomas has it, by the remaining books "of
logic."

The further division of these remaining books is accomplished by an analogy to natural processes, which Thomas sees
as being in some ways like the processes of art.[36] Some natural
processes unfold necessarily and without possibility of defect;
others unfold only usually and are subject to error, though it
happens in fact quite rarely. Other processes still are completely
misdirected, monstrous, and result from some defect or
disorder. So it is with discursive reasoning. To the necessary
processes, there corresponds scientific demonstration, called
iudicativa, which judges with the certainty of *scientia*.[37] It is
treated in the two books of the *Analytics*, appropriately so named in so far as demonstration works by resolution, by *analysis*.
It is further divided into two parts, the first of which deals with
the necessity of the syllogism's form (what might be called simple validity), and the second of which deals with the matter of
demonstration, with the substance of demonstrative syllogisms.

To the natural processes which are only usually accomplished, there corresponds the *logica inventiva*. Since
discovery is not always certain, one must be careful to consider
the degree of certainty which attends any particular result. The
highest certainty attainable in *inventio* is merely opinion, whose
exact degree varies with the probability of the propositions
from which one has proceeded.[38] With opinion, reason is total-
ly moved to one of the two poles of a contradiction — the result
of the art studied in topics or dialectics and described by Aristotle in his *Topics*. The second degree in *inventio* is merely a kind
of "suspicio" which takes one of the alternatives over others,
without being entirely convinced. "Suspicio" is produced by
rhetoric. At the next degree down, there is not even a
"suspicio" produced by argument, but merely an "existimatio"
created by representation, chiefly in poetry. Thomas does not
think that poetry must be ignoble, though it is cognitively weak.
The work of the poet, after all, is "inducere ad aliquod vir-
tuosum per aliquam decentem repraesentationem."[39] And

poetry takes further luster by being set against sophistic. Poetry at least seeks truth; sophistic does not, and so falls outside "rationalis philosophia."[40] Thomas does not deign even to describe sophistic, since it is a miscarriage of the discursive movement. He notes only that Aristotle has treated of it in the *Sophistical Refutations*.

The classification of the proemium is clear, perhaps even deceptively so. Demonstration denominates the entire arrangement. Thomas holds, with Gundissalinus, that logic is for the sake of the theory of demonstration in the *Analytics*. That theory subordinates both the theory of terms which comes before it and the theory of the less-than-scientific processes which comes after it. Dialectic is, in this passage, clearly relegated to second rank, being a logic of discovery but not of proof. It could never in principle attain to that sort of certitude which is the desired end of human knowing. This conclusion would be misleading if one took it as Thomas's only or constant teaching on logic. As is always the case, Thomas's vocabulary is fluid, even with regard to technical matters, and his use of *'logica'* and its sibling-terms varies considerably from one passage to another. Schmidt finds passages even in this same commentary in which *'logica'* is described as if it were equivalent to *'dialectica'* and so contrasted with *'analytica'*.[41] In other passages, "modus logicus," "per logicas rationes," and "secundum considerationem logicam" are used with a dialectical or otherwise contracted sense.[42]

But the play in the use of terms cannot be taken as suggesting that Thomas is willing to reaccredit the claims of dialectic, at least not in the Aristotelian sense. When Thomas comes to explicate Aristotle's distinction between the use of common principles in demonstration and in dialectic, he emphasizes their differences and then uses the occasion to contrast both logic (i.e., demonstration) and dialectic with first philosophy: "Sciendum tamen est quod alia ratione dialectica est de communibus et logica et philosophia prima. Philosophia enim prima est de communibus, quia eius consideratio est circa ipsas res communes, scilicet circa ens et partes et passiones entis. Et quia circa omnia quae in rebus sunt habet negotiari ratio, logica autem est de operationibus rationis; logica etiam erit de his, quae communia sunt omnibus, idest de intentionibus rationis, quae ad omnes res

se habent.... Sed hoc dialectica facit, quia ex communibus intentionibus procedit arguendo dialecticus ad ea quae sunt aliarum
scientiarum, sive sint propria sive communia, maxime tamen ad
communia."[43] But even this clear distinction is too strong if one
considers the search for first principles in metaphysics — a
search which Aristotle describes in the *Topics* as 'dialectic'.
Thomas's own dialectic will be considered below.

There is also in this passage, as Schmidt points out, the mention of a distinction between pure and applied logic.[44] Schmidt
develops the distinction to help in explaining some of the
vagaries of terminology already mentioned.[45] Of more importance than these anomalies is the question of the place of logic
in the hierarchies of arts and *scientiae*. The history of the
trivium, as should by now be clear, is the record of the attempt
of one or another of its three arts to assume a privileged position. Grammar offers itself not only as the first study, but as the
universal key to meaning; rhetoric is not only the study of
disputation, but also the technique of persuasion and so of
power; logic, in its earlier guise as dialectic, exerts a control
over both the form and matter of all the other arts, whether in
the *trivium* or the *quadrivium*.

Is is not surprising, then, that Thomas does not place logic so
neatly as one might like. It can be called an *'ars'*; so much is obvious from the proemium to the *Analytics* commentary. It is
also a liberal art, though that does not make it more artful.[46] But
logic is also and even preeminently *scientia*. In the proemium
itself, Thomas moves very quickly from calling logic the "ars artium" to calling it "rationalis scientia."[47] What place has logic,
then, among the other *scientiae*? Here there are different
schemata. If one uses the practical/theoretical division familiar
from Aristotle, then a place must be made for logic as a rational
but not really speculative science, insofar as logic is not merely
practical or factive.[48] If one uses the different division of *Ethics*
I, logic becomes the unique 'methodological' science, rather
than a substantive one.[49] Then a special place must be made for
logic as an instrument for philosophy. As instrument, it is at
once among the *scientiae* and yet not fully one of them, "since
the mind does not merely discover what it studies, but both
makes and finds it. [Logic] is, therefore, only reductively
speculative and only a quasi-speculative science."[50]

The ambivalent place of logic with regard to the sciences is another trace of the birth of the notion of science in the logical works of Aristotle. There are difficult issues here: whether Aristotle himself follows or means to follow his own logical precepts in the substantive works; whether Aquinas means to do so; whether anyone could do so. But there is no doubt that this notion of science as demonstration from evident principles informed Aristotle's and Aquinas's thinking about procedure. For this reason, if no other, it is worth recalling the main features of the notion of science and worth seeing its extension into the question of the hierarchy of speculative *scientiae*. It is that hierarchy which Thomas will find one of the most fruitful extensions of logic into the understanding of discourse.

The first extensive treatment of science *per se* in the commentary on the second *Analytics* occurs in *lectio* 4, in regard to the second chapter of Book I of Aristotle's work. It will help in avoiding later misconstruals to note that this passage, both in Aristotle and in Thomas's commentary, begins by considering what it is to know something in the strongest sense. The characteristics of *scientia* given here are derived from what is meant by *'scire'*. Even the grammatical relation of *'scientia'* to *'scire'* says this. It is very difficult to reproduce such a relation in English, unless one introduces the term 'knowingness' as the translation for *'scientia'*. The beginning of the study of demonstration is a definition precisely of the activity of knowing: "aliquid dicimus scire simpliciter, quando scimus illud in seipso.... [S]cire aliquid est perfecte cognoscere ipsum, hoc autem est perfecte apprehendere veritatem ipsius: eadem enim sunt principia esse rei et veritatis ipsius.... Oportet igitur scientem, si est perfecte cognoscens, quod cognoscat causam rei scitae.... Et ideo oportet scientem simpliciter cognoscere etiam applicationem causae ad effectum. Quia vero scientia est etiam certa cognitio rei; quod autem contingit aliter se habere, non potest aliquis per certitudinem cognoscere; ideo ulterius oportet quod id quod scitur non possit aliter se habere."[51]

The familiar elements of the Aristotelian notion of *scientia* are all here. *Scientia* is the strongest sort of knowing for things that have causes of their being; it knows such a thing essentially and not accidentally. This is to know not only its causes, but also their applications. That this knowing is also intimately connected with demonstration is clear both in Thomas's explication of the chapter[52] and in the remarks immediately following, which touch on the relation of the demonstrable to the indemonstrable.[53] Since "[n]on enim contingit aliquem habere scientiam, nisi habeat demonstrationem eorum," it follows that one does not have *scientia* of premises strictly speaking (loosely, *scientia* includes both).[54] The status of these principles is discussed again by Aristotle in the third Chapter. Thomas adds: "Si ergo quaeratur quomodo immediatorum habeatur scientia, respondet quod non solum eorum est scientia, immo eorum cognitio est principium quoddam totius scientiae. Nam ex cognitione principiorum derivatur cognitio conclusionum, quarum proprie est scientia. Ipsa autem principia immediata non per aliquod medium extrinsecum cognoscuntur, sed per cognitionem propriorum terminorum."[55] The origin of those first principles Thomas has made a matter of understanding the connections which obtain among terms, of seeing (in the example he gives) what a whole is and what a part is and thus in grasping immediately that every whole is greater than its part.[56]

When Aristotle returns to this issue at the end of the second *Analytics* in an often disputed passage,[57] Thomas goes over the same ground again, though he seems to do so at a very concrete level, nearer the applications of the particular sciences. In explaining the passage from particulars to universals, Aquinas gives a medical example. It is just as if a *medicus*, he writes, had remembered that a particular herb had cured one man and then another and then another. The *medicus* can then be said to have an "experimentum" of the curative workings of the herb. When this becomes the insight that the species of herb heals fever *simpliciter*, then the *medicus* has passed to the universal in the form of a rule of medical art.[58] Aristotle had explained with the example of the single soldier reversing a rout by being the first to stand firm. Thomas repeats the example, but is quick to add a clarification. Such a formation of the universal can happen only in a mind, that is, only in the presence of the power of the possible and agent intellect which can know intelligibles in act by abstraction.[59] One is reminded here of the earlier sense of first principles as things known in themselves by inspection of the intelligible connections of their terms. In both cases, Aquinas grounds the account of *scientia* in the operation of the intellectual power.

What is the connection, then, between those absolute first principles of *scientia* which are discussed early in Book I of the second *Analytics* and those more particular principles of a specific art or science which are discussed at the end of its Book II? Such a question is the question about *scientiae* especially as a practical *scientia*. This question is the fruit, I think, of what Thomas learns from Aristotle about science. It is precisely in trying to apply the Aristotelian paradigms to more concrete cases of demonstration that Thomas uncovers the significance for the theory of discourse of what Aristotle says about *scientia* in the *Analytics*.

2.6 THE ORDER OF THE SCIENCES

The greatest of his texts on the *scientiae* is found at the end of Thomas's unfinished *expositio* of the *De Trinitate* by Boethius. On the occasion of a few remarks by Boethius about the Aristotelian triad of speculative knowing, Thomas takes up two related issues: the division of the speculative 'sciences' and their methodological differences. Both the distinctions and the differences point to a hierarchy in the approaches to the knowable. The entire treatment is animated by that sense of the refractions in human understanding which also lay behind the treatment of the *modi significandi*. Thomas seems certain that a naive approach to being is not philosophically justified. One must have constant reference to the mode of one's approach, since it is this which conditions what is known. I would like to offer a preliminary reflection on this lesson here before proceeding to its detailed illustration in the next chapters.

Thomas's treatment begins with a defense of the Aristotelian trichomotomy of speculative *scientia* — physics, mathematics, and theology. This last term already suggests that the studies are ranged hierarchically to culminate in an end. Yet it is a hierarchy grounded not by reference to presupposed ontological categories, but by a consideration of the possibilities for cognition in the soul. Thomas writes: "quando habitus vel potentiae penes obiecta distinguuntur, non distinguuntur penes quaslibet differentias obiectorum, sed penes illas quae sunt per se obiectorum inquantum sunt obiecta."[1] Speculative knowing ought then to be divided by reference to the modes of operation in speculation. Mind itself is always immaterial, separated from matter. (I use 'speculative' here and throughout as opposed to practical and not, of course, in the sense of conjectural or hypothetical. It ought to be regarded simply as an English term for Thomas's *speculativus*.) Speculative knowing is concerned with the necessary, with what is separated from the contingency of motion (hence its independence of experiment, but not of experience.) An exhaustive enumeration of speculative *scientiae* can be given by combining the criterion of separation from motion with that of separation from matter. Physics considers things which depend on matter in *esse* and in definition; mathematics considers those which depend on matter in *esse* but not in definition; theology, finally, considers those which are independent of matter in being and in definition.

Each of the speculative *scientiae* studies beings, but not all are therefore branches of metaphysics. Each is differentiated by what Thomas calls its *modus considerandi*. "Accipit enim unaquaeque scientiarum unam partem entis secundum specialem modum considerandi alium a modo, quo consideratur ens in metaphysica."[2] The mind-centered construal of the *scientiae* also explains the recurring attention to the nature of medicine.[3] Medicine is a special case not because its object is anomolous, but because it seems to mix two modes of knowing, the practical and the speculative.

If the division is based on the ways of considering, still this does not imply an equality among those ways, an indifference with respect to the mode of approach. The step away from the hierarchy of beings is not the abandonment of objective hierarchy altogether. Indeed, there is a hierarchy of the ways of consideration which is as definite and as objective as that of beings. One can see this quickly in one of the discussions of medicine. Thomas there disposes of an objection by borrowing the Aristotelian notion of subalternating one *scientia* to another.[4] Subalternation is neither inclusion nor mere deduction. The construction of the regular solids is a part of geometry, but is not therefore subordinated to geometry. Rather, subalternation entails the use in one *scientia* of truths which are not fully known except in another, higher *scientia*. Thus music makes use of whole number ratios in the construction of the diatonic scale, but the musician is not therefore obligated to demonstrate the whole of Books V through VII of Euclid's *Elements*. The musician knows these ratios as true *quia*, while the arithmetician knows them *propter quid*. The musician knows the ratios in their effects, the arithmetician in their constituent causes.

The most famous application of subalternation comes in considering theology as a *scientia* subalternated to the beatific vision.[5] That application makes clear that subalternation is not merely a relation of deducibility; the higher *scientia* must be more intelligible if it is to serve as a ground for the lower *scientia*. I want to set aside the application to theology, however, and indeed the technical sense of subalternation, in order to study the more general use which Thomas makes of notions of intelligible hierarchization in the commentary on Boethius. Here he argues that all natural and mathematical *scientiae* are subordinated to metaphysics. What the physicist and the mathematician know as principles *quia*, the metaphysician must secure *propter quid*. Since the human intellect is embodied, men must learn the more accessible truths of the physical and mathematical before studying metaphysics. The other sciences are naturally prior *quoad nos* because it is in them that we learn such things as generation, corruption, number, and the celestial cycles, all of which are necessary to the study of metaphysics. But there is no vicious circle, Thomas reasons, because the teaching of the lower sciences depends upon *per se nota* 'principles' which are not themselves borrowed from metaphysics. This might seem to deny the subordination of the lower sciences by granting them autonomous principles, except that Thomas immediately adds the reminder that the knowledge of the lower sciences proceeds by demonstration *quia*, that of the first science by demonstration *propter quid*.[6] The local understanding of physics is teleologically ordered to the embracing understanding of metaphysics. One might recall here the Socratic description of the third level of the Divided Line, which takes as hypotheses propositions which must themselves be penetrated by moving to the fourth level.[7]

One must understand the remarks on abstraction and separation within such a hierarchy; they otherwise take on a distorting preponderance. A clear text is that in Article 3, which attempts to distinguish the abstraction in physical speculation from that in mathematics.[8] The first sort of abstraction is *totum a partibus*, that is, the *abstractio universali a particulari*. It is common to all *scientiae*, but belongs especially to the knower who can discern the *universal* in particulars. The second sort of abstraction is *forma a materia*, that is, the *abstractio formae a materia sensibili*. This is the abstraction of the knower who discerns shapes and numbers which happen to be found in physical things.[9] Together, the two forms of abstraction are distinguished from the *separatio* or negative judgment which is the basis of metaphysical inquiry.[10]

The danger is to see these as democratically equivalent and generically similar perspectives in regard to an entity, as if they were sectional slices which could prove more or less useful depending on what one were looking for. They are not. Thomas places the treatment of abstraction and separation after the hierarchy established in Article 1 as an elaboration within it. Again, he places it before the pedagogical hierarchy which will be described in Question 6. The processes of the abstracting intellect described in Articles 2 through 4 of Question 5 would not be answered unless one could also discern the hierarchy of knowing which frames them. More simply, the degrees of abstraction and separation are not arbitrary because they are placed within the objective and well-grounded hierarchy of ways in which the human mind responds to *ens*.

The starting-point of Question 6 is the Boethian remark on the modes of speculative *scientiae*: one proceeds in physics *rationabiliter*, in mathematics *disciplinabiliter*, and in divine things *intellectualiter*. Part of what Thomas must do is to explain in what senses he takes these adverbs. But it is already clear that the three modes of proceeding are hierarchically disposed. *Ratio* is subordinated to *intellectus* as motion to rest; they form the bottom and top of the hierarchy. Mathematics is the middle term; it conduces from the use of principles in *ratio* to the grounding of principles in *intellectus*. The ascent is seen as Thomas parses the qualifiers which describe the three modes. He treats *rationabilis* in the first part of Article 1. There are three senses of the word. The first is that of what is *rationalis ex parte principiorum*; the second sense, of what is *rationalis ex termino*.[11] Neither of these two senses of *'rationalis'* is restricted to the speculative knowing of natural things. Thomas finds a more specific sense in the fact that *ratio* is the predominant note of human knowing (as opposed to the *intellectus* of higher minds). To say that physics is *rationalis* is to say, on this construal, that it is the peculiarly human knowing, the product of the *anima rationalis*. This means both that it begins from what is best known to men, and that it exhibits especially the discursive forms of the earth-bound mind. This is why reasoning from effect to cause is characteristic of physics, which explores *per causas extrinsecas*.[12]

The plane of *ratio* is subordinated to that of *disciplina*. Since Thomas is constructing a hierarchy of cognitive modes of knowing rather than one of objects, he is not concerned with the problematic ontology of the mathematicals. He is concerned, rather, with the greater lucidity and rigor of mathematical knowing, which is both *facilior* and *certior* than either natural or divine *scientia*. The mathematical realm provides a middle step of the hierarchy in which both *ratio* and *intellectus* are included as the poles of *disciplina*. It is not, then, primarily a formal structure of implications which interests Thomas; his mathematics is not that of Hilbert. Mathematical knowing depends for him on the intrinsic clarity and manifestness which makes its result the most teachable of the speculative *scientiae*.[13]

In making *disciplina* the hallmark of mathematics, Thomas echoes not only Aristotle's association of strict knowing with what is teachable,[14] but also the ancient place of mathematics in pedagogy. These objects are called '*ta mathêmata*' because they lend themselves superbly to *mathêsis*, to learning. Thus Thomas rejects the suggestion of one objector that the modes of procedure ought to be taken from psychologically discovered faculties. Thomas replies that the modes of procedure ought to be taken, not from faculties, but from the modes of their relation to what is known. "Unde modi scientiarum non respondent potentiis animae, sed modis quibus potentiae animae procedere possunt, qui non solum diversificantur penes potentias tantum, sed etiam penes obiecta."[15] Even so, the *modus disciplinabilis* is not a method in the Cartesian sense and is not to be distinguished from the other *modi* as one method among others. It is, rather, a way of proceeding which is native to a certain use of the mind, which itself occurs at a fixed point in the pedagogical ascent.

There remains the highest mode of procedure, that of the *intellectus*. *Intellectus* stands to *ratio* as unity to multiplicity.[16] It stands to *disciplina* as privileged act to abstracted paradigm. The mode of *ratio* leads to *intellectus* by way of *resolutio*, "inquantum ratio ex multis colligit unam et simplicem veritatem."[17] Conversely, *intellectus* grounds *ratio* as the synthetic seeing of what it will variously discover and devise. Even the mode of *disciplina* must rely on this synthetic vision of the *intellectus*, which alone can secure the cogency of the first mathematical truths.[18] Thomas insists again on the primacy of theology as regards subject matter: its study of what is common to all *entia* and of separate substances presupposes the other ways-of-knowing. But divine *scientia* has a modal primacy: "Illa igitur consideratio, quae est terminus totius humanae ratiocinationis, maxime est intellectualis consideratio."[19] This modal, teleological primacy is that of insight over deduction, of synthesis over analysis. However much human hermeneutics moves in the circle between whole and part, the whole possesses a priority in virtue of which it determines the meaning of the parts.

The consequences of Thomas's ranking of the *scientiae* and their cognitive modes is to qualify the status of physical and mathematical speculations. On the one hand, each of them is a *scientia* with a specific kind of object and a characteristic mode. On the other hand, both the objects and the modes depend on higher objects and higher modes. The *physicus* can know truly about motion and time, can explain and demonstrate them adequately. But whatever he knows is fulfilled in the highest *scientia*. In this sense, there is no closure at any point below the *scientia* of the divine.

The fulfillment, in object and in mode, of every *scientia* in the *scientia divina* is seen from below precisely as the other sciences' hermeneutical incompleteness. The truths of the *physicus* or the mathematician can never be fully grounded by their exponents. This is because they contain terms which cannot be finally grounded except in the highest *scientia*. Does this mean that physics is not a *scientia*? On the contrary, it is precisely as a *scientia* that it enters the hierarchy *in via* to metaphysics. But is physics then finally absorbed into metaphysics? On the contrary, it cannot be absorbed precisely because of the differences in object and in mode and its own demonstrative character. The members of the hierarchy of *scientiae* are not homogeneous elements in a single text. They are, rather, discourses in their own right which participate finally in the first member of their hierarchy. It is, at once, their ground and their completion.

The doctrine of the hierarchy of *scientiae* here described is the extension of the art of logic beyond itself and into knowledge. With it, the study of the *trivium* has already passed over into the study of the *scientiae* themselves. Their order has been justified by a quasi-logical reflection on the modes of knowing. It must now be embodied in the actual pursuit of what can be known. That pursuit will move at once beyond the arts in speaking about more substantial things in a more detailed way. The pursuit will remain within the *trivium*, however, in the sense that it can never abolish its origin in the arts of language. The rules of the *trivium* govern the discourses of speculative knowing as much as they govern the exercises of elementary schooling.

PART TWO
EXEMPLARY PHILOSOPHICAL DISCOURSES

CHAPTER 3

Discourse about Physical Causes

To speak about each of the speculative sciences in detail would be to replicate whatever Thomas has written in philosophy. Indeed, since he did not always write the same thing, a comprehensive study of his writing would also be the history of the progress of his thinking. Such a reading of Thomas is not possible — not practically and not in principle. But it is possible, I think, to describe in a schematic way the conditions for discourse at the different levels of speculative knowing. An adequate schematic description requires the choice of representative texts and typical arguments. More exactly, it requires that one choose those speculative discourses which are most revealing of their own ground. Thus, a typology of speculative discourse is also a claim about the origin of each type of speculative discourse. It is, at once, a study in logic and in epistemology.

For reasons to be argued below, I think that the hierarchy of speculative discourse in Thomas is the hierarchy of physics, psychology, and metaphysics. The most revealing point in the discourse of physics is the account of physical causes. In psychology, the whole discourse takes its character from the limitations of the soul's knowledge of itself. For metaphysics, finally, the limit on discourse is the limit set by the negative judgment which grasps both *esse* and the separate substances, which thus begins to approach theology. These three topics — physical causation, the soul's knowledge of itself, and the negative account of *esse* — provide the matter for the general theory of the types of speculative discourse.

3.1 CONTEXTS FOR THE STUDY OF PHYSICS

The connection between the finding of causes and the inquiry of philosophy was made by the predecessors of Socrates.

It was treated in various of the Platonic dialogues, most emphatically in the *Phaedo*. Questions about this connection between causes and philosophy elicited the answer which is Aristotle's Organon. The questions were rehearsed again in the other ancient schools, especially among the Stoics.[1] They also form the main matter of Aquinas's reflection on physics.

Since the Organon is a frank answer to those questions, it is not surprising that the recovery by the medieval Latins of the philosophical inquiry into causes came with the finding of Peripatetic sources during and just before the twelfth century. For the preceding generations, physical speculation had to content itself with the eruditely disorganized assemblies of natural lore which are typified by Seneca's *Quaestiones Naturales*, by Aulus Gellius' *Noctes Atticae*, by the elder Pliny and the Latin version of the *Solutiones* of Priscianus Lydus.[2] The early Latin encyclopedists had given *physica* a place among the parts of philosophy, but had then reduced the philosophical study of causes to the four parts of the *quadrivium*.[3] The new Aristotelian learning added to this mass of half philosophic, half naturalistic reminiscence not only fresh observation, but the informing power of the Aristotelian paradigm of *scientia* as demonstration through causes.

Already at the beginning of the twelfth century, Adelard of Bath makes his pilgrimage in search of ancient knowledge, travelling through Italy, Spain, and France. If he did not succeed in learning much Arabic Aristotle, he still serves as a figure for the desire to recover philosophical physics.[4] He was followed by those authors who are called the "School" of Chartres, by the translators working in Spain and Italy, by the English writers around Hereford. These same years mark the ascendancy of the medical school at Salerno, of its greatest clinicians and its commentators upon the newly canonized medical texts, the *articella*.[5]

Yet Aquinas's handling of these authorities in natural philosophy is more complicated than talk of a twelfth-century 'renaissance' would suggest. Even his explicit allusions to named references, the bluntest sort of *auctoritas*, are not simple. Indices for his major works would show that Thomas cites at least the following authors in natural science, leaving aside the line of Aristotelian commentators: Albumasar, Aulus Gellius, Algazel, Constantinus Africanus, Galen, Isaac Israeli, Macrobius, Nemesius of Emessa, and Ptolemy. But such a list of citations is deceiving. Reference to Aulus Gellius is made, for instance, through Augustine's *De Civitate Dei*, as Aquinas plainly says.[6] Some of the references to Galen seem to derive from Gregory of Nyssa.[7] Nemesius' work on human nature is *cited*, of course, as a work by Gregory.[8] Some of the references to Ptolemy may be direct, but others almost certainly derive from Chrysostom's *In Genesim*.[9] The mere appearance of a reference says nothing for direct acquaintance.

What is perhaps more interesting is the absence from the reference-list of all but one of the authors of twelfth or early thirteenth-century science. The exception is Constantinus Africanus, but he is cited only once and for a common-place opinion.[10] The absence of direct citations of recent Latin authors might be due to medieval strictures on the citation of contemporaries. Even so, one would expect to find such references behind the allusions to unnamed authors or texts. In these cases, of course, the difficulties of identification are enormous. D. A. Callus, whose work on the sources in Aquinas is exemplary, deciphers blank references by depending on the force of a parallel or on some stray bit of manuscript evidence. Such bits are, for example, the two marginal notes in different codices which allow one to argue that a reference in the commentary on the *Peri Hermeneias* points to Siger of Brabant.[11]

When one does attempt to go behind natural philosophic allusions, to trace down the parallels, one does not find the twelfth-century Latin authors. A case in point is that excerpt from a letter by Aquinas which is called "De mixtione elementorum ad Magistrum Philippum." The text is generally accepted as authentic, though its recipient, a professor medicine, is not otherwise well known.[12] In the text's few paragraphs, there are seven references to named sources; all are to Aristotle.[13] There is one anonymous reference. It introduces the counter-position around which Thomas will build his solution.[14] The counter-position claims that it is possible to have degrees of substantial form in elemental compounds.

Now this problem of the mixture of the elements was of enormous interest in the twelfth century. It appears in many of the writers associated with Chartres, especially in relation to the doctrine of the *elementatum*.[15] It also figures in the thought of the Salernitan medical writers; Urso of Salerno's masterwork, for example, is entitled *De Commixtione Elementorum*. An avid reader of Aristotle, Urso composed the book in Norman Italy not fifty years before Aquinas's birth.[16] But the anonymous "quidam" of Aquinas's letter refers, I think, only to Averroes. It is not the Averroes of the middle exposition of *De Generatione et Corruptione*, the obvious locus. There Averroes argues against substantial degrees in mixtures.[17] Yet Averroes teaches the opposite doctrine in his commentary on the third book of *De Caelo*.[18] Indeed, Albert the Great chides Averroes for having contradicted himself.[19] If this "quidam" refers to Averroes, why does Aquinas bring him into the conversation anonymously? Perhaps it is because he remembers the contradiction between the two texts and does not want to decide the Commentator's true thought. Perhaps the doctrine comes to Aquinas through Averroistic treatises in the Parisian arts faculty which Aquinas chooses to attack generally, therefore anonymously.[20] Or perhaps Thomas is somewhat embarrassed by the recollection of his once having held a more sympathetic reading of Averroes's remarks on the *De Caelo*.[21] Whatever the reason, one has here a case in which Thomas considers only Averroes, where there are any number of nearer Latin authors.

The case would be no different in the little treatise *De Principiis Naturae*, for which Thomas used the commentaries of Averroes and Michael the Scot's versions of Aristotle's *Physics* and *Metaphysics*.[22] On the other hand, there do seem to be recent Latin sources behind the treatise *De Motu Cordis*. Indeed, the Leonine edition suggests that Thomas's tract is something like a reply to Alfred of Sareshel's *De Motu Cordis*.[23] Alfred's treatise, written before 1217, had fairly wide circulation in the thirteenth century;[24] it is cited, for example, by Albert.[25] Of course, Thomas's explicit point is to justify and perhaps to clarify the *Aristotelian* treatment of the heart and the Aristotelian doctrine on natural processes generally. Thus, twelve explicit citations are to Aristotle's works, namely the *De Motu Animalium* (four times), the *Physics* (five times, but once not by title), the *De Anima* (twice), and the *De Partibus*

Animalium (once).

There are also anonymous references: to the "quidam" or "aliqui" who hold that the natural motion of the heart comes from an extrinsic universal nature or even an intelligence; to the "alii" who trace cardiac motion back to animal heat; to the "quibusdam" who call man "minor mundus"; and to those "medici" who distinguish vital from animal operations.[26] The Leonine editors trace the second of these to Alfred and the third to Aristotle; the other two are supported only by general references. It is clear, however, not only that these four could be viewed as common doctrines, but that they are commonplaces. They cannot justly be attributed to any single source. Man as a microcosm is a well-worn image; external universal causality is a frequent enough question in ancient philosophical physics. Even the two medical doctrines, which might seem technically specific, are found in many Latin medical commentaries in circulation from the twelfth century onward.

There is a first lesson, then, about philosophy and knowledge of natural causes. His restraint with regard to technical works from the Latin tradition suggests that Thomas's interest in physics is controlled by his logical and epistemological motivations. He is not an encyclopedist, not like the omnivorous Vincent of Beauvais, in whose *Speculum Maius* one can find a wealth of contemporary naturalistic material. Thomas is concerned, rather, with the ground of the intelligibility of philosophic discourse about physical causes. That ground he finds well described, though not completely comprehended, in Aristotle. The Latin reading of Aristotle had shown the appropriateness of studying physics on the way to metaphysics. Aquinas, of course, argues for that sequence of study in the pedagogical treatise which is his supplement to Boethius's *De Trinitate*.[27] To Moses Maimonides, in a different but not unrelated inquiry, it seems at least dangerous for one to approach metaphysics without the prior study of mathematics, astronomy, and other parts of what Aristotle meant by 'physics'. He rebukes his exemplary student, the Rabbi Joseph, for wanting to jump over physical studies on the basis of mere gossip, thus disrupting the approach "secundum ordinem quae addiscenda erat."[28] Maimonides resists the disruption both in principle and in the structure of the *Guide*.

There are many reasons which might be found for the pedagogical precept that physics ought to precede metaphysics in the philosophic pursuit of causes. One reason is particularly important for the question about causes and philosophic speech. It is in physics that philosophy discovers its semantics and comes to understand how 'sciences' can be sciences and how they cannot. In physics, one sees the mind at work on its commensurate object and so sees how speculative discourses, including philosophic ones, can be bearers of truth.

3.2 DESCRIPTIONS OF ARISTOTELIAN PHYSICS

'Physics' means for Aquinas both the speculative study of bodily things and the introductory or general section of that study. The introduction corresponds to Aristotle's *Physics*; the rest of the whole is divided among the other works of the *libri naturales*. But the division of topics by books is not only bibliographical. The public work of expounding Aristotle was very much a part of the medieval restoration of philosophical inquiry about causes. For Aquinas, as for his contemporaries, the recovery of physical science was in large measure the recovery of certain texts. The attention to texts already suggests what I will call the 'exegetical' character of philosophical physics in Aquinas. Aquinas's physics is 'exegetical' because it describes human knowledge of the world as beginning from a textual tradition, as concerned with grammatical and logical evidence, as pedagogical in construction, and as anti-literal in motivation. Aquinas will insist, of course, that philosophical physics is a study of things and not of men's opinions about them.[1] Yet he makes such remarks in commentaries on Aristotle. More broadly, the plurality of pedagogical approaches, the immersion in the commentators, the emphasis on unity in annotating each work — these are features of an approach to physics in which the direct access to things is mediated at least by a textual tradition.

Let me insist that it is mediated not only by a textual tradition. The exegetical character enters into the conception of physics as such, leaving aside the manner of its rediscovery or of its teachings. In its sequence of considerations, in its division of topics, in its choice of starting-points, the science of physics is a *habitus* of the human mind. That is why it is not incongruous that the division of natural sciences should correspond to the division of treatises by Aristotle, or that these treatises should be considered as instantiating physics. The telling phrase, "quae prae manibus habemus," is applied by Aquinas both to books and to sciences.[2] The sciences seem very often to be identical to the books which teach them. Both are pedagogically ordered, interpretative, full of readers' devices.

The question about the division of the treatises is not an uninteresting question, then. It touches in a preliminary way on the issue of a semantic hierarchy within the concrete case of discourse in physics. Thomas himself offers a first division of natural philosophy in his prefatory remarks to the commentary on the *Physics*. One notices immediately that part of the motive behind the division, as behind the entire commentary, is a desire to correct Averroes.[3] Indeed, Aquinas abandons even the traditional pattern of the *accessus* which is used by Averroes.[4] There is agreement, however, on the general principles of dividing the *Physics* from the other books.[5]

Thomas begins his own treatment by rehearsing the three levels according to which being is grasped in speculation.[6] But Thomas now develops the description of physics in its privileged relation to the human mind. Everything which has matter is changeable; thus *ens mobile* is the *subiectum* of natural philosophy. It seems then that nature must in some way be the "principium motus et quietis in eo in quo est,"[7] though this suggestion will only be secured in Book II. The consideration of natural entities ought to begin with general principles of changeable things as such, so that one will not have to repeat the principles for every particular case. This general provision Aristotle has made in the *Physics*, where he has treated "de iis quae consequuntur ens mobile in communi."[8] The other special treatises follow. *De Caelo* deals with the first and most obvious kind of motion, which is motion according to place. *De Generatione* deals with motion towards substantial form and with the first moving things, namely the elements, as regards their typical transformations. The books *Meteororum* deal with the special, elemental transformations. *De Mineralibus* considers moving things which have been mixed with the unmoving. Finally, *De Anima* and its allied tracts deal with living things.9

Even in this simple schema, Thomas is disagreeing with Averroes. The *Physics* treats those general principles of motion which are to be used in all studies of particular motions. Averroes had said that 'principles' must be taken here in a restricted sense, as conditioned to the specifically physical investigation.10 Thomas disagrees. The principles of *Physics* are truly principles, just as its physical causes are truly causes, its elements, elements. But it is also true, as Thomas repeats, that the knowledge which physics has of its principles is neither exhaustive nor autonomous. Here Thomas brings forward the familiar difference between the order of things and the order of learning.11 The orders are not only different, they are inversely related.

There are two questions buried in the disagreement and in the simple schema. The first question concerns the relation of the principles of physics to those of the higher sciences. Is it the case that physical principles are only equivocally intelligible? Thomas answers that they are not. Physics has its own principles which are truly intelligible. This he seems to argue against Averroes. But the second question has to do with the status of these principles within physics. If it is indeed the case that the order of nature is the reverse of the order of learning, then the *first* principles of physics are not first axiomatically or deductively, but pedagogically. They are the principles one is taught first. They stand in need of the qualification of the studies of specific moving entities. In short, they are abstract almost in Hegel's sense. Thus the division of the sciences as between general and particular is not a mathematical division between axioms and theorems. It is more like a division between assumptions and experiments, or between rough and refined description.12 But these comparisons do not capture the mind's paths through physics; more is needed.

The division of physical study is treated as well in the proemia to various of the other commentaries on Aristotle. According to the order established in the *Physics*, the next treatise ought to be the *De Caelo*. There Thomas begins with an analogy to the processes of practical reason, which he divides into four

orders, *apprehensio, intentio, compositio, sustentatio.*[13] The
same fourfold order, he argues, is to be found in speculative
reason. First there is the order which proceeds from the universal to the particular, from what is more common to what is less
so. The second order is that which moves from whole to parts;
the third, from the simple to the complex, "inquantum com-
posita cognoscuntur per simplicia, sicut per sua principia."[14] In
fourth place stands the order which considers the principal
parts before the secondary.

The fourfold order, found first in practical and then in
speculative reason, is now discovered "in processu scientiae
naturalis."[15] First the book called the *Physics* treats of the common features of movable things as such. The subsequent books
will apply these *communia* to the proper subjects of motion.
This application answers to the first order of proceeding. The
general subject of motion is material body as such. By sub-
dividing it, one discovers the other three orders: the priority (in
consideration) of the whole of the corporeal cosmos over its
parts; the priority of the simple bodies over their compounds;
and the priority of the principal simple bodies over the secondary. *De Caelo*, says Thomas, treats the prior member of each of
these — of the first in the first Book, of the second in the second
Book, of the third in the third and fourth Books.[16]

Such a plurality of topics led the ancient commentators to
assign various different subject-matters for *De Caelo*. Alexander
thought that it described the universe taken in three senses.
Other imagined that the main topic was the heavenly body
which is moved by circular motion. Still others concluded that
the book concerned bodies — Iamblichus taking 'bodies' as
denoting what are contained and received by the heaven,
Syrianus taking it accidentally as denoting whatever leads to
knowledge of the heavens.[17] This last opinion Thomas finds
very un-Aristotelian. Simplicius reports that others held the
main matter of the book to be simple bodies considered as fall-
ing under the "communis intentio" of 'simple body'. Of these,
the chief was held to be the heaven. Simplicius himself agrees
with this, but Thomas does not. Thomas prefers the first position, that of Alexander. This second work among the *libri
naturales* is, indeed, about the universe and the bodies within

it, divided now according to the properties associated with their natural places. Not inappropriately, Thomas concludes, have the Latins said that this book treats "de corpore mobili ad situm, sive secundum locum."[18]

The implicit contrast between *graeci* and *latini* is interesting and might suggest something about Thomas's classification of sources for the work. More interesting, however, is the complexity of the list of the orders of thought in natural philosophy. These are not four steps in a single method, not so many *regulae ad directionem ingenii* which together form a coherent system. They are, rather, four concurrent ways of discovering the organization of the intelligible. Here one sees that Thomas is committed both to seeing thought as a progress towards truth and to offering a plurality of starting-points from which progress might begin.

The third book of the physical canon is *De Generatione et Corruptione*. It describes the order of inquiry again and differently. Aquinas begins his comments with the principle that the parts of knowledge, as befits a *habitus*, are distinguished according to differences in the object known. The objects of physical knowledge are motion and the movable; its differences, then, are the differences found in motions and in movable things.[19] The first motion is that with regard to place. It is prior to the others and common to all natural bodies. After the general consideration of motion in the *Physics*, it was appropriate to treat of local motion in the *De Caelo*. Having done so, it is time to treat of motions which are not common to all but which belong to those bodies below the sun.[20] The ruling principle of the lower motions is generation and corruption. The two can be considered generally, with generation taken as governing alteration and including augmentation. Since in any genus the highest member is counted the cause of all, however, the investigation ought to begin with the elements, "quae sunt causa generationis et corruptionis et alterationis in omnibus aliis corporibus."[21] Thus it is that this third work of natural science considers concretely generation and corruption as found in the elements.

The last work of the main canon of physics, leaving aside the special treatises on the soul and its operations, is the *Meteorologica*. In his commentary on this work, Thomas does not provide a separate proemium, but comments instead on Aristotle's own prefatory remarks in the first Book. It is here that Thomas gives a fourth account of the order of studies in nature. He begins by rehearsing the difference between a merely abstract universal knowledge and one which is carried down to an actual knowledge of specific differences. "[M]anifestum est quod complementum scientiae requirit quod non sistatur in communibus, sed procedatur usque ad species."[22] One cannot proceed down to individuals, of course, since there is no *science* of the individual as such. But one must proceed to detailed considerations in order to have fully actual knowledge. Thomas considers this imperative to be the motive for the other books after *De Generatione*.

Apparently, the requirement can be discerned in the whole schema of natural studies, which is already familiar from the other works. The *Physics* comes first, since it treats sequentially "de causis naturae" and "de motu in generali."[23] As the second step there is *De Caelo*, which first expatiates "de caelo et stellis, quae moventur motu circulari," and then "de numero elementorum et de motu locali eorum."[24] The third work is *De Generatione*. In it, one studies both the general features of generation and corruption and "de permutatione elementorum in invicem."[25] This schema leaves for the *Meteorologica* the task of considering four sorts of things: those extraordinary happenings which occur nearest the stars, the common *passiones* of air and water, the properties and events of earth, and the matter-laden effects of wind on the elements.[26] Thomas notes that Aristotle ends by mentioning what is to be studied in the following works, those dealing with plants and animals. Aristotle speaks of something yet to be done, "quia non omnia naturalia ab homine cognosci possunt."[27] One ends with a reminder of the progress of thought and of its fallibility.

The variety of descriptions given for the order of study in natural science is apparent. I do not say that Thomas contradicts himself, though the first list is more comprehensive than any of the others and the third seems incomplete. I do say that the plurality of explications for the order of study shows the exegetical character of Thomas' physics. One suspects that he could have found *rationes convenientiae* for yet other arrangements and different lists of the books. This would not be exegetical relativism; it would be the corollary of a doctrine about human understanding. There are several different ways of coming to know nature. These ways are differently but mediately related to the real. Moreover, the whole study of physics is subordinate to higher sciences and higher intelligibilities. Thus, the multiple study of physics has many affinities with the interpretative arts of the *trivium*, which are plural, heuristic, and subordinate. Moreover, the study of physics seems very much like an exegesis of the world. This seeming needs now to be tested in the fundamental study of physical causes.

3.3 THE EXEGESIS OF PHYSICAL CAUSES

Given Aquinas's insistence on the pedagogical order of study, it ought to come as no surprise that he uses grammatical evidence in securing the analysis of the first principles of physics. The use of such evidence is particularly important at the end of the historical survey of Book I of the *Physics*, where Aristotle turns, as Aquinas tells it, from the survey of the opinions of his predecessors to the determination of the truth.[1]

The Aristotelian doctrine of nature begins from the analysis of change as from a decisive experiment. Correctly distinguishing the elements in a physical change can lead one to the basic terms for the whole of physical study, though the two are not identical. Thus the discovery of the "communia" which underlie the "fieri" in any change is of the greatest importance.[2] Their discovery begins when one finds two ends or terms in change, what will be seen as the *oppositum* and the *terminus factionis* which succeed one another in the same *subiectum*. The evidence of the two terms is grammatical; it is evidence drawn from what one says and how one understands what has been said.[3] Something "is said" to come to be made from something else, with the two terms being "taken" as either simple or composite. 'Simple' and 'composite' in this context refer not to physical composition but to the logical character of subject and predicate in sentences, to the signifying of change as simple or complex.[4] When I say that the evidence is grammatical, I do not mean, of course, that ordinary usage is the ultimate arbiter of philosophic doctrine, any more than one could say that the *trivium* is an ordinary language philosophy.

What finally matters is not the saying but the said. I do mean, however, that Aquinas follows Aristotle in using the common language as known by the *trivium* for a sign of what occurs in the world. The language serves as a record of the long, common experience of nature. To give an artful account of why one speaks in a certain way is to begin — if only to begin — in giving an account of why things happen as they do.

In the same passage, Aquinas refers explicitly to certain modes of speaking which can be understood as pointing to the composite model of *subiectum, oppositum,* and *terminus*.[5] Indeed, the various ways of speaking indicate that there is a difference between the mode of human conceiving and the mode of actual existence. There is a distinction between the unity of the real entity and its necessary multiplicity in predication and so in conception.[6] The disparity between grammar and reality can also be useful in explicating certain loose ways of speaking about change.[7]

Aquinas concludes these grammatical remarks, which have been offered in support of the tripartite model for change, with a summary statement which could serve as an explication of his procedure in the whole twelfth *lectio*: "Ex hoc ergo ipso quod diverso modo loquendi utimur circa subiectum et oppositum, manifestum fit quod subiectum et oppositum, ... etsi sint idem subiecto, sunt duo tamen ratione."[8] The evidence of grammar is above all evidence of the modes of understanding by which human minds grasp change. Since the study of physics is a search which begins from the purview of human understanding, the linguistic practice in describing change can well point to the sought for physical *principia*. Nor is grammatical evidence confined to this single *lectio*. Similar arguments are made in the next three *lectiones*, 13 through 15. Indeed, in *lectio* 14, the solution to the ancient puzzles about becoming is found by careful attention to the differences between *per se* and *per accidens* predication, as well as to those between the attribution of a quality in act and in potency.[9] A careful study of the grammar of the terms employed provides a way out of the difficulties which entrapped the *antiqui,* the pre-Socratics.

The same exegetical character could be illustrated from the discussion of nature as *principium* in Book II of the *Physics* and in the retrospective, opening chapters of *Metaphysics*, XII. I will

leave these passages aside in order to take up the treatment of
the classification of the causes. Even here, I will have to restrict
myself to Aquinas's comments on Book II, Chapter 3, of the
Physics and on its close paraphrase in *Metaphysics*, V, 2. Given
such a selection, I will have to pass over the extended teaching
on the role of the four causes in demonstration which makes up
so much of the *Posterior Analytics*. Let me only assert that the
method of demonstration *ex suppositione finis*, which Father
Wallace justly emphasizes,[10] is a perfect example of the construction of an exegetical framework within which causes can
be discovered and interpreted.

Wallace insists that the method is not equivalent to some pro-
babilistic or purely formal hypothetical procedure.[11] Certainly
the conclusion of a syllogistic demonstration is not to be
qualified by a probability factor; Aquinas's point in the relevant
section of the commentary on the *Analytics* is precisely to overcome the uncertainties of the temporal distance between cause
and effect.[12] But to protest too much against hypotheses is to
forget that Thomas has already shifted an empirical question of
efficient causality into a logical question about the proper form
for final demonstration. The cause that emerges from the 'supposition of the end' is a principle of demonstration which
works through a series of intermediate middles selected for
their logical power.[13] If it is true to say that one of Thomas's
main doctrines with regard to causal explanation is the introduction of the *suppositio finis*, this only reinforces the
general claim that causes are not, for Thomas, things given by
brute sensation of the world, so much as they are features of the
sorts of discourses about the world which are carried to completion in the demonstrations of physics. I will try now to show
the same point in the less obvious case of Aquinas's division of
causes.

Aquinas's treatment of the Aristotelian division of causes in
Book II of the *Physics* is spread over the fifth and sixth *lectiones*. The shared starting point of both is a study of those
causes from which "scientia naturalis ... demonstret."[14] The
discussion of causes is for the sake of knowledge, not of action.
The pedagogical motive stands out. Thomas distinguishes the
two *lectiones*, however, by contrasting the "species causarum"
with the "modos diversarum causarum secundum unamquam-

que speciem."[15] The same distinction is made in the *Metaphysics* as a distinction between a classification of the causes "quasi ... per differentias essentiales species constituentes" and a classification "per differentias accidentales non diversificantes speciem."[16] Now in no way does Thomas restrict the term "modos" to naming the second sort of classification. One can read that the "species causarum" are so many "modi."[17] But the reasoning behind the distinction is consistent, even if the terminology at first sight is not so. The classification of the causes according to *species* is prior to that according to *modi* as the essential is prior to the accidental, or the species to the individual. They are not two different classifications so much as two halves of a single classification which considers all the ways in which causal relations are predicated.

Still the classification of causes into four *species* is not, at least within physics, an 'absolute' classification. The study of causes in themselves is reserved for first philosophy, just as the study of form *absolute* had been set aside in an earlier passage.[18] The species of causality assumed by the physicist are those pertaining to the causes of natural changes. Aquinas calls the four species material, formal, efficient, and final, following Hellenistic and Arabic practice in broadening Aristotle's motive cause to a *causa efficiens* or *agens*.[19] Aquinas repeatedly describes these as four ways in which something "is said" to be a cause; the list of species is an answer to the question "quot modis dicitur causa."[20] His examples are mostly Aristotelian, though he sometimes augments them by adding technical detail, particularly from medicine.[21] Aquinas also adds further subdivisions of the causal species. He divides the efficient cause, following Avicenna, into *perficiens, disponens, adiuvans, consilians*.[22] In all of this, there is a breadth to the notion of causality which corresponds to its many different uses in ordinary and technical speech.

The breadth in the sense of 'cause' is underscored in the treatment of what might be called syllogistic causality. Following Aristotle, Aquinas counts the relation of premises to conclusion as an example of "ex quo" causality.[23] He not only allows this classification, he defends it against the objection that a material cause must inhere in its effect.[24] Aquinas seems to know that

that point is denied by Avicenna, who holds that the premises are not the matter for the conclusion, but for the figure of the syllogism. According to Avicenna, the premises can be compared to the conclusion only as an efficient cause.[25] Thomas agrees, in reply to an objection, that the premises are the effective cause of the conclusion by virtue of the *vis illativa*.[26] But he does insist that the terms in the premises are used as parts of the conclusion and that the premises can thus be considered as "ex quo" causes of the conclusion.[27] In this argument, the notion of causality is broadened further and a plurality of causal perspectives is frankly admitted.

What remains implicit in the treatment of particular causes is made explicit in Aquinas's remarks on three general conclusions drawn from the study of causal species.[28] The first of these is that "cum causae dicuntur multipliciter, contingit unius et eiusdem esse multas causas per se et non per accidens." In the parallel passage from the *Metaphysics*, the same principle is qualified with the remark that it is impossible that "eiusdem secundum idem genus, sint multae causae per se eodem ordine; licet possint esse plures causae hoc modo, quod una sit proxima, alia remota: vel ita, quod neutrum sit causa sufficens, sed utrumque coniunctim."[29] The second principle states that "quaedam sibi invicem sunt causae secundum diversum speciem causae," according to "diversas rationes."[30] The third principle is that "idem est causa contrariorum quandoque."[31] The three principles are, respectively, principles of causal multiplicity, of reciprocal causality, and of alternating causality.

In an analogy one expects a central analogate and in an intelligible multiplicity one expects a hierarchy. Such a one is provided in a final doctrine, which Aquinas gives after a treatment of certain anomolous causes.[32] It is the doctrine that the final cause is the chief cause. This lesson Aquinas reiterates: "Et haec species causae potissima est inter alias causas: est enim causa finalis aliarum causarum causa."[33] A very similar formulation can be found in the Latin versions of Avicenna.[34] In the doublet from the *Metaphysics*, the phrase '*causa causarum*' is justified by saying that the final cause "est causa causalitatis in omnibus causis."[35]

The doctrine on the primacy of the final cause completes the treatment of the division into causal species. There comes next the division into causal modes. I have already touched on Aquinas's distinction between the two, a distinction between causes classed by essential differences and causes classed by accidental ones. But this may be nothing more than a remark which follows on specifying one division as that of species and another as that of modes; it would follow from the very notion of 'species' that different species would have to be constituted by 'essential' differences. An easier way to grasp the relation of species to modes is to take Aquinas's remarks on it in the parallel passage from the lexicon of the *Metaphysics*. There he says that the division according to modes is made "penes diversas habitudines causae ad causatum. Et ideo est in his quae habent eamdem rationem causandi, sicut per se et per accidens, remotum et propinquum."[36] The causal modes are, then, something like degrees of causal 'proximity' which are applied within the species of causes already distinguished. The distinction of causal modes is a second perspective from which to describe the position of a cause in relation to its effect.

In the commentary on the *Physics*, the list of modes is given first as: (a) priority and posteriority in the parallel orders of predication and causality; (b) the *per accidens* and its genera; (c) the *in potentia* and the *in actu*; and (d) those complex causes which mix the potential and the actual.[37] The Latin Aristotle then reduces these non-isomorphic classes into a classification of three pairs: (a) "singulare et genus," which Aquinas correlates with the earlier discussion of "prius et posterius" ' (b) "accidens et genus accidentis"; (c) "simplex et complexum."[38] Each of these can be considered as either actual or potential, so that there are twelve modes in all.

The treatment in the doublet from the *Metaphysics* is more elaborate. Its first distinction into the modes of the prior and the posterior is divided into two cases, the first of which has to do with nearer and remoter causes in an ordered sequence of difform causes, and the second of which has to do with the ordering of universal and particular as seen in genera and species.[39] The second division of the modes includes the *per se* and the *per accidens* with their genera. The *per accidens* is further divided into causes *ex parte causae* and *ex parte effectus*, which branch is itself further divided by reference to the modality of the relation of cause and effect.[40] There follow the third and fourth divisions of the causal modes, the *in potentia/in actu* and the simple/composite. The whole list is summarized in a chart of three pairs of modes, each of which is further specified by the application of the *per potentiam/per actum*.[41]

The *Physics* commentary adds to this list of the modes three further conclusions which seem to express not only the sense of the modes, but the purport of the entire classification of causes. The first conclusion is that an actual *per se* cause which is singular exists simultaneously with its effect.[42] This is a reminder of the theory of the syllogistic middle in *Posterior Analytics*, II, and of the original or primary intuition of causality. The second conclusion is that full causal explanation must always proceed to the primary cause.[43] Thomas remarks that such a first cause may be found only within a particular order. It is a sufficient answer to the question, why the man builds, to say that he has the art of building. But the conclusion also reminds the reader that a metaphysical explanation of causality has yet to be provided, one which ascends to a first cause in the truest sense. The third conclusion is that causes correspond to their effects, general causes to general effect, potential to potential, and so on.[44] Each of these conclusions is a rule for sorting the predications of causal relations. In the profusion of possible causes, whose types now number twelve, rules must be given for distinguishing among the axes or perspectives of causality. One must be given grammatical rules for the discussion about causes: rules of tense, rules of comparison, rules of degree. The exegetical character of the conception of cause could not be plainer.

One can generalize from these conclusions. It is obvious that Aquinas is not what some call a causal 'singularist'; he does not hold that there is one and only one proper cause for an event. It is also clear, though perhaps not so obvious, that Aquinas does not teach any strict doctrine of causal necessity. Rather, he follows Aristotle, who shies away from any suggestion of cosmic necessity, any universal scheme of virtually determined results.[45] Because Aquinas denies causal singularity and causal necessity, one must be careful in assigning to him any unqualified adherence to a doctrine of sufficient reason, whether in its Leibnizian formulation or some other. If the principle means nothing more than what is meant by the maxim, "omne quod movetur ab alio movetur," then it can be taken as an important general truth about the world, though one in need of specification.46 If the principle means, however, that there is only *one* reason to be found, then it tacitly supposes a doctrine of causal singularity and so goes against Aquinas's teaching. The enormous concern lavished on a principle of sufficient reason in some neo-Thomist writings, a concern described by Laverdière,47 must be seen as obscuring Aquinas's own causal doctrine. Aquinas is careful not to reduce the complex discourse about causes to one or several tightly worded 'principles'. With Aristotle, he refuses to make causal relations into convertible, fixed connections. Indeed, he moves in the opposite direction, to disclose the complexity of the relations among different orders of causality.

The philosophic discourse about causes, which always treats the unified and continuous by means of discrete reasonings, is a reflection on the ongoing operation of agency and actuality in things. But that operation is itself the reflection of a higher intelligibility and a higher agency. The privileged place of final causality foreshadows the treatment of the ultimate end, thus also foreshadowing the original agency of divine creation. These matters pass beyond the exegesis of physical causes. Still, it may be possible to understand something of their role by turning to the doctrines of causal likeness and causal participation, which do fall at least partly within philosophical physics.

3.4 CAUSAL LIKENESS AND PARTICIPATION

There can be little doubt that the full account of causality in Aquinas reaches far beyond the causality of physics to consider the activity of God. Certainly the greatest transformation of Aristotelian causality occurs in the metaphysical investigation, especially in the study of divine creation as the causing of *esse*. Thomas's synoptic treatments of creation are by way of analogy to human artistry; he exploits the similarities even while he underscores the dissimilarities and the theological inadequacy of any relation to human action. The most important similarities are those of causal likeness, which is clearly seen in human art, and of causal participation, which is not seen there.

Granted that these doctrines are unfolded only at the highest levels, they figure even in the exegesis of physical causes. One can see this in a Question from the very end of the *prima pars*, in a passage that Father Fabro has singled out for comment.[1] The topic of the whole Question is the action of corporeal creatures; that of the first Article is the issue of whether any body is active. Thomas settles the question by examining three errors with regard to the activity of bodies. The first error is that of Avicebron, who holds that no body acts, but that "omnes actiones quae videntur esse corporum, sunt actiones cuiusdem *virtutis spiritualis.*"[2] The second error is that of Plato, who holds that bodily causes can at most dispose some matter to the completing causality of an immaterial form. The third error is that of Democritus, who reduces physical causality to the motions of atoms in pores. Since the last opinion is refuted by Aristotle, Thomas gives his own attention to the first two. With regard to each, he invokes both the principle of causal likeness and the principle of causal participation, once correctly understood. The principles are combined in the argument which reasons from the premise that anything which participates in something is necessarily a participant of what is proper to that of which it is a participant, and the premise that to act is to communicate that actualization which is proper to any act, to conclude that any participated act, however limited by matter, must still be active. Otherwise, it would not be a participated act.[3] The argument shows that the correct exegesis of physical causality stands upon the principles of causal likeness and causal participation.

Aquinas finds the principle of causal likeness in Aristotle generally and in the *Physics* particularly. One Aristotelian context is the discussion in Book II of the physicists's use of each of the four kinds of cause. This is argued in one way from the coalescing of the formal, final, and efficient causes in generation. The coalescence occurs because univocal agents produce effects similar to themselves.[4] Even for equivocal agents, there is as much similarity as the given difference of type will admit;

the effects "participate in some likeness" of the cause.5 The principle of causal likeness also figures at the end of the tenth *lectio* in Book II of the *Physics*, where Thomas turns from a consideration of fortune and chance to the reiteration of the argument that there are only four causes. Here the principle of likeness is used as a premise in arguing for the final cause.6 In such ways, causal likeness leads back to the deeper metaphysical notions of activity and finality.7 Still, it is not an absolute maxim and its application must frequently be qualified, especially in cases of equivocal agency.

Both the principle and its applications are known from the other works of the physical canon. For example, Thomas cites the principles from the *Meteorologica*'s fourth Book, though he never had occasion to comment on it in that context.8 The principle becomes particularly important in the second tier of physical works, those concerned with the soul. Here it is decisive for Thomas's reconstruction of the Aristotelian account of perception.9 Perhaps more telling than the reiteration of the principle in the commentaries is the frequency of its appearance throughout the works in Thomas's own voice, from first to last; examples abound in the *Sentences*-commentary,10 in the *Contra Gentiles*,11 and in the great *Summa*.12

What is the sense of this maxim which is, even for Thomas himself, so common as to be a commonplace?13 I have already suggested that one of its meanings lies in the insight which links form to act and which derives from this the motto that each acts according to what is proper to it. There is a second meaning in those universal or generic causes which Aquinas adopts from Aristotle and neo-Platonism.14 The highest member of each genus stands as cause to the rest precisely because of some analogically-graded likeness which they have to it. There are, in third and fourth place, two logical meanings for the maxim of causal likeness. To the logical doctrine of intentionality, there corresponds the analogy between art and nature. To the logical rules for sorting out causes, there corresponds the likeness of definitional commonality.

The principle of causal likeness, taken too narrowly or too mechanically, can produce absurdities; Aquinas does qualify it. Even so, the principle is an important part of Aquinas's account and cannot be passed over. There is some tendency to do so in

Father Lonergan's famous account of efficient causality. Certainly Lonergan is right to insist that the Baroque controversies over causal influx cannot be obtruded into the reading of Thomas.[15] He may also be right in substituting for the vitiated theories of 'real causal influx' an alternate account which posits only a real dependence in the effect. But the positing of such a dependence ought not to be construed as denying causal likeness. It is by means of reflection on likenesses that one can come to grasp the order of natural causes and the working out of causal actualization. More importantly, causal likeness provides a means of access to the more fundamental account of participation.

The experience of the likeness between cause and effect, which is had naturally in the sequence of generations and intentionally in human craft, points to the hierarchy of ontological sharing which secures that likeness. The relation between causation and participation has become a *quaestio disputata* of great fame in Thomistic controversies of recent years. A treatment of the whole question would go beyond the boundaries of a philosophical physics and its causes. But I do want to recall one text where Thomas himself discusses the relation between causation and participation most connectedly. I mean his commentary on the *Liber de Causis*. The treatise is obviously not a text in physics. Moreover, Thomas's exegetical role in this commentary is more ambiguous than it was in his commentaries on Aristotle, with which the exposition of the *Liber* is contemporary.[16] Despite such hesitations, however, it is worth singling out a few passages from the commentary that show the ground of causal likeness in the teaching on participation.

There is little Aristotelian demonstrative science in this text, which Thomas first correctly identifies for the Latins as a paraphrase of excerpts from Proclus's *Elements of Theology*.[17] Still, he makes much reference to Aristotle in his own proemium.[18] Each of the references recalls the importance of causal knowledge. All emphasize the pathos of human inquiry into causes.[19] Such remarks constitute a thoroughly Thomist preface to a treatise which often seems forgetful of the need for evidence or for qualification. Indeed, the contrast between the confidence of the *Liber* and Thomas's parsimony with regard to causal knowledge is a specific prefiguring of the conclusion of his exegesis of the causes. His procedure in the face of the *Liber* is to provide such proofs as he can, either by appeal to experience,[20] or by adducing the appropriate demonstrations from the complete text of Proclus.[21] Thomas also insists on supplying his own qualifications. He asks whether the maxim of causal intelligibility applies to all four types of cause; he finds that it does.[22] He then asks whether it applies to causes ordered both *per se* and *per accidens*; he finds that it does not.[23] The work of commentary leads Aquinas to treat of those issues which separate him from the *Liber* and each of these from the other positions of the tradition. One such issue is the ineffability of the First Cause; it is treated in the sixth Proposition.

Aquinas argues, in agreement with the author of the *Liber* and with Pseudo-Dionysius, that the First Cause cannot be known in itself since it is beyond all the modes of things which can be known in themselves. Nor can it be known in its effects.[24] Even in its best and noblest effects — the Intelligences — it is refracted only in part with many defects of mode. The First Cause exceeds *a fortiori* all the rest of its effects and cannot be known from the lot of them. It follows, then, that the First Cause is above both direct and indirect speech in so far as it is above any adequate knowing from outside. Yet the order of causes, descending from the First Cause into increasing darkness, is also the ground for the order of intelligible likeness. The stages of descent into the effects are marked by stages in the modes — modes of being, modes of understanding, modes of being signifiable. The rules of causality include rules for limitation in mode in the effects. The rules are the principles both of likeness and of differentiation in the cosmos.

Aquinas employs many such rules in the commentary on the *Liber*, most of them familiar from Aristotelian texts. One reads that the cause is participated in by its effect,[25] that the power of the effect depends upon the power of its cause,[26] that the cause is always present in its effect within the facet of its causation,[27] and that there is in any genus a first cause from which the other causes of the genus derive.[28] These are the principles of likeness by which the field of causal intelligibility is constructed. One also reads that the cause is more intelligible than its effects,[29] that the cause is always better than what is caused,[30] that a cause

which exceeds its effects can never be embodied in them,[31] and
that the cause is in the effect in the mode of the effect, while the
effect is in the cause in the mode of the cause.[32] These are the
principles of difference within the causal field. They are, of
course, primarily verified in the unbridgeable difference between the First Cause and its effects. The balance between these
two sets of principles is maintained by a third set, according to
which the First Cause is the ground for the subsistence and efficacy of all other causes.[33] Indeed, Aquinas insists that secondary causes derive their power from the First Cause: "et in-
telligentia et anima et natura habent virtutem participatam ab
alio, sicut virtutes causae secundae participantur a virtute
causae primae quae non est participata ab alio, sed ipsa 'est
causa omnis virtutis'."[34]

The combination of the three sorts of causal rules — those of
likeness, those of difference, and those of dependence — produces an essential restraint on the philosophic claims made by
human intellects for knowledge through causes. Knowledge is
of causes and through causes — Aquinas repeats that maxim in
commenting on the *Liber* as he had in Aristotelian contexts.[35]
But all causality depends on the causality of the First Cause. The
effects of that Cause do not give anything like a sufficient account of Its nature. Clearly, then, the knowledge of second
causes on which human reasoning depends, however sufficient
it is for human purposes, is not complete. Thus the principles of
causal likeness and participation are at once affirmed and
denied. They are affirmed in so far as an ontological ground is
secured for them in the luminous causality of the First Cause.
They are denied for human knowing in as much as it is blocked
in its approach to that originary Cause.

3.5 THE LITERALISM OF SPEECH ABOUT CAUSES

I have considered Thomas's teaching about causality at different points in his texts: in the very selective use of the
naturalistic tradition; in the logical comments on the *Physics*
and others of the *libri naturales*; in the commonplace of causal
likeness; and, finally, in the insight which leads from likeness to
participation in the *Liber de Causis*, only to end with the inef-

fability of the First Cause. At each point, Thomas has moved to limit the pretensions of human inquiry to a literal comprehension of physical causes. The sum of these limitations is the conclusion that the knowledge of causes in philosophical physics cannot become a resting-place for human thought. Any final account for the causes in daily experience is projected beyond physics.

This projection is seen within physics itself as a prohibition against literalism. By 'literalism', I mean three conjoined prejudices: (1) the assumption that it is possible to exhaust the significance of what is known; (2) the assumption that the modes and orders of knowing are identical with the modes and orders of things; and (3) the assumption that the things to be known are divided into units which admit of univocal determination. This is literalism generally, which Thomas sees exemplified in Platonism, that is, in the temptation to reify the mind's significations.[1] The literalism is specified in physics not only as the application of a general attitude to physical objects, but also as the tendency to explain all things from below. This tendency Thomas sees in the ancient cosmologists.[2]

Thomas prevents literalism in physics by denying its three assumptions. He denies that the significance of the corporeal can be exhausted, by recalling the endlessness of inquiry and by insisting that causality derives from God. Aquinas argues against the identification of the modes of knowing and the modes of being, by keeping always in view the difference between the order of learning and the order of the real. Finally, he argues against the reduction of the knowable to transparent monads by multiplying the modes or layers of causality and by tracing their many logical roots. The arguments against these three are brought together in what I have called the 'exegetical' approach to physical causality.

The exegetical approach is summarized for Thomas by one of the most famous topics in ancient physics, the dispute concerning the status of astronomical hypotheses. In it, Thomas encounters the ancient desire of philosophy to know the hidden causes of the first things. The question of astronomical hypotheses arises for Aquinas in several contexts, but especially when he considers discrepancies among the competing theories of stellar motion known to him from antiquity.3 In his commentary on Book II of *De Caelo*, Aquinas rehearses a variety of opinions on the nature and motions of the heavens (lect. 1-9) and of the stars (lect. 10-19), as well as those regarding the position and possible motion of the earth (lect. 20-28). Much of the detail about ancient teaching comes to Thomas through Simplicius's commentary on the same text. But Simplicius contributes more decisively the view that astronomical theories attempt to 'save the appearances'—Thomas has it as "omnia apparentias circa stellas salvari."4

When it comes to settling disagreements over the stellar motions, Aquinas stresses the enormous difficulty of the matter and narrates the 'revolutions' in the history of astronomy before and after Aristotle.5 It is in the course of explicating the problem of anomalies that Aquinas remarks on the efforts of the "astrologi," who, following Eudoxus, attempt to dissolve the appearance of celestial irregularity: "Illorum tamen suppositiones quas adinvenerunt, non est necessarium esse veras; licet enim, talibus suppositionibus factis, apparentias salvarentur, non tamen oportet dicere has suppositiones esse veras; quia forte secundum alium modum, nondum ab hominibus comprehensum, apparentiae circa stellas salvantur."6 Aquinas adds that Aristotle himself seems to have ignored this stricture. The review of the competing theories ends with a reiteration of the warning: "Ista autem quae inquirenda sunt, difficultatem habent: quia modicum de causis eorum percipere possumus, et accidentia eorum magis sunt remota a cognitione nostra, quam etiam ipsa corpora elogentur a nobis secundum corporalem situm."7 The study of the heavens is, of course, exceptionally difficult for human minds. Astronomical hypotheses are more uncertain than are the explanations of more familiar causes. But the qualifications which are placed on astronomy are only superlatives with regard to the positives of ordinary physics. Indeed, the favorite Aristotelian example for the general theory of causal syllogism is the astronomical example of the eclipse. On epistemological grounds, again, Aquinas frequently depicts astronomical inquiry as suffering more intensely the difficulties which are felt in the rest of physics. Though the causes of astronomical happenings are "omnino improportinatae accidentibus inferiorum corporum," the metaphor of distance still serves to cover the relation of human thinking to both earthly and celestial causes. In both cases, human inquiry is governed by the nature of mind: "connaturale sit nobis quod ex accidentibus, id est sensibilibus, deveniamus ad cognoscendum naturam alicuius rei."[8] If Thales, the first philosopher, was notorious for studying the stars, it is not inappropriate that the difficulties over astronomical hypotheses should remain difficulties for the knowledge of philosophical physics generally. The ancient cosmologists succumbed to the temptation of literalism in physics; the correction of that lapse is a correction for the sake of all speculative speech that rests on physics.

With the remotest physical causes as with the nearest, one meets the limit set by the origin of human discourse. Because he recognizes that limit, Aquinas treats the knowledge of causes as an exegetical knowledge. The obscure text for the exegesis is embodied experience of the bodily world; the method of the exegesis is suppositional explanation by causal middle terms. The sense discovered by the exegesis is the dependence of the world and human knowing on the intelligibility of a separated First Cause. Because the search for causes is the original and perennial philosophic inquiry, Thomas's exegesis of causes discovers that natural knowledge of the world, no matter how adequate, can never be self-possessed. The exegesis stresses the mediacy of natural knowledge and the pedagogical character of causes. Aquinas thinks in this way to leave open the possibility of a radically non-discursive ground even for physics.

CHAPTER 4

Discourse about the Soul

The middle discourse in the hierarchy of speculative sciences is said by both Aristotle and Boethius to be the discourse of mathematics. Mathematical studies are given this position in view of their particular abstractive character. Aquinas accepts the arrangement in the commentary on Boethius and in his scattered remarks on Aristotle's teaching about speculative knowledge. But he does not, in fact, follow the arrangement in his own writings. The clearest sign of this is that there is little study of mathematics in Thomas.[1] The omission would not be telling except that the hierarchy of speculative sciences is, more than a consequence of the logic of abstraction and separation, indeed a progressive pedagogy for human intelligence. The absence of serious attention to mathematics in Thomas would thus be a failure of philosophical education unless some justification were found *de facto* for altering the speculative hierarchy.

Two texts in which Thomas discusses school curriculum suggest such a justification. In commenting on the sixth Book of the *Ethics*, Thomas gives the "ordo addiscendi" as instruction in *logicalibus, mathematicis, naturalibus, moralibus,* and *sapientibus et divinis.*[2] A roughly contemporary text in the commentary on the *Liber de Causis* gives the list as *logica, mathematica, philosophia naturalis, philosophia moralis,* and *scientia divina.*[3] These lists have their origins in various of the medieval schemes for classifying the arts and sciences.[4] But they bear important consequences for the hierarchy of sciences. First, mathematical studies are placed before physics, since "nec experientiam, nec imaginationem transcendunt."[5] Second, the place between physics and metaphysics is taken by moral studies, "quae requirunt experientiam et animum a passionibus liberum."[6] Now it would be easy to explain the appearance of moral philosophy here as a distant effect of conflating the Stoic trichotomy of philosophy with Peripatetic and Platonic divisions. It is more helpful to see that these descriptions of the *ordo addiscendi* correspond to the actual structure of Thomas's corpus, with its extended treatments of natural and moral philosophy. But it is very difficult to distinguish textually in Thomas between a moral philosophy and moral theology. The truths about human goods knowable without revelation are always linked by him to the fuller context of divine instruction. Hence it would be difficult if not impossible to trace a distinctive character for a discourse of moral philosophy. What can be done is to take the preliminary part of moral reflection, which I will call 'psychology' with an etymological sense, as a metonym for the whole. The *ordo addiscendi* and the structure of the Aristotelian corpus together argue that the extension of physics into the study of soul marks a new step in the hierarchy of sciences.

There can be little doubt about the importance of psychological discourses in Thomas. He composed three commentaries on Aristotelian psychological works, the *De Anima*, the *De Sensu et Sensato*, and the *De Memoria et Reminiscentia*. Among the disputed questions, there are the two sets entitled *De Anima* and *De Spiritualibus Creaturis*. The controversial works include the monograph *De Unitate Intellectus Contra Averroistas*. But much more telling than a list of separate titles is an examination of the structure of the major works. Underneath the traditional schema of the *Contra Gentiles*, a protreptic variation on the Lombard's ordering,[7] the largest portion of the work is given, in fact, to a treatment of the human soul, its powers and ends. Thus, the second half of Book II is devoted to a detailed discussion of the human intellectual soul, while the third Book includes an extended protreptic argument that the contemplation of God is the only fitting end for human life, as well as arguments for human participation in the cosmic hierarchy of providential operations, for human freedom from external control, for law, for the states of life, and for sin and grace. The order is also telling. Even though the *Contra Gentiles* contains no full treatment of moral matters, it is clear that the sequence of consideration beginning at the mid-point of Book II moves from a psychological and even physiological consideration of the soul to a moral consideration, for which the psychology is presupposed.

The same order is found in the great *Summa*, as well as the same weight of attention. The *secunda pars* alone, that extraordinary depiction of the operations of the soul from farther and nearer views, makes up something like half of the *Summa*. If one adds to this part the sections from the *prima pars* on the human soul, its creation and nature, then the portion of the whole work given to a consideration of topics related to the soul is something like two-thirds. The importance of this emphasis would be confirmed by a study of the circumstances surrounding the composition of the *Summa* and by an investigation of its relation to the history of Dominican writing on morals.[8] It is interesting, too, that the *secunda pars* had the widest medieval distribution, to judge from extant manuscripts.[9] But the amount of attention given to psychological and moral matters is perhaps less telling for the hierarchy of sciences than is the order of attention. In the *Summa Theologiae* as in the *Contra Gentiles*, the reader is led from a view of the soul like that in natural philosophy, through detailed psychological considerations, to a view of the soul from moral philosophy and moral theology. The passions, for example, are mentioned first in connection with the sensitive appetite (Ia q.81 a.2), next in a general psychological sketch (Ia-IIae qq.22-25), and then in detailed moral analyses (Ia-IIae qq.26-48).

If psychology does constitute the extension of physics 'upwards' towards ethics and metaphysics, it must do so in virtue of a particular pedagogical character. While psychology does not take the place of mathematics in the order of abstraction, psychology does have in Thomas, as in Aristotle,[10] an intelligibility more complex than that of simple physics. The human soul is, as both embodied and separable, the boundary between corporeal and incorporeal. So Thomas quotes that striking image from the *Liber de Causis* which makes of the human soul "quasi quidam horizon et confinium corporeorum et incorporeorum."[11] In this way the study of the soul answers to the place of the Platonic *mathêmata* on the divided line, though not to the Aristotelian mathematical abstractions.[12]

As a step between simple physics and morals (or even metaphysics), psychology ought not only to have a different semantic character than physics, it ought to teach a further lesson about the inherent limitation of philosophic speech. The limitation will appear, first, in the indirectness of speech about the 'self' and, second, in the merely potential character of the self described in speech. The potency of the self will then bring the discourse about soul to the task of exhortation, at which point psychology gives way to the full study of human good.

4.1 DISCOURSE ABOUT THE SOUL AND EPISTEMOLOGY

There is no stratum of discourse in Aquinas's text which is organized as an epistemology or a cognitional theory. The word *'epistemologia'* does not appear in Aquinas, of course. It is of modern coinage. Nor can one find anything which might answer to such tags as 'cognitional theory' or 'theory of knowledge'. It is not only the absence of the name in Aquinas, however; it is the absence of the thing named. The difference of philosophical organization can be verified, as before, by attending to the large structure of the texts in which Aquinas considers what are now called epistemological issues. To return to the second half of Book II of the *Contra Gentiles*: one finds there fifty-six chapters devoted to the consecutive consideration of created intelligences. The entire treatment occurs under the rubric of the "distinction of creatures," by which it is connected to the preceding account of divine creation. An exactly parallel position is occupied by the much-read questions on the human soul in the *Summa*. In both cases, the discussion is ordered by the distinctions in created being — not by the desire to assuage skeptical doubt or the need to justify existing bodies of knowledge.

The ontological ordering can be seen on a smaller scale in the sequence of topics within the disputed question *De Anima*. The first two articles ask about the *esse* of the soul. The next five, Articles 3-7, consider problems about the being of various 'parts' or powers in the soul. The following three Articles consider the soul's union with body (8-10) and the soul's relation to its powers (11-13). On the basis of this ontological depiction, questions are raised about the soul's operations when separated from the body after death (14-21). Only among these, in a single Article that wants to draw an epistemological contrast between the present life and the life to come, does Thomas raise issues about ordinary cognition. He then stresses its limitation.

For all that these arrangements have of the traditional, they
are not brought forward mechanically.[1] If attended to, they suggest that Aquinas approaches questions about mind only within
the study of the ontological gradations in the cosmic hierarchy.
His discourse about the soul is a discourse which begins with
the nature of soul as embodied intellect. It moves from there to
consider how such an intellect might know things. Thomas is
not attempting to find reasons by which the conscious subject
can be assured of the veracity of its thinking. He is trying,
rather, to uncover and then disclose the operations of that ambiguous creature, the embodied intellect. Thus the treatments of
the soul fall where they do. So also they tend always upwards to
the pure case of angelic knowing.[2]

To say that Thomas's psychology is not an epistemology
amounts to more than noticing the place of psychological
remarks in his writings. It suggests that the vocabulary of the
discourse about soul will have a different context, and so different meanings, than the vocabulary of epistemology. I will illustrate the difference in meaning with regard to one term only,
but the crucial one. That is the word 'certainty'. Aquinas
himself clearly asserts that 'certainty' belongs to *scientia* as such
and is a mark of the highest *scientia*, though perhaps not for us
in our present condition.[3] If one tries to discover what Aquinas
means by '*certitudo*' and related terms, it becomes quite clear
that the meaning is broad and that its typical contexts are moral
rather than epistemological. The shortest lexical survey will
show both the breadth and the moral coloring. '*Certitudo*' is
used by Thomas as equivalent to "constantia,"[4] a term with
psychological and moral resonances. Thomas speaks of the certainty of the artisan,[5] of prophetic certainty,[6] of the certainty of
an inclination towards its object,[7] and of the certainties of hope
and faith.[8] The last use, the "certitudo fidei," is most interesting
and establishes that certainty is for Aquinas something different
from what it is in the project of modern epistemology.

There are several full dress treatments of faith in the corpus,
each of which emphasizes the certainty of the believer.[9] I take
the treatment in *De Veritate* as the most continuous. Aquinas
there distinguishes five conditions of the possible intellect with
regard to affirmation. First, the intellect can be *un*moved, either
because there is no force present to it or because of cancelling

forces. This condition Aquinas calls doubt. Second, the intellect can be moved to one of the two contraries, yet not completely, so that there remains some "fear" that the alternative may be true. This is opinion. Third, the intellect can be completely moved to one possibility immediately, without discursive reasoning, by the action of an intelligible object. This is *intellectus*. Fourth, the intellect can be moved to one of two possibilities mediately, through reasoning from first starting-points. This is *scientia*, discursive knowing. Finally, the will can move the intellect in the absence of the force of the intelligible object, on the basis of a willed commitment. This Aquinas calls the *dispositio credentis*, the disposition of the believer.

Thomas underscores the difference between discursive knowing and believing. In discursive knowing, the reasoning (*cogitatio*) and the assent are not co-eval, since reasoning produces the assent which then terminates it. "In scientia enim motus rationis incipit ab intellectu principiorum, et ad eumdem terminatur per viam resolutionis; et sic non habet assensum et cogitationem quasi ex aequo: sed cogitatio inducit ad assensum, et assensus cogitationem quietat."[10] In believing, however, assent *is* co-eval with reasoning, since such assent comes directly from the will. Thus reasoning is not brought to its proper term in faith by producing assent; the assent existed already before the reasoning. "Inde est quod eius motus nondum est quietatus, sed adhuc habet cogitationem et inquisitionem de his quae credit, quamvis eis firmissime assentiat." Aquinas insists on the certainty of faith again when replying to the seventh objection. Certainty, he argues, can mean either firmness of conviction or evidence for what is asserted. Faith has the firmness, but not the evidence.

The distinction between faith and knowledge is taken frequently as a distinction between subjective and objective certitude (to use the modern senses of these terms). More important for Thomas is that faith does have certitude and is distinguished from opinion precisely by certitude. He will say later, in a similar context: "siquidem hoc fit cum dubitatione et formidine alterius partis, erit opinio, si autem fit cum certitudine absque tali formidine, erit fides."[11] He insists on this even while arguing that faith is not of things seen. There is a *lumen fidei*, but this is not the same as *scientia*. "Sicut enim per alios habitus virtutum homo videt illud quod est sibi conveniens secundum habitum illum, ita etiam per habitum fidei inclinatur mens hominis ad assentiendum his quae conveniunt rectae fidei et non aliis."[12]

The dissociation of certainty from sight, the emphasis on the pedagogy of faith and its proper certitude, not only removes certitude from apodictic contexts, but effectively prevents the search for an epistemological answer in the Cartesian sense. If certitude can be given by faith, or to prophets and to hopeful believers, then the use of certitude as a criterion for knowledge is impracticable. In a slightly later Article from the same section of the *Summa*, Aquinas argues that faith is more certain than science or any other intellectual virtue as regards its cause, which he takes as the paramount consideration. Considered in this way, "fides est certior tribus praedictis [*scil.,* sapientia, scientia, intellectus], quia fides innititur veritati divinae, tria autem praedicta innituntur rationi humanae."[13] Of course, if one considers the present weakness of the human mind and the sublimity of the objects of faith, then greater certainty does seem to belong to the intellectual virtues. But simply speaking, faith is more certain. Moreover, one can also consider those three intellectual virtues as themselves gifts of the Holy Spirit, in which case faith stands to them as their principle and can again be counted as the more certain. The certitude of faith is converted to hope in the believer, giving him a participated certitude even during this present life.[14] Further, though divine election is not generally known to the elect in this life, it can be revealed by a special privilege.[15] Such a revelation would bring with it the *certitude* of one's predestination.

There are, of course, a few texts in Thomas that have been made into occasions for epistemological argument. The strongest is probably *De Veritate*, q.1, a.9. The body of this article has been used to ground epistemological justifications by neo-Thomist writers as diverse as Kleutgen,[16] Mercier,[17] Maréchal,[18] Boyer,[19] Hoenen,[20] and Lonergan.[21] They claim that one has here a description of an intuitive certainty, or a transcendental criticism, or at least the beginning of a program of philosophic reflection. But the sense of the passage is rather different from any of these construals, I think, and Thomas's in-

tention in writing it is correspondingly different from the
epistemological projects imposed on him.

The Article falls within a disputed question on truth. The
'truth' of which it speaks is not the missing piece of human
epistemology. It is, rather, a plurality of likenesses or confor-
mities springing from the primordial conformity of creatures to
exemplars in the creator. Indeed, Thomas's analysis of truth is
meant to harmonize definitions of truth from philosophical and
theological authorities alike; definitions of truth by Augustine,
Avicenna, Isaac Israeli, Anselm, Aristotle, and Hilary of Poitiers
are cited in the body of the first Article. There is no restriction
of the analysis of truth to contexts of epistemic justification. On
the contrary, the truthfulness of the human intellect is asserted
long before the question of its justification arises. The human intellect, Thomas writes, "nata est de se facere veram aestima-
tionem."[22] The first step is not to justify this claim, but to locate
truth with regard to any intellect. So Thomas defines truth
generally (a.1), next he assigns it primarily to intellect (a.2), then
resists attempts to make the intellectual locus into a warrant for
a logical view of it which would abstract from the conditions of
the real (aa.3-6). It is only afterwards that Thomas turns to a list
of topical issues — beginning with 'truth' as predicated in the
Trinity (a.7), then moving through participation of truth (a.8)
and truth in the senses (a.9), to falsity in things, in senses, and in
the intellect (aa.10-12). This is the context within which one
must read the supposed epistemology.

Article 9 asks "utrum veritas sit in sensu."[23] The question
arises from having assigned truth to intellect (aa.1-2) and from
the earlier insistence on the lack of truth in simple apprehension
(a.3). Thomas replies that truth is in both sense and intellect, but
differently. The senses have truth as the effect of an unreflective
act; intellect has the effect, truth, and also the reflection which
discloses the relation of the truth to its causes. In drawing this
distinction, Thomas describes the mind's reflection on itself.
Mind knows not only its act, but the "proportio" of its act to
the "res" which is known in the act. But it cannot know the
"proportio" without knowing the nature of the active "principium," here the intellect itself. Thomas secures the recursion
a little later by appeal to a hierarchical contrast between the
reflectivity of mind and sense. Intellectual substances "return"

(*redeunt*) to their own essences in a "complete return" (*reditio completa*). They move back from things, to knowing, to the knower. The return is complete when they come to know their own essences — as it is said in the *Liber de Causis*.

So far the corpus of the Article as it describes the mind. Several remarks are needed before attempting to judge it. First, the question is not confined to human intellects and human senses. It asks for a general comparison of the power of sensation and intellection. Indeed, the theorem cited from the *Liber de Causis* and the two other passages cited in the objections are perhaps best applied to angelic intellects. Second, the point of the Article is to argue against Anselmian and Augustinian claims that truth is only in the mind. It describes mind in order to draw out certain features which are also found in sensation. Third, the "reditio" is described not as a phenomenological possibility but as an ontological fact about intellectual creatures. The Article does not exhort one to perform a *reditio*; it asserts that such a *reditio* takes place in intellectual substances. The Article is an ontologist's answer to a perplexity arising from the previous discussion about the locus of truth. It extends the previous rejection of a purely logical conception of truth. The passage is not, then, a new beginning for philosophy.[24]

If the *reditio* is not a founding answer to radical doubt, it remains the description of the potency that characterizes a certain kind of being.[25] Truth is found in minds and by minds more fully than it is had in and by sense. The philosophic question about the *reditio* is the question, what sort of being has the potency for intellectual appropriation. The place of epistemology is taken by the study of intelligent beings, that is, by the highest stage of philosophical psychology. The discourse about the mind is part of the discourse about living creatures who are both intellectual and bodily. It is philosophically central, not because it is the key to all systems, and not because it describes ourselves to ourselves, but because it is the study of that ontological boundary which most attracts philosophical analysis.

In an attempt to give Thomas's psychological texts the status which he intended for them, I will now proceed according to two headings found in his texts. The first heading is that of the soul's knowledge of itself. It is directly attached to descriptions of the mind's present operations. The second heading concerns the soul's knowledge of its own teleology. This is tied to the first topic by Thomas's constant comparison of the intellectual and moral orders. But it is also a way of tracing out the soul's operations to their completion. Thus, it suggests that the discourse of psychology replaces the literalism of self-inspection with the promise of an end reached through acts. The soul is not the sort of thing that can be studied in timeless abstraction from its concrete operations. If Thomist physics is the critique of causal literalism, then Thomist psychology is, in some sense, the advocacy of a philosophical discourse which further actualizes the beings that ought to appropriate their own teleology.

4.2 THE SOUL'S KNOWLEDGE OF ITSELF

In Thomas, then, the question of the soul's knowledge of itself is not treated as the first question in an epistemology. It appears in most contexts rather as a topic under a larger question about the embodied soul's knowledge of separate substances. Among the *Quaestiones Disputatae De Anima*, for instance, the main issue of the sixteenth question is "utrum anima coniuncta corpori possit intelligere substantias separatas."[1] Aquinas determines that the embodied soul cannot know them by its phantasms.[2] No phantasm can be had which is an adequate representation of separate substances. What can be known of them is what can be garnered from their effects. "Et hoc est scire de eis magis quid non sunt quam quid sunt."[3]

Aquinas draws the consequences for the soul's knowledge of itself in the reply to the eighth objection of this disputed question. The objector had argued that the soul must be able to know itself in this life and so must be able to know separate substances, since it shares their nature as intelligence.[4] Aquinas responds by denying the major premise: "intellectus possibilis noster intelligit seipsum non directe apprehendendo essentiam suam, sed per speciem a phantasmatibus acceptam ... Et hoc est commune in omnibus potentiis animae, quod actus cognoscuntur per objecta, et potentiae per actus, et anima per suas potentias. Sic igitur et anima intellectiva per suum intelligere cognoscitur."[5] There is no intuitive self-knowledge in the intellectual soul. It knows itself in the same way as it knows other things. Moreover, it knows itself through reflection on knowing its objects, just as is the case with the lesser psychic powers. Thomas has refused any privilege of self-intuition.

The reply here is both straightforward and representative. It shows how Thomas places the question of man's knowledge of himself within the context of his ways of knowing generally; it indicates the main lines of his response to the question. But there is something more at stake, as is clear at a single point in the text. The authority quoted by the objector is the authority of Augustine: "Mens enim intelligit se et amat se, ut dicit Augustinus, in IX *De Trinitate.*"[6] At stake in the disagreement, then, is the authority of Augustine. His authority is introduced here to secure the use of the soul's knowledge of itself as the ground for philosophical certainty and the rational ascent towards God. If Aquinas will reinterpret that authority, he will change the logical character of the discourse about soul.

The place to begin with the change is in a set of parallel texts, one line of them from the questions *De Veritate*, the other line from the *prima pars* of the *Summa*.[7] In the first line of texts, the question of the soul's knowledge of itself is rooted in a consideration of the mind as image of the Trinity.[8] The context is explicitly Augustinian and Thomas is much concerned to save the authority of the patristic texts. In the second line, the topic occupies the same argumentative position as it has in the *Questiones Disputatae De Anima*. The soul's knowledge of itself is treated in the *Summa* as a pendant on the main description of the soul's ontology, which description is itself a part of the consideration of intellectual creatures within the general hierarchy of the *distinctio rerum*.[9] The text of the *De Veritate* would have been composed about five years before the text of the parallel passage from the *Summa*. Indeed, the *Summa* seems to presuppose that earlier text for certain crucial technical distinctions. But it is best to begin with the *Summa* as the simple account, the one not directly burdened by exegetical concerns for authority.

Question 87 of the *prima pars* is divided into four Articles, of which the first seems to settle the general principle, while the other three discuss particular cases. This, at least, is the inference one would draw from the short *divisio quaestionis*. In fact, as is generally the case in the *Summa*, the Question advances from an abstract resolution of a general difficulty to the concrete interpretations of particular pieces of evidence. The true structure of the Question is seen only retrospectively, from its end. This passage from abstract to concrete will be discussed below as the decisive contribution of discourse about soul; it should be noted now as a caution to the reader.

The first Article asks "utrum anima intellectiva seipsam cognoscat per suam essentiam."[10] The phrase "per suam essentiam" recalls the phrase "per suam formam," which had been used to describe the angel's knowledge of itself.[11] The more emphatic phrase "per seipsum" had been used to describe God's self-knowledge.[12] In both earlier discussions, an immaterial substance's knowledge of itself was described by contrast with the refracted knowledge of the human soul. Thomas now takes the other side of the contrast, descending the hierarchy of intelligences from top to bottom. The phrase "per essentiam" is glossed in *De Veritate*, more prosaically, as referring not to the object known (where the contrast would be with knowledge of accidents), but to the manner of knowing (where the contrast is with something known through a *species*.)[13]

The argument of the first Article in the *Summa* uses three different premises. The first asserts the parallelism of being and intelligibility: "unumquodque cognoscibile est secundum quod est in actu."[14] The second depicts the hierarchical position of the human intellect with regard to the separated substances: "Intellectus autem humanus se habet in genere rerum intelligibilium ut ens in potentia tantum." The third premise is the anti-Platonic claim that all human knowledge in this life is by abstraction. If the human soul is a potency, then it is intelligible only as a potency. Potencies are understood once actualized, and then by abstraction from observations of the discrete actualizations. It follows, Thomas argues, that the soul knows itself not by its essence but by inference from its acts or operations.

Nonetheless, he distinguishes two sorts of abstractive knowledge of one's own operations. There is the particular knowledge when one "percepit se intelligere"; there is the general knowledge when one considers the nature of mind as such. For the first knowledge to be had "ipsa mentis praesentia'' suffices, which is the very first act by which the mind perceives itself; for the second, "diligens et subtilis inquisitio" is needed. Thomas adds that this second study requires divine aid at least in some sense: "iudicium et efficacia huius cognitionis per quam naturam animae cognoscimus, competit nobis secundum derivationem luminis intellectus nostri a veritate divina, in qua rationes omnium rerum continentur." This remark recalls the preceding treatment of the operation of the agent intellect.[15] It marks the limit of Aquinas's concession to Augustine on epistemological issues. But the division of the mind's knowledge of itself into two sorts, the particular and the general, is un-Augustinian.

Indeed, it forestalls precisely the inference which Augustine requires from the mind's experience of self-presence to a philosophic discourse about the nature of the soul.[16] Thomas separates the simple "praesentia" from the acquired knowledge of the soul's nature — separates, in short, the phenomenon of self-presence from the discourse of psychology. Whatever content is had in the first sort of knowledge, it is not a speculative content.[17] If it were, one could not explain how "multi etiam circa naturam animae erraverunt." Philosophers have been wrong about the soul because philosophic knowledge about the soul is difficult to obtain; such knowledge is clearly not the same as that presence to itself which is had by all intellectual beings when they enter into operation.

Thomas emphasizes that even the intellectual presence of the soul to itself is not prior to the soul's operations; even the first sort of knowledge of itself must be had after an act of the soul. The first objection had cited Augustine to the effect that anything incorporeal knows itself by itself. Thomas replies that the mind comes to know itself 'by itself' in the sense of 'by its own act'. He then adds a distinction between two senses of "per se notum." Something is "per se notum" if "per nihil aliud in eius notititam devenitur," as is the case with first 'principles'. Something is "per se notum" in a second sense if it is not knowable "per accidens." The analogy given is "sicut color est per se visibilis, substantia autem per accidens."

The analogy ought not to mislead. It is not the case that the first sense of "per se notum" corresponds to the first type of the soul's knowledge of itself, the second sense to the second type.

On the contrary, both types of soul's knowledge of itself would
seem to stand in relation to the soul as to something "per se
notum" in the first sense. One comes to the knowlege of first
principles directly, just as the soul knows itself "per suum actum." Yet it comes to know itself through its activities and not
by its essence. Does this mean that the soul is not "per se
notum" in the second sense, that it is known through 'accidents'? Here the question is the old Aristotelian crux of
making too strict a dichotomy between substance and accident.
There is a sense, of course, in which intellection is not accidental to the soul in the way that having a tall or short body might
be. And yet intellection is an accident in so far as any operation
can be classed as accidental over against substance. Thus, the
distinction between the two senses of "per se notum," while
not fully helpful, is clearly meant not to distinguish two types of
the soul's knowledge of itself but rather to set Thomas over
against those who hold for intuitive self-knowledge.

What has been established in this first Article from the *Summa* is the abstract claim that the soul's knowledge of itself is
mediate because dependent on the observation of the soul in
act. Within such mediate knowledge of itself, there are two
types: the knowledge of presence to itself and the knowledge
which grounds philosophical discourse about the soul. Thomas
has not yet made clear what content is had in the first self-
knowledge. He has not said what is to be studied in order to
gain the second type of knowledge of itself, that is, in order to
begin the sort of discourse in which he is presently engaged.

A number of these questions are answered in the parallel
passage from *De Veritate*, though other difficulties are raised.
The determination of the first query there depends on a twofold
distinction. Thomas first distinguishes the soul's 'cognition' of
what is proper to it, even private, from the knowledge of what
is true of soul in general. He connects the cognition of what is
proper with the question *an est?*; the knowledge of what is
common to any soul answers the question *quid est?*. The soul's
cognition of itself as individual is further divided into actual and
habitual. Actual cognition is had through the soul's acts. "In hoc
enim aliquis percipit se animam habere, et vivere, et esse, quod
percipit se sentire et intelligere, et alia huiusmodi vitae opera

exercere.''[18] Note that Thomas has moved from the already loose "cognitio" to the looser "percipere." The soul's grasp of itself as singular is not scientific knowledge in any sense. The soul's habitual cognition of itself as singular is the presence of the soul to itself. It is prior to specific acts of an actual understanding of itself as potency is prior to actualization. To say that such prior "cognition" is habitual is not to say that it is an acquired habit. On the contrary, "ad hoc sufficit sola essentia animae, quae menti est praesens."[19]

The knowledge which the soul has of the nature of soul is also divided, as between apprehension and judgment. The apprehension of the nature of the soul is had in the way any apprehension is had, that is, by abstraction of a *species* from sense. Moreover, the soul understands its own nature by reasoning back from the natures of other things. By reflection on the universality of known natures, the mind infers that what is known is immaterial. From the immateriality of the intelligible, it further infers its own immateriality and subsistence. Such a roundabout route is required by the weakness of human mind, which is like prime matter in its pure potency or formlessness. Only with the judgment of the soul's nature, then, can one bring in the Augustinian rhetoric of certitude, which Thomas sees as describing, not the beginning, but the end of the stages of soul's knowledge of itself. Moreover, though Thomas is more irenic towards the Augustinians in the *De Veritate*, he has performed the same radical criticism of the Augustinian introspection here as in the *Summa*. By distinguishing strictly between the soul's 'perception' of itself as singular and its knowledge of itself as having a nature, he has taken away the main weapon in the Augustinian armory — despite his citations of Augustine and his relegation of the anti-Augustinian authorities to the status of objections.

The same response to Augustine is found in the last text by Thomas on the soul's knowledge of itself, a single disputed question from a Bodleian manuscript.[20] A reference to the parallel question in the *prima pars* places the text after 1267-68.[21] Thomas begins his answer by setting forth two "sollemnes opiniones."[22] Although names are not given these are the positions of Augustine and Aristotle. Thomas sets aside the first by arguing both from the intellect's need for sensible species and from its lack of knowledge about the soul's nature.[23] He argues for a version of the second opinion, that of Aristotle, but only after distinguishing three types of knowledge of the soul. There is first the "cognitio de quidditate et natura anime," second the "cognitio actualis existencie ipsius," and third the "[cognitio] habitualis per quam exit in actum cognoscendi."[24] The intellect has the first sort of knowledge only "indirecte" and "per speciem intelligibilem a fantasmatibus abstractum."[25] This is a knowledge "per quandam reflexionem" which knows its own nature as it would know the nature of another.[26] Indeed, "virtus anime primo cognoscit proprium eius obiectum, et tunc per reflexionem cognoscit seipsam."[27] Habitual self-knowledge, by contrast, depends only on "ista sola presencia" by which the soul "est sibi ipsi presens," but *not* "ut obiectum intelligibilis informans intellectum."[28] When the soul knows that it is, it knows by presence; but when the soul wants to know what it is, it must — *pace* Augustine — have recourse to species abstracted from sensory experience.

In both the *Summa* and the *De Veritate*, the general questions about self-knowledge are followed by more detailed questions about the soul's knowledge of its habits. The second Article of Question 87 in the *prima pars* asks "utrum intellectus noster cognoscat habitus animae per essentiam eorum."[29] The principles used in the body of the first Article are brought forward again. Since a habit is midway between potency and act, and since things are known only in act, it follows that a habit is known not by its essence but only as it acts. Thomas also repeats the distinction between two sorts of mediate knowledge of a habit. A habit is known, first, "per ipsam praesentiam habitus."[30] The case given is "dum aliquis percipit se habere habitum, per hoc quod percipit se producere actum proprium habitus." Presumably one would 'know' that one had the habit of grammar by seeing oneself speak grammatically. But Thomas adds "quia ex hoc ipso quod est praesens, actum causat, in quo statim percipitur." He seems, then, to be thinking of habits less voluntary than the exercise of grammar.

A habit is known in the second way "per studiosam inquisitionem," for which the example is "dum aliquis inquirit naturam et rationem habitus, ex consideratione actus." This corresponds exactly to the second type of self-knowledge discussed in general by Article 1 and, in fact, to the knowledge of what is common to soul in *De Veritate*. Indeed, the whole distinction here is the distinction of the earlier Article transposed to the discussion of habits. Only a very few specifications are added. In the reply to the second objection, Thomas argues that the soul's habits are not present to it as objects, but as means of knowing, "ut quibus intellectus intelligit." They are known as instrumental or intentional.[31] He adds, in the reply to the third: "Sed habitus non est de ordine obiectorum, inquantum est habitus; nec propter habitum aliqua cognoscuntur sicut propter obiectum cognitum sed sicut propter dispositionem vel formam qua cognoscens cognoscit."[32] This seems to add a further specification of the status of the soul's powers as intelligible. It is not just that a habit is somehow midway between act and potency; it is also that a habit, when actualized, points beyond itself to what it intends. Again, the intellect is not only a potential being to be known in act; it is also an intending being, to be known in what it intends.

The parallel discussion from *De Veritate* also applies to habits the schema of particular cognition and general knowledge established in the immediately preceding treatment of the soul. But Thomas wants to stress there that the schema must be rearranged as it is applied. One can see the operations of the soul and infer that there must be something behind them, without having exact knowledge of its nature. That is the general order of knowledge about causes. But one cannot see the operations of a habit without knowing the habit, since a habit *is* nothing but the principle of operation manifested in the acts. "Habitus autem per essentiam suam est principium talis actus, unde si cognoscitur habitus prout est principium talis actus, cognoscitur de eo quid est."[33] Alternately, if one has no notion of the specific habit that governs and delineates a particular group of actions, one has no way of identifying the actions as actions of the habit. The *quid sit* must come before the *an sit* to pick out the actions about which one is speaking.

So it is that Thomas reverses the two parts of his schema. He begins with knowledge of the *quid sit* of habits, distinguishing again between apprehension and judgment. Apprehension of the whatness of habits is drawn from knowledge of objects and acts. Judgment of the whatness of habits is had from the "measure" which governs the habit. The measure can be from sense experience (as in the case of useful arts), from nature (as in the case of cardinal virtues), or from grace (as in the case of theological virtues). After judgment, as it were, comes the question *an sit?*. Here, as before, Thomas distinguishes actual cognition of the presence of the habit from habitual cognition of its nature. The actual cognition is a 'perception' of a habit in virtue of one's being aware of performing acts under that habit. The habitual cognition is based directly on the essence of the habit, which as such is in the mind. But habitual cognition is different in cognitive and affective habits. Cognitive habits are the proximate principles of their own habitual cognition; affective habits are only remote principles.

In applying the re-ordered schema to the case of the habits, Thomas adds a few telling remarks about the very reflexive power of the mind. The remarks draw a contrast with the more limited case of sensation. For any power of the soul, such as sensation, the primary tendency is towards the object. The power cannot seize upon its object, cannot come to rest in it, unless there is a certain recognition of the object, a certain "reditio" by which the power recognizes that it has its object in view, as it were. "[I]n actum visionis suae non dirigitur nisi per quamdam reditionem, dum videndo colorem videt se videre. Sed ista reditio incomplete quidem est in sensu, complete autem in intellectu, qui reditione completa redit ad sciendum essentiam suam."[34] But even the *reditio completa* of intellect, the reflexive power of mind, is dependent on the primary operation of intellect in grasping things. "Unde actio intellectus nostri primo tendit in ea quae per phantasmata apprehenduntur, et deinde redit ad actum suum cognoscendum." As the term plainly says, the "reditio" is a return by the mind from its primary engagement in the world.

The third Article from the discussion in the *Summa* wants also to preserve some reflexive character for the intellect. The argument begins from the same correlation of ontology and intelligibility, but adds the premise that the intellect is a complete action, one whose highest activity is for its own sake. In general, then, "[h]oc igitur est primum quod de intellectu intelligitur, scilicet ipsum eius intelligere.''[35] Yet the hierarchical premise is applied to this general truth in order to distinguish types of self-knowledge. Below God's absolute unity of act and the angel's knowledge of itself, the human intellect must come to a thinking of its own act through the thinking of external objects. "Et ideo id quod primo cognoscitur ab intellectu humano, est huiusmodi obiectum; et secundario cognoscitur ipse actus quo cognoscitur obiectum; et per actum cognoscitur ipse intellectus, cuius est perfectio ipsum intelligere.''

To the objection that the object of the intellect is something common, and not its own particular act, Thomas replies that the act of the intellect falls under those common, external objects.[36] To the objection that the intellect's knowledge of itself implies an infinity of reflexive acts, Thomas replies that there is nothing wrong with a potential infinity.[37] Indeed, the act by which the intellect understands an external object is to be distinguished from the act by which it understands its own understanding of that object. Finally, Thomas denies that the analogy between sensation and intellection extends so far as to rule out any self-'perception' by the intellect.[38]

The talk of two acts, or of a potentially infinite series of dependent acts, seems to be the answer to the question about the content of the soul's simple knowledge of itself. Intellectual *perceptio* by actual presence gives no theoretical content; it cannot be the basis of a scientific treatment of soul. That is reserved to the second, speculative form of self-knowledge. But the *perceptio* does provide an affirmation of one's own activity. There are two consequences to the assertion of this bare self-awareness. The first is that one does not have to posit any higher faculty than intellect — as one had to posit a common sense in order to see and collate the activities of particular senses. The second is that one has established some small space of interiority. But the interior space in Aquinas is very small and very dark in comparison with that of Augustine. It is a space in which other activities can be seen, not a space filled with its own activity.

The purport of the third Article is to save the intellect's knowledge of itself with the limitations already stated. The premise of intentionality does not preclude a secondary act of reflection which, as it were, runs alongside the intentional apprehension of an external object. A similar distinction between primary and secondary apprehensions is used, in the fourth Article, to explain the intellect's grasp of acts of the will. Given that willing is, in Thomas's formula, an inclination following upon a form understood in the intellect, he argues the hierarchical principle that an inclination is in its subject according to the ontological status of the subject. Thus, will is in intellectual creatures intellectually. "Unde actus voluntatis intelligitur ab intellectu, et inquantum aliquis percipit se velle, et inquantum aliquis cognoscit naturam huius actus, et per consequens naturam eius principii, quod est habitus vel potentia."[39] Here one has again the distinction between a simple knowledge by "perceptio" and an acquired, philosophic knowledge by apprehension of the natures involved. But one also sees the distinction between a primary and secondary apprehension. The intellect knows its own act mediately, and in knowing itself, knows the actions of the will which are grounded in the intellect. One knows the "sicut principiatum in principio, in quo habetur notio principati."[40] In knowing one's own will, there is a double mediation: the mediation by which intellect is known, and the mediation by which the will is known through the *notiones* of the intellect.

Taken together then, the Articles from *De Veritate* and the Question from the *Summa* argue for three different types of indirection which lie behind a discourse about soul. The first is the general indirection resulting from the soul's being a potency; any discourse about the soul is dependent on observing the soul as actualized. It cannot be gotten by an immediate intuition, but comes, rather, in a subsidiary or dependent act of understanding. Within the indirect knowledge of the soul, there is an inchoate *perceptio* of the self as present in activity. There is also, at a higher level of indirection, the universal, speculative knowledge of the nature of the intellect. From the intellectual *perceptio* of self, there follows, in another direction, the *perceptio* of the will's inclination to certain objects known in intellect. From the speculative knowledge of the nature of intellect, there can follow the speculative knowledge of the nature of the will.

Whatever the discourse about soul might be, it is conditioned by these three types of indirection. The speculative discourse about soul, the general form of the human being's knowledge of itself, is a branch of physics. It studies the soul as an external object, as one among other natural things. The simple "perceptio" of intellectual operation, in contrast, seems to be only the reflexive affirmation of the act of one's own knowing activity. There remains the soul's knowledge of its own will.

4.3 THE SOUL'S KNOWLEDGE OF ITS OWN TELEOLOGY

The so-called 'treatise on law' from the end of the *prima secundae* has a long history of use and mis-use as an almost autonomous tract. Its chief interest has been in its seeming to offer solid ground for attacks on moral relativism. Properly construed, in context, it does have much to offer to an account of the public virtues. But it speaks as forcefully to the question of the soul's knowledge of itself, since knowledge of the natural law is knowledge of the soul's own teleology.[1] The natural law is an expression of the lived means to that end which is appropriate to rational creatures. Indeed, the parallel between speculative and practical knowing is never far from Thomas's mind in the "treatise." The parallel is drawn in the very first Article and then recurs in many subsequent arguments as the crucial premise.[2] It is not too much of an imposition, then, to take the text as a concrete supplement to the discussion of speculative knowledge about the human soul.

The first description of natural law has much in common with the first description of speculative self-knowledge in psychology. The natural law is introduced as the rational counterpart of natural tendency to an end. It is, accordingly, a "participatio legis aeternae in rationali creatura" by which the creature has "naturalem inclinationem ad debitum actum et finem."[3] The first discussion of speculative psychology had insisted that the soul's knowledge of itself "competit nobis secundum derivationem luminis intellectus nostri a veritate divina, in qua rationes omnium rerum continentur."[4] Where lower animals have mute tendencies, 'instincts', rational souls appropriate such teleological orderings rationally and recognize them as participations in God's grounding intelligibility. That "eternal law" from which natural law is participated is, Thomas has already said, nothing other than God Himself.[5]

Thomas's next step is to place limits upon the soul's appropriation of this 'natural law'. The whole argument of the immediately subsequent Article is that the natural law is, at best, an abstract and incomplete guide to action. Human law is needed as the completing specification of natural law; human law can offer those particular conclusions drawn from the "principiis communibus et indemonstrabilibus" of natural law. There are two corollaries to this view of human law. The first is that the natural condition of man is to be in a city-state; thus, human law would always be present naturally as a constant supplement to the natural law.[6] But the other reason is that Thomas views natural law as a necessarily limited participation of the eternal law. "[R]atio humana non potest participare ad plenum dictamen rationis divinae, sed suo modo et imperfecte."[7] The same claim is repeated while showing the necessity for a divine law. Thus, "per naturalem legem participatur lex aeterna secundum proportionem capacitatis humanae naturae."[8]

From this preliminary treatment, three things are clear. First, the natural law is like speculative psychology in being a grasp of a certain intelligible participation in God. Second, the participation which is natural law is by no means comprehensive or detailed. It remains, on the contrary, an inchoate teleological knowledge. Third, then, natural law is completed and made explicit by other sorts of law, namely, the human and the divine.[9]

The positive content of the natural law, to the extent that it can be articulated, is described in the six Articles of Question 94. I will not go through each of them, but will comment only on those three which seem to me to form the center of the argument. Article 2 addresses the question whether the natural law has one or more precepts. Article 3 asks whether the natural law actually specifies all virtues. Article 4 considers whether the natural law is the same for all. Thomas's determination of each Article depends on a distinction between general principle and particular case, a distinction which recalls not only the parallel between theoretical and practical reasoning, but also the whole movement of discourse about the soul from abstract to concrete, from definition to act.

The body of the second Article begins with a distinction

made in speculative reasoning, that between what is self-evident *quoad se* and *quoad nos*. The distinction is used elsewhere in the *Summa*, for example, to settle the issue of the self-evidence of God's existence.[10] Curiously, this distinction is not applied explicitly in the resolution of the argument. Thomas proceeds from its enunciation to a description of the levels of 'premises' in the natural law. But the application of the principle might be deduced from the parallel to Boethius, in which the wise see more precepts as self-evident, the ignorant only a few. This would suggest that the wise find many precepts in the natural law, the ignorant few. But the matter is more complicated. First, the distinction between self-evident *quoad se* and self-evident *quoad nos* requires a decision about the inclusion of a predicate in a subject. The wise see inclusions where the ignorant do not. But what about all men, wise and foolish, in comparison with God? How does one decide predicate inclusion for God? The second difficulty is that Thomas wants to argue for a real plurality of precepts, which are nonetheless hierarchically ordered to a single precept. Wisdom could be to see either their plurality or their hierarchical ordering to unity. Thus, a near approach to what is *quoad se* might be an approach either to plurality or to simplicity.[11]

Thomas seems on surer ground when he enunciates the first principle of practical knowledge, which is "bonum est quod omnia appetunt."[12] The first precept of the law, then, is "bonum est faciendum et prosequendum, et malum vitandum."[13] But the good, the end, is immediately broken down according to three different levels of psychic activity. The first good is the one that man shares with other natures; this is the good of existence and its precept is survival. The second good man shares with animals; this is the good of life and its precept is generation and nurture. The third good is the good which man has as rational; its precepts enjoin living in society and knowing about God.[14] Thus, the first precept of natural law has a triple content: survival as individual, survival as family, and survival as city-state. Again, the triple content of the law is the content of existence, generation, and philosophic legislation.

Thomas gives a few examples under each head. He says, for example, that generation comprises "educatio liberorum" and that political life requires "quod homo ignorantiam vitet, quod alios non offendat, cum quibus debet conversari."[15] But he does not perform anything like a transcendental deduction of the conditions for the fulfillment of each end. Indeed, in the next Article, he argues that such a complete deduction of the natural virtues cannot be performed.[16] He distinguishes between virtuous acts considered as virtuous and as particular acts. The natural law does include the inclination to act rationally, which is to act virtuously. But it does not include a complete list of virtuous acts; these are discovered, rather, in the long political experience of the race.[17] Thus, a complete enumeration of entailments under the three branches of the first precept of natural law is not part of the law, but part of the history of human communities.

Given the diversity of city-states, the contradictions in the history of conventions, what remains of the kernel of natural law? Is there an absolutely common content of the practical participation in the law of God? Thomas's reply to such questions, in the fourth Article, is one of the most subtle of his doctrines on the law. It is also the point at which he must deny the parallelism between practical and theoretical reasoning.[18] In speculative matters, the premises are knowable by all equally; the same conclusions are knowable, though not equally. Differences of knowledge with regard to the conclusions are explained by reference to the difficulty of demonstration in various cases. In practical matters, the first principles are known to all. The conclusions, however, are common neither in content nor in clarity of apprehension: "quantum ad proprias conclusiones rationis practicae, nec est eadem veritas seu rectitudo apud omnes, nec etiam apud quos est eadem, est aequaliter nota."[19]

The more particular the case, the more difficult it is to arrive at a conclusion on which all will agree. Alternately, the more specific a norm or precept proposed in ethics or law, the more liable it is to justified exception. In many particular cases, the right course of action cannot be rigorously deduced. Matters become even more complicated when one considers the defects to which practical reasoning is liable, whether of passion, or bad habit, or bad political convention. Although Thomas does want to urge that the most common principles are the same "apud omnes et secundum rectitudinem et secundum

notitiam,"[20] he restricts the "communia" in his examples to
such matters as "secundum rationem agatur." What is common
in the natural law is so abstract as to provoke disagreement
when expressed as precept, much more when applied to particular cases. Thomas thus suggests the question, what is it to
have a principle of practical reason which cannot be applied?

The parallelism between the speculative and practical is
broken, then, at a very interesting point. The first principles of
each order are held to be alike in common acceptance. The two
differ in efficacy with regard to conclusions. But that is a
decisive difference, because the whole end of practical reason is
action. The "principles" of practical reason thus play a different
role than those of speculation. The most powerful premise in
speculative reason would be that from which most light could
be cast, from which most demonstrations could be made. The
most powerful practical premise would be one from which
right action could be most certainly deduced. Yet the premises
of the natural law are, in their generality, unable to ground sure
deduction of right action. For this very reason, one needs the
different specificities of human and divine law.

What one learns about the soul from natural law is precisely
that the soul is in potency. Each of its three levels — the existen-
tial, the animal, and the rational — has an end. These ends are
known in a general way through the natural law. It is even the
case that certain abstract imperatives follow from the apprehension of these ends: that one ought to struggle to survive, that
one ought to nurture one's offspring, even that one ought to act
rationally. Yet these imperatives are still remote from concrete
conclusions. The soul's knowledge of itself discloses a
teleology, but not how to enact it. At most, it might suggest that
one ought to be ready to act, that one ought to recognize one's
potency. It is as if the soul's teleological knowledge of itself produced insight into its fundamental lack. The ontological premise
of the soul's potency, which appeared in Thomas's arguments
for mediated self-knowledge, is now confirmed in seeing the incompleteness of natural law.

The discussion of natural law is not the only point in the
Summa where Thomas considers the soul's natural knowledge
of its own teleology. The most salient of the other passages
would be the discussion of the natural habit of *synderesis* in the

prima pars; there it occurs in the preliminary description of
human nature and its powers.[21] The single article on *synderesis*
recalls a much longer discussion of the habit written by Thomas
some ten years earlier in Question 16 of *De Veritate*.[22] The two
passages do not differ in substance; together, they extend the
discussion of soul's knowledge of itself to its knowledge of the
natural law. I do not think that they alter its conclusions. Indeed, the discussion of *synderesis* may show more exactly the
limitations of the soul's appropriation of its own teleology.

Question 16 of *De Veritate* is divided into three Articles: the
first considers whether *synderesis* is a power or a habit; the second, whether *synderesis* can err; the third, whether *synderesis*
can be extinguished in an individual. After admitting a diversity
of opinion on the first topic, Thomas argues by analogy with the
habit of the speculative "intellectum principiorum" that there
must be "quidam habitus naturalis primorum principiorum
operabilium, quae sunt universalia principia iuris naturalis."[23] It
does not matter much whether '*synderesis*' is the name of this
latter habit or of a certain rational power acting with the habit.
The power cannot operate thus without the habit. What matters, beyond names, is that *synderesis* is a natural appropriation
of the first starting-points of action, which are like principles of
the natural law, and that it is thus a constant guide to what is
good. Of course, as with the speculative habit of principles,
synderesis directs only in general; it is a universal judgment
about all human action and is to be distinguished from the more
particular judgment of conscience in regard to specified kinds
of acts, as well as from the free choice of a particular act.[24]

Can *synderesis* err, the second Article asks? Thomas
paraphrases the first book of Aristotle's *Physics*: nature aims at
the good through regularity of action. Such action must depend
on firmly fixed principles. So, in speculative matters, there must
be certain cognition of the first principles from which all the
more specific deductions are made. In practical matters, there
must be a corresponding apprehension. *Synderesis* is just that
unwavering grasp of a first principle of action, "cuius officium
est remurmurare malo, et inclinare ad bonum." Of course, the
infallibility of *synderesis* applies only to its grasp of a universal
in the light of which all acts are examined; it is not a guarantee

for particular cases. Error in moral judgment can arise both in regard to kinds of acts and in regard to the quality of a particular act.[26] It would still seem, however, that there would be a direct intuition of the most general moral principles in *synderesis*.

The essential qualification comes in the third article which considers the extinguishing of *synderesis*. It follows directly from what has been established that *synderesis* cannot be entirely extinguished in an individual; it is, after all, a light that is of the nature of soul itself. In particular instances, however, its act can be inhibited, either entirely or partially. The act of *synderesis* is entirely inhibited in those who lack the use of reason — as a result, for example, of a physical wound. *Synderesis* is partially inhibited or deflected whenever one errs in choosing. Thus, the force of concupiscence or some other passion can ''absorb'' power to such an extent that the truths known in *synderesis* are not applied.[27] Thomas admits that this happens in any number of cases. Among heretics, for example, the truths held by *synderesis* are not applied to their own infidelity because of an error made about what is pleasing to God; for the vicious, the vice itself blinds them to the application of such truths. *Synderesis* is a habit of the first principles of action, but its natural possession is existentially compatible with many species of sinful acting. In other words, the content of the truths known in *synderesis* is sufficiently general and sufficiently fragile as to admit grossly contradictory applications. The principles of *synderesis* are, when restricted by opposed minor premises, practically equivocal.

The general conclusion drawn from the discussion of the knowledge of natural law still stands. The soul's knowledge of a human beings's teleology has the universality of potency; it attains the specificity of act only by experience or instruction. The soul has no intuitive knowledge of moral matters, as there was none in speculative matters. Indeed, the moral incompleteness seems even stronger, since it requires as remedy not only long personal experience, but the accumulation of experience in human law and in philosophic ethics. The soul needs others in order to come to itself.

4.4 MORAL PEDAGOGY IN DISCOURSE ABOUT THE SOUL

Thomas adverts, in a few passages of the commentary on *De Anima*, to the question of evidence for a philosophical discourse about the soul. He explains the privileged position of psychology in part by reference to the soul's knowledge of itself. "Haec autem scientia, scilicet de anima ... 'certa est', hoc enim quilibet experitur in seipso, quod scilicet habeat animam, et quod anima vivificet."[1] In view of distinctions made elsewhere, this must mean that the presence of the soul to itself provides some ground for certainty about the existence and informing nature of soul as such. Yet this certainty would seem to be at most the raw material for a scientific discourse.

Thomas is more explicit in a later passage, where he remarks on the evidence for Aristotle's account of mind. After recalling that the mind does not know itself "per suam essentiam" but rather by "aliquam speciem intelligibilem, sicut et alia intelligibilia,"[2] Thomas says that mind's knowledge of itself opens the way to understanding intellection. "Species igitur rei intellectae in actu, est species ipsius intellectus; et sic per eam seipsum intelligere potest."[3] Thomas connects this explicitly with the composition of the treatise at hand. "Unde et supra Philosophus per ipsum intelligere, et per illud quod intelligitur, scrutatus est naturam intellectus possibilis."[4] Aristotle used reflection on his own understanding as the basis for his account of the possible intellect. Generally, "[n]on enim cognoscimus intellectum nostrum nisi per hoc, quod intelligimus nos intelligere."[5] How can this be construed so as to be consistent with all of the limitations already discovered?

Thomas would seem to refer, by that "supra," to the immediately preceding *lectiones*, perhaps even more exactly to that part of the seventh *lectio* wherein, Thomas says, Aristotle "ostendit naturam intellectus possibilis."[6] But there is no explicit use in those discussions of introspective evidence. The main thesis to be established is the potential character of the *intellectus possibilis*. Indeed, Anaxagoras's appeal to the experience of willing is rejected, since Aristotle wants to make the argument on the more general grounds of act and potency. The reason is not hard to find. How could one prove the potency of the possible intellect by active introspection? The argument must be made, rather, by appeal to the general definition of soul and to the degrees of actuality.

Thomas had said not only that the account of possible intellect, but also the notion of soul as a particular kind of form, could be drawn from one's apprehension of one's own intellection. The masterful Aristotelian definition of soul is constructed at the beginning of the second Book of *De Anima*, particularly in the passages which Thomas reviews in the third *lectio*. But that *lectio* avoids introspective evidence both formally and materially. Formally, Thomas argues that the nature of soul cannot be demonstrated from its causes, as in mathematics, but only from its effects, as in the rest of physics.[7] Soul must be defined in that round-about fashion because what we know with certainty about the soul is that it is, but not what it is. The nature of soul is hidden from us, as are many other physical causes. The same point is made, materially, in the actual argument for the definition of soul as "principium vivendi."[8] The argument presupposes a hierarchy of living things and certain physical principles about motion. The human soul is described in the hierarchy as if from the outside: "In quibusdam autem, cum his ulterius invenitur intellectus, scilicet in hominibus."[9] Thomas's language is like that of an observing naturalist. The definition of soul is established — must be established, according to Thomas — without the direct appeal to what might be provided in introspection.

The relation between the soul's presence to itself and discourse about soul is not spelled out, then, in the actual arguments of that discourse. It has been mentioned, but not appropriated. I have suggested that there would be something odd in arguing that active self-knowing is the basis of our assertion about the soul's being in potency. This suggests, in turn, another way of reading the mentions of 'presence to itself'. Discourse about the soul, however indirect, does pre-suppose that the soul can know itself when actually in act. There must be at least that negative understanding of the soul's knowledge of itself; the soul cannot be ignorant of its own activities. Knowledge of itself appears in psychology, then, only as a pre-

supposition, not as a principle of construction; it is a requirement for avoiding contradiction, not a premise with positive
content. The content must be supplied by the external study of
things — ensouled human bodies among them.

If the discourse about soul presents itself as an infallible
enactment of private certainties, then it not only truncates
philosophical questioning, it also forestalls the discursiveness of
reason by appeal to an angelic intuition. Thomas sees this defor-
mation of psychological discourse in Platonism. To deny
abstraction from sensibles in favor of an intuition of Forms is to
forget the human condition — and so too the conditions for the
possibility of human philosophy. That is why Thomas is so
careful about appeals to introspection. I have already mentioned its few appearances in the commentary on *De Anima*, where
it seems to figure in prefatory or summary paragraphs only and
not in the main arguments. Elsewhere, its appearances are very
much controlled. In the protracted disputes with Alexander,
Avicenna, and Averroes about the nature of intellect, where introspective evidence might seem decisive, it is sparse. The *Contra Gentiles*, for example, devotes some twenty-three Chapters
to the critique of opposing views about the intellect, in which
by far the largest number of arguments are made on ontological
or logical grounds. Thomas will argue that the opposed views
are "destructivum totius moralis philosophiae et politicae con-
versationis."[10] He will compare translations to establish Aristotle's sense.[11] He will repeat his appeal to the principles of unity
in forms and substances. But only rarely, and then on the
margin, does he actually adduce the evidence of introspection.
Once, in contrasting intellect with sense, he says that intellect
apprehends universals, "ut per experimentum patet."[12]
Elsewhere he seems to point to the experience of understanding
when he argues against Averroes that "[h]abens enim intellectum est intelligens."[13] But even there the argument is more that
Averroes does not explain what he purports to explain.

It is possible that Thomas avoids introspective evidence in
controversy because it is ambiguous as to the specific point in
dispute. But I think the reason is broader. Thomas does not rely
on introspection because he does not think that philosophic introspection is possible. He reduces the evidentiary weight of introspection to the minimum, to the negative affirmation that

one is not unaware of what happens. The same motive can be traced in the discussion of speculative knowledge about soul. This knowledge is a part of physics and, as such, is a study of observed events, of particular bodily substances, from which an induction can be made. In order to come to a knowledge of what it itself is, the soul must go out into the world and study itself as if from the outside. That is why Thomas finds it easy, and not only right, to discuss the soul always in the third person. The soul is, indeed, an external object for philosophy — an entity in the world to be studied as one part of a hierarchy of living things.

The point is made rhetorically in q.76 of the *prima pars*, in an article which is decisive for the construction of the account of the human soul.[14] The issue is "utrum intellectivum principium uniatur corpori ut forma." One would expect that first-person evidence would be used here, if anywhere, to affirm that the embodied soul thinks. Thomas does refer to particular acts of understanding, but always in the third person: "Experitur enim unusquisque seipsum esse qui intelligit."[15] This is not a direct appeal to introspective evidence; it is a universal claim about what could be available from introspective evidence. It is a generalization, not a testimony. As a generalization, it requires something more than private self-examination. Indeed, such a general claim could only be based on a speculative study which forms part of physics.

Still the movement to the external is at the same time a movement to the particular. This is one of the most interesting twists in Thomist psychology; it results from the central place in the discourse about soul of contingent events, as well as from the overlapping of theoretical and practical. The theory of the virtues is, at once, a theoretical study of certain kinds of habits and a practical study undertaken in order to act virtuously. The difference is made by the end. Whether the end is practical or theoretical, however, the evidence to be considered is variegated, the conclusions to be drawn partial. If the study of soul cannot begin from a private intuition of the solitary self, it must begin from the public inquiry into many selves. The weakness of the human soul's presence to itself is, thus, the beginning of a philosophical psychology, which must be public, discursive, and in some way empirical.

Philosophical psychology is a discourse constructed by and for the souls about which it speaks. It is constructed after a recognition that there is a decisive difference between the implicit cognition of one's self and the explicit *scientia* of philosophic inquiry. In that recognition, the discourse of psychology affirms the potency of the human soul. A cognate potency is discovered in the investigation of the soul's knowledge of its own teleology. The soul must learn explicitly what end lies implicit in its own nature. So it is that Thomas returns to the question of pedagogy when remarking on the features of ethical knowledge.

In the third *lectio* of his commentary on the first Book of the *Nicomachean Ethics*, Thomas describes what he calls Aristotle's teaching on the mode of the science of ethics. Thomas rehearses, first, the remarks on the different degrees of certainty to be had in various sciences and the reasons for the impossibility of mathematical or metaphysical certainty in ethics.[16] He turns, second, to Aristotle's requirements for the "hearer" or student of ethical teaching.[17] Aristotle excludes three classes of learners as unsuitable. The young are excluded because of lack of experience, while the followers of passion and the incontinent are excluded because of an unwillingness or inability to act upon any moral lesson learned. If the young are excluded because of inexperience, it must be that the ethical teaching about the soul cannot be had except from experience. Thomas says, "iuvenis non habet notitiam eorum quae pertinent ad scientiam moralem, quae maxime cognoscuntur per experientiam. Iuvenis autem est inexpertus operationum humanae vitae propter temporis brevitatem, et tamen rationes moralis scientiae procedunt ex his quae pertinent ad actus humanae vitae et etiam sunt de his."[18] Ethics cannot rest only on private knowledge of one's self.

Yet a certain self-possession is supposed by moral teaching and so one must exclude the followers of passion and the incontinent. The former are excluded because they intend not to act consequentially: "sector passionum ... audiet hanc scientiam et inutiliter, idest absque consecutione debiti finis."[19] The latter, the incontinent, are excluded because they seem unable to act consequentially; they have forfeited that minimum of self-possession which is necessary for intelligent action. A negative presupposition is essential in psychology: one must not be unaware of one's activities as they happen. So, too, a negative imperative is presupposed in moral teaching: one must be able to act rationally, that is, in accordance with what one comes to know about soul.

Even so, as Thomas makes clear in any number of places, the negative presupposition is not equivalent to a first axiom in a full-blown science of ethics which might be available to direct introspection. If it were, there would not be such difficulty about the study of ethical matters. There would not be the concern over the teaching of ethical norms, or the disposition of the student, and the lengthy consideration of cases. The pedagogy of ethics is undertaken precisely because one can only make a negative presupposition about presence to one's self or self-possession. Ethical discourse is truly, and not accidentally, hortative so far as its teaching is needed to bring about the soul's progressive actualization. The limitation on the soul's teleological knowledge of itself is the reason for taking moral teaching seriously as a work of persuasion to an end which might otherwise not be attained.

The motive of moral teaching animates Thomas's writings at many of its starting-points. The great *Summa*, for example, was written, in some sense, for the sake of writing the *secunda pars*. The same might be argued, less neatly, of the *Summa contra Gentiles*. Thus, the two major works for which Thomas himself provided the structure are built around a moral pedagogy. Nor is this surprising, given Thomas's evident concern, as a Dominican Master, for bringing about the perfection of souls, concretely and practically. The reader of Thomas sees the moral motive at work, as well, in the constant attention to cases and decisions, in the irritation with the merely technical, and in the frequent appeal to moral consequences in the criticism of speculative positions.

The reader also sees that the moral pedagogy converges with the speculative pedagogy. It is true, of course, that teaching is justified by Thomas on moral and theological grounds.[20] But there is more to the convergence than that single intersection. To ascend the speculative hierarchy is, for Thomas, to actualize the human end, which is speculative. Moral pedagogy is instrumental with regard to speculative pedagogy. It aims at the practice of virtues which are subordinated to the acquisition of the intellectual virtues in speculative knowing. The two sides of discourse about the soul are not only seen to converge, they are recognized as hierarchically related. The limitation on speculative knowledge of self is seen also as a limitation on moral self-knowledge; moral teaching, in seeking to remedy the second, becomes a remedy for the first as well.

If the discourse about soul is in some way the middle speculative discourse in the Thomist *corpus*, it now seems to be so instrumentally as well. It serves, as did mathematics in the Boethian hierarchy, to bring forward the problem of teleological actualization which is the motor for speculative ascent. The discourse of physics showed that there was an ascent to be made in denying 'literalism', in denying that one had a finished explanation already in hand. The discourse about the soul makes the ascent possible by denying that one is already complete, accomplished, actualized; it shows the ground for a kind of discourse that moves one towards one's own, imperfectly grasped end.

CHAPTER 5

Discourse about First Principles

5.1 THE DEFINITIONS OF METAPHYSICS

The medieval question about the definition of metaphysics is complicated by a number of ancient quarrels. The first of these is the quarrel between Plato and Aristotle over the relations between acts of understanding and intelligible objects. The second is the quarrel occasioned by the reading of Aristotle; it is a dispute about the most appropriate name of the science. The third quarrel comes from what seems a vacillation in Aristotle on the question, whether the subject of the science is being as being or the best beings, the separate substances. The three quarrels are different faces of the same difficulty: How can one describe the relation of human scientific discourse to the most intelligible things?

The last quarrel provides the best entry into Thomas's texts. Its recent history was known to the medieval Latins through the controversy between Avicenna and Averroes.[1] In the first chapter of his *Metaphysica*, Avicenna claims, against various objections, that the *subiectum* of metaphysics is "ens inquantum est ens."[2] It cannot be God (whose existence would then be taken for granted), nor the supreme causes of being understood in an absolute sense, nor the totality of causes.[3] This position of Avicenna's is criticized by Averroes in his commentary on Aristotle's *Physics*.[4] Averroes offers in its place the claim that the *subiectum* of first philosophy is precisely the separate substances. The dispute between the two was known and reflected among the Latins.[5] Gundissalinus rehearses Avicenna's reduction.[6] Robert Kilwardby traces the various definitions in Aristotle's *Metaphysics* in order to conclude "patet quod primae scientiae est considerare ens in genere secundum quod ens est, et per consequens omnia in universali, scilicet causam primam et eius effectus."[7] Following Avicenna, Albert reviews and criticizes the three opinions of 'the philosophers' with regard to the subject of metaphysics.[8] He affirms a formula much like that of Avicenna: "ens est subiectum inquantum ens et ea quae sequuntur ens, inquantum est ens et non inquantum hoc ens, sunt passiones eius."[9] Albert does pause, however, to attack "quidam Latinorum logice persuasi" who hold that the *subiectum* is God.[10]

Thomas's first approach to the definition of metaphysics comes in the exposition of Boethius's *De Trinitate*.[11] That text will require much attention in the study of the character of metaphysical discourse. Still, a preliminary reading would show that Thomas there conforms to the Latin tradition for the most part, with interesting alterations. He begins by saying that every science considers as its subject some genus, of which it must know the *principia*.[12] There are two kinds of *principia*, subsistent and inherent. There are also two kinds of common *principia* that extend to all being, some as common by predication and others as common by causality. There are *principia* common to all beings in each of these ways; there is an order or hierarchy among *principia* which can be traced back to incorruptible substances, 'divine things' in Aristotle's sense. Owing to the weakness of human understanding, however, these subsistent 'divine' *principia* can be treated in metaphysics only as "principia communia omnium entium," that is, as they are inherent in their physical effects.[13] Thus, metaphysics treats "ea quae sunt communia omnibus entibus" and has as its *subiectum* "ens in quantum est ens."[14] The science which has the separate beings immediately as its *subiectum* is that other 'theology', based on revelation. The philosopher's theology treats of God and of other separate beings "non tamquam subiectum scientiae, sed tamquam principia subiecti."[15]

Thomas seems to be following the direction of Avicenna. But he may do so for different reasons and to a different end. Avicenna rejected God as *subiectum* with a dual reduction requiring as essential the premise that men have no immediate intuition of God.[16] God has been suggested in physics and now must be sought by demonstration.[17] Thomas takes up these simple remarks and greatly expands them. The very definition of metaphysics in the Boethius commentary is constructed on the admission of the weakness of human understanding. Its name *'theologia'* is both justified and qualified by the same admission.

The same is true of the more famous discussion of the science in the proemium to his commentary on Aristotle's *Metaphysics*.[18] 'Highest intelligibles' can be understood in three ways, he writes.[19] The first is according to the order of understanding. Since the sureness of knowledge depends on its grasp of causes, that science which grasps the first causes provides the greatest sureness and the highest intelligibility. There must be, then, a science dealing with the first causes — a science which thus rules the others. The second way to understand 'highest intelligibles' is by comparison of intellect to sense. Intellect is distinguished from sense by dealing not with particulars but with universals; the more universal is the more intelligible. The most universal things are "ens, et ea quae consequuntur ens, ut unum et multa, potentia et actus."[20] To lack knowledge of these most universal things would be to lack the central knowledge. Yet none of the particular sciences can deal with them. There must be, then, a science above the others which deals with these universals. The third way of approach to metaphysics is from the very cognition of what is understood.[21] A thing is more intelligible as it is further removed from matter. The things which strike the cognitive power with greatest force are those which are completely immaterial, such as God and the Intelligences.

These three approaches point not to many, but to one science. Along the first approach, it is called "first philosophy"; along the second, "metaphysics" ' along the third, "divine science" or "theology."[22] The highest cause of the first way is identified with the most intelligible of the third, when the separated substances are seen as the starting-points of causal chains. The first and third ways are subsumed under the second when it is realized that all of the objects known in them are either *passiones* or causes of *ens commune*. In another and more convincing way, one can see that *ens commune* is so abstract that it can be treated as separated from matter both *in esse* and *in ratione*, though not in exactly the same way as are God and the Intelligences.[23] These reasonings bend the cognitive and ontological characterizations of metaphysics into a circle.

Thomas's closure of the circle cures certain ambiguities in the Aristotelian text. Aristotle himself seems to move among three possibilities for the subject-matter of metaphysics: being *qua* being, the first causes and principles, and the divine. Thomas tries to reproduce this plurality in his explication of the three names for metaphysics. He also considers it with regard to Aristotle's first enumeration, in I, 2, of the six attributes commonly assigned to Wisdom.[24] Aquinas sees with Aristotle that each of these attributes inheres in that knowledge of the first and universal causes.[25] But the arguments which Thomas provides to show the inherences are largely of his own making. They turn the looser remarks of the Aristotelian text into a fairly tight argument divided into symmetrical parts.

This reworking becomes even more apparent in the remarks on IV,1, where Aristotle turns from defining metaphysics as the science of first causes to defining it as the science of being *qua* being. For Aquinas's reading, this chapter marks Aristotle's passage from disputation to demonstration. It appropriately reconsiders the subject-matter and scope of the science.[26] The subject-matter of the science is "ens" or, more specifically, "ens secundum quod est ens"[27] or "ens universale inquantum huiusmodi."[28] How is this definition to be reconciled with the emphasis on first causes in I,2? Thomas answers that the earlier definition of metaphysics designated it as the search for the principles and highest causes of things.[29] But principles and causes are *per se* principles and causes of some other nature. In this case, that other nature is *ens*. The ancient search for the first causes is a search for the causes of *ens*.

Of course, the field of study has only an analogous unity, since *'ens'* is an analogical term.[30] Analogical predication requires a certain something, a 'focus', to which all the other predications of the term can be referred as to a standard: "unumquodque secundum habitudinem ad illud unum refertur."[31] This standard must have a numerical unity, not merely a notional one.[32] The Aristotelian examples show that the single nature can stand to the other as end or as efficient principle. The single nature which grounds the other predications of *'ens'* is, of course, *ens* as substance. It is neither the end nor the efficient cause of the others, but that which serves as their *subiectum*.[33] Substance stands at the top of a four-tier hierarchy of the senses of being. In an order descending from strong sense of *ens* to weak, the tiers are: substance; qualities, quantities, and properties; generation or corruption, with the other movements; and, finally, negation and privation, which are *entia* "tantum in ratione."[34] So it is that one can abbreviate the consideration of *ens inquantum ens* as the study of substance and its causes.

The concentration of the study of *ens commune* on the study of substance and its causes is quite important in preventing a slip which comes easily enough from the definition of metaphysics as the science of *ens inquantum ens*. I remarked earlier that this definition already contained a concession to human weakness inasmuch as the subject of metaphysics lies not in separate *principia* but in physical *principiata*. That concession ought not to be undone by reifying *ens inquantum ens*. *Ens* is not a subsisting replacement for the inaccessible separate substances. It is not a thing to be seized in any intuition, whether intellectual or sensible. Thus, Aquinas's use of the phrase '*ens inquantum ens*' is entirely different from its later uses by those who hold for intellectual intuition in philosophy. *Ens commune* is an analogical consideration of substances with very different structures and very different conditions. It is, then, important to keep in mind that *subiectum* itself is used analogously of different sciences and that the *subiectum* of metaphysics is determined in relation to the peculiar conditions of the *status viae*.

Thomas must next explain how this definition of metaphysics, even if it should be accepted, requires the assignment of *separatio* as the cognitive characteristic of first science. This could be accomplished by showing that the 'separate substances' occupy a central place in the study of *ens*. Aquinas attempts just this in explicating the long argument which is the bulk of Aristotle's Book Lambda. The Book begins with a reiteration of the claim that metaphysics chiefly considers substance.[35] The second *lectio* undertakes the division of substances into three kinds — the sensible corruptible, the sensible incorruptible, and the non-sensible immobile.[36] The two sorts of sensibles are also mobile and the study of them as mobile belongs to physics.[37] Aquinas asserts that the consideration of *ens commune* belongs also to that science which considers the separate substances. It follows that even material

substances fall within the purview of physics only in one of
their aspects — only insofar as they are mobile — and *not* in all
respects, especially not in those which are most basic ontologically.

Why ought the consideration of substance as such be assigned
to the study of the separate substances rather than to the study
of the corporeal? There are several answers to this, the crucial
question. The first answer, already at work in Book I, is that
things are known by their causes and that the ultimate causes of
substance are found among the higher substances. Aquinas explicitly recalls that reasoning in the second *lectio*: "Hoc enim in-
quiret considerando de substantiis separatis, quae sunt principia
moventia et fines corporum caelestium...."[38] It is then argued at
some length that the principles of substances are analogously
the principles of other things in at least three ways.[39] Then, of
course, the argument for the existence of a highest immaterial
being proceeds from the hypothesis of the eternity of its effect,
time.[40] The entity which is pure act is, after all, the *primum
movens*. The connection is made.

The second answer to the question about the assignment of
ens commune to the study of separate substances would be that
the pure actuality of the first mover serves as the generic ground
for all substances as such. Particularly when Thomas follows
Aristotle's practice, but not his understanding of it, in naming
this first being 'God',[41] it is easy to view its pure actuality as
paradigmatic. When Thomas connects this, in his own thought,
with the actuality of *esse*, it is clear that the entity of pure actuality grounds other substances.

Having argued the difference between metaphysics and each
of the particular sciences, Thomas turns already in Book XI to
Aristotle's comparisons between metaphysics and the others.[42]
There are three grounds of comparison, namely, with regard to
the mode of separation, with regard to nobility, and with regard
to universality.[43] In each, the radical difference between the
subject-matters of metaphysics and the lesser sciences is em-
phasized. On the count of separation, metaphysics deals not only with the separation of *ens commune*, but with that of entities
completely separated from matter, with the 'divine' in Aristotle's sense.[44] The same invocation of the divine is made with

regard to the second comparison, that of nobility: "Et in scientiis speculativis ultima, scilicet theologiae, cum sit circa
nobiliora entia, est nobilior."⁴⁵ An equally decisive cognitional
line is drawn in the comparison of universality. Here Aquinas
also makes an argument in direct answer to the question about
the relation of *ens commune* to the separate entities: "Si autem
est alia natura et substantia praeter substantias naturales, quae sit
separabilis et immobilis, necesse est alteram scientiam ipsius
esse, quae sit prior naturali. Et ex eo quod est prima, oportet
quod sit universalis. Eadem enim est scientia quae est de primis
entibus, et quae est universalis. Nam prima entia sunt principia
aliorum."⁴⁶ The movement of the argument is clearly dependent on the causal answer already discussed.

Thomas makes clear in this text, though hardly for a final
time in the commentary, that the investigation of *ens inquantum ens* is not strictly separable from the desire to know the
separate substances. The universality of the *subiectum* of
metaphysics does not make it opposed to the 'particular' study
of immaterial being. Indeed, Thomas has rehearsed many times
now the ways in which the various descriptions of metaphysics
converge. The study of *ens inquantum ens* is not opposed to
the study of spiritual being; it is, on the contrary, what we can
know of spiritual being without grace. Metaphysics turns to the
study of the most common principles of all substances precisely
in order to trace up from them, by causal inference, the agency
of the first substances. Zimmermann captures this turn nicely
when he writes that God is neither the subject nor a part of the
subject of metaphysics; God is the "Ursache des Subjekts" and
as such stands above the other separate substances, which are
"Zweitursachen des dem Menschen gegeneben Seienden."⁴⁷

The question was asked, what is the connection between the
subject-matter of metaphysics and its epistemological
characterization as *separatio*. The answer has been roundabout.
Its first step was to argue that *separatio* is suitably applied to the
study of those highest entities. It was then argued, second, that
the same study ought to embrace *ens commune* since those first
entities were the causes of all other beings, especially
substances. *Ens commune* is not a substitute for the first
substances; it is the only possible means for inquiring about

them. Latent in this argument was a second route to the answer — the suggestion that the *separatio* or *ens commune* from particular *entia* was something like the *separatio* by which those entities separated from matter are known. It is this suggetion which needs now to be taken up in a re-reading of Thomas's remarks on the character of *separatio*.

5.2 *SEPARATIO* AND THE NEGATIVE JUDGMENT

The first difficulty about '*separatio*' is to know whether the word names anything other than what is named by the word '*abstractio*'. The issue continues to be controversial. It is agreed by the controversialists that Thomas frequently uses '*separatio*' and '*abstractio*' or their derivatives interchangeably.[1] The disagreement begins with the question, whether such occurrences are simply examples of loose speaking. The evidence for thinking that there ought to be a sharp distinction between the strict senses of the two terms comes from the holograph of Thomas's commentary on Boethius's *De Trinitate*. The stages of redaction in the holograph show that Thomas suppressed his original teaching on three stages of abstraction in order to oppose two sorts of *abstractio* against a way of thinking called by him '*separatio*'.

The first modern commentator to draw out the lessons of Thomas's redaction at any length was Louis Geiger. Although he did not have a critical edition,[2] Geiger knew of the main faults of Uccelli's printed version from Antoine Dondaine.[3] Geiger argued that any confusion of abstraction and separation, any attempt to make them stages of a single ascent, would bring on the errors of Platonism by confusing the judgment of real separation with mathematical abstraction.[4] Geiger's views won wide acceptance and have become the prevalent reading of Question 5 of the *De Trinitate* commentary.[5] The 'new' reading was rejected at its first appearance by Leroy[6] and has been attacked quite recently by Ponferrada[7] and Vansteenkiste.[8] Their objections fall into two classes: they argue either that there are only weak textual grounds for positing a *separatio* or that *separatio* can be assimilated to one of the Cajetanian degrees of abstraction. Thus, for example, Ponferrada argues that the exposition of *De Trinitate* is, as a work, "young, unfinished and controversial"; he infers that it must be corrected by reference to the later works.[9] The later works teach Ponferrada that 'separation' and 'abstraction' are synonymous and that the act of separation is best accounted for by being integrated into the classical, Cajetanian treatments.[10]

The evidence, however, weighs on the side of Geiger. The record of the holograph shows Thomas's meticulous concern to recast the discussion of metaphysics around the discovery of *separatio*.[11] There is no later treatment of these questions *ex professo* which would have a literary character stronger than that of the exposition: there is no more precise text which might replace it. The treatment of the question in the *Metaphysics*-commentary neither contradicts nor transforms the earlier account. Nor is it quite enough to integrate Geiger's reading into the patterns inherited from Tridentine scholasticism. Cajetan, for example, is least reliable on cognitive questions, in part because he works against an established Scotism and a persistent Ockhamism, in part because of his own peculiar notions of demonstration.[12] One must take the doctrine of Thomas's *Super De Trinitate* without cutting it to the modern patterns already inchoately traced out in Cajetan or, more boldly, in John of St. Thomas.

The doctrine as a whole was sketched above with an eye to the hierarchy of the speculative sciences.[13] I return to it now in order to underscore its remarks on separation as characteristic of metaphysics. Those remarks fall into two articles, the third and fourth of Question 5. I will rearrange the remarks more topically in order to address the questions, what is *separatio* and how does it stand in relation to negation.

Separatio first appears with a technical sense in the defense of mathematical abstraction.[14] Thomas has presented the distinction between apprehension and judgment; the first "respicit ipsam naturam rei," the second "ipsum esse rei."[15] Thomas then describes the various types of separability, real and logical, which can be seized upon by the acts of mind. The mind can distinguish in judgment or in apprehension. Only the first is properly called 'separation', namely that operation in which the mind, composing and dividing, "distinguit unum ab alio per hoc quod intelligit unum alii non inesse."[16] The in-

finitive "inesse" combines with the mention of composition
and division to remind the reader that *separatio* is a judgment
of how things stand in being. Thomas repeats the reminder
somewhat later in the body of the same Article: "In his autem
quae secundum esse possunt esse divisa, magis habet locum
separatio quam abstractio."[17]

The judgment of *separatio* establishes the subject of
metaphysics: "secundum operationem intellectus componentis
et dividentis, quae separatio dicitur proprie; et haec competit
scientiae divinae sive metaphysicae."[18] But such a judgment affirms that there are two kinds of things which are separate
secundum esse from motion and matter: the first kind is always
separate from matter, the second kind is sometimes found
without matter.[19] To the first kind belong God and the angels;
to the second, such objects of the metaphysician's interest as
ens, substance, potency, and act. The difficulty is to distinguish
the second kind from the mathematical products of abstraction.
The distinction is made when one can judge that *ens* and the
others are not intrinsically linked to matter, as were the
mathematicals: "non sit de ratione eius quod sit in materia et
motu, sed possit esse sine materia et motu, quamvis quandoque
inveniatur in materia et motu."[20] The second kind of separate
beings, once established, is found to be the "subiectum" of
philosophical metaphysics; for it the first kind of objects, God
and the angels, is treated "sicut de principiis subiecti."[21] Only
the theology of sacred Scripture can treat of God and the angels
"sicut de subiectis."[22]

Separatio requires judgment that there are beings apart from
matter. It requires two types of judgment. There is, first, the
judgment that there are beings which exist wholly apart from
matter. There is, second, the judgment that there are
'categories' of being which refer both to material and immaterial beings. The second requires the first, but is a markedly
different claim; it refers not to another realm of entities, but to
all entities considered in a certain aspect, under a certain formality. The logical character of the second judgment is also different from that of the first. For the first separation, the
philosopher must show that there are purely immaterial beings.
For the second, he must argue that certain 'categories' found in
experience of the physical world are not necessarily physical,

but are also found in non-physical beings. Arguments of the first sort are had in Aristotle's demonstration of a first unmoved mover.[23] It is not clear that Aristotle himself argues for the second separation, though he does apply the metaphysical terminology of act to the Prime Mover.[24] Thomas does argue for the second separation when he shows, for example, that God is pure act or that the act/potency distinction applies to angels.[25]

I said that the second sort of judgment requires the first. I mean that one cannot arrive at a separative judgment with regard to *ens* without affirming the existence of separate substances. Lacking such an affirmation, the discussion of *ens*, substance, act, and the others would fall back into abstraction; it would be no more than a predicative consideration of certain common features belonging to all physical substances. A treatment of *ens* or substance resting only on a predicative consideration would be much more like apprehension than a judgment. It would fall short of the strong emphasis on the fact of separation from matter that Thomas's formulas from the *Super De Trinitate* reiterate.

Father Wippel has recently argued against such a reading on several grounds.[26] The texts in which Thomas speaks of a dependence of metaphysics on physics are, Wippel thinks, not Thomas's own opinion. Moreover, Thomas says something rather different in the proemium to the *Metaphysics*, where he is "surely writing in his own name."[27] The texts which argue the study of physics before metaphysics are only pedagogical and give "no indication that one study metaphysics after natural philosophy because the former depends upon the latter for knowledge of its starting point."[28] Indeed, any real dependence of metaphysics on physics might undercut Thomas's careful rebuttal of circularity within the hierarchy of the sciences.[29] Wippel suggests that *separatio* is grounded, not in demonstrations of the existence of immaterials, but in a distinction between the "distinctive intelligibilities" indicated by the two questions, why it is a being and why it is this given kind of being. Wippel draws out the distinction in this way: "that by reason of which something is recognized as being need not be identified or restricted to that by reason of which it is recognized as being of a given kind."[30]

There are various difficulties in Wippel's reading. Some concern his way of using material from the Aristotle commentaries: it is not so simple as taking Thomas's *proemia* for writings 'in his own name'. But the main difficulties have to do with Wippel's tendency to turn back towards a kind of apprehension, an intuitive judgment of 'intelligibility', as the ground of *separatio*. This tendency is connected with the habit of regarding sciences as bodies of apprehended propositions to which pedagogical concerns are extrinsic. In the same way, Wippel finds that *separatio* is sufficiently justified by the positing of the "negatively" or "neutrally" immaterial objects, such as *ens*, substance, and so on.[31] The use of these two terms suggests, again, something like a pre-judgmental understanding, like the absolute consideration of the *De Ente*. Geiger was closer to the mark, I think, in insisting that the *separatio* could only be grounded on a judgment that there *are* immaterial beings and that things like *ens* and substance *are* sometimes found ("quandoque," Thomas says) outside of physical beings. The two judgments are, I would repeat, intrinsically connected.

Wippel is right, even so, to be skeptical of the attempts to find a discrete demonstration on which *separatio* could be said to rest. It is not as if there were certain set pieces of argument which, once understood, would issue in a separative judgment. *Separatio* is a judgment — not the formal conclusion to a syllogism. As a judgment, it requires evidence. Such evidence is provided in the inquiries of physics and psychology. The evidence elicits an act of judgment very much in the way of a rational pedagogy.[32] The rational pedagogy justifies the judgment but does not reduce it to an 'intuition' or a quasi-apprehensive formal conclusion.

Separatio has often been linked to a 'negative judgment'.[33] Its two sorts of judgment can be construed as negations in at least three ways. The first judgment denies that God and angels are material; it finds that not all beings are physical. Thomas expresses the judgment as a negation in commenting on the *Metaphysics*: "ipsa enim natura, id est res naturalis habens in se principium motus, in se ipsa est unum aliquod genus entis universalis. Non enim omne ens est huiusmodi."[34] Thus Aristotle's arguments for celestial movers are to be taken as providing evidence for a judgment that separate beings exist. This leads one further along the first judgment, to strip away any physical properties from such beings. The denial of physical properties points in turn to the discovery of the characteristics of immaterial substances, their hierarchies, their individuation by species, their relation to time, and so on. In short, the first judgment leads towards that inquiry into immateriality which Thomas records especially in the *De Substantiis Separatis* and in the commentary on the *Liber de Causis*, as well as in his major treatments of God and the angels.

The second sort of separative judgment denies that every instance of *ens* or actuality is physical. In order to establish that these features are sometimes found outside matter, it is enough to show that there is one instance of them which is not material. If there is one immaterial instance, then "de ratione eorum non est esse in materia et motu."[35] Schmidt describes the second sort of judgment as a "séparation descendante" which reaches down to embrace all being in a single, analogous notion.[36] This descent does not apprehend a new realm of entities; it judges that already apprehended entities do in fact share certain intelligible characteristics. The judgment is secured by a series of particular judgments which assert, for example, that there are immaterial substances, that angels do suffer the distinction of act and potency, and so on. The comprehensive judgment that affirms *ens* or substance unites these particular judgments under truly analogical predication. The cause of the predicative analogy is not an apprehended formality, but an affirmed hierarchical unity of being. There is yet another negation. It applies to both sorts of judgments. This is the negation or remotion of the limitation of sensible origin in metaphysical language. The negation is suggested in the *Super De Trinitate* at the first mention of *'separatio'*, when Thomas adds a summary comment on the three levels of speculative objects: "Et ideo secundum ordinem remotionis a materia et motu scientiae speculativae distinguuntur."[37] *'Remotio'* covers both logical and ontological distance from the conditions of matter. It is a word used by Thomas already in the first Book of the *scriptum* on the *Sentences* when discussing predications about God.[38] Still the doctrine about logical remotion — and not merely the word — figures prominently in Question 6 of the Boethius exposition. There

Thomas argues, in Article 2, that metaphysics must abandon imagination entirely and, in Article 4, that no speculative science can yield a vision of the divine form.

The doctrine of logical remotion begins by retelling the hierarchy of sciences. In Article 2, Thomas distinguishes the starting-point of knowledge from its various ends. The starting point of all human knowledge is in the senses.[39] The lowest end lies in a judgment which confirms what the senses show about things; this end is physics.[40] The middle end is a judgment on those objects which are abstracted from sensible matter but still represented in imagination; these are the mathematical objects.[41] The highest end reaches beyond sense and imagination, along the "viam causalitatis," to those incommensurate first causes which are reached only "vel per excessum vel per remotionem."[42] This highest end is that sought by metaphysics. The mode of understanding in it is that described in Ps-Dionysius's *Divine Names*; it is a kind of apophasis, of negation. To the objection that the negation of images would seem to undercut the bases of human cognition, Thomas replies that men never escape the imagination and yet cannot judge according to it.[43] Alternately, we cannot deny bodily properties of God and the angels without having some image-based understanding of bodies.

The answer needs more elaboration. Thomas provides it in the next two Articles, which assert that the mind can see God but not through the speculative sciences of the present life. I will turn directly to the second, the negative, part of the assertion, which is presented in Article 4. There Thomas rehearses the retracing of all scientific knowledge, whether definitional or demonstrative, back to a first knowledge of "principia demonstrationum indemonstrabilia" and of "primae conceptiones intellectus."[44] The first knowledge of such *principia* and *conceptiones* is known to men by the agent intellect's illumination of phantasms drawn from sense. But sense must be left behind in apprehending the immaterial. It follows that neither the *principia* nor the *conceptiones* can support quidditative demonstration or definition of the immaterial substances. Thus, "per nullam scientiam speculativam potest sciri de aliqua substantia separata quid est, quamvis per scientias speculativas possimus scire ipsas et aliquas earum condiciones."[45] Separative judgment affirms the existence of the immaterial beings and their properties as *im*material. But it cannot affirm or even presume the apprehension of the essence of any separate substance. The quiddity of the first causes remains "semper ignota."[46] The science of metaphysics is, then, an incomplete grasp of immaterial beings through their effects; it is a "habitus sapientiae" which is not yet that complete human happiness available through grace in the beatific vision.[47] Metaphysics embodies the natural striving for a contemplative end which is only attained through grace beyond the conditions of this life: "Quamvis enim homo naturaliter inclinetur in finem ultimum, non tamen potest naturaliter illum consequi, sed solum per gratiam, et hoc est propter eminentiam illius finis."[48]

The third aspect of negation in *separatio* is, then, the most important. Metaphysics must strive to negate the limits which sense and imagination place on its inquiry. It is, however, incapable of freeing itself from its origin in sense experience. That experience is in principle incapable of providing a quidditative knowledge of the first causes. If metaphysics can attain some grasp of the properties which God and the angels share with physical creatures, it cannot apprehend what God and the angels essentially are. Separative judgment affirms that immaterial beings exist and are truly substances in act. The affirmation contains several negative judgments: that *not* all substances are material, that immaterial substances do *not* have the features of bodies. The affirmation is conditioned by negation in yet a more important way: it is in principle not able to proceed to a positive statement about the substances on which its truth rests. Separative judgment knows *an sit* but never *quid sit*. Its denial of the claim that all being is material is attended by a denial of its own capability to proceed to final knowledge of the immaterial. There are, then, two quite different senses in which *separatio* is a 'negative' judgment.

The two negations remain, in the Boethian exposition, the boundaries of a question which is not fully answered. Remotion is, if not delimited, too radical a critique of language. The negative movement of *separatio* must be balanced against some positive intentionality linking metaphysical discourse to its final objects, the separate substances. Such intentionality is discovered in treating of the divine names.

5.3 THE DIVINE NAMES

De Divinis Nominibus is the Latin name for that *topos* which originates in neo-Platonism and passes to the medieval west through Ps-Dionysius and the Lombard's *Sentences*.[1] The topic is taken up several times by Aquinas, for whom it is always associated with the more general consideration about the knowledge of God.[2] It is doubly associated, then, with the questions already broached in metaphysics. In first place, God is the ground of beings and the highest separate substance. So the problem of the divine names is the foremost instance of the problem of metaphysical language. In second place, the most appropriate of the divine names is seen to be one of greatest metaphysical significance: *Ipse qui est*, He who is. In these two ways, the problem of the divine names is the limit of the problem of metaphysical discourse. But it is also the beginning of theology. The names are theological not because they are a discourse about God; such discourse Thomas conceives as also metaphysical. They become theological because they make the methodologically decisive turn to the use of evidence from the traditions of revelation.

The involvement of both metaphysical and theological matter can be seen in the various ways of phrasing the issue. When Aquinas discusses the names in *De Potentia*, he does so parenthetically within the discussion of divine simplicity.[3] That discussion is not theological in any strict sense. Thomas cites only three *auctoritates* in the body of the Article which begins the discussion: Aristotle, twice, and Hilary from the *De Trinitate*, once. But one of the citations of Aristotle and the reference to Hilary are offered more as illustrations than as premises. The remaining citation of Aristotle is used in support of the claim that quasi-material potency is necessary for composition.[4] Indeed, the text of the first Article shows plainly that Thomas derives the doctrine of simplicity not from theology, but from the chief conclusions of his ontology. The simplicity of God is required by the place of God as the highest member — and thus the source — of the most comprehensive hierarchy. This position is seen in three ways: as an eminence of actuality, as an absolute priority in action, and as a perfection with regard to all qualities. The doctrine of the divine simplicity follows from these as a tenet from the inquiry of metaphysics and not from the revelation of Scripture. It is then not the case that the problem of the divine names arises from anthropomorphic locutions in Scripture which must be excused.

Yet the resolution of the question about naming such simplicity does engage the theological tradition. If the divine names are not said accidentally, are they then said of God substantially? By way of an answer, in the fifth Article of *De Potentia* Aquinas returns to the starting-point of the question.[5] He sketches two responses, the first more radical than the second, to the question whether the names name at all. These two seem to Aquinas the only responses worth long consideration. The first is that of Maimonides, the second that of Ps-Dionysius. On Aquinas's reading, Maimonides holds that no divine name signifies the divine substance. Either such names signify by likeness to effects, or they signify in the way of negation. To take a signification of the first sort: God is called 'wise', says Maimonides, because his effects seem to men to show wise action. To take a signification of the second sort: God is called 'living' in order to stress that He is not inanimate. The two explanations are not mutually exclusive; both names seem susceptible of both sorts of explanation.

Aquinas rejects Maimonides's radical proposal that the divine names do not name anything about God. He argues against Maimonides's first model — that of analogy to the effects — by saying that this would put names such as 'wrathful' and 'fiery' on the same footing with names such as 'wisdom', since God's effects certainly seem at times like wrath and like fire. Moreover, Aquinas argues, Maimonides's first form of signification would make meaningful predication about God dependent on the existence of His effects, thus denying the intelligible articulation of divine features in the absence of the cosmos.[6]

Aquinas rejects Maimonides's second model for signification on the grounds that every name involves some negation by being distinct from other names. Thus God can be called 'lion' in order to stress that He is not a bird, but also 'bird', since He is not a lion. More fundamentally, Aquinas holds that every act of negation depends upon the prior grasp of an affirmation. Maimonides would deny such a prior grasp in favor of pure negativity and would thus rob the language of meaning.[7] The rejection of the Maimonidean model, then, takes the form of an argument from the practice of speaking about God. More, Thomas seems to hold that not all things said of God are equally well said. This tenet does not seem particularly scriptural. The examples which Aquinas uses to illustrate *illegitimate* ways of speaking are more nearly theological and scriptural than the examples he uses for the legitimate predications. Indeed, Aquinas seems to contrast these with a philosophic practice within which 'good', 'wise', 'just' and other such terms become the privileged predications.

Having set aside the radical alternative of Maimonides, Aquinas turns to the more moderate proposal, as he construes it, of Ps-Dionysius. On this proposal, the divine names do signify the divine substance; they do name, but imperfectly. Aquinas explains the manner of predication by comparing it to the relations of likeness which obtain between cause and effect. Thomas distinguishes, as he customarily does, between adequate and inadequate effects.[8] Since no effect is adequate to God's creative causality, creatures represent a splintering of the attributes which are united in God. This likeness allows an imperfect speech about the divine substance to be constructed on the basis of human understanding. The refracted signification of the divine names is stated more technically in the reply to an objection.[9] The divine names are to be said of God with regard to what they signify, but not with regard to *how* they signify. Their mode of signification is to say anything as if it were a finite attribute. Yet the things which are named by such constricted names are imperfect likenesses of 'things' which are in God non-attributively. So it is that one gets the three-step dialectic of Ps-Dionysius. One first affirms the names of God with the understanding that there is something *like* goodness or justice in God. But secondly, one has then to negate the names, since what is in God is not like what human language means by such terms. In the third step, one negates the mode of signification implicit in the names while affirming what they intend to signify. One begins, that is, to predicate the names of God "supereminently".[10]

The discussion which began with a comparison of two positions within theology, of two scriptural exegeses, has come back to the basic doctrines of grammar, of analogy. It is as if one had crossed and recrossed the line between metaphysics and theology in pursuit of the logical character of language about God. The same movement can be seen, more quickly, in the thirteenth Question of the *prima pars*. Aquinas begins here with a simple recital of the doctrine of the *Peri Hermeneias*.[11] Once he has reminded the reader that "voces referuntur ad res significandas mediante conceptione intellectus," he states that "Deus in hac vita non potest a nobis videri per suam essentiam." It follows that human names for God must be derived, rather, from human experience of His effects. Moreover, the mode of signification of all human names for God is radically deficient. We know subsisting creatures as composite and fashion names accordingly: "omnia nomina a nobis imposita ad significandum aliquid completum subsistens, significant in concretione, prout competit compositis."[12] Whenever we talk about simple substances, we do so as if they were elements by which composite substances were enabled to exist. In regard to God, the incongruity is even more striking. Nouns, verbs, participles — every grammatical form implies in its mode of signification something which is not true of the divine ontology. Moreover, we cannot even say exactly how such names fall short, except that nouns ought to speak of God not compositely, verbs and participles not temporally, and so on.[13]

There is nothing in this Article which might be considered strictly theological. The authorities quoted for and against are from the theological tradition, but the argument does not hinge on them. Nor are such theological materials deployed in the second Article, which argues that even if negative and relational terms are not said substantially of God, perfective terms are.[14] They are said substantially, but imperfectly, since they are always limited by our mode of understanding and signifying. This doctrine is extended in the third through sixth Articles to cover eminent names and the analogy of names generally.

There then follow some five Articles which do indeed use theological material and which seem to constitute part of theological discourse. For example, the seventh Article asks whether relational names said of God with respect to His

creatures acquire temporal determination. The handling of the
question, which depends on a correct parsing of the types of
relation, is philosophical. But the question itself is not. The examples which power it are the names *'Dominus'* and
'Creator'. That either should be considered as having a temporal import suggests that they are being understood from the
theological perspective of divine action within history.

   A theological origin is equally clear in the eleventh Article,
"utrum hoc nomen, Qui est, sit maxime nomen Dei proprium."[15] The question would not arise except on the basis of
the Vulgate version of Exodus. It might be argued that the problem could arise metaphysically from knowing that God is the
entity in whom there is no difference between essence and *esse*.
That is true but beside the point. To ask whether the name *'Qui
est'* is the most proper name of God is not only to take a Scriptural passage, but to assume that one is dealing with a *name*. So
it is that Thomas defends the name by theological arguments of
the *status viae* and the particular character of divine eternity.

   Yet the twelfth Article, which deals with forming affirmative
propositions, seems to return to the philosophical grounds of
grammar. Aquinas finds that ordinary predications, whether accidental or substantial, require a notional distinction between a
subject and predicate which are really united. So he takes the
formula, 'notional diversity with real unity', and moves it from
ordinary predications to positive propositions formed about
God. It counters objections that affirmative propositions about
God imply diversity where there is none. It might as well be objected against ordinary predications. Thus, the final difficulty
about the names is resolved precisely by linking it to conditions
in ordinary speech.

   I have stressed the mixture of metaphysics and theology, as
well as the link betwen scriptural and speculative discourse,
because it is in the movement across these various lines that
Thomas enacts the intentionality of metaphysical language. The
danger in an unqualified doctrine of remotion is that the
negative will destroy any positive content and so rob the
language of sense. This is the danger Thomas underlines in
Maimonides. The Dionysian alternative to Maimonides is a
remotion which is tethered to a certain positive intentionality.
Dionysian predication by supereminence is an attempt to pro-

ject an intention through a negative moment, through remotion. The intention aims at what would be meant by the true
predicates if their mode of signification could be corrected. But
it cannot be corrected under the conditions of the present life.
The project of correction remains, then, only a wish, but a wish
now embodied in the negated, the prolonged intentionality of
language about God. The intentionality is not satisfied by the
shift into theology. It is, rather, enriched and made explicit.
Theological language is a franker expression of longing for
union with God because it is, through grace, a more efficacious
longing.

It is not necessary to go to theology, however, in order to see
the meaning of metaphysical language as an intention, a project,
rather than a simple achievement. It is not even necessary to
turn to the divine names, where, as I have already argued, the
intentionality is seen in the reliance on the three stages of
Dionysian predication. The ground of Thomas's doctrine of
analogy is the notion that a term can be truly predicated of
many different things according to an order of priority and
posteriority, that is, according to a hierarchy. The hierarchy requires an ordering of the predications to a central case or a central being. The ordering is compounded when the language for
expressing the analogy is itself constructed among the lower
reaches of the hierarchy — as is the case with human speech applied to God. Then the ordering of the lower analogates to the
higher is crossed by the linguistic ordering of all instances to the
lower, the sensible end. The crossed orderings set up again that
dialectic between sensible origin and metaphysical end. The
dialectic controls the use of every term in metaphysics. It cannot be resolved, but it can be made fruitful precisely as an intention towards the end, towards the metaphysical. The hierarchy
of intelligible cases implicit in any metaphysial analogy suggests
the intentional possibility which Ps-Dionysius states
theologically. It is the possibility of considering the hierarchy
dynamically as a pedagogy. The same possibility is explicitly
present in the hierarchy of sciences.

5.4 METAPHYSICS IN THE HIERARCHY OF DISCOURSE

Two hierarchies now stand forth — the one a hierarchy of discourses or sciences, the other a hierarchy of intelligible entities. The two hierarchies are correlated in various fashions. Movement from physics to metaphysics is movement up the hierarchy of discourses and also up the hierarchy of entities. But it must be added immediately that the perspective from which such a correlation is made is essentially misleading. The hierarchy of entities is described fully only in the discourse of metaphysics, subject as it is to severe qualifications. From no perspective within the scope of human knowledge is it possible to make a direct comparison of the two orders. The closer one comes to a description of the ontological hierarchy, the more refracted is the reference of one's discourse. So the ideal of a parallel ascent is only an ideal; the reality would be more nearly described by diverging paths of ascent — the ascent of the sciences pulling away from the ascent of beings into greater refraction and negation.

This divergence is itself known within the order of discourse. It brings to mind the fact that there is a hierarchical dependence within the hierarchy of discourses which is separate from the ontological dependence of the order of beings. The lower discourses depend for their *principia* on the higher; physics and psychology have been said to depend for the final analysis of their accounts on metaphysics. They must also then be bound in some way by the epistemological and discursive strictures placed on that discourse. The logical dependence of the lower on the higher sciences, then, is particularly concerned with the divergencies of discourse from being, since the whole of the hierarchy of discourses hangs by the top.

The question of dependencies within the discourses has appeared several times. It needs now to be addressed directly. One of the difficulties about the question is that it is so fundamental — it cuts so deeply into any philosophic account of intelligibility. Thus, the Platonic image of the 'divided line' is not only a prelude to the curriculum for the attainment of wisdom, it is also the epitome of the Platonic account of mind in its struggle with being.[1] Aristotle's triplet of speculative sciences replies to Plato on both these counts.[2] The defenses and modifications of Aristotle's threefold division by medieval Latin authors are very much essays in the philosophical account of intelligibility. The discussion of the differences between the mode of procedure in the three sciences, for example, must require something like an account of abstraction and separation, however these are described.[3] Again, a discussion of the various names for metaphysics often raises the questions about its relation to lower sciences.[4]

The most pointed text in Thomas on this latter question is again from the exposition of Boethius's *De Trinitate*. In a text there which has already been mentioned (q.5, a.1 ad 9), Thomas argues that metaphysics is the first of all sciences, though it is the last to be learned by us. The other sciences depend on metaphysics, but we learn metaphysics on the basis of the other sciences. Is there then a vicious circle in scientific demonstration? There is not, Thomas argues, "quia principia, quae accipit alia scientia, scilicet naturalis, a prima philosophia, non probant ea quae idem philosophus primus accipit a naturali, sed probantur per alia principia per se nota; et similiter philosophus primus non probat principia, quae tradit naturali, per principia quae ab eo accipit, sed per alia principia per se nota."[5] Moreover, Thomas adds, since the sensible effects used in physical demonstration are better known to us at first than the remote causes disclosed in metaphysics, we ascend by demonstration *quia* to the causes. Having understood the first causes in metaphysics, we then demonstrate *propter quid* about their effects. There is no vicious circle because the principles of ascent and descent are quite distinct pedagogically.

This passage is difficult to construe. Most readings view it as containing two different arguments, the first about a plurality of principles and the second about the shift from *quia* to *propter quid* demonstration. But the 'first' argument has been read in quite different ways.[6] It is clear that the metaphysician secures principles for the physicist and that these principles are not used by the physicist to prove conclusions which the physicist gives up to metaphysics; there is thus no circle. But where are the conclusions passed up by the physicist in fact proved? One reading has it that they are proved in metaphysics on the basis of other self-evident principles. Another reading has it that they are proved on the basis of such principles in physics. The first reading would not seem to be consonant with any discussion of the *pedagogy* of sciences. If every principle received from a lower science mut be 'proved' again in metaphysics on the basis of self-evident principles, then the other sciences are otiose. Yet the second reading does not seem to be consonant with any *hierarchy* of sciences. If physics can prove propositions *tout court* using its own principles, then it is indeed an autonomous science and does not have any real dependence on metaphysics. Indeed, its relation to metaphysics would be entirely extrinsic.

If neither reading seems plausible, it is because neither takes into account the remainder of Thomas's remarks, which are an important part of his response to the objector. Sensible effects are used in physics as the bases for *quia* demonstrations about the first causes. They are, indeed, *principia* for physics — not in the Cartesian sense of propositional principles, but in the Aristotelian sense of starting-points for showing something to be true. The *quia* demonstrations may lead to a judgment that first causes exist and are immaterial. On the basis of such a judgment, one can provide *propter quid* demonstrations about the sensible effects of those causes, which effects are now understood not as starting-points but as consequences, results, indeed effects. Metaphysics is said to borrow certain *principia* from physics. These *principia* are not vitiated by circularity when used by metaphysics because they lead to a reversal of view which transforms them from *principia* to *consequentia* by virtue of the disclosure of a higher intelligibility, a higher 'cause' or 'form'. The *principia* given by physics to metaphysics are not rules to be applied, but cases to be illuminated. They are more like phantasms or facts than like 'laws of nature'. Metaphysics does not prove them again; it clarifies them, finds grounds for them, leads them back to an intelligible firstness.

Why not dispense with physics altogether, then, once metaphysics has been found? This is the suggestion of the first reading, which wants to see all principles proved in metaphysics. The reading assumes that metaphysics can be finished. I have argued that Thomas thinks otherwise. It is not possible to proceed into metaphysics and to cast physics aside as if it were a now unneeded ladder. The need for physics remains precisely because one can never make the final step from *quia* to *propter quid* without it; one knows of the immaterial substances only through their sensible effects. Why not then concede that physics secures its own principles by its own intuitons? This is the suggestion of the second reading. The reading assumes that it is possible for physics to have complete principles without reference to metaphysics. This suggestion not only misconceives what is meant by *'principia'*, it also denies the claim that metaphysics is about the first causes and principles. The claim is made by Thomas in the body of this Article and in many other texts.[7] There remains the suggestion of a third reading which refuses the dichotomy. It holds that the *principia* from lower sciences are necessary for further progress in metaphysics, even while metaphysics aims to know the first substances and acts upon which those *principia* are ultimately grounded.

Confirmation for the third reading can be found in an unlikely place. Decker notes[8] and Wippel shows[9] that the reply to the ninth objection is closely related to a longer passage in Avicenna's *Metaphysica* I, 3. The passage on circularity from Avicenna is bracketed by others in which he makes clear the pedagogical reason of the hierarchy of sciences and the frailty of human intelligence when confronted with the task of metaphysics. On the first point, the Latin Avicenna writes: "omnes scientiae communicant in una utilitate, scilicet quae est acquisitio perfectionis humanae animae in effectu praeparantis eam ad futuram felicitatem."[10] He adds that the usefulness of metaphysics is like the "utilitas regentis ad id quod regitur, et sicut eius cui servitur ad servientem."[11] This is a description of the place of the ideal metaphysics in the hierarchy of sciences. It seeks to find a knowledge which secures all demonstrations "ex via propositionum universalium intelligibilium per se notarum."[12] But the condition of the embodied human intellect imposes a pedagogical order which makes it necessarily last in our consideration: "Sed nos propter infirmitatem nostrarum animarum non possumus incedere per ipsam viam demonstrativam, quae est progressus ex principiis ad sequentia et ex causa ad causatum, nisi in aliquibus ordinibus universitatis eorum quae sunt, sine discretione."[13] These pedagogical emphases need not be an important part of Avicenna's final views on human understanding. They are, nonetheless, a prominent feature of the text which Thomas has in mind when composing his reply to the objection against the hierarchy of sciences. They help confirm the pedagogical view of the hierarchy of sciences.

The pedagogy has been traced through the various sciences not so much by tracking particular *principia* as by describing the different modes of discourse. Thomas himself does the same. He does not give an example of the borrowing of a particular *principium*; he does give much attention to the conditions for inquiry at each level. Concern for its own semantic status has been seen in each of the speculative sciences. In physics, the inquiry into causes was very much an inquiry into the middle terms of demonstrations, qualified then by the maxim that the order of discovery for middle terms is not the order of being. In psychology, the inquiry into soul was an inquiry into the frailties of the human being's knowledge of itself. In metaphysics, the inquiry into *ens*, with its connection to the separate substances, is an inquiry into what grounds intelligible being from beyond the limits of human discourse. One might say that the self-criticism of physics discovers the links of demonstration, that the self-criticism of psychology discovers the imperfection of its knowledge of itself, and the self-consciousness of metaphysics, the inherence of negation. The ascent along the hierarchy of speculative discourses is, then, a movement from the construction of discourse, through its enabling powers, to its supradiscursive ground — the movement from literalism through mediated self-reference to negation.

Still, this sort of reading cannot be taken as much more than a poetic construct until it can be secured by reference to the hierarchy of being. However much the study of speculative discourse has shown the refractions of being in language, it is most importantly true that language is for Thomas a public means for expressing truth. The semantic modes of the various sciences have been so many ways of safeguarding the approach to truth despite the complexity of human discourse and the weakness of human intelligence. The denial of literalism, of finished causal explanation, in physics aims to prevent a closure of explanation at the level of the merely material. The rejection of privileged self-knowledge in psychology wants to forestall any claim for intellectual intuition as an autonomous ground for intelligibility. Finally, the insistence on *separatio* and analogy in metaphysics serves to enact an intentionality which projects speculation beyond the conditions of the present life. Each of these semantic descriptions makes sense only to the extent that there is a hierarchy of intelligible being which stands outside the hierarchy of discourses. The first hierarchy grounds the second; it does not mirror it. It is the principle of real hierarchy itself which must be secured in the first so that the second becomes more than a nominal possibility. The hierarchy is really seen only in the zealous study of *esse*. No summary of such a difficult and self-correcting enterprise is possible. It may be possible, however, to draw some help from what Thomas says about real hierarchy itself.

Thomas's explicit considerations of hierarchy appear in those contexts in which *'hierarchia'* reached him from Ps-Dionysius — the celestial hierarchy of angels and the ecclesiastical hierarchy of sacramental sanctification. But even in these technical contexts, Thomas makes clear his sense of hierarchy generally as a participatory order of a certain sort. Consider the Article on the angelic hierarchies in the great *Summa*. Aquinas begins with an etymological parsing of *'hierarchia'*: "Respondeo dicendum quod hierarchia est sacer principatus.... In nomine autem principatus duo intelliguntur, scilicet ipse princeps, et multitudo ordinata sub principe."[14] Strictly speaking, every creature is under the rule of God and so all creatures would fall into a single hierarchy. But just as there are delegations of power in the civil order, so there are divisions of the cosmic order according to the different degrees of participation. The notion of hierarchy is further specified by Aquinas when he treats the traditional division of angelic hierarchies into angelic orders: "[U]na hierarchia est unus principatus, id est, una multitudo ordinata uno modo sub principis gubernatione. Non autem esset multitudo ordinata, sed confusa, si in multitudine diversi ordines non essent. Ipsa ergo ratio hierarchiae requirit ordinum diversitatem. Quae quidem diversitas ordinum secundum diversa officia et actus consideratur."[15] He replies to the first objection: "[O]rdo dupliciter dicitur. Uno modo ipsa ordinatio comprehendens sub se diversos grados; et hoc modo hierarchia dicitur ordo. Alio modo dicitur ordo gradus unus; et sic dicuntur plures ordines unius hierarchiae."[16] Substantially the same doctrine is found in the discussion of the angelic hierarchies in the *Sentences* or the *Contra Gentiles*.[17] One would also find it repeated with regard to the graded reception of grace which is the celestial hierarchy.[18]

I have taken these theological examples not to consider them on their merits, but as illustrations of how Thomas develops notions of hierarchical order. His definition of hierarchy contains a principle of likeness and a principle of difference.[19] The principle of likeness is the participation by which those ruled share in community with the ruler — whether the community is one of being or illumination or commonweal. The principle of difference is the distinction between ruler and ruled. One sees both clearly at work in the hierarchy of *esse*. The principle of likeness is the participation in the *actus essendi* by which creatures share diversely in those perfections contained eminently in God. The principle of difference is the absolute distinction between creature and creator.

Is it now possible to describe more lucidly the hierarchization of the field of speculative discourses? A simple answer would be this: The principle of sameness is the logical dependence of lower speculative sciences on metaphysics; the principle of difference is the unique character of metaphysics as *separatio*, the severe discursive restrictions placed on it. But there is a more searching answer which reflects the ways in which the hierarchy of the speculative sciences can be seen as representative of the hierarchy of discourse as a whole. In fact, the principle of sameness here is the mode of human experience; the principle of difference is the divergence between that mode and the order of being. This is to say that the principle of sameness in the hierarchy of discourses is a generalized *id a quo imponitur nomen*; it is the human stance as speakers in the world. The principle of difference is the *id ad quem* taken to its furthest point — the otherness of the world about which one speaks. As is appropriate in a hierarchy, the principle of sameness predominates at the bottom of the hierarchy of discourses, while the principle of difference predominates at the top. Physics is colored by the embodied framework of human understanding, metaphysics by the insufficiently of that framework when faced with the ground of the real.

One can see in this second answer a stronger reason than the one given above for the necessary concern in each of the speculative discourses about its semantic status. As members of the discursive hierarchy, these discourses are ruled by the principles of sameness and of difference. Each discourse is set spread out between the pole of that human experience from which it originates and that intelligible ground with regard to which it falls short. Construed in these ways, the speculative discourses can also be seen as an inverted image of the *trivium* at a more concretely intelligible and substantive level. In its concern for the disclosure of causes as middle terms, physics is a higher logic. In its search for the means of self-reference, psychology is a higher rhetoric. Finally, as a discourse about what lies beyond the sayable, metaphysics is the final grammar — the meditation on how things can be named.

Structural conceits such as this comparison can be helpful in reminding one of the persistence of questions about language throughout philosophy. These questions and the structure of the hierarchy itself are not understood until one looks beyond metaphysics to theology. The discussions of the definitions of metaphysics and of the divine names have shown already how difficult it is to describe a sharp textual division between the two senses of the name *'theologia'*.

One had all sorts of mixed cases — theologically motivated questions with theologically ordered answers, or with philosophically ordered answers, or with answers which were neither one nor the other. If there is a methodological difference between metaphysics and theology, there is no material segregation of them in the texts. The discourse of metaphysics is not closed at some point below theology in the hierarchy of sciences. The reader passes imperceptibly from one discourse to another. Indeed, it is not as if one were passing outside of metaphysics, even though one knows that metaphysics itself cannot prove the necessity of a higher realm. It is rather that one finds the unexpectable completion of metaphysics in revelation.

In the remarks on Boethius's *De Trinitate*, Aquinas makes the relation of completion quite clear. He writes: "duplex est felicitas hominis. Una imperfecta quae est in via, de qua loquitur Philosophus et haec consistit in contemplatione substantiarum separatarum per habitum sapientiae, imperfecta tamen, et tali, qualis est in via possibilis, non ut sciatur ipsarum quidditas. Alia est perfecta in patria, in qua ipse Deus per essentiam videbitur, et aliae substantiae separatae. Sed haec felicitas non erit per aliquam scientiam speculativam, sed per lumen gloriae.''[20] Revealed theology promises a vision of the principles which the metaphysician seeks, even desires.

One consequence is that philosophical metaphysics must tend by its very nature to want what is given to theology in revelation. The objects of the metaphysician's direct study are grounded in *principia* which he cannot know as metaphysician. As the highest natural wisdom, metaphysics will want to grasp those *principia*. Thus the second consequence is that once revelation is believed and a theology becomes possible, the natural desire in metaphysics for a direct knowledge of separated substances will pass over into theology. Theology will in fact serve to complete metaphysics, because in so doing it will satisfy the thwarted inquiry of the metaphysician. That will make it very difficult to distinguish *textually* between the highest reaches of metaphysics and the claims of theology. Of course, spiritually there is every difference between a philosophy pursued according to nature and the divine gift of grace.[21]

There are exegetical cautions to be derived from this realization. What is more important is that the fluidity of the actual passage from metaphysics to theology, *pace* the methodological differentiation, suggests that the discourse of metaphysics is not closed, is not decisively bounded. Its boundary is marked by the failure of human inquiry to grasp what it mutely desires — a contemplation of the separate substances, chiefly of God. The discourse of metaphysics is not closed because the end of metaphysics is not reached by philosophy. The hierarchy of the speculative sciences is preparatory to some further contemplation, which is promised in faith and achieved in beatitude. These discourses are then in principle neither comprehensive nor complete, though they must be in some way adequate. To ask about this adequacy is to bring into view the questions about the character and purpose of philosophical authorship in Aquinas.

PART THREE

PHILOSOPHICAL AUTHORSHIP

CHAPTER 6

Aquinas's Authorship

Aquinas's philosophical discourses have been examined in their elements and in some exemplary instances. The elements were both a general doctrine, in logic, about the end of language and a set of concrete patterns, in the whole *trivium*, for the construction of speech. The exemplary discourses were taken from physics, psychology, and metaphysics. Behind the use of elements and the construction of discourses has stood Thomas Aquinas, the author of texts. In the history of philosophy, questions about authorship are asked in several different ways. The first way is to ask for the author's 'identity'; one ties the text to a name which is already or may soon become tied to other texts and to other historical mentions. This identification of authorship is essential, of course, but it is only preliminary. Once a name has been given to a number of texts, the questions about authorship become more decisive philosophically. What, after all, is the relation of the author to the various parts of the corpus of identified writings? And how did the author conceive of his own philosophical authorship?

The first of these deeper questions is most often raised when there seems to be some dislocation between the identification of the author and the form of the texts. The famous example would be Kierkegaard, whose tract on the *Point of View for my Work as an Author* enacts the question and establishes the term 'authorship' with its ampler sense. But the question is by no means appropriate only where there are such carefully constructed intermediaries as the Kierkegaardian pseudonyms. Plato's authorship is equally enigmatic; he does not himself ever make an argument in the dialogues. Among the medievals, Maimonides's *Guide* and Averroes's *Decisive Treatise* or *Commentary on the Republic* contain similar difficulties. Maimonides begins by talking about how he must conceal the truth that properly ought to be passed down with the protection of an oral tradition.[1] Averroes conceals a metaphysical doctrine of intellectual perfection at the center of a *Commentary*

183

filled with the praises of the revealed Law.[2]

But mediation between the author's voice and the texts of his corpus do not appear only in so-called 'esoteric' writings. A shift from one compositional genre to another also requires such mediations. What is said in a textbook is often not so near the author's intention as what is said in a fully technical treatment for his peers. Thus, for instance, the *Summa theologiae* may be, *ceteris paribus*, less central in Aquinas's authorship than the disputed questions. Alternately, one may find passionate expressions in a popular writing which would be qualified or suppressed in more technical genres. Thus, Thomas seems to teach the immaculate conception in his Lenten homilies for 1273, while he denies that doctrine in the nearly contemporary *tertia pars* of the *Summa*.[3] Again, the countless shifts in Thomas's technical vocabulary from work to work are in part due to the passage from one genre to another, though they are also the signs of his further education. A good *expositio* of Boethius or the *Liber de causis* would speak differently than commentaries on Aristotle. Clearly, then, a simple chronology of works in Thomas's corpus will not answer the question of which works are nearer his authoritative voice. The chronology must be qualified by an examination of generic differences, at the least. A later work in a more constrained or more rudimentary genre is not *eo ipso* more important than an earlier work in an ampler genre. Allied to the question of genre would be questions of ideal audience, intended effect, and relation to other works in the overall pedagogy. Only after having addressed such questions could one complete the collating of passages from different works. Every lesser reading remains provisional and every practicable reading is a lesser reading.

Still, the deepest form of the question about authorship is this: what does the author imagine that his writing can accomplish even in the ideal case? This question is put in the second half of the *Phaedrus*, with Socrates's myth about the origin of writing and his reluctance to entrust dialectic to a frozen text.[4] It recurs, with the added weight of religious hesitation, in Maimonides's worry about preserving the true teaching of the *Torah* in written words, which are not only indiscriminately public, but falsely the same for all.[5] Similar hesitations can be found in Clement of Alexandria's *Stromata* and in various later writers. The ritual protestations of humility which preface many medieval treatises are indeed *topoi*. They are also reminders of the ancient difficulty of writing about what is most important. Another reminder is contained even in the alternate definition of philosophy offered by Isidore and echoed in the Latin tradition: "Philosophia est divinarum humanarumque rerum, in quantum homini possibile est, probabilis scientia."[6] The deepest question about authorship appears in Aquinas with every remark about the limitation of human intellect and the boundaries placed upon philosophy. To ask what does Thomas think can be accomplished in a philosophical authorship, is to ask, what is the sum of his limitations upon philosophy?

6.1 PHILOSOPHY AND ITS TRADITIONS

The *questio disputata*, I argued earlier, is a rhetorical device for persuading its participants to resolve some difficulty in the tradition. The *quaestio* depends on the grammatical analysis of texts in context. It requires a belief that the traditional texts can be read reflectively so as to illuminate very modern perplexities. I tried to argue, in the case of physics, that this exegetical engagement with the tradition extends into the nature of the speculative discourse itself. Physics is exegetical not primarily because it was recovered through ancient texts. It is exegetical because the reading of texts is, in a most obvious way, what the mind does as it seeks to understand the world. This is not so much a reflection on the lack of experiment in Aquinas; it is, rather, the suggestion that there is an analogy between the activity of reading in the philosophical traditions and the activity of philosophy in understanding the world. The relation of philosophical physics to the texts by which it is handed down is not adventitious. The argument needs now to be made for philosophical discourse as a whole.

In the *Sic et Non*, Abelard had shown that contradictions in the ancient texts could be resolved by interpretation in context and by careful attention to the relative authority of the writers.[1] He had established a hierarchy of authoritative texts. In Thomas, a similar hierarchy is established for the traditions of

philosophy. This hierarchy is the ground for understanding
Thomas's doctrinal choices, such as his Aristotelianism. It is also
an image of the hierarchy of speculative discourses. The ordering of philosophical traditions is both the way in which Thomas
takes up a position within the history of philosophy and the
means by which he sets out the stages of philosophical ascent
for the present.

Thomas treats the history of philosophy as a coherent progress towards a greater understanding of the ways in which
human minds can come to know the first things.[2] In this, he
follows Aristotle. Aristotle's historical reviews are arguments
for the Aristotelian position — either by exhaustion of alternate
theories or by tracing a line which ends with the Aristotelian
texts.[3] Thomas accepts Aristotle's historical accounts, by and
large; he had little choice.[4] More importantly, he accepts the
principle that the history of philosophy ought to be a doxography with a lesson. The opinions of the *antiqui* are not just
accidentally generated positions; they are steps along a path
which leads to greater philosophic adequacy. Thomas writes, in
his commentary on the *Metaphysics*, that Aristotle was justified
in saying that one ought to give thanks to one's predecessors.
Whether they have helped directly by advancing truth, or indirectly by illustrating errors, the older philosophers have placed one in their debt, having served both for "exercitium circa
inquisitionem veritatis" and "causa instructionis."[5] For this
reason, as well, the chronological history of philosophy seems
unimportant in comparison with the history of truth in Aristotle
and his expositors.

Any hierarchy of philosophical traditions would be, then,
somehow aligned with the hierarchy of speculative discourses.
The most laudable philosophical opinion would be one from
the peak of the historical progress. It would be the opinion
nearest the true account of the various speculative discourses.
Indeed, one often gets the impression that Thomas is defending
Aristotle not as Aristotle, but as the fullest moment of human
reason. To show that Aristotle were foolishly wrong would be
to show that human reason were radically imperfect. Thus, the
title *'Philosophus'* is not only a personal honorific; it is
something of an allegorical role. Aristotle is "the Philosopher"
as representing the philosophical achievement of the mind

without revelation.[6]

Aristotle, however, cannot be made simply into the most authoritative philosophic voice.[7] It might well be the case that the historical progress of philosophy did not achieve maturity in all of the discourses at the same time. Thus, Aristotle might be the authoritative voice for physics, but not for metaphysics. Or, as seems the case, he might be the authority for the sublunary world, but not for the world of separated substances. The Aristotelian doctrine of material substance is the key to understanding the physical world; it is a hindrance when it comes to the more than physical. Aristotle is right and Plato wrong about the operations of embodied intellects; Aristotle is at least incomplete in treating the separated substances. Thomas seems to say as much in his late treatise, *De Substantiis Separatis*. Following a summary of the Platonic and Peripatetic positions, Aquinas remarks that the position taken by Aristotle "seems" to be surer than that of Plato since it does not strain sense evidence. Nevertheless, Aristotle's position is "minus sufficiens."[8] It does not satisfy because it does not account for certain spiritual phenomena, because it unduly limits the number of immaterial beings, and because it is not conclusive even on its own premises.[9] Plato's inferences from abstraction may be fallacious, but the Platonic conclusions are substantially correct.

The result of such a comparison is that the history of progress in philosophy is not uniform across the hierarchy of speculative discourses; there are different authorities for the different levels. By what criteria, then, are the authorities to be determined? In Abelard's theological ranking, the criteria are nearness to Scripture and fidelity to saintly authority. There is a diminishing authority as one moves down through history from the time of revelation.[10] In Thomas's philosophical ranking, a similar chronology will not work, because there is no single moment of disclosure which cuts across all discourse. Aristotle's may be the most ample of adequate philosophical discourses, but his adequacy is not unlimited. Philosophical authority is not to be measured merely by fidelity to Aristotelianism.

It is not enough to say that the obvious criterion in philosophy is the truth, as if access to the truth were had entirely apart from the philosophical traditions.[11] It is a biographical fact, for Thomas as for anyone else, that one is brought into philosophy by education. Thomas learned his Aristotelian principles not only by simple observation or from 'common sense', but under the tutelage of Aristotle.[12] Moreover, and this is decisive, Thomas does not propose the abandonment of one's education as the criterion for entry into philosophy. He is not interested in beginning anew, in founding a philosophy, in revolution. There is nothing in Thomas like Descartes's decision, to see whether all those bookish maxims were true.[13] There is no such decision because Thomas does not think it likely that one would progress in philosophy except through the tradition. This sentiment is partly the Latin West's deep sense of indebtedness to the ancients, with whom they felt themselves to be in continuity. But it is, more importantly in Thomas, a testimony to human frailty in intellect.

Still, that frailty cannot be described from the outside. One cannot overcome dependence on the traditions by describing it from some privileged vantage point. So Thomas deploys a number of internal criteria for the evaluation of the traditions. In the comparison between Plato and Aristotle from the *De Substantiis Separatis*, Thomas requries that philosophical accounts explain observed phenomena, be free from unwelcome conclusions, and be consistent. Related criteria could be found on almost any page of the corpus, since so much of Thomas's writing is taken up with the gentle criticism of rival accounts.[14] When an *auctoritas* is brought against him, he will argue exegesis. When cases are adduced, he explains the appearances differently or denies their relevance to the disputed issue. Thomas will correct fallacies and point to inconsistencies. But these internal criteria are the stock in trade of Western philosophy; there is nothing Thomistic about them. They do not make clear the foundation of Thomas's relation to the philosophical traditions.

Moreover, Thomas himself intends to offer in speculative discourse something more than hypotheses which satisfy formal or factual criteria for adequacy. It is not enough that the account be consistent; it is not enough that it cover the known cases. These matters are brought forward in discursive argument, but the ground of intelligibility lies beyond them. By what criterion does Thomas judge philosophical accounts to be true or partly true? The question is, if course, too broad to be useful. One might limit it to the single important case: How does Thomas justify his claims that Aristotle is philosophically authoritative? But even this question is elusive, because it presupposes a notion of philosophical authority. The first question ought to be, what is it for Thomas to be philosophically authoritative?

The answer must be that authority in philosophy is very different from authority in theology. For the believer, the authority of revelation in Scripture and tradition is final. One can differ about its interpretation, but the believer cannot doubt that revelation is the ground of what is disclosed to faith.[15] Faith is had in God's revelation; it speaks truths which can only be known by revelation. No other authority is possible except the authority of the manifesting God.[16] In philosophy, on the contrary, the authority of the traditions is not final, but original or pedagogical. One comes to know much about the world through the traditions. Yet the traditions and the philosophic knowledge to which they conduce are not final. The speculative discourses are, at best, propaedeutics to beatitude. The authority of philosophic traditions is, then, the authority of good pedagogy.

At this point, the external criteria become important. A philosophic discourse must, indeed, offer a comprehensive and well divided vocabulary. It must explain, at least generally, the most salient facts known to the reader about the matter considered. The discourse must, as well, appropriate and take forward the history of philosophic learning.[17] These characteristics give a philosophical discourse the authority of the good teacher. What about truth? Truth is not given but discovered. This does not mean that the discourses are set aside in order to find a new source of truth. It does mean that the discourses are treated as questions, as beginnings for inquiry. They are, in the Aristotelian prescription, "common opinions" which must be examined dialectically on the way to first principles of demonstration.

Aristotle has authority in Thomas as just such an authoritative opinion. Aristotle himself had said in the *Topics* that dialectical premises are distinguished from the 'self-evident' premises of

demonstration in being only those which are "accepted by
every one or by the majority or by the philosophers."[18] But the
distinction is cast in a different light when Aristotle adds in the
following section that dialectic is useful to philosophy precisely
with regard to the "ultimate bases of the principles used in the
several sciences."[19] Dialectic comprises the "process of
criticism wherein lies the path to the principles of all inquiries."[20] The testing of first principles in philosophy begins,
then, from the authoritative opinions of the philosophic community. Thomas, being a good reader of Aristotle, takes Aristotle himself as one of the *endoxai*.

It is on this basis that one can appreciate the qualifications
upon Aristotle, the knowing transformations of Aristotelian
vocabulary, and the various appropriations of Aristotle in different parts of the corpus. There are also texts in which Aristotle is judged as inadequate. In the commentary on the *Peri
Hermeneias*, Thomas takes as insufficient the Aristotelian
deduction of contingency from the potency of matter.[21] More
famously, in the commentary on the *Physics*, Thomas ends his
paraphrase of Aristotle's arguments from the eternity of motion
with a long critique of them from faith.[22] There are other
passages, such as that in the *De Substantiis* quoted above,
where Thomas seems to place the whole of the Aristotelian
enterprise within a fuller hierarchy of philosophical projects.

To call Thomas an Aristotelian makes just the same sense as
calling Aristotle a Platonist in the *Metaphysics*. The criticism of
the views of the Academy is the starting-point for many of the
main passages of the Aristotelian work. So, in Thomas, the examination of Aristotelian teachings is the beginning of
philosophic discourse. Aristotle most often rejects the Platonic
formulae in order to adopt formulae with new sense. Thomas
most often keeps the Aristotelian formulae, adding new senses
under the traditional words. But the logical relation in both
cases is the same. It is a procedure of dialectical inquiry which
begins from received philosophic opinions, that is, from the
philosophic traditions. Thomas's relation to the traditions,
then, is anything but accidental or external. It is the mainstay of
his procedure in philosophical discourse.

6.2 PHILOSOPHICAL 'METHOD' AND PEDAGOGY

There is no philosophical 'method' in Aquinas as there is a 'method' for many of the moderns. It is not that Thomas is anarchical or unreflective. It is rather that Thomas's notion of the mind and its workings save him from thinking that there could be such a thing as a method, a set of rules for finding truth, in philosophy. One can see this even lexically. Thomas rarely uses the word *'methodus'* and then only in the commentaries on Aristotle.[1] When the word does appear, it is equated with *'ars'* and so seems to mean nothing more than skill or practiced technique. For Thomas, a *methodus* is not a guarantor of truth; it is the summary of experience in inquiry. It does not set out the conditions which are to be met; it only recalls how things have been found to be. The point is made theoretically when Thomas agrees with Aristotle that there is no one way of asking the question about essence. The latin Aristotle writes in the beginning of *De Anima* that there is no one "methodus" by which a substantial definition can be produced in all cases. Each case seems to require a different "modus".[2] Thomas agrees: "haec est difficultas in qualibet re, cum sit una communis quaestio animae et multis aliis, circa substantiam eorum, et circa quod quid est. Est ergo prima difficultas, quia nos nescimus per quam viam procedendum sit ad definitionem."[3]

If there is not a philosophical 'method' in Thomas, what does it mean to say that there is something like an *ars* of philosophical procedure? *'Ars'* is a shifting term which is sometimes used interchangeably with *'scientia'* and sometimes contrasted with it. In the commentary on the opening chapter of the *Metaphysics*, Thomas follows Aristotle in contrasting *'ars'* with the unknowing, merely customary operation of the craftsman.[4] Art knows the causes which it controls; it is able to teach them and to give an account of itself at the level of the universal. This is a summary of the comparison between simple experience and art "quantum ad cognitionem."[5] But Thomas does not immediately restrict art to the practical, since he goes on to distinguish practical from speculative art, including within the latter the "scientiae logicales" which serve as an introduction to the other "scientiae."[6] It is only at the end of the *lectio* that Thomas repeats Artistotle's reference to the sixth

Book of the *Ethics* and distinguishes *'ars'* from *'scientia'*.[7] Here
he recalls the Aristotelian definition of *'ars'* as "recta ratio factibilium"[8]

   The *factum* in the *ars* of philosophical procedure, as in the
logical arts generally, is argumentative discourse. *Recta ratio*
about philosophical discourse is presumably that *ratio* which
leads one to the truth through discourse. This *ars* is not made to
produce silent, interior illuminations. It is meant to persuade by
the use of speech. So, too, in Aristotle, the general description
of philosophical dialectic is enacted in the writing of those
school *logoi*, which serve as instruments for advancing a public
inquiry, being both summaries and suggestions. The logical
outline in the *Topics* does not do justice to the diversity of
Aristotelian practice in the treatises, just as the paradigms of the
Analytics do not serve by themselves to constitute Aristotelian
demonstration. The logical works are preliminary descriptions
of discourses which have yet to be done.

   Thomas's remarks on dialectic or demonstration would be
found to differ little from those in Aristotle. But Thomas's practice does seem to differ from the Aristotelian in a number of
ways. The differences sometimes appear in the first impressions
of new readers. Thomas's texts seem tighter than those of
Aristotle. He develops, especially in the *Summa*, an almost
syllogistic cadence very different from the Peripatetic circlings.
Moreover, the Thomist texts seem more self-conscious in adop-
ting the logical patterns. One can see this in the complex sub-
divisions of the texts, in the very pattern of the *quaestio
disputata*, in the constant analysis of argument into premises.
This first impression does correspond to a change in the
Aristotelian philosophic procedure. It is not the case that
Thomas is undialectical; the *quaestiones* remain questions and
Thomas does reverse easy arguments into more balanced, more
nuanced pedagogical structures. But it is also true that there is a
greater logical formality in Thomas, both in construction and
refutation. As a result, one sees less of Thomas's first thoughts;
the text presents itself always as second thoughts, finished
arguments. Of course, Thomas's changes of emphasis can be
traced by collating texts. But the form of each text presents
itself as tight argument.

The logical formality is connected with another impression, that Thomas is somehow more contentious than Aristotle. Aristotle can be thoroughly argumentative, as he is in the historical reviews. In *Metaphysics* I, 9, for example, he adduces several dozen arguments against Platonistic theories of the Forms. But there are much longer stretches in Aristotle where the other views drop out and one is left constructing views rather than refuting them. For Thomas, in contrast, every page is filled with opposing views to be refuted, corrected, or reinterpreted. The difference here is the difference of the *auctoritates*, which seem to be present in almost every consideration. Even the anonymous "quidam" reminds the reader that this is a dispute, a disagreement among different texts, different views. Perhaps it is precisely this sense of constant disputation that accounts for the prominence of logical formality. Every conversation in Thomas is a disagreement and so requires that artful exactness used by disputants.

Again, one has the impression that Thomas is more didactic, some would say "more dogmatic," than Aristotle. Thomas is constantly presenting principles and maxims which are to be applied in a particular case. He is always demanding that the reader assent to some rule or other. Sometimes it seems that the Thomist texts are always reaching for elementary principles, which are repeated again and again. Or it seems that one goes round in a circle of sciences, principles being borrowed back and forth without any final justification. Thomas seems not to want a method of discovery but a method of handing over what has already been discovered, that is, a didactic method. With Aristotle, one has the impression of joining an inquiry; with Thomas, one has the impression of receiving a lecture.

Now these various impressions — of logical formalism, of contentiousness, of a didactic impulse — have different sources and would deserve different replies in detail. Some of them are simply the result of one's reading badly. But it is more interesting to see that the various comparisons between Aristotle and Aquinas can be construed in opposite directions. The sum of the impressions seems to be that things are settled in Aquinas which were not so neatly arranged in Aristotle. One sometimes hears, in fact, that Thomas has 'completed' Aristotle. Yet 'completion' could mean two very different things — either a tidying up of difficulties or a continuing of the dialectic. The first impressions in reading Thomas may not indicate a neater 'system'; they may — I think they do — indicate a more radical application of the dialectic.

Philosophical dialectic is the search for first principles by the raising of difficulties. To advance, any dialectic must address three questions: What is it to be a first principle? What are the true difficulties? How does one establish a principle beyond, behind demonstration? Thomas addresses each of these questions more radically than does Aristotle. He thus advances in the practice of the *ars* of making philosophical discourses.

Thomas addresses the question of what is to be first in treating the hierarchy of sciences. It is a commonplace in the reading of ancient philosophy that Aristotle breaks down the unity of the sciences required by Plato. Thus, the autonomous inquiries of the Aristotelian natural treatises violate that smooth ascent which is described in the *Republic* VII. This view seems to me too simple, given the Aristotelian concern for first principles throughout the *Metaphysics*, especially in IV, 3 and XII. But it is certainly true that Aristotle weakens the Platonic requirement somewhat. Thomas, on the other hand, adopts something much more like the Platonic hierarchy. He does so for reasons external to philosophy when he subordinates all speculative knowledge to beatitude. He does so for internal reasons when he emphasizes the *ordo disciplinae*, whether in discussing the arts or in considering the parts of physics or in defending the primacy of metaphysics. In Thomas, the lower studies are preparations for the higher; the human mind is not satisfied with any study below the highest. Moreover, no philosophical study is complete with the study of metaphysics — and metaphysics is not complete, except with the vision of God. In both of these ways, I take Thomas to be reestablishing something like the Platonic hierarchy of study.

The second question for dialectic is the question, how to raise searching difficulties. Thomas's 'contentiousness' is, in fact, an attempt to advance with this question. The conflict of *auctoritates*, the concern to respond to all opposed views even if they be less than reasonable — these are ways to survey the field of possible questions to find which are the truly searching ones, to find where questions ought to be asked. In a curious way, then, Thomas's 'contentiousness' is his being thoroughly dialectical, his wanting to have it out on every point. But since the inquiry is dialectical, is a search for principles discovered only at the end, only in the final knowledge, the particular disputes are not solved except by the invocation of principles which cannot be demonstrated. Thomas's use of argument is not the attempt to prove everything, unless one construes 'prove' as if it still meant test. Demonstration is impossible in the case of the first principles; that is exactly where dialectic must be used. So the questions raised at every turn in Thomas are not raised in the expectation of a proof; they are raised in hopes of finding a way to the indemonstrable first principles.

Here one has Thomas's response to the third issue in dialectic, that of establishing the indemonstrable principles. I argued above that each disputed question ought to be read, in some sense, as an attempt at public persuasion. That argument was a way of making explicit what is contained in the literary form of the *quaestio*. One can now see how such persuasion is possible. It is persuasion by showing, through repeated application, the coherent power of the first principles. In the *Contra Gentiles*, for example, one can find the main metaphysical maxims repeated in dozens of different contexts. A good example is the maxim of causal likeness.[9] Where is the maxim established? In the analysis of causality, one wants to say. But the analysis of causality itself depends on metaphysics, on the insight into causal participation through insight into act. And how is act established? By a kind of ostension. One 'sees' how the act/potency distinction is embodied in various examples. Similarly, one sees how causal likeness illuminates any number of cases. Its content is established precisely in the cases. The reader learns what the maxim means by watching it applied, just as one learns the content of physics in its special branches, and the final content of the soul's knowledge of itself in moral inquiry. The first principles are not known fully in the beginning, such that all specific cases can be deduced from them. On the contrary, they are known through the cases, which is to say, through their dialectical application in response to searching questions. The maxims which survive the test of repeated application are the maxims which point to the indemonstrable first principles.

It is not the case, of course, that Thomas imagines that adequacy in consistent application is the same as truth. He does
think that adequacy in application is both a consequence of being true and a sign leading to the discovery of truth. Moreover,
Thomas writes with the hope that the repeated application of a
principle will enable one to apprehend the principle itself
through the particular cases. The Thomist arguments are
themselves part of a vast *epagogê* after the Aristotelian model of
the induction of the notion of act. One learns what Thomas
means by his metaphysical principles in watching their application. More to the point, one learns the truth of the principles
themselves.

The pedagogical question of securing the first principles is
touched by Thomas in a number of Aristotelian commentaries.[10] But it also figures, and perhaps more interestingly, in
Thomas's reply to the Augustinian question, whether any man
can be said to teach another.[11] Thomas replies to it first in the
questions *De Veritate*, where the eleventh Question is entitled
De Magistro.[12] The text is not what one would expect from the
Aristotelian parallels. Thomas holds that men can properly be
called teachers, but only secondarily and as acting from the outside: "solus Deus est qui interius et principaliter docet."[13] He
adds, more elegantly: "homo verus et vere doctor dici potest et
veritatem docens et mentem quidem illuminans, non quasi
lumen rationis infundens sed quasi lumen rationis coadiuvans
ad scientiae perfectionem per ea quae exterius proponit."[14] If
one learns to know something and not only to have an opinion
about it, one does so on the basis of first terms and principles
grounded by participation in the divine light. A teacher can
neither give nor augment that intellectual light; he can only be
the external, the supplementary cause which brings those terms
and principles from potentiality to actuality.[15] Thus human
teaching, as regards its end, belongs more to the active life than
the contemplative.[16] It is acting not directly on the mind's
power, but indirectly through the senses, by signs and deeds.

The two articles on teaching in the *prima pars* echo in
substance and formula the treatment of *De Veritate*. Thomas
locates the question in the wider context of natural action[17] and
rehearses the various opinions. Again, Thomas admits no more
to human teaching than that it be "coadiuvans agens prin-

cipalis," which is the natural itself working internally.[18] Teaching cooperates with the student's own *inventio* either by propounding "aliqua auxilia vel instrumenta," as new evidence for apprehension, or by suggesting as "ordinem principiorum ad conclusiones," as a remedy for rudimentary powers of deduction.[19] But if men can teach one another in these two manners, they can in no way be said to teach angels, to whom they are always inferior in intellectual act.[20] In these remarks, Thomas is mainly concerned to reject explanations of teaching which would imply finished causal explanation or confuse the human mind with the angelic.[21] But he is also concerned to place human teaching in a progression, a pedagogy, for which it is not the end.[22]

Thomas's 'method', then, is an art for constructing philosophical discourses. Their construction depends, of course, on the prior arts of the *trivium*. But it depends, as well, on the special art of philosophical dialectic. Thomas advances beyond the Aristotelian dialectic by deepening it along three lines: the hierarchy of sciences, the raising of searching questions, and the persuasion to first principles. Thomas's 'method' is the pedagogy required by the hierarchy of knowledge, and the logical rigor required by submitting every point to the conflict of authorities, and the persuasion through induction from repeated applications of general principles. Thomas's method is not outside and before the texts; it is in them, as the source of composition. It animates the texts up to the point where philosophical discourse passes over into theology. There, another principle of authorship is required.

6.3 PHILOSOPHY, THEOLOGY, AND BEATITUDE

The difference between the discourses of philosophy and theology is most often stated by Thomas as a difference of origin. Theology begins from revealed sources which the philosopher cannot use. Thus, in the *Contra Gentiles*, Thomas separates two sorts of truths which believers hold about divine matters. The first sort falls ideally within the sphere of human reason and corresponds to truths "quae etiam philosophi demonstrative de Deo probaverunt, ducti naturalis lumine rationis."[1] The second sort of truth includes truths "quae

humanae rationis penitus excedant ingenium."[2] The second
sort of truth can begin only in divine revelation. For both sorts
of truth, moreover, revealed sources provide a surer footing
than is had in philosophy, given the circumstances of human
knowledge in this life. Revelation makes possible the use of
premises for demonstration which far exceed in power and
scope the discoveries even of the highest philosophy.[3] With
regard to the highest things, philosophical discoures remain only as exercises, so long as they do not presume to comprehend
or to demonstrate that of which they are only distant
likenesses.[4]

The other characterizations of the difference between
philosophy and theology fall within the difference in origin
which separates revealed from unrevealed sources. The first
Question of the *Summa*, which draws a dialectically qualified
analogy between *sacra doctrina* and philosophical *scientia*,
proposes a formal difference between philosophy and theology.
The "ratio formalis" which unites theological discourse is the
criterion of revelation: "omnia quaecumque sunt divinitus
revelabilia, communicant in una ratione formali objecti huius
scientiae."[5] Indeed, theology gathers together subject matters,
which are dispersed in philosophical consideration, precisely
by understanding them all as divinely revealed.[6] In the *Contra
Gentiles*, Thomas makes the same argument differently, by
arguing that the believer and the philosopher treat the same
things differently, since the believer sees everything as relating
to God, and so approaches the perspective had in God's own
knowledge.[7] Of course, the believer's insight into the divine
knowledge has already been shown to be possible only by
revelation.[8] The formal difference, too, is the difference of
origin.

Philosophy and theology are also distinguished, of course, by
the epistemological status of the relation to first principles.
Philosophy seeks to know them; theology must believe them.
The difference is profound and thoroughgoing, especially as
regards the results to be expected from theological argument.[9]
But the difference is due precisely to the dependence in
theology on revelation. Theology requires faith because
theology begins from what God reveals, which is believed

without being seen. If it is easily seen, it need not be revealed.[10] Once revealed, it provides not knowledge, but the anticipation of knowledge which is belief.

The difference in origin between revealed and unrevealed sources manifests itself in third place as the greater richness of the theological context. A proposition verbally the same does not mean the same thing to the philosopher and the theologian. This is true in two ways. First, a proposition such as God's unity, which is professed by believers and demonstrated by philosophers, is qualified for the believer by the revelation of the Trinity. Similarly, philosophical knowledge of divine providence or of divine eternity is both supplemented and corrected in the theological discussion of the Incarnation, of grace, and of creation in time. In a second way, philosophical truths are qualified for the believer not by the addition of other truths but by the moral force of the truths as believed. The believer accepts the doctrine of the divine unity as the basis for action — whether in worship or in obedience. A revealed doctrine, as revealed, can affect souls which would remain unaffected even by the most polished metaphysical demonstration.[11] Thomas says, in the prologue to his commentary on the Apostle's Creed, that faith brings four good gifts: union with God, inchoate knowledge of God, direction for the present life, and victory over temptations.[12] Faith is the effective rhetoric which offers both knowledge and the power of action.

The difference of origin is a difference between the human discourse of philosophy and the divine discourse of revelation. Whatever the mechanism of its composition, Thomas treats Scripture as a discourse which comes from the divine. Its author is God Himself. It is a speech supreme over all philosophic speech, in truth, authority, and persuasive power. So the difference of origin becomes a charge against philosophy. On the one hand, theology depends faithfully upon revelation for its first principles and so falls short of philosophical knowledge. On the other hand, philosophy cannot have the knowledge of God as fully or as certainly as it is offered by revelation through faith. Philosophical knowledge can never be complete in this life. Philosophy cannot offer what the human intellect desires and grace promises. The fulfillment seems to be left to theology, which gives an account of the highest things, of the first ground, beyond the capacity of philosophy.

Theology, then, is able to reply to philosophy on philosophy's own terms. If it is true that the first Article of the *Summa* asks theology to justify itself in the face of already constituted philosophical discourses, it is equally true that theology turns out to be the architectonic wisdom which philosophy cannot be. It is not only that theology is more efficacious morally than philosophy, the charge made famously in Augustine's *Confessions*. Nor is it that theology offers an alternative discourse about the highest things. It is rather that theology offers a present discourse about the things which remain always future for philosophy. So it is that Thomas says, recurring to a favorite Latin *topos*, that a little old lady under the Christian dispensation speaks more truly about God than the highest metaphysician without it.[13] More strongly, the weakness of the human intellect is such that only faith can bring philosophy to completion even in simple cases: "cognitio nostra est adeo debilis quod nullus philosophus potuit unquam perfecte investigare naturam unius muscae: unde legitur, quod unus philosophus fuit triginta annis in solitudine, ut cognosceret naturam apis."[14] The mind's desire to know itself impels the mind to accept the offer of divine revelation. The moral imperative for philosophy becomes the moral imperative to believe. Just as a *rusticus* would be accounted foolish for not believing the wise, how much more foolish would a man be for not believing God.[15] By assuming authorship, God becomes the true teacher, giving instruction not only by the natural light of understanding, but also by the explicit discourse of Scripture. God seems to speak into the incompleteness of philosophic discourse.

What God speaks is Scripture, however, and not theology. The discourse of theology is itself a promise and not a fulfillment. The virtue of faith is not an end. Faith is, Thomas said with regard to the Creed, an unformed beginning of the knowledge of God: "per fidem inchoatur in nobis vita aeterna: nam vita aeterna nihil aliud est quam cognoscere Deum."[16] Faith is a preparation for beatitude. So, too, the present discourse of theology is no more than a discourse subalternated to the "scientia Dei et beatorum."[17] If philosophy learns its limitations by its dependence on the arts of language and by speculative inquiry into the world, soul, and God, theology knows its limitation from its very beginning, in faith. The contrasts between philosophy and theology, then, cannot forget that there are further contrasts to be drawn between theology and beatitude. If theology goes one step beyond philosophy, it nonetheless does not bring the human mind to rest.[18]

This can be seen quite clearly in the doctrine about the vision of God. Thomas insists that the speculative sciences do not give one a vision of the separated substances.[19] The happiness of the human intellect, its fulfillment, "non erit per aliquam scientiam speculativam, sed per lumen gloriae."[20] But that restriction applies as much to theology as to philosophy. The inability of the human intellect to see God in the present life is absolute, extending even to mystical vision. To see God's essence would require one's death — that is, one's passing beyond the present life. "Quod ergo anima elevetur usque ad supremum intelligibilium, quod est essentia divina, esse non potest, quamdiu in hac mortali vita vivitur."[21] Thomas seems to allow for the miraculous exception in the highest mystical vision, referring to the later consideration of rapture.[22] There, after noting the diversity of opinion on the matter, he allows that Paul and Moses saw the divine essence in rapture.[23] Of course, rapture itself is a transient anticipation of beatitude and an explicit violation of the moral condition — a foretaste of death. So the general principle stands: there is no present vision of the divine essence.

The human authorship of philosophy is superseded by the divine authorship at the origin of theology. Yet the discourse of theology, passed down by human authors, is itself a promise of that vision of God which comes after death. Neither discourse is complete. Each points beyond itself into the discourse of the blessed, the speech of the elect.

NOTES

NOTES TO THE INTRODUCTION

1. There is an annotated bibliography by Albert Keller, "Arbeiten zur Sprachphilosophie Thomas von Aquins." A number of items having to do with Aquinas can also be found in the general bibliographies of medieval language and logic: E.J. Ashworth, *The Tradition of Medieval Logic and Speculative Grammar*, in the section containing nn.1-633; G.L. Bursill-Hall in R.W. Hunt, *Collected Papers on the History of Grammar in the Middle Ages*, pp. xxvii— xxxvi. Full citations for these and other works mentioned in the notes can be found in the Bibliography.

2. Ernest A. Moody, "The Medieval Contribution to Logic," reprinted in *Studies in Medieval Philosophy, Science, and Logic*, pp. 371-392. Moody writes: "What medieval logic has to contribute, to the further development and enrichment of modern logic, is this semantical bridge between the abstract, axiomatically derived, formal system of modern logic, and the concrete, empirically oriented forms in which natural languages exhibit the rational structure of experience on its phenomenological level" (pp. 389-390).

3. An ongoing survey of Thomistic bibliography is provided by the *Rassegna di letteratura tomistica* (Naples, 1969-), which continues the *Bulletin Thomiste* (Le Saulchoir, 1923-1968). The earlier bibliographic compendium was the *Bibliographie Thomiste*, ed. Pierre Mandonnet and J. Destrez. For addenda, see the review of the *Bibliographie* by C. Frati. The *Bibliographie* was revised by Marie-Dominique Chenu, who added a supplement with imprints from before 1920 which had been overlooked by the original editors. Summary bibliography for more recent years can be had in Vernon J. Bourke, *Thomistic Bibliography, 1920-1940*, and Terry L. Miethe and Vernon J. Bourke, *Thomistic Bibliography, 1941-1978*. See also Carlo Giacon, "Sussidi lessicali e bibliografici per lo studio di S. Tommaso."

4. Maurice De Wulf, *An Introduction to Scholastic Philosophy, Medieval and Modern*, pp. 158, 207, 259-262.

NOTES TO THE PROLOGUE TO CHAPTER 1

1. Weisheipl, *Friar Thomas*, p. 386, n.57, and p. 392, n.68. In order to avoid long digressions, I will usually follow Weisheipl's dating and his titles for works by Thomas. Here I note, however, that H.-F. Dondaine will say no more of the *De fallaciis* in the Leonine edition than that "il n'apparait pas exclu que saint Thomas puisse être à l'origine de l'ouvrage" (EL 43, p. 386). Some who approve Thomas's authorship would assign it to a much later date. Dondaine counts the evidence for the *De propositionibus modalibus* as even more ambiguous.

2. Aquinas died in March of 1274. The commentary on the *Analytics* was written from 1269 to 1272, that on the *Peri Hermeneias* from 1270 to 1271. The second is incomplete. See Weisheipl, *Friar Thomas*, p. 375, #37, and p.

374, #36.

3. Weisheipl, *Friar Thomas*, p. 404, #98. There is some logical matter in the group of seven philosophical treatises of dubious authenticity; see Weisheipl, *Friar Thomas*, pp. 403-404, ##91-97.

4. Weisheipl, *Friar Thomas*, pp. 19-20.

5. For the maxim's origin see the letter by Van Steenberghen in the *Bulletin de philosophie médiévale*. Many of the Parisian statutes against false teaching and intellectual presumption were directed against the Masters in Arts. This is famously true of the 1272 statute against 'theologizing' in the faculty of Arts and of Tempier's condemnations of 1277. See Henri Denifle and Emile Chatelain, *Chartularium Universitatis Parisiensis*, I, pp. 499-500 and 543-558. The statute reads in part: "Statuimus et ordinamus quod nullus magister vel bachellarius nostre facultatis aliquam questionem pure theologicam ... determinare seu etiam disputare presumat, tamquam sibi determinatos limites transgrediens, cum sicut dicit philosophus non geometram cum geometra sit penitus inconveniens disputare" (I, p. 499). Conversely, of course, the theologians were prohibited by Gregory in *Parens scientiarum* from involving themselves with the arts and philosophy. See Denifle and Chatelain, *Chartularium*, I, pp. 136-139. Gregory writes: "Magistri vero et scolares theologie in facultate quam profitentur se laudabiliter exercere nec philosophos se ostentent, sed satagant fieri theodocti ..." (I, p. 138). For a synoptic account, see Fernand Van Steenberghen, *Philosophie au XIIIe siècle*, pp. 357-373.

6. For a summary of conclusions, see Weisheipl, *Friar Thomas*, pp. 374-381, ##36-47, with pertinent corrigenda and addenda, p. 482; compare pp. 282-284. See also Lohr, "Medieval Aristotle Commentaries: Authors Robertus-Wilgelmus," pp. 159-172. If Gauthier is right that the *De anima* was composed before the return to Paris in 1269, and perhaps beginning in 1267, five years would stretch to something like six or six and a half.

7. In summary, Weisheipl, *Friar Thomas*, p. 379, n.45. Compare Mansion, "Dates de quelques commentaires de Saint Thomas," throughout. The new Leonine edition will show the diversity of commentaries employed by Thomas and thus the variety of dates and of circumstances in the commentary's composition.

8. For example, *Super Peri* I, lect.1, n.4 (EB 4,327,1). Thomas writes, "In graeco habetur...," but the reference is to Moerbeke's traslation, *Aristoteles Latinus* II/1-2, p. 41, line 1. The same is true of citations to the 'Greek' in *Super Peri* I, lect.3, n.13 (EB 4,329,1); lect.8, n.9 (EB 4,332,2); lect.10, n.13 (EB 4,334,2); lect.13, n.7 (EB 4,337,1); and II, lect.2, n.5 (EB 4,340,2); and *Super Post An.* I, lect.6, n.5 (EB 4,276,2).

9. The famous review of the dependencies is Callus, "Les sources," throughout. Particular dependencies are illustrated in detail in some of the editions of the *Corpus Latinum Commentariorum in Aristotelem Graecorum*. See, for example, *Ammonius: Commentaire sur le PERI HERMENIAS d'Aristote, CLCAG* II, especially *xi-xxv* and *xxvi-xlxvi*.

10. The dedicatory letter for the exposition of the *Peri Hermeneias* does not show much of Thomas's intention, in part because it conforms so strictly

to the literary patterns for such letters (see the "Epistola nuncupatoria," EL 1, p. 5). Jean Isaac wants to connect it with the prologue to the *prima pars* and so to draw a pedagogical contrast between the well-ordered Aristotle and the chaotic Lombard ("Saint Thomas interprète," pp. 356-357). The text is too much a formula to bear such weight.

11. Most recently, Van Steenberghen, *Thomas Aquinas and Radical Aristotelianism*, throughout, and Van Steenberghen, *Maître Siger de Brabant*. See also Henri-Edouard Wéber, *La controverse de 1270*, but with the criticisms of Bazán, "Le dialogue philosophique entre Siger de Brabant et Thomas d'Aquin."

12. On Aquinas's intention, see Jean Isaac, "Saint Thomas interprète," pp. 356, 361, where Thomas's intention is described as that of providing a *summa philosophica* by means of an analytic, exegetical, and comparative reading of Aristotle. Compare Marie-Dominique Chenu, *Introduction*, pp. 175-183; Joseph Owens, "Aquinas as Aristotelian Commentator," especially pp. 213-216 and 234-238, where Owens concludes that the commentaries cannot be read fully except in the light of Aquinas's theological concerns; and, more summarily, F. Edward Cranz, "The Publishing History of the Aristotle Commentaries," particularly pp. 157-158. Albert's intention is treated by Weisheipl in "Albert's Disclaimers in the Aristotelian Paraphrases."

13. Pierre Duhem, *Système du Monde*, V, p. 569: "Il n'y a pas de philosophie thomiste .... La vaste composition élaborée par Thomas d'Aquin se montre donc à nous comme une maquetterie où se juxtaposent ... une multitude de pièces empruntées à toutes les philosophies."

14. See the corrective essay by Josef Pieper in *Hinführung*, pp. 66-80, where Pieper argues against an easy labeling of Thomas as an Aristotelian.

15. Bernard Dod writes, "There is a tenacious legend that the West learnt its Aristotle via translations from the Arabic, but the fact is that the West turned to Arabic-Latin translations only in default of the more intelligible Greek-Latin ones .... The legend has more basis, however, when one considers Aristotelian doctrine in a vaguer sense" ("Aristoteles latinus," p. 52). What Dod calls a 'legend' has a very strong basis in the influence not only of Arabic treatises circulated in the twelfth century, but in those Arabic commentaries which had great authority in the thirteenth. My point about the double entry refers exactly to the impact of the Arabic reading of Aristotle on the Latin readers of the *Metaphysics* and the other *libri naturales*.

16. There are various medieval curricula for the arts available from other universities at other times. Among these, the most famous would be the 1255 statutes for the Arts faculty in Paris and the earlier Parisian examination—handbook discovered by Martin Grabmann (see his "Eine für Examinazwecke"). Lewry has recently described similar collections from the mid-century in "Examination Compendia from the Faculty of Arts," pp. 106-112. Weisheipl has studied later Oxford sources in "Curriculum of the Faculty of Arts at Oxford in the early Fourteenth Century." But no conclusive comparison could be drawn from these Parisian or Oxford curricula

to that at Naples, where there was both a different polity and a different intellectual origin.

17. The early biographies of Thomas are found in *Fontes vitae s. Thomas Aquinatis*, ed. D. Prummer. For the descriptions of Naples, see Calo's life, c. 4, p. 20; Tocco's life, c. 5, p. 70; Gui's life, c. 4, p. 170. On the intellectual character of Naples, see Angelo Walz and Paul Novarina, *Saint Thomas d'Aquin*, pp. 35-38; Martin Grabmann, "Kaiser Friedrich II. und sein Verhältnis zur aristotelischen and arabischen Philosophie."

18. Tocco writes: "Unde puer de utriusque parentis consilio Neapolim mittitur, et sub Magistri Martini in grammaticalibus et logicalibus, et Magistri Petri de Ibernia studiis in naturalibus edocetur" (c. 5, in *Fontes*, p. 70). But Calo gives the logic to Peter: "Nam cum Martinum praeceptorem in grammatica breve excederet, traditus est magistro Petro Ybernico, qui in logicalibus et naturalibus eum instruxit" (c. 4, in *Fontes*, p. 20). Gui does not mention the arts masters at Naples. Since Tocco's seems to be the original life, and since Calo's *Legendarium* is often unreliable, it is tempting to give the logic to Martin on textual grounds. That assignment would be supported by the curricular association of grammar and logic, but weakened by the fact of Peter's commentaries on the *Peri Hermeneias* and Porphyry. See on the textual matters F. Pelster, "Die älteren Biographen des hl. Thomas von Aquinas," p. 397; cf. Michael Bertram Crowe, "On Re-Writing the Biography of Aquinas," pp. 263-265, and Weisheipl, *Friar Thomas*, pp. 344-347.

19. It was thought for a time that he might be that Martin of Dacia who is later known as one of the Parisian *modistae*. But this identification presents chronological inconveniences, since Martin of Dacia seems still to have been alive in 1340. See Weisheipl, *Friar Thomas*, p. 19.

20. Besides the disputation before King Manfred (see fn. 21, below), Glorieux lists commentaries by Peter on Porphyry's *Isagoge* and on the *Peri Hermeneias, Posterior Analytics, Sophistical Refutations* and *De longitudine et brevitate vitae* of Aristotle. See Palémon Glorieux, *Faculté des arts*, pp. 288-289. Lohr adds a commentary on the *De morte et vita* in his "Medieval Latin Aristotle Commentaries" (1972), pp. 354-356. The attribution of the physical commentaries has been questioned by Dalgaard in her edition of the *Peri Hermeneias* (p. 6). The authorship of the commentaries on the *Analytics* and the *Sophistics* has been rejected by Ebbesen in his edition of the latter (pp. *xlviii-lix*). Paul Oskar Kristeller has further attributed to Peter an extant commentary on the *Isagoge* of Johannitius ("Philosophy and Medicine in Medieval and Renaissance Italy," p. 38, n. 8), but this is the same text assigned by Thorndike and Kibre to John de Gallicantu (*Incipits of Mediaeval Scientific Writings*, 995).

21. The text of the disputed question was published by Baeumker in "Petrus de Hibernia der Jungendlehrer des Thomas." It shows Peter's careful reading of Aristotle and Averroes.

22. See the remarks by Dalgaard in the introduction to her edition, p. 9. The dating is by no means as precise as that for the public dispute, which is fixed by King Manfred's reign.

23. Avicenna, *Logica* c.1, f.2r; Dominicus Gundissalinus, *De divisione philosophiae*, ed. Baur, pp. 71-72. Josef Pieper calls Peter's doctrine an extreme and even dangerous form of Aristotelianism (*Hinführung*, p. 65). It would be better to say that it is a rawer Aristotelianism, but perhaps therefore less syncretic than the views prevalent in the norther universities.

24. Peter of Ireland, *Glosulae in librum Aristotelis Peri hermenias*, ed. Dalgaard, pp. 13-14.

25. Peter of Ireland, *Glosulae*, ed. Dalgaard, p. 14, lines 17-29.

26. Peter of Ireland, *Glosulae*, ed. Dalgaard, p. 15, lines 16-19 and 22-27. I follow Dalgaard's emendations.

27. Weisheipl, *Friar Thomas*, p. 19. Compare Walz, *Studi biographici*, p. 26.

28. See Helene Wieruszowski, "Rhetoric and Classics in Italian Education of the Thirteenth Century," with its mention of Thomas's wide reading, pp. 184-185. For the *trivium* at Padua, see Nancy G. Siraisi, *Arts and Sciences at Padua*, pp. 33-65.

29. See Tommaso Leccisotti, *S. Tommaso d'Aquino e Montecassino*, pp. 26-33. Within the curriculum for oblates, Leccisotti emphasizes both Latin and vernacular versification, together with "quelle tradizioni letterarie" (p. 28).

30. See Bloch, "Monte Cassino, Byzantium, and the West," especially pp. 218-222; more generally, H.E.J. Cowdrey, *The Age of Abbot Desiderius*, pp. 19-27.

31. De Renzi claims, with his usual extravagance, that the medical school at Salerno was the model for the university at Naples and so "la progenitrice delle Universita moderne" (*Collectio Salernitana*, I, p. 313). This is far-fetched. Still it is true that Frederick II's legislation establishing the university at Naples formed part of a program which also included legislation regulating the practice and teaching of medicine in the kingdom, with privileged reference to Salerno (De Renzi, *Collectio Salernitana*, I, pp. 313-318). It is also the case that Frederick's legislation envisages the co-operation of arts faculties and the medical school in the training of physicians. For the scientific ambience of the Neapolitan university generally, see Rashdall, *Universities of Europe in the Middle Ages*, I, p. 75 ff.; also Walz, *Studi Biographici*, p. 26.

32. See James A. Weisheipl, "Thomas d'Aquino and Albert His Teacher," p. 5.

33. H.F. Dondaine and H.V. Shooner, *Codices Manuscripti Operum Thomae de Aquino*, I, no. 4, with reference to Naples, Bibl. Naz. MS I. B.54.

34. Albert approaches the Dionysian text under the headings *causa efficiens, subjectum, modus agendi, finis*, and *habitus quo regitur in acquisitione finis* (c.1, lect.1, ed. Borgnet, *Opera omnia*, XIV, p. 6).

35. For Aristotle, ed. Borgnet, XIV, p. 7, col. 1; p. 8, col. 1 (twice); and p. 10, col. 1. For Boethius, p. 9, col. 2; and p. 11, col. 1. For Averroes, p. 7, col. 2.

36. C.1, lect.3, ed. Borgnet, *Opera omnia*, XIV, pp. 20-21.

37. *Resp. art. 108*, q. 1 (EB 3,642,3).

NOTES TO SECTION 1.1

1. Through Ammonius and Boethius, Aquinas knows something of the Greek commentary tradition, as can be seen by his references to Alexander e.g., I, lect.2, n.7 (EB 4,327,3); lect.5, n.19 (EB 4,330,3); lect.6, n.4 (EB 4,331,1); lect.8, nn.5 and 20 (EB 4,332,1; 4,333,1); to Andronicus I, lect.2, n.6 (EB 4,327,3); to Aspasius I, lect.6, n.4 (EB 4,331,1); to Diodorus I, lect.14, n.8 (EB 4,338,1); to Herminus II, lect.2, n.7 (EB 4,340,2); to Philo I, lect.14, n.8 (EB 4,338,1); to Porphyry, e.g., I, lect.2, nn.7 and 11 (EB 4,328,1); lect.5, n.19 (EB 4,330,3); lect.6, n.4 (EB 4,331,1-2); to the Stoics I, lect.14, nn.8 and 10 (EB 3,338,1); and to Theophrastus II, lect.2, n.7 (EB 4,340,2). Isaac has argued at some length that these references can be traced back to either Ammonius or Boethius. Thomas himself frequently mentions that he is quoting at second hand (e.g., the references to Diodorus and Philo are cited as coming through Boethius). See Jean Isaac, *Le PERI HERMENIAS en Occident* pp. 98-105. The comparison of the uses of Ammonius and Boethius is complicated by the fact that Boethius also relied on Ammonius, though without mentioning him. See Verbeke's introduction to Ammonius, *Commentaire sur le PERI HERMENIAS*, p. xi, and the comparison, pp. xii-xxi.

2. For the history of the use of Boethius's commentaries in translations, see Isaac, *Le PERI HERMENIAS en Occident*, pp. 35-97, and, more recently, Osmund Lewry, "Boethian Logic in the Medieval West."

3. Proemium n.3 (EB 4,327,1). Much of the doctrine about language in Aquinas is summarized by Manthey in his *Die Sprachphilosophie des hl. Thomas von Aquin*, Chapters 1-5, pp. 54-155. There are two problems with Manthey's treatment, besides the limitations of any older scholarship. The first is that Manthey constructs his synthetic account by collating remarks from very different works in the corpus. He rarely adverts to context and does not seem much worried by the differences which might be required by it. The second difficulty is that Manthey conceives the various linguistic remarks as propositional parts of a 'system' rather than as practical parts of a pedagogy. Since I take the opposite side on each issue, it is not easy to compare my readings with those of Manthey. I will advert to him on certain special topics, but will not attempt a running criticism. The same remarks would apply to Viktor Warnach, "Däs aussere Sprechen und seine Funktionen nach der Lehre des hl. Thomas von Aquin." The synoptic treatment in Marcia Colish, *The Mirror of Language*, pp. 110-151, is marred by a different difficulty, even in its revised version. What is said there in detail about language is slight and Colish seems more interested in a survey of the main points of Thomas's 'epistemological' doctrine as against the standard reading (compare the new prefatory remarks, pp. xiii-xiv).

4. Proemium n.3 (EB 4,327,1); Ammonius, ed. Verbeke, pp.8-9, lines 31-35. Compare Manthey, *Sprachphilosophie*, pp. 107-110. For Aquinas's correction of Boethius here and its consequences in the account of truth, see Mirko Skarica, "*Peri hermenias*, algunas divergencias entre los comentarios

de Boecio y Tomás de Aquino." Albert takes the looser definition of '*interpretatio*': "Et quamvis enuntiatio sit potissima interpretatio, non tamen convertitur cum interpretatione quae dicit expositionem rei per omnem modum..." (ed. Borgnet, I, p. 374, col. 1). Albert's logical commentaries were most probably composed before 1264 and could have been known to Thomas. See Weisheipl, "The Life and Works of St. Albert the Great," p. 40, and "Albert's Works on Natural Science ...," p. 577. Alfred Wilder argues that there is no interdependence of Thomas's and Albert's commentaries in his "St. Albert and St. Thomas on Aristotle's *De interpretatione*: A Comparative Study."

5. For typical attempts to assimilate Thomas's thought on language to that of 'analytic' philosophy, see Pietro Cardoletti, "Analisi logica del linguaggio ...," and Mariano Brasa Diez, "Tomás de Aquino y el analisis linguistico." As should already be clear, I regard Thomas's treatment of language as fundamentally opposed to the treatments in most Anglo-American philosophy.

6. Boethius's translation, AL II/1-2, p. 5, line 1.

7. I, lect.1, n.2 (EB 4,327,2); Ammonius, ed. Verbeke, pp. 18-19, lines 77-91.

8. I, lect.5, n.2 (EB 4,327,2).

9. I, lect.5, n.3 (EB 4,327,2).

10. I, lect.1, n.5 (EB 4,327,2).

11. "[D]icendum est quod vox est quoddam naturale; unde pertinet ad considerationem naturalis philosophiae.... Unde etiam non est proprie orationis genus, sed assumitur ad constitutionem orationis, sicut res naturales ad constitutionem artificialium." I, lect.1, n.6 (EB 4,327,2); Ammonius, p.30, line 85 - p.31, line 3.

12. I, lect.2, n.2 (EB 4,327,3); Ammonius, pp.34-35, lines 69-75.

13. I, lect.2, n.3 (EB 4,327,3).

14. The triple order is described by Boethius in the first commentary, the *minora*, in a passage which begins: "Tria sunt ex quibus omnis collocutio disputatioque perficitur, res, intellectus, voces..." (PL 64,297B-C). This is connected with the threefold status of the *oratio* as it is thought, written, or spoken, as described in the *maiora* commentary (PL 64,407A). The development of the doctrine of these triplets is surely motivated in part by earlier debates surrounding the Stoic doctrine of the *lekton*, for which see the works in n.15 of Section 1.2.

15. Cf. I, lect.2, n.4 (EB 4,327,3). For various senses of '*vox*', see Manthey, *Sprachphilosophie*, pp. 103-104.

16. Boethius's translation, AL II/1-2, p. 5, line 7; Moerbeke's translation, AL II/1-2, p. 41, line 8; in the Greek, 16a8.

17. Boethius, AL II/1-2, p. 5, lines 10-11; Moerbeke, p. 41, line 9. Compare the lemma in the Verbeke's edition of Ammonius, p. 32, line 24.

18. Lect.2,n.5 "Non enim potest esse quod [voces] significent immediate ipsas res, ut ex ipso modo significandi apparet: significat enim hoc nomen homo naturam humanam in abstractione a signularibus. Unde non potest esse quod significet immediate hominem singularem." (EB 4,327,3).

19. Lect.2, n.11 (EB 4,328,1-2).

20. Lect.2, n.10 (EB 4,238,1).

21. Lect.2, n.10 (EB 4,328,1).

22. Ammonius, ed. Verbeke, p. 49, lines 15-18.

23. Lect.3, n.1 (EB 4,328,2).

24. Lect.3, n.2 (EB 4,328,2).

25. For example, lect.3, n.7 and n.9 (EB 4,328,3).

26. Lect.3, n.8 (EB 4,328,3).

27. Boethius, AL II/1-2, p. 6, lines 4-5.

28. I, lect.4, nn.2-8 (EB 4,329,1-2).

29. Lect.4, n.5: "Si igitur nomina rerum artificialium significant formas accidentales, ut concretas subiectis naturalibus, convenientius est, ut in eorum definitione ponatur res naturalis quasi genus, ut dicamus quod scutella est lignum figuratum, et similiter quod nomen est vox significativa. Secus autem esset, si nomina artificialium acciperentur, quasi significantia ipsas formas artificiales in abstracto" (EB 4,329,1).

30. Lect.4, n.9 (EB 4,329,2); compare McInerny, *Logic of Analogy*, pp. 54-60 and 157-158, on the various applications of this distinction.

31. On the dating, see Weisheipl, *Friar Thomas*, p. 374, #36, and p. 388, #62.

32. *De regno* I, c.1 (EB 3,595,2).

33. *Sent. Pol.* I, lect.1, n.24 (EB 4,249,3-250,1).

34. For the genesis of language, see Manthey, *Sprachphilosophie*, pp. 86-101.

35. Boethius's commentary on the *Categories* (PL 64,159). The whole doctrine of conventional naming and the technical distinction between first and second imposition Boethius attributes to Porphyry (PL 64,159C, with reference to Porphyry's own commentary on the *Categories*, CAG, IV/1, p.101). Porphyry's sources, in turn, include the Stoics, who also exercised a large influence on grammarians such as Dionysius Thrax. It is from Dionysius that the later Latin grammarians in turn drew many of the starting-points of their studies. The medieval tradition of Latin grammar will be treated below, in Sections 2.1 and 2.2.

36. R.W. Hunt, *Collected Papers*, pp. 18-20.

37. Hunt, *Collected Papers*, p. 21.

38. Hunt, *Collected Papers*, pp. 45-46, 70-71.

39. Abelard, *Logica Ingredientibus*, ed. Geyer, pp. 1-32, particularly pp. 18-19.

40. Peter of Spain, *Tractatus*, ed. L.M. De Rijk, p. 111, lines 24-34.

41. I have in mind, of course, Socrates' 'prophetic' and 'Inspired' etymologies, *Cratylus*, 396d-427d. His strategy in the *Cratylus* is quite complicated and the etymologies serve more than one purpose. Still, they show at least a long reflection on the question of the conventional origin of language.

42. See Hans Aarsleff, *From Locke to Saussure*, in summary form, pp. 278-292.

43. AL II/1-2, page 43, lines 12-13; compare Boethius, p. 70, line 20,

through p. 8, line 1.

44. Lect.6, n.4 (EB 4,331,1-2); compare Ammonius, ed. Verbeke, p. 113, lines 93-94.

45. Lect.6, n.8 (EB 4,331,2), where the reference to the *Cratylus* seems to be from Boethius, not Ammonius.

46. Lect.6, n.8 (EB 4,331,2); compare Ammonius, ed. Verbeke, p. 120, lines 19-23.

47. Lect.7, n.4 (EB 4,331,3). Ammonius gives as examples "vocativam et optativam et interrogativam et imperativam," p. 124, lines 84-85. The list is also found both in Boethius's *minora* commentary (PL 64,295) and in his *maiora* commentary (PL 64,396B). The non-enunciative *orationes* have some resemblances to the Stoic divisions of *lekta* as reported by Diogenes Laertius (VII 66). Leaving aside the Stoic *axiomata*, which correspond to *enunciationes*, the sorts of *lekta* were questions, inquiries, commands, oaths, prayers, suppositions, addresses, and quasi-*axiomata*.

48. Lect.7, n.5 (EB 4,331,3).

49. Lect.7, nn.4-6 (EB 4,331,2-332,1). Compare the illocutionary/perlocutionary distinction in Austin and Searle.

50. Lect.8, n.15 (EB 4,332,3).

51. Lect.2, n.1 (EB 4,327,2).

52. Lect.3, n.1 (EB 4,328,2).

53. *Peri hermeneias*, 16a5.

54. Boethius, AL II/1-2, p. 5, line 6; Moerbeke, p. 41, line 4 respectively.

55. *Peri hermeneias*, 16a7.

56. Boethius, AL II/1-2, p. 5, line 8; Moerbeke, p. 41, line 6, respectively.

57. *Peri hermeneias*, 16a20; Boethius, AL II/1-2, p. 6, line 4; Moerbeke, p. 41, line 19.

58. I, lect.2, n.3 (EB 4,327,3).

59. E.g., Ammonius, p. 32, line 21; p. 37, line 7.

60. The combination of Aristotelian and Augustinian elements yields a doctrine in Thomas which is neither simply Aristotelian nor Augustinian. Thus Colish concludes too strongly when she writes: "For all Thomas's differences from Augustine and Anselm, it is possible to see that he agrees with the basic Augustinian theory of signs on all the important points" (*Mirror of Language*, p. 150).

NOTES FOR SECTION 1.2

1. *Summa theol.* IIIa, q.60, a.6 ad 1 and ad 2 (EB 2,863,1.)

2. *Summa theol.* II-IIae, q.72, a.1 (EB 2,619,2), and q.55, a.4 ad 2 (EB 2,598,1), respectively.

3. *Summa theol.* II-IIae, q.110, a.1 ad 2 (EB 2,667,2).

4. Augustine writes: "Sed omnia verbis conparata paucissima sunt. Verba enim prorsus inter homines obtinuerunt principatum significandi quaecumque animo concipiuntur, si ea quique prodere velit" (CCL 32,34, lines 11-16 in the chapter).

5. *De doctrina* I,i,1.

6. *De doctrina* I,ii,2.

7. The dialectical argument of *De magistro* no only shows the ambivalent interdependence of *res* and *signa*, it also embodies the circles traced by those *signa* which teach *signa*.

8. *De doctrina* II,i,2.

9. *De doctrina* II,ii,3; CCL 32,33, lines 1-3 in the chapter.

10. *De doctrina* II,x,5; CCL 32,41, lines 5-8 in the chapter.

11. R.A. Markus, "St. Augustine on Signs," p.72.

12. B. Darrell Jackson, "The Theory of Signs in St. Augustine's *De doctrina Christiana*," pp.17-26.

13. This predominance of communication is clear not only in the doctrine, but in the rhetorical structure of many of Augustine's works, especially the dialogues.

14. *De doctrina* II,i,2: "sine voluntate atque ullo appetitu significandi" (CCL 32, 32, lines 12-13 in chapter).

15. The sources for Augustine's doctrine of signs are discussed by Markus, pp. 60-64, and Jackson, pp. 29-48. Remarks on the Augustinian doctrine of signs outside *De doctrina Christiana* can be found in Guy H. Allard, "Arts libéraux et langage chez saint Augustin," which concentrates on *De ordine* II,xi,30.

16. *Q.D. De verit.* q.9, a.4 obj.4 and obj.5 (EB 3,59,3-60,1).

17. *De doctrina* II,i,1; CCL 32, 32, lines 5-7 in chapter.

18. *Q.D. De verit.* q.9, a.4 ad 4 and ad 5 (EB 3,60,2).

19. The famous passage is *Confessions* I,viii,13, but the connection of words and the will is felt throughout the whole work.

20. *Q.D. De verit.* q.9, a.4 (EB 3,60,1-2).

21. *Q.D. De verit.* q.9, a.4 (EB 3,60,2).

22. *Summa theol.* Ia, q.107, a.1 (EB 2,337,3).

23. *Summa theol.* Ia, q.107, a.1 ad 2 (EB 2,337,3).

24. *Q.D. De verit.* q.9, a.4 (EB 3,60,1).

25. *De doctrina* II,iii,4: "Nam et odore ungenti dominus, quo perfusi sunt pedes eius, signum aliquod dedicit et sacramento corporis et sanguinis sui per gustatum significavit, quod voluit, et cum mulier tangendo fimbriam vestimenti eius salva facta est, nonnihil significat. Sed innumerabilis multitudo signorum, quibus suas cogitationes homines exerunt, in verbis constituta est. Nam illa signa omnia, quorum genera breviter attigi, potui verbis enuntiare, verba vero illis signis nullo modo possem" (CCL 32,34, lines 16-24 in chapter).

26. *Summa theol.* IIIa, q. 60, a.6 (EB 2,863,1).

27. *Summa theol.* IIIa, q.60, aa.5, 7 (EB 2,862,3 & 2,863,2).

28. *Summa theol.* IIIa, q.60, a.5 ad 1 (EB 2,862,3).

29. *Summa theol.* IIIa, q.60, a.2 (EB 2,862,1).

30. *Summa theol.* IIIa, q.60, a.2 (EB 2,862,1).

31. *Summa theol.* IIIa, q.60, a.1 ad 1 (EB 2,862,1).

32. The relation of Aquinas's account of scriptural meaning to those of his

Dominican contemporaries is provided by Beryl Smalley, *The Study of the Bible in the Middle Ages*, pp.292-308. See more generally C. Spicq. *Esquisse d'une histoire de l'exégèse latin au moyen âge*, pp. 298-316; M.-D. Mailhiot, "La pensée de saint Thomas sur le sens spirituel"; and Henri de Lubac, *Exégèse médiévale*, II/2, pp. 272-301. Aquinas's Scriptural commentaries are considered methodologically by M.-D. Chenu, *Introduction à l'étude de saint Thomas d'Aquin*, pp. 199-225.

33. *Summa theol.* Ia, q.1, a.10 (EB 2,186,3).

34. *Summa theol.* Ia, q.1, a.10 (EB 2,186,3).

35. *Summa theol.* Ia, q.1, a.10 (EB 2,186,3).

36. Smalley, *Study of the Bible*, p.300. De Lubac argues, to the contrary, that Thomas is like Bonaventure in being an exegetical conservative, a traditionalist; *Exégèse médiévale* II,2, p.272. Smalley has since changed her views on the literal sense in Thomas; see her *The Gospels in the Schools*, pp. 257-271, but especially pp. 265-266.

37. *Quodl.* VII, q.6, a.2 (EB 4,479,2-3). In the discussion of the Scriptural senses at the beginning of the *Sentences* commentary, Thomas says no more than that "secundum quod accipitur ipsa veritas fidei, est sensus historicus" (*Super Sent.* I prol., q.1, a.5 (EB 1,3,3), ed. Mandonnet 18).

38. *Super Galat.* c.4, lect.7, n.8 (EB 6,438,2).

39. F.A. Blanche, "Le sens littéral des Ecritures d'après saint Thomas d'Aquin," pp.211-212. Blanche provides a survey of the progressive strengthening of this doctrine among Thomas's commentators; see p.203, fn.2, and p.211, fn.3.

40. P. Synave, "La doctrine de Saint Thomas d'Aquin sur le sens littéral des Ecritures," pp.9-22 and 26. Synave took up the argument again against various opponents in his review of five articles for the *Bulletin Thomiste* (1933).

41. *Q.D. De pot.* q.4, a.1: "hoc enim ad dignitatem divinae Scripturae pertinet, ut sub una littera multos sensus contineat, ut sic et diversis intellectibus hominum conveniat, ut unusquisque miretur se in divina Scriptura posse invenire veritatem quam mente conceperit ..." (EB 3,217,3). The question concerns the physics of duration and so the truth to be had in Scripture is not that of the spiritual senses but that of the literal.

42. *Quodl.* VII, q.6, a.1 ad 5: "auctor principalis sacrae Scripturae est Spiritus sanctus, qui in uno verbo sacrae Scripturi intellexit multo plura quam per expositores sacrae Scripturae exponantur, vel discernantur" (EB 3,479,2).

43. *Q.D. De pot.* q.4, a.1 (EB 3,217,3).

44. *De doctrina Christiana* III,xxvii,28; CCL 32, 100, lines 12-14 in chapter. For the rather flexible understanding of God's authorship in the patristic writers, see Augustin Bea, "Deus auctor Sacrae Scripturae," especially p.28. He concludes that divine authorship is not so much mechanical as intentional.

45. *De doctrina* II,i,2.

46. *Quodl.* VII, q.6, a.1 (EB 3,479,1-2); *Super Galat.* c.4, lect.7 (EB 6,438,1-2); *Summa theol.* Ia, q.1, a.10 (EB 2,186,3).

47. Compare *De doctrina* III,x,14-16, where Augustine is echoing a neo-Platonic rule for interpreting apparent nonsense.

48. This treatment of metaphor is frequently ascribed to Thomas as an innovation in the doctrine of the Scriptural senses. In fact a similar principle already appears in Hugh of St-Victor's large notion of *'historia'*: *Didascalicon* VI,3 (PL 176, 801A-B; ed. Buttimer, p. 115, line 26, to p. 116, line 4), *De scriptoris et scriptoribus sacris*, 3 (PL 175, 11-12).

49. *Summa theol.* Ia, q. 1, a. 10 ad 3 (EB 2,187.1).

50. *Summa theol.* Ia, q. 1, a. 10 ad 3 (EB 2,187,1); cf. *Super Galat.* cap.4, lect.7, n.8 (EB 6,438,2).

NOTES FOR SECTION 1.3

1. *Summa theol.* Ia, q. 34, a.1 (EB 2,237,1).

2. In a series of articles for *Theological Studies* (1946-1949), which were anthologized as *Verbum: Word and Idea in Aquinas*.

3. The method was used to produce a cognitional theory and an epistemology in *Insight*; these were then applied to theological inquiry in *Method in Theology*. Although Lonergan is by choice admirably close to the Thomist text, it is still clear that he is interested in those parts of it which will aid him in thinking his own views on cognition. Hence one gets a preponderant emphasis in *verbum* on the dynamic character of judgment.

4. *De Trinitate* XV,xii,22 (CCL, 50A, 493-494, lines 87-98; quoted in Lonergan, *Verbum*, p. xi). The CCL text differs from that quoted by Lonergan in punctuation and in reading *'ex'* for *'et'* in the phrase "ex quibus gignitur verbum verum" (lines 89-90).

5. Lonergan, *Verbum*, p. xi.

6. Augustine, *Sermo* 119,vii,7 (PL 38,675): "Ecce ego verbum quod vobis loquor, in corde meo prius habui; processit ad te, nec recessit a me: coepit esse in te, quod non erat in te; mansit apud me, cum exiret ad te. Sicut ergo verbum meum prolatum est sensui tuo, nec recessit a corde meo: sic illud Verbum prolatum est sensui nostro, nec recessit a Patre suo. Verbum meum erat apud me et processit in vocem; Verbum Dei erat apud Patrem et processit in carnem. Sed numquid ego possum id facere de voce mea, quod potuit ille de carne sua?" The sermon is an exposition of *John* 1:1-14. See also *Sermo* 288, 3-4; *De doctrina Christiana* I,xii,12; and *In Iohannis evangelium tractatus CXXIV*, tract. 1, ##8-10 (CCL 36,4-6, especially lines 10-39 in #8).

7. Lonergan, *Verbum*, pp. xii-xiii.

8. Lonergan, *Vergum*, pp. 3-11.

9. For example, Lonergan, *Verbum*, p. 2; p. 11, fn. 48; p. 191.

10. *Super Sent.* I, d.27, q.2, a.1 sed contra 1 (EB 1,74,2).

11. *Super Sent.* I, d.27, q.2, a.1 sol. (EB 1,74,2).

12. The *auctoritas* does not appear in the *glossa* printed under the name of Wilifrid Strabo in PL 114,356. But compare the *Catena Aurea* for *John*, c.1, n.1 (EB 5,367,1-5,368,1), and Thomas's *Super Joh.*, c.1, lect.1 (EB 6,229,1).

13. John Damascene, *De Fide orthodoxa*, c.13, ed. Buytaert, p.62.

14. Augustine, *De Trinitate* IX,x; CCL 50,306, lines 8-9.

15. *Super Sent.* I, d.27, q.2, a.1 sol. (EB 1,74,2).

16. Lonergan, *Verbum*, p. 191, fn. 31.

17. *Super Sent.* II, d.11, q.2, a.3 sol. (EB 1,156,2).

18. *Super Sent.* II, d.11, q.2, a.3 sol. (EB 1,156,3).

19. *Q.D. De verit.* q.4, a.1 (EB 3,24,2-325,2).

20. For example, Objection 1 becomes Objection 8, though the reference to Priscian is dropped; Objection 2 becomes Objection 1; Objection 3 becomes Objection 9; and so on.

21. *Q.D. De verit.* q.4, a.1 (EB 3,24,2).

22. *Q.D. De verit.* q.4, a.1 (EB 3,25,1).

23. *Q.D. De verit.* q.4, a.1 ad 5 (EB 3,25,1-2).

24. For example, *Q.D. De verit.* q.4, a.3, "Verbum enim manifestationem quamdam importat" (EB3,26,2); q.9, a.4, "In nobis enim locutio dicitur ipsa manifestatio interioris verbi quod mente concepimus" (EB 3,60,1); q.9, a.5, "Locutio igitur proprie est qua aliquis dicitur cognitionem ignorati, per hoc quod fit ei praesens quod alias erat sibi absens; sicut apud nos patet unus refert alteri aliquid quod ille non vidit, et sic facit ei quodammodo praesentiam per loquelam" (EB 3,60,3).

25. *Quodl.* VII, q.6, a.1 (EB 3,479,1).

26. *Quodl.* I, q.6, a.1 (EB 3,440,3).

27. *Super I Cor.* cap.13 lect.1 n.1: "talis manifestatio dicitur locutio ad similitudinem hominum, qui occulta cordium manifestant alii per voces" (EB 6,385,1); *Super Matt.*, c.11, lect.3: "Manifestatio enim fit per verbum" (EB 6,165,3); Report. Ined. Leon. n.3, c.13, vs.1: "apud nos manifestatio eorum quae unice habemus in corde nostro per signa particularia et distinctia verba" (EB 6,372,3); *Super Hebreos* c.1, lect.1: "expressio, qua insinuetur quod conceptum est; tertio ipsius rei expressae manifestatio, qua res expressa evidens fiat" (EB 6,515,1).

28. Especially *Contra gent.* IV, cc.11-12.

29. *Contra gent.* IV, c.12, n.5 (EB 2,120,3).

30. *Summa theol.* IIIa, q.12, a.3 ad 2 (EB 2,790,1).

31. *Summa theol.* II-IIae, q.91, a.1 (EB 2,645,2).

32. *Summa theol.* II-IIae, q.76, a.1 (EB 2,622,2).

33. *Summa theol.* I-IIae, q.93, a.1 ad 2 (EB 2,477,3)

NOTES FOR THE PROLOGUE TO CHAPTER 2

1. The opposite view may be had in Eugenio Toccafondi, "Il Pensiero di San Tommaso sulle arti liberali," especially p. 639.

2. The references occur in Thomas's *Sentences*-commentary and point only to such commonplace doctrines as might be learned through *florilegia*. Their remaining as explicit citations shows that Thomas does not yet write as economically, as pedagogically, as he will in the later masterworks. For the references to Priscian, see *Super Sent.* I, d.9, q.1, a.1 obj.1 (EB 1,28,1) and *Super Sent.* I, d.27, q.2, a.1 obj.1 (EB 1,74,1). For the reference to Donatus, See *Super Sent.* II, d.23, q.2, a.1 ad 3 (EB 1,190,3).

3. *Super De Trin.* q.5, a.1 obj. 3 (EB 4,532,1).

4. *Super De Trin*. q.5, a.1 ad 3 (EB 4,532,2).

5. *Didascalicon* III, c.3, ed. Buttimer, pp. 52-53.

6. *Super De Trin*. q.5, a.1 ad 3 (EB 4,532,3). For Thomas's remarks on the ideal curriculum see prologue to chapter 4, below.

7. *Super Meta*. IV, lect.2, n.16: "Nam mathematica habet diversas partes, et quamdam principaliter sicut arithmeticam, et quamdam secundario sicut geometriam, et alia consequenter se habent his, sicut perspectiva, astrologia, et musica" (EB 4,419,3). The list adds perspective, of course, and provides an organization of the *quadrivium* which owes more to Aristotle than to the arts traditions.

8. See, for example, *Super De Trin*. q.5, a.1 ad 3 (EB 4,532,3).

9. See the *Indices* in EL 16, p. 219, col. 3.

10. *Indices*, EL 16, p. 220, col. 1.

11. For example, the origin of mathematics is traced to Egypt in *Metaphysics* I,1, 981a15-28, on which see Thomas's commentary, I, lect.1, n.33 (EB 4,392,3). Thomas confirms the speculative bent of the Egyptian priesthood by reference to Scripture: "sicut etiam legitur in *Genesi*." Scripture had figured throughout the traditional myths about the origin of the arts. See, e.g., Cassiodorus, *Institutiones* I,xxviii,4 and II,iii,22, ed. Mynors, p. 71, line 2, and p. 132, line 2; Cassiodorus, *Variae* III,52, ed. Mommsen, pp. 107-108; Bernard Silvestris, *De mundi universitate* I,iii, ed. Barach and Wrobel, p.16, lines 49-54; and Alexander Neckham, *De naturis rerum*, c. 174, ed. Thomas Wright, p. 308.

12. The conflict achieves famous expression in two poems studied at length by Paetow, the *Morale scolarium* of John Garlandus and Henri d'Andeli's *Bataille des set arts*. But the fame of these poems ought not to mislead one into thinking that all of the conflict was reserved for a fight between Orleans and Paris, or that it arose only at such a late date.

13. There is a tendency, evident in Paetow and repeated since, to arrange the teaching of the *trivium* as a linear history, with defined tensions and resolutions. This is a convenient view. But it seems *prima facie* unlikely that anything as universal as the teaching of grammar, rhetoric, and logic, on both elementary and advanced levels, would be governed by laws of linear development. The illusion of the line comes from our lack of sources and our tendency to construe the extant ones as elements of a complete story.

NOTES FOR SECTION 2.1

1. Martianus, *De nuptiis* III, n.223, ed. Dick, p. 82, lines 11-12, and p. 83, line 19.

2. Martianus, *De nuptiis* III, nn.224-226, ed. Dick, pp. 82-83.

3. Martianus, *De nuptiis* III, n.228, ed. Dick, p. 84, line 14

4. Martianus, *De nuptiis* III, n.326, ed. Dick, p. 150, lines 3-4.

5. On the complex relations between grammar and ethics, see Philippe Delhaye, "*Grammatica* et *ethica* au XIIe siècle."

6. Conrad of Hirsau, *Dialogus super auctores*, ed. Huygens, p. 79, lines

238-240 and 242-244. Similar sentiments appear in the passage on pp. 81-82, lines 317-321. The author of the *Accessus* also edited by Huygens exalts grammar over dialectic precisely because of its foundational nature: "Ars autem ista utilis valde est et nulla potest sciri absque ista et magis necessaria [est] quam dialectica, quemadmodum aqua magis necessaria est quam balsamum" (p. 49, lines 40-42).

7. A survey of the materials can be had in Geoffrey L. Bursill-Hall, *A Census of Medieval Latin Grammatical Manuscripts*. Manuscripts of materials from the first pole are described by Bursill-Hall in "Teaching Grammars of the Middle Ages: Notes on the Manuscript Tradition." A list of texts important for speculative grammar before the thirteenth-century *modistae* is given by Jan Pinborg, *Die Entwicklung der Sprachtheorie im Mittelalter*, pp. 323-327.

8. Reprinted in R. W. Hunt, *Collected Papers* (hereafter *CP*), pp. 1-38 and 39-94. The other essays in the same volume, though not so directly concerned with the general development, nonetheless illuminate it on many points.

9. Hunt, "Studies on Priscian, I," pp. 214-215 in the original pagination; *CP*, pp. 21-22: "This preoccupation with questions of logic is the distinguishing mark of the early twelfth century glossators. They were not engaged in teaching the rudiments.... [W]hilst theoretically they confined grammar to the correct joining of words according to rules and usage, and reserved the investigation of truth and falsity for dialectic, they were not in practice content to limit themselves in this way."

10. Hunt, "Studies on Priscian, I," p. 220; *CP*, p. 27.

11. Hunt, "Studies on Priscian, I," p. 215; *CP*, p. 22.

12. Hunt, "Studies on Priscian, II," p. 22; *CP*, p. 60.

13. Hunt, "Studies on Priscian, II," p. 39; *CP*, p. 77: "[T]he two main points that distinguish the work of these glossators from their predecessors — the development of syntax and the reapplication of the study of authors — first appeared in [Ralph of Beauvais's] work."

14. Hunt, "Studies on Priscian, II," p. 39; *CP*, p. 77.

15. G. L. Bursill-Hall, *Speculative Grammars of the Middle Ages*, pp. 26-31. Compare the synopsis in Pinborg, *Logik und Semantik im Mittelalter: Ein Uberblick*, pp. 13-18, 55-126. An earlier general account is given by Heinrich Roos, *Die Modi Significandi des Martinus de Dacia*, pp. 92-99 and 99-107, which takes the account up to Martin himself.

16. There is now an edition of Peter Helias's commentary on *Priscianus minor* by James Tolson.

17. This account will certainly be amplified and probably altered by the publication of complete texts of works from the period 1140-1270.

18. Weisheipl, *Friar Thomas*, p. 11.

19. *Super Sent.* I, d.27, q.2, a.1 obj.1 (EB 1,74,1; Mandonnet 1:653).

20. *Institutiones* VIII,i,1, ed. Hertz, *Grammatici Latini* (hereafter *GL*), II, p. 369, lines 5-6.

21. *Commentarius in Artem Donati*, Proemium, ed. Keil, *GL*, IV, p. 405, lines 14-15: "verbum dictum est eo, quod verberato aere motu linguae haec pars orationis inventa sit."

22. *Explanationum in Artem Donati*, "De Partibus Orationis", ed. Keil, *GL*, IV, p. 488, lines 22-24: "Verbum dicit ab eo, quo aerem verberat vox. sed dicis, et ut aliae partes exprimuntur, vox aerem verbeat ut dicamus Romam."

23. For his influence, Curtius, *European Literature*, pp. 22, 192, 199, and so on. For the manuscripts, see Keil's introduction, *GL*, IV, pp. xlix-1, xliv, and the apparatus, p. 486, line 1. Keil uses the earliest manuscripts of the *Explanationum*, which he dates to the eighth, ninth, and tenth centuries (pp. xxxii-xxxiii, xliv, xlix). He also remarks on the persistent confusion in the manuscripts between 'Servius' and 'Sergius' (p. lii). Keil regards the *Explanationum* as one of the many paraphrases of Servius (p. liii).

24. Isidore, *Etymologiae* I,ix,1: "Verbum dictum eo, quod verberato aere sonat, vel quod haec pars frequenter in oratione versetur" (Lindsay, lines 17-18); III,xx,2: "Vox est aer spiritu verberatus, unde et verba sunt nuncupata" (Lindsay, lines 23-24).

25. *Super Sent*. I, d.9, q.1, a.1 obj.1 (EB 1,28,1; ed. Mandonnet I, p. 245). A similar discussion occurs in Bonaventure's comment on the first Book of *Sentences*, d.9, art. unicus dub.1. For an earlier example, see the *Tractatus Anagnini*, ed. De Rijk, in *Logica Modernorum*, II, pp. 315-317, where there are several Trinitarian examples involving *'alius'*.

26. Priscian, *Institutiones* II,iv and II,vi, *GL*, II, p. 55, lines 13-29 and p. 61, lines 9-20, respectively.

27. See, for example, *Notulae super Priscianum minore Magistri Jordani*, ed. Mary Sirridge, pp. 16-17, 18-19; Radulphus Brito, *Quaestiones super Priscianum minorem*, eds. Enders and Pinborg, pp. 255-256, 300-303, 303-304. The way in which a pronoun indicates a substance was treated earlier by Peter Helias in his commentary on *Priscianus minor*, ed. Tolson, pp. 55-56, with reference to the *Institutiones* XIII,31.

28. *Super Sent*. II, d.23, q.2, a.1 ad 3 (EB 1,190,3 ed. Mandonnet II, p. 574).

29. Donatus, *Ars grammatica*, III,6, ed. Keil, *GL*, IV, p. 402, lines 5-6; Isidore, *Etymologiae* I,xxvii,26, ed. Lindsay, lines 21-22.

30. *De nuptiis* III, n.230, ed. Dick, p. 85, lines 10-12.

31. Marius Victorinus, *Ars grammatica* I, 4-5, ed. Mariotti, p. 65; Sergius, *Expl. in Donatem*, Proemium, ed. Keil, *GL*, IV, p. 486, lines 15-16; Cassiodorus, *De artibus* c.3 (PL 70, 1192); Augustine, *De ordine*, II,xii,35 (CCL 29,127); see the discussion in Baur's edition of Gundissalinus, p. 275, fn.1.

32. *Etymologiae* I,v,1, ed. Lindsay, lines 3-4; cf. I,ii,1, ed. Lindsay, lines 14-15: "Prima grammatica, id est loquendi peritia."

33. *De divisione philosophiae*, ed. Baur, p. 44, lines 17-18: "Grammatica est ars vel sciencia gnara recte loquendi, recte scribendi." Again, *De divisione philosophiae*, ed. Baur, p. 45, lines 5-7: "Grammatica igitur est ars vel sciencia gnara i.e. perita recte loquendi et recte scribendi: recte i.e. sine vicio soloecismi et barbarismi."

34. Ed. Thurot, *Notices et extraits*, pp. 121-122: "Grammatica est scientia gnara recte scribendi et recte loquendi.... Huius ... artis officium est litteras congrue in sillabas, sillabas in dictiones, dictiones in orationes ordinare et easdem competenter pronunciare ad evitationem soloecismi et barbarismi." For a comparison of Peter's definition with that from Gundissalinus, see Hunt, "The Introduction to the 'Artes,' " *CP*, pp. 118-125. Hunt suggests that both Gundissalinus and Helias were drawing upon material from Chartres.

35. *De grammatica*, ed. Baron, p. 76, lines 5-7.

36. *Q.D. De verit.* q.24, a.6 (EB 3,145,2).

37. *Summa theol.* I-IIae, q.56, a.3 (EB 2,424,3).

38. Compare *Contra gent.* IV, c.70, n.2 (EB 2,142,3); *Sent. Ethic.* II, lect.6, n.11 (EB 4,158,3); *Q.D. De malo* q.3, a.1 (EB 3,285,3); *Super Phys.* II, lect.14, n.3 (EB 4,75,3).

39. See *Q.D. De malo* q.3, a.6 (EB 3,289,1); *Super Meta.* V, lect.12, n.14 (EB 4,436,3); IV, lect.3, n.1 (EB 4,419,3); *Summa theol.* I-IIae, q.94 a.1 (EB 2,479,1); *Super Peri.* I, lect.7, n.6 (EB 4,332,1); *Sent. Ethic.* II, lect.4, n.2 (EB 4,157,1).

40. Donatus's *minor* treats of the eight "partes orationis," which Servius defends as the only proper object of grammar ("quae specialiter ad grammaticos pertinent"; *Commentarius in Artem Donati*, Proemium, ed. Keil, *GL* IV, p. 405, lines 10-11). Donatus's *major* treats of twenty-one topics. Priscian's teaching is spread over eighteen Books, each containing a number of chapters. Priscian enumerates topics in his dedicatory letter, but does not give a reasoned account of the division.

41. Martianus, *De nuptiis* III, nn.231, 326, ed. Dick, p. 86, lines 5-13, and pp. 149-150, lines 20-23.

42. Isidore, *Etymologiae*, I,v,4, ed.Lindsay, lines 14-19.

43. *De divisione philosophiae*, ed. Baur, p. 47, line 20.

44. According to Baur, *De divisione philosophiae*, pp. 47-48; cf. p. 277.

45. Hugh of St-Victor, *De grammatica*, in *Opera propaedeutica*, ed. Roger Baron, pp. 75-156, specifically pp. 76-77. Hugh writes: "De numero partium grammatice artis alii ut libuit et visum est diffinierunt. Michi vero interim commodius videtur viginti duas enumerare et in hoc numero partium grammatice artis summam diffinire" (p. 76, lines 23-26).

46. Thurot, *Notices et extraits*, p. 132, from the *Summam in Priscianum*: "Partes huius artis sunt quatuor: quarum nomina quoniam non habemus, dicatur prima pars scientia de litteris, secunda, de sillabis, tertia, de dictionibus, quarta, de oratione."

47. Thurot, *Notices et extraits*, p. 132.

48. Thurot, *Notices et extraits*, p. 132.

49. Thurot, *Notices et extraits*, p. 133.

50. Thurot, *Notices et extraits*, p. 133, where the titles from Donatus may be reversed.

51. *Doctrinale*, ed. Reichling, pp. 7-8, lines 11-23.

52. Robert Kilwardby, *Comm. Prisc. minor*, ed. Fredborg et al., pp. 29-30.

53. Robert Kilwardby, *Comm. Prisc. minor*, ed. Fredborg et al., p. 30.
54. Robert Kilwardby, *Comm. Prisc. minor*, ed. Fredborg et al., p. 37.
55. Robert Kilwardby, *Comm. Prisc. minor*, ed. Fredborg et al., p. 42.
56. *Super De hebd.* lect. 5, n.2 (EB 6,529,3).
57. *Super De anima.* II, lect.11, n.4 (EB 4,348,2); *Super Peri* I, lect.2, n.3 (EB 4,327,3).
58. *Super Post. An.* I, lect.4 (EB 4,275).
59. *Super Meta.* IV, lect.1, n.19 (EB 4,419,1).
60. *Summa theol.* I-II, q. 56, a.3 (EB 2,424,3); *Q.D. De virt. comm.* q.1, a.7, ad 5 (EB 3,406,2); *Super Sent.* III, d.33, q.2, a.4 obj.3 (EB 1,385,2); *Q.D. De malo* q.1, a.5 (EB 3,274,3).
61. *De fallaciis* 3 (EB 6,576,1), with the caveat about the authenticity of this work noted above in 1.P, note 1.
62. *Sent. Ethic.* VI, lect.7, n.17 (EB 4,197,1); *Super De caus.* proem, n.8 (EB 4,507,1). See the fuller discussion of these passages in 4.P, below.
63. *Super Sent.* IV, d.38, q.2, a.3 ad 2 (EB 1,616,1); *Super Sent.* I, d.4, q.1, a.2 ad 1 (EB 1,16,1); *Summa theol.* I, q.39, a.8 ad 1 (EB 2,244,2), q.41, a.1 ad 3 (EB 2,246,1); *Q.D. De pot.* q.7, a.10 ad 8 (EB 3,248,1).
64. See the range of examples in the *Index Thomisticus*, II: Concordantia Prima, vol. 10, *s.v.* "grammatice."

NOTES FOR SECTION 2.2

1. Aristotle, *Peri hermeneias*, 16b6.
2. The verb *pros-semaino* or one of its forms occurs twice in the *Topics* (134b18, 140a19-20) and once in the *Rhetoric* (1374a12). It occurs frequently in *Peri hermeneias*, especially at 20a3-15. In all of these cases, the words seem to mean implication or suggestion.
3. *Peri hermeneias*, 16a8.
4. Anselm, *De grammatico*, ed. F. S. Schmitt, I, p. 159, lines 10-11, and 161, lines 12-13,18; compare the remarks by D. P. Henry, *Commentary on De Grammatico*, pp. 263-265. For Abelard, see *Editio super Aristotelem de Interpretatione*, ed. Mario Dal Pra in *Scritti di Logica*, pp. 73-76; and Abelard, *Dialectica*, ed. L. M. De Rijk, pp. 111-117, to which compare the remarks by Jolivet, "Comparaison des théories du language chez Abélard et chez les Nominalistes du XIVe siècle."
5. See Pinborg, *Entwicklung der Sprachtheorie*, pp. 60-66; and Bursill-Hall, *Speculative Grammars*, pp. 26-36.
6. For the difficulties of this dating, see Pinborg, *Entwicklung der Sprachtheorie*, pp. 95-96.
7. The dates are from Pinborg, *Entwicklung der Sprachtheorie*, pp. 67-69, 77-78, and 87, respectively.
8. Pinborg writes: "Thomas von Aquin kennt zwar das Ternar 'modus essendi, intelligendi, und significandi,' er wendet aber nicht die modale Definition der Wortclassen an (z. B. in seinen Quodlibet aus der Zeit um 1270). Ich glaube, dass man Manthey gegenuber Grabmann Recht geben

muss: Thomas von Aquin hat die eigentlichen modistischen Texte nicht gekannt" (*Entwicklung der Sprachtheorie*, p. 69, fn. 19).

9. *Super Peri* I, lect.4, nn.7 and 12-14 (EB 4,329,1-3).

10. *De ente* c.3, n.31 (EB 3,585,3). Compare nn.36, 43, 44, 48.

11. The example occurs, for instance, in the "Milan glosses," ed. B. Geyer, *Peter Abaeleards Philosophische Schriften*, II, pp. 366-367; and in the *Dialectica*, p. 122, lines 22-25.

12. *Super De hebd.* lect.2, n.22 (EB 4,539,2).

13. *Super De hebd.* lect.2, n.22 (EB 4,539,3).

14. *Super De hebd.* lect.2, n.23 (EB 4,539,3-540,1).

15. *De ente* c.4, nn.54-65 (EB 3,586,1-2).

16. The fourth set of *quodlibetales* is dated by Synave at Christmas 1270, and by Mandonnet, Glorieux, and Gorce as Easter 1271. See Weisheipl, *Friar Thomas*, p. 367.

17. *Quodl.* IV, q.9, a.2 (EB 3,460,3 - 461,1). Reference will be had to this passage until otherwise noted.

18. There is a similar argument with regard to tense differences in *Q. D. De verit.* q.1, a.5 (EB 3,4,1): "Cursus enim Socratis est res una, sed anima quae componendo et dividendo cointelligit tempus, et dicitur in III *De anima*, diversimode intelligit cursum Socratis ut praesentem, praeteritum, et futurum; et secundum hoc conceptiones diversas format, in quibus diversae veritates inveniuntur." The reference is to *De Anima* III, 6, 431b1-7, for which see Thomas's commentary *ad loc.*, III, lect. 11, nn.4-6 (EB 4,365,2).

19. *Super Sent.* I, d.22, q.1, a.2 (EB 1,60,3 - 61,1); *Contra gent.* I, cc.30-32 (EB 2,9,1-3); and *Summa theol.* Ia, q.13, a.5.

20. *Contra gent.* I, cc.30-32 occur in the preparation (cc.30-36) for the long description of God (cc.37-102) which begins with the tenet of divine goodness.

21. *Contra gent.* I, c.30, n.3 (EB 2,9,1).

22. *Contra gent.* I, c.32 (EB 2,9,2).

23. *Contra gent.* I, c.32 nn.2-3 and 7 (EB 2,9,2-3), respectively.

NOTES TO SECTION 2.3

1. The most detailed treatment of Thomas's relation to classical rhetoric is in E. K. Rand, *Cicero in the Courtroom of St. Thomas Aquinas*. Rand calls *De inventione* "a little gospel of rhetoric for St. Thomas" and concludes that Cicero is in general "a weighty and respected source" for him (p. 44). Again: "But [Thomas] also judges the domains of rhetoric and ethics, those in which Cicero, though taught by the wise of many schools, can also speak for himself. Then it is that St. Thomas listens with respect" (p. 64). Rand was chiefly interested in Thomas's explicit citations of Cicero and not in Thomas's thought on the *ars* of rhetoric. A constant respect for ancient authority is not, at least in Thomas, the same as approbation of the whole of an ancient teaching. For a complete list of citations to Cicero in Thomas, arranged by genre of work, see Clemens Vansteenkiste, "Cicerone nell'opera di

S. Tommaso." Vansteenkiste concludes (pp. 378-379) that Thomas knew at first hand the *Somnium Scipionis, De natura deorum, Paradoxa, Disputationes Tusculanae, De officiis,* and the *'Rhetorica',* that is, the *Ad Herennium* and the *De inventione* treated as one.

2. *Super Coloss.* c.2, n.1 (EB 6,476,2).

3. *Contra impugn.* pars 3, c.5 obj.4 (EB 3,550,1).

4. *Contra impugn.* pars 3, c.5 resp. (EB 3,550,2).

5. *Contra impugn.* pars 3, c.5 resp. (EB 3,550,2).

6. *Summa theol.* II-IIae, q.48, a.unicus (EB 2,591,1).

7. *Summa theol.* II-IIae, q.49, a.4 obj.3 (EB 2,591,3).

8. *Summa theol.* II-IIae, q.49, a.4 ad 3 (EB 2,592,1).

9. *Sent. Ethic.* I, lect.3, n.5 (EB 4,145,3).

10. *Super Sent.* III, d.33, q.3, a.1d (EB 1,387,2).

11. *Super I Cor.* c.1, n.3 (EB 5,498,2); cf. *De fall.* c.3 (EB 6,576,1), *Post. Thren.* c.1, n.1 (EB 6,122,3), *Contra impugn.* pars 3, c.5, resp. ad 3 & ad 4 (EB 3,550,2-3).

12. *Summa theol.* II-IIae, q.177, a.1 obj.1 (EB 2,741,1). The reference is to *De doctrina christiana* IV,xii,27, but Augustine is quoting directly, if anonymously, from Cicero's *Orator* xxi,69.

13. *Summa theol.* II-IIae, q.177, a.1 ad 1 (EB 2,741,1).

14. *Sent. Ethic.* I, lect.18, n.10 (EB 4,154,2); cf. *Super Sent.* IV, d.16, q.3, a.1 sol.1 ad 1 (EB 1,524,1).

15. "Exhortatio," *Super II Tim.* cap.2, lect.2 (EB 6,503,2); "enthymema" and "exemplum," *Super Post. An.* I, lect.1, n.12 (EB 4,274,1); "laudes et vituperia," e.g., *Sent. Ethic.* I, lect.16, n.10 (EB 4,153,1).

16. *Super Sent.* IV, d.15, q.4, a.3 and ad 2 (EB 1,516,1-2); *Super II Tim.* cap.2 lect.1 (EB 6,502,2); *Super Matt.* cap.6 lect.3 (EB 6,149,3); Report. Ined. Leon. n.2 cap.6 vs.9 (EB 6,363,2-364,1). In applying rhetoric to prayer, Aquinas is only following the much more technical elaboration of William of Auxerre's *Rhetorica divina.* See Caplan, "Classical and Mediaeval Theory," in *Of Eloquence,* pp. 109-110.

17. *Summa theol.* III, q.30, a.4 (EB 2,815,1). Such rhetorical considerations appear as well in the short *reportationes* of Thomas's homilies on the *Ave Maria.*

18. See *Summa theol.* IIIa, q.30, a.4 (EB 2,815,1): "reddere mentem ejus attentam."

19. *Summa theol.* II-IIae, q.1, a.6 (EB 2,525,1). The reference is to the *Ad Herennium* IV,xix,26.

20. *Summa theol.* I-IIae, q.7, a.2 obj. 3 (EB 2,367,2).

21. *Summa theol.* I-IIae, q.7, a.2 ad 3 (EB 2,367,2).

22. *Super Peri* I, lect.7, n.6 (EB 4,332,1). Thomas's remarks on poetry are famously derogatory and he does not follow Gundissalinus in making it a liberal art.

23. *Super Phys.* VIII, lect.5, n.3 (EB 4,129,1).

24. *Summa theol.* Ia, q.83, a.1 (EB 2,306,2).

25. *Super Post. An.* I, lect.1, n.9 (EB 4,273,3).

26. Respectively *Super I Cor.* cap.2 lect.1 (EB 5,500,2); *Sent. Ethic.* I, lect.3, n.5 (EB 4,145,3).

27. *Super Meta.* III, lect.2, n.8 (EB 4,409,2); IV, lect.4, nn.3-4 (EB 4,420,2).

28. *Super Meta.* III, lect.2, n.8 (EB 4,409,2); *Super Phys.* III, lect.8, n.1 (EB 4,81,2), and VIII, lect.5, n.3 (EB 4,129,1); *Super De anima* I, lect.1, n.15 (EB 6,6,1); *Super Sent.* I, d.17, q.2, a.3 ad 4 (EB 1,48,1).

29. *Super Post. An.* I, lect.1, n.6 (EB 4,273,1-2), and lect.20, n.6 (EB 4,283,2); *Summa theol.* II-IIae, q.48, art.unicus (EB 2,591,1).

30. *Super Post. An.* I, lect.13, n.7 (EB 4,279,3).

31. *Super De anima* I, lect.1, n.2 (EB 6,6,1).

32. *De inventione* I,xv,20. The whole section I,19-26 is devoted to the construction of the *exordium*.

33. *Ad Herennium* I,iv,7.

34. *De nuptiis* V, #545,: "ut attentum, ut docilem, ut benivolum faciat auditorem," ed. Dick, p. 272, lines 5-6.

35. *Etymologiae* II,7,2: "ut benivolum, docilem, vel adtentum auditorem faciamus," ed. Lindsay 1ine 25.

36. *Summa dicataminis* II,lxviii, cited in C. B. Faulhaber, "Guido Faba," in *Medieval Eloquence*, p. 97.

37. *Postilla super Isaiam*, prol. (EB 5,51,1; EL 28,3); *Postilla super Jeremiam*, prol. (EB 5,96,1); *Postilla super Threnos* (EB 5,122,2).

38. Guy-H. Allard, "Le 'Contra Gentiles' et le modèle rhétorique," p. 242: "[L]e *Contra Gentiles* met sans cesse en relief la possibilité, l'utilité et l'efficacité des moyens qu'ils conseille à quiconque recherche le veritable Bonheur."

39. Allard, "Modèle rhétorique," p. 249: "Etant donné que le *Contra Gentiles* supporte bien la comparaison avec le discours délibératif, pourquoi ne pas y voir un indice que le *lieu* de sa stratégie est le domaine civil, mieux qui'il est une réponse à une menace sociale?"

40. See the various essays in Caplan, *Of Eloquence*, especially pp. 79-92, 93-104, 105-134, 135-159. For Aquinas' doctrine, see J. Walsh, "St. Thomas on Preaching"; O'Daniel, "Thomas Aquinas as Preacher." Caplan offers a fourteenth- or fifteenth-century treatise on preaching which claims to be based on a similar work by Thomas; see *Of Eloquence*, pp. 52-78, with the claim in the title, p. 52.

NOTES FOR SECTION 2.4

1. Joseph de Ghellinck, *Le mouvement théologique du XIIe siècle*, Chapter 5, pp. 416-499.

2. For example, *De nuptiis* V, #441, ed. Dick, p. 216, line 18 - p. 217, line 15.

3. Martianus, *De nuptiis* V, #445, ed. Dick, p. 219, lines 4-6.

4. *De nuptiis* V, #461-463, ed. Dick, p. 228, line 16 - p. 230, line 11.

5. *De nuptiis* V, #464, ed. Dick, p. 230, lines 12-18.

6. *De nuptiis* V, #473, ed. Dick, p. 236, lines 23.

7. Caplan, "Classical and Mediaeval Theory," in *Of Eloquence*, p. 107, with the references there.

8. See Brian Lawn, *I Quesiti Salernitani*, pp. 19-33.

9. Hugh of St-Victor, for instance, adopts the question-and-answer form in his *De grammatica*, but uses it only as a pedagogical device for the exposition of what is already known. The *quaestio disputata*, in contrast, requires a discovery. One needs to distinguish, then, between the pedagogical questions of the dialogues in Alcuin, Scotus Eriugena, or Hugh, and the argumentative questions of the disputations in the law books. The dialogues of Anselm might constitute a separate class.

10. Chenu, of course, provides a general sketch of the *quaestio* in his *Introduction*, pp. 71-81 and 241-245. The rhetoric of the *quaestio* itself has been described elegantly by Josef Pieper in his *Hinführung zu Thomas von Aquin*, pp. 109-126; compare the English, *Guide to Thomas Aquinas*, pp. 75-88. There are also studies of parts of the *quaestio*. One of the best is Leo Elders, "Structure et fonction de l'argument 'Sed contra.' "

11. M.-D. Chenu, *Introduction*, pp. 76-77. For instances of editing in the related genre of the *quodlibetales*, see P. Glorieux, "Le quodlibet et ses procédés rédactionnels."

12. Peter Abelard, *Sic et Non*, Prologue, ed. Boyer and McKeon, lines 330-334 (fasc. 2, p. 103). Abelard himself points to the legal antecedents. Speaking of the importance of context, he writes, "Haec autem institutionibus ecclesiasticorum decretorum vel canonum maxime distingui necesse est" (Prologue, ed. Boyer/McKeon, lines 184-185, fasc.1, p. 96).

13. Quoted in Chenu, *Introduction*, p. 72, fn. 2. One thinks also of John of Salisbury's criticism of the overzealous use of dialectic in the *Metalogicon*, e.g., II, cc.9-12.

14. On Abelard's sources for the comparison of authors, see J. de Ghellinck, *Le mouvement théologique du XII siècle*, pp. 118-148; Ermenegildo Bertola, "I precedenti storici del metodo del 'Sic et Non' di Abelardo"; and Jean Jolivet, *Arts de langage*, pp. 239-241.

15. For an interpretation of Abelard's project along these lines, see Jean Jolivet, *Arts du langage*, pp. 238-250.

16. *Sic et Non*, Prologue, ed. Boyer/McKeon, lines 185-187, p. 96.

17. *Sic et Non*, Prologue, ed. Boyer/McKeon, lines 189-191, p. 96.

18. See the quotation from Augustine's *Contra Faustum* on canonical and uncanonical texts in Abelard's Prologue, ed. Boyer/McKeon, lines 282-290, p. 101. Note that the passage ends with a plea for hermeneutical toleration.

19. *Quodl.* IV, q.9, a.3 (EB 3,461,1). On dispute in Thomas generally, see Mirko Skarica Zuñiga, "La 'disputatio' en Tomás de Aquino."

20. *Quodl.* IV, q.9, a.3 (EB 3,461,1).

21. Michel Corbin has argued at great length that there is a decisive change in Thomas's thought on this point, which ends with something like Melchior Cano's use of texts as historical *loci*. See his *Le chemin de la théologie chez Thomas d'Aquin*, pp. 807-854.

22. See Jerome, *Epistula* 53, 8 (PL 22, 545): "omnesque leges dialecticae"; Gregory, *Moralia in Job*, e.g., XVI,viii,12 and xliii,55 (CCL 143A, pp. 805, 831).

23. *In Job* cap.9 (EB 5,13,2; EL lines 54-59); cap.12 (EB 5,19,1; EL lines 287-295).

24. *In Job* cap.7 (EB 5,12,1-2; EL lines 524-527); cap. 10 (EB 5,17,1; EL lines 423-425).

25. *In Job* cap.13 (EB 5,20,2; EL lines 302-306).

26. *In Job* cap.6 (EB 5,10,2-3; EL lines 301-325).

27. *In Job* cap.13 (EB 5,20,2; EL lines 307-310).

28. *In Job* cap.34 (EB 5,40,2; EL lines 390-399).

29. *In Job* cap.21 (EB 5,27,3; EL lines 30-36).

30. *In Job* cap.22 (EB 5,28,3-29,1; EL lines 9-33): "ut ex mutua collatione aliquid occultum indagetur," "ut fiat collatio datorum et acceptorum." Compare cap.23 (EB 5,30,1; EL lines 50-51): "ut plenius veritatem intelligant."

31. *In Job* cap.33 (EB 5,38,2; EL lines 99-130).

32. *In Job* cap.39 (EB 5,46,3; EL lines 339-340).

NOTES FOR SECTION 2.5

1. *Super Post An*. I, lect.1, n.2-3 (EB 4,273,2). A discussion of the definition and a collation with similar definitions can be had in Robert W. Schmidt, *The Domain of Logic according to St. Thomas Aquinas*, pp. 3-4, and pp. 3-9 generally. See also L. Lachance, "Saint Thomas dans l'histoire de la logique," pp. 71-77, and Battista Mondin, "La logica di S. Tommaso D'Aquino," pp. 263-265. Lachance was hampered by the lack of materials for the medieval Aristotelian tradition; Mondin reworks the citations in Schmidt.

2. Maria Teresa Beonio-Brocchieri Fumagalli, *The Logic of Abelard*, p. 23, fn.6.

3. For an excellent survey of the record of Boethius's influence, see Osmund Lewry, "Boethian Logic in the Medieval West."

4. Beonio-Brocchieri Fumagalli, pp. 7-8. A longer list is given by De Rijk, *Logica Modernorum* I, pp. 20-23, and by Gilson, *Christian Philosophy in the Middle Ages*, p. 627, fn. 95. See, more recently, Sten Ebbesen, "Ancient Scholastic Logic as the Source of Medieval Scholastic Logic," CHLMP, especially pp. 105-109. The additional items are the Boethian commentaries on the *Peri hermeneias* and a second tract on categorical syllogisms.

5. Gilson, *Christian Philosophy*, p. 627, fn. 95.

6. See the summary by Minio-Paluello in his edition of the *Ars disserendi, Twelfth-Century Logic* I, xxiv-xxxiv.

7. Beonio-Brocchieri Fumagalli, *Logic of Abelard*, pp. 8-10.

8. Beonio-Brocchieri Fumagalli, *Logic of Abelard*, p. 23, fn. 6.

9. De Rijk argues from a survey of twelfth-century compendia that "[e]ven when from about 1140 the *logica nova* was drawn into the discussion, interest was focused only on those parts of new logic that concern

syllogistics ... and sophistical argumentations ... in particular" (*Logica Modernorum* II/1, p. 162).

10. De Rijk, *Logica Modernorum* I, pp. 14-18 and 19-20. See also Kretzmann, *William of Sherwood's Introduction to Logic*, pp. 16-20, which discusses especially the hypothesis that Sherwood was the first analyst of the *proprietates terminorum*.

11. See Jean Jolivet, "Comparaison des théories du langage"; recall the discussion in Section 2.4, above.

12. Martianus, *De nuptiis* IV, #376; ed. Dick, p. 155, lines 11-12.

13. Rabanus Maurus, *De institutione clericorum* III,20 (PL 107, 397C).

14. See the introduction by Cora Lutz, *Annotationes in Marcianum*, xxiii. Eriugena does not stress the superiority of dialectic in his glosses, however, perhaps because he considers it a common-place.

15. Beonio-Brocchieri Fumagalli, *Logic of Abelard*, p. 22.

16. Adam Balsamiensis Parvipontanus, *Ars disserendi*, ii-v, ed. Minio-Paluello, pp. 3-5.

17. *Ars disserendi*, vii, ed. Minio-Paluello, p. 5, lines 26-28.

18. William Shyreswood, *Introductiones in logicam* I,1, ed. Kretzmann, p. 21.

19. Isidore, *Etymologiae* II,xxii,1, ed. Lindsay, lines 15-19.

20. Boethius considers a number of different definitions for '*dialectica*' in his commentary on Cicero's *Topics* at PL 64,1045A-1047D. See also Stump's translation of Boethius's *De topicis diferentiis*, pp. 218-226.

21. Alcuin, *De dialectica* 1: "Dialectica est disciplina rationalis quaerendi, diffiniendi et disserendi, etiam et vera a falsi discernendi potens" (PL 101,952D-953A).

22. Rabanus Maurus, *De institutione clericorum* III,20: "Dialectica est disciplina vera et a falsi discernendi potest" (PL 107,397C).

23. De Rijk, *Logica Modernorum* II/1, pp. 162-165.

24. Gundissalinus, *De divisione philosophiae*: "logica ratio disserendi diligens, i.e., sciencia disputandi integra," which includes both *invencio* and *iudicium*, Baur, p. 69, lines 14-16.

25. *De divisione philosophiae*: "[S]et quia pars quarta vehemencioris probacionis est, ideo omnibus antecellit sublimitate et dignitate. nam per totam logicam principaliter non intenditur nisi pars quarta. relique vero partes non sunt invente nisi per quartam," ed. Baur, p. 71, line 22, to p. 72, line 2.

26. See the citation, "Secundum Alfarabium ...," at *De divisione philosophiae*, ed. Baur, p. 71, line 16.

27. *De divisione philosophiae*: "racionacio autem habet tres species: dialecticam scilicet, que est sciencia colligendi per probabilia, — et demonstrativam, que est sciencia colligendi per se nota, — et sophistica, que est sciencia colligendi per ea, que videntur esse et non sunt," ed. Baur, p. 76, lines 11-15.

28. *De divisione philosophiae*, ed. Baur, p. 73, lines 7-8: "Propriam est thopice fidem facere rei dubie racionibus probabilibus, veris vel verisimilibus."

29. *De divisione philosophiae*, ed. Baur, p. 72, lines 10-23.

30. *De divisione philosophiae*, ed. Baur, p. 72, lines 5-10.

31. Shyreswood, *Introductiones* IV,1, tr. Kretzmann, p. 69. Curiously, Shyreswood never really treats demonstration here, though he devotes many pages to dialectic.

32. Schmidt, *Domain of Logic*, p. 13.

33. *Super Post. An.* Proem., n.1 (EB 4,273,2).

34. In assuming this principle and in dividing according to the works of the Organon, Thomas seems to set aside the traditional divisions. In fact his division of "intellectus," based on Aristotelian noetic, will end with many of the traditional schemata which divide the "verba." See, e.g., the division tacitly associated with the six works of the Organon in Martianus, *De nuptiis* IV, #338, ed. Dick, p. 155, line 18 - p.156, line 1. Compare [Ps?-] Augustine, *De dialectica* IV, ed. Pinborg, p. 86. See also Lachance, "Saint Thomas dans l'histoire de la logique," pp. 77-88.

35. *Super Post. An.* Proem., n.4 (EB 4,273,2): "quid est res."

36. *Super Post. An.* Proem., n.5 (EB 4,273,2). The association of demonstration with necessity and certitude, and of dialectic with probability, faith, and opinion, is found in Gundissalinus, *De divisione philosophiae*, ed. Baur, p. 72, lines 7-10, 23. But its real source, of course, is Aristotle.

37. The division of the "ratio disserendi" into "iudicativa" and "inventiva" can be found in Boethius, *De topicis differentiis*, (PL 64,1173C).

38. For a more complex treatment of the degrees of intellectual conviction, see *Q.D. De verit.* q.14, a.1 (EB 3,91,1-92,1).

39. *Super Post. An.* Proem., n.6 (EB 4,273,3).

40. *Super Post. An.* Proem., n. 6 (EB 4,273,3).

41. *Super Post. An.* I, lect.13, n.1 (EB 4,279,1-2); lect.35, n.1-2 (EB 4,292,2-3). Compare Schmidt, *Domain of Logic*, pp. 38-39.

42. Schmidt, *Domain of Logic*, p. 40. Jean Isaac has tried, in his "La notion de dialectique chez saint Thomas," to construct a synthetic picture of dialectic which makes of it both "la science logique des méthodes inventives" and "l'art, également logique, de les appliquer en tout domaine" (p. 482). Such a collation of texts does not seem to do justice to the diversity of contexts and sources in Thomas.

43. *Super Post. An.* I, lect.20, n.5 (EB 4,283,1).

44. Schmidt, *Domain of Logic*, p. 33.

45. Schmidt, *Domain of Logic*, pp. 36-41.

46. *Summa theol.* I-IIae, q.57, a.3 ad 3 (EB 2,426,3).

47. Compare *Super Peri* Proem., n.2 (EB 4,327,1). In the Prologue to the *De fallaciis*, which is very early if authentic, logic is defined as "rationalis scientia" but is not called an '*ars*' (EB 6,575,3).

48. Schmidt, *Domain of Logic*, p. 30. See also the discussion in Richard McKeon, "Philosophy and Theology, History and Science in the Thought of Bonaventure and Thomas Aquinas," pp. S39-S45.

49. Schmidt, *Domain of Logic*, p. 27.

50. Schmidt, *Domain of Logic*, p. 41.

51. *Super Post. An*. I, lect.4, nn.4-5 (EB 4,275,1-2).
52. *Super Post. An*. I, lect.4, nn.2-3 (EB 4,275,1).
53. *Super Post. An*. I, lect.4, nn.10-16 (EB 4,275,2-276,1).
54. *Super Post. An*. I, lect.7, n.6 (EB 4,277,1).
55. *Super Post. An*. I, lect.7, n.8 (EB 4,277,1).
56. *Super Post. An*. I, lect.7, n.8 (EB 4,277,1).
57. *Posterior Analytics* II,19, 99b32-100b18.
58. *Super Post. An*. II, lect.20, n.11 (EB 4,311,2).
59. *Super Post. An*. II, lect.20, n.12 (EB 4,311,2).

NOTES FOR SECTION 2.6

1. *Super De trin*. q.5, a.1 (EB 4,532,2). The fifth and sixth questions have served as the material for many construals of Thomas's doctrine on the *scientiae*; I will not consider these in any detail. See, for example, Siegfried Neumann, *Gegenstand und Methode der theoretischen Wissenschaften nach Thomas von Aquin*, pp. 58-160, for a thorough reading, and pp. *xvi-xix*, for bibliography to 1965. More recently, there is an excellent survey of sources on the issues in Questions 5 and 6 by Leo Elders, *Faith and Science*, pp. 85-140. The one synoptic treatment of the classification of the sciences by medieval Latin authors is the quite out-of-date, *Problème de la classification des sciences* by Joseph Mariétan. His discussion of Thomas may be found on pp. 176-194. Mariétan finds Thomas to be the solution to all the tradition's difficulties about classification ("une solution qui eclairit tous les doutes constatés," p. 76).
2. *Super De Trin*. q.5, a.1 ad 6 (EB 4,533,1). Armand Maurer expresses the balance of mind and being nicely: "The sciences are no longer considered as differentiated according to a distinction of forms ready-made in the world, but according to distinctions the mind itself makes in the course of its investigation of reality" (*Division and Methods of the Sciences*, p. *xvi*).
3. *Super De Trin*. q.5, a.1 ad 4 and ad 5 (EB 4,532,3-533,1).
4. *Super De Trin*. q.5, a.1 ad 5 (EB 4,533,1). Aristotle considers the relation of subalternation, to cite one text, in *Posterior Analytics*, I,9, 76a8-13 and 76a24-26.
5. Recall, e.g., the much debated but simplified exposition of *Summa theol*. Ia, q.1, a.2.
6. *Super De Trin*. q.5, a.1 ad 9 (EB 4,533,1).
7. *Republic* VI, 510b-511c.
8. *Super De Trin*. q.5, a.3 (EB 4,533,3-535,1). It is here that Wyser's work with the autograph proved most important in correcting the printed versions and the erroneous interpretations based upon them. See ed. Wyser, pp. 20-21, where a chart shows the crucial emendations.
9. *Super De Trin*. q.5, a.3 (EB 4,534,3). Compare the summary paragraph at the end of the discussion, ed. Wyser, p. 40, line 42 - p. 41, line 3.
10. *Super De Trin*. q.5, a.3 (EB 4,534,1-3).
11. *Super De Trin*. q.6, a.1 [qc.1] (EB 4,536,2).

12. *Super De Trin.* q.6, a.1 [qc.1] (EB 4,536,3).

13. On the actual place of mathematics in the speculative hierarchy, see Section 4.P, below.

14. *Metaphysics* I,1, 981b7-10.

15. *Super De Trin.* q.6, a.1 [qc.2] ad 4 (EB 4,537,1).

16. This is Thomas's shorthand rendering of an extended reflection on the relations between the two. Recall J. Peghaire, *INTELLECTUS et RATIO selon saint Thomas d'Aquin.*

17. *Super De Trin.* q.6, a.1 [qc.3] (EB 4,537,2).

18. But Thomas is largely silent on the question of the exact dependence of mathematics on metaphysics. McKeon is right to say that "Aquinas preserves Aristotle's division of the theoretic sciences into metaphysics, mathematics, and physics as the divisions of doctrinal science, but his theoretic organization of the sciences is a reduction of the ways of things to metaphysics and physics" (McKeon, "Philosophy and Theology," p.S45). See below, Section 4.P.

19. *Super De Trin.* q.6,a.1 [qc.3] (EB 4,537,2).

NOTES FOR SECTION 3.1

1. See, for very different analyses of causality in antiquity, William A. Wallace, *Causality and Scientific Explanation*, I, pp. 20-24; Gregory Vlastos, "Reasons and Causes in the *Phaedo*"; Richard Sorabji, *Necessity, Cause, and Blame*, pp. 45-88; Michael Frede, "The Original Notion of Cause."

2. For the use of this sort of source among the early medieval Latin authors, see Brian Lawn, *I Quesiti Salernitani*, pp. 19-33. The patristic genre of commentaries *in Hexaemeron* was another means of passing down physics; see Appendices 7-9 by Wallace in the "Blackfriars" edition of the *Summa*, X, pp. 202-224.

3. One can see this in Isidore's *Etymologiae*. The third quarter of the whole work is devoted to naturalistic subjects (Books XI-XIV); a separate Book summarizes medicine (Book IV). Moreover Isidore includes the study of physical causes in his definition of philosophy: "Philosophiae species tripertita est: una naturalis, quae Graece Physica appellatur, in qua de naturae inquisitione disseritur ... In Physica igitur, causae quaerendi, in Ethica ordo vivendi, in Logica ratio intellegendi versatur" (II,xxiv,3-4, ed. Lindsay, lines 23-35, 28-1). Then Isidore credits Plato with having analyzed physics more exactly according to "quattuor deffinitiones ... id est Arithmeticam, Geometricam, Musicam, Astronomiam" (II,xxiv,2, lines 12-15). These four are the liberal arts of the *quadrivium*. A similar treatment can be found in the pedagogical dialogues of Alcuin (PL 101,952A-B).

4. Adelard justifies himself before his nephew by recalling the extent of his voyages (*De eodem et diverso*, ed. H. Willner, 4, lines 6-8, and 34, lines 3-4). But many of the exotic trappings are illusory and the foreign learning is meager; see Lawn, *I Quesiti Salernitani*, pp. 38-48.

5. These writers have been described in a number of essays by Paul Oskar Kristeller. See particularly his "The School of Salerno"; "Beitrag der Schule von Salerno zur Entwicklung der scholastischen Wissenschaft im 12. Jahrhundert;" "Bartholomaeus, Musandinus and Maurus of Salerno and Other Early Commentators of the 'Articella' ..."; and his lecture, *La scuola medica di Salerno secondo ricerche e scoperte recenti*. The Salernitan influence on the *physica* of Chartres and other northern schools is imperfectly known. One single indication of this influence is the respectful treatment which William of Conches accords to Constantinus Africanus; e.g., *Philosophia mundi*, I,xxii, ed. Gregor Maurach, lines 256, 262-63, 301-03, 320-21, 351.

6. *Summa theol*. I-IIae, q.59, a.2: "ut Augustinus narrat in IX De Civ. Dei, ab Aulio Gellio dictum" (EB 2,429,2).

7. This is true of the references to Galen on the soul, e.g., *Contra gent*. II, c. 63-64 and 68 (EB 2,44,2-45,2), for which see Gregory of Nyssa, *De anima* serm.1 (PG 43,195C). There are other references to Galen which do not refer to this doctrine. Galen is cited twice in favor of the principle that every body is consumed by fire (*Super Sent*. II, d.15, q.2 art.2 ad 1 [EB 1,167,3], IV d.44, q.3, a.1, qc.3 ad 3 [EB 1,647,2]; cf. *Summa theol*., Suppl. q.86 a.3 ad 3 [EB 2,921,3]. He is cited once as the source of the maxim "summa medicina est abstinentia" (*Super Sent*. IV, d.15, q.3, a.1, qc.2 ad 3; [EB 1,511,3]. The two doctrines are precisely of the aphoristic sort that is learned through reading *florilegia*.

8. E.g., *Super Sent*. II, d.17, q.2, a.2 (EB 1,174,1), *Contra gent*. III, c.90 (EB 2,89,3).

9. Ptolemy is cited in the discussions of the heavenly order; e.g., *Summa theol*. Ia, q.70, a.1 ad 3 (EB 2,285,3). But the discussion of the *Hexaemeron* in the *Summa* shows explicitly that the reference comes through John Chrysostom, *In Genesim* c.1, hom.6 (PG 53,58). Ptolemy is cited more frequently against the opinion that the human will is determined by celestial influences (e.g., *Super Sent*. II, d.25, q.1, a.2 ad 5 [EB 2,199,3], *Contra gent*. III, cc.84-86 [EB 2,86,1-88,3], *Summa theol*. I-IIae, q.9, a.5 [EB 2,369,3]. These references to the *Centiloquium* and the *Liber quattuor tractatuum* of Ptolemy suggest, by their variety and detail, a direct acquaintance.

10. *Super Sent*. IV, d.33, q.1, a.3, qc.1 (EB 1,599,2), where the allusion is to the *De coitu* of Constantinus. A similar allusion is found in the Supplement to the *tertia pars*, q.65, a.3 (EB 2,871,3). The same position is attributed to certain anonymous "medici" in *Super Sent*. II, d.38, q.1, a.2 ad 6 (EB 1,236,3). On the ancient and medieval sources of the *De coitu* itself, see Schipperges, *Die Assimilation*, p. 44; cf. Manfred Ullmann, *Die Medizin im Islam*, pp. 193-96. The opinion to which Thomas refers appears in the very first lines of Constantine's treatise; he need not have had more than a browser's acquaintance with it, if he had direct acquaintance at all.

11. Daniel A. Callus, "Les Sources de Saint Thomas. Etat de la question," particularly pp. 108-09.

12. Weisheipl, *Friar Thomas*, 395, #74. What can be discovered of the

recipient, Phillip of Castro Caeli, is summarized by Fr. Mandonnet in "Les Opuscules de saint Thomas d'Aquin," particularly pp. 138-39.

13. The text appears among the other opuscula in EL 43 (1976), pp. 155-57. One finds the *Physics* three times (lines 26, 97, 107), the *Metaphysics* twice (lines 87, 116), and the *Categories* and *De generatione* once each (lines 66, 150, respectively). The editors connect the "quibusdam" of line 3 with the texts of Avicenna and Algazel, but the position is sufficiently popular for it to be drawn from a number of texts. For a summary of the philosophical positions on the question of the mixture of the elements, see Anneliese Maier, *An der Grenze von Scholastik und Wissenschaft*, pp. 3-35.

14. *De mixt.*: "quidam autem uolentes utrasque rationes vitare, in maius inconveniens inciderunt" (EL 43, 156,53-54).

15. For example, William of Conches, *Glosae super Platonem*, ed. E. Jeauneau, sect. LIX, CLXIV. Compare the anonymous gloss cited by Jeauneau, p. 264 (c). See also the *Philosophia mundi* of William, I,xxii, ed. Maurach, lines 370-426. For general treatments of the topic, see Theodore Silverstein, "*Elementatum*: Its Appearance among Twelfth-Century Cosmologists"; Silverstein, "Guillaume de Conches and the Elements: *Homoiomera* and *organica*"; and Peter Dronke, "New Approaches to the School of Chartres," especially pp. 128-132. The doctrine of the *elementatum* also appears in the twelfth-century Salernitan commentaries on the *articella*.

16. *Urso von Salerno: De commixtionibus elementorum libellus*, ed. Wolfgang Stürner. For the date, see pp. 7-8; for the doctrine of the *elementatum*, pp. 22-23.

17. Averroes, *Commentarium medium in Aristotelis De generatione et corruptione*, lib.1, n.90, ed. F. H. Fobes with S. Kurland, pp. 93-94.

18. Averroes, *In De Caelo*, 227B-C.

19. Albertus Magnus, *De caelo et mundo*, lib.3, tract.2, c.8, ed. Paul Hossfeld, *Opera omnia* V/1, p. 241, lines 13-26. Compare Albertus, *Quaestiones de animalibus*, lib.12, q.2, ed. Ephrem Filthaut, *Opera omnia* XII, p. 225, lines 46-55.

20. See, for example, P. Glorieux, *La Faculté des Arts et ses maîtres au XIIIe siècle*, ##4e, 24e, 68w, 109d, 115d, 124b, 269a, 392c, 411u, 416ea, et 427g, for commentaries on *De generatione*.

21. *Super De Trin.* q.4, a.3 ad 6 (EB 4,531,1): "Probabilior tamen videtur esse opinio Commentatoris in III Caeli et mundi, qui hanc opinionem Avicennae improbans dicit elementorum formas in mixto non remanere nec totaliter corrumpi, sed fieri ex his unam mediam formam, in quantum suscipiunt magis et minus." The degrees are not of substantial form itself, but of the forms "secundum quod manent virtute in qualitatibus elementaribus quasi in propriis instrumentis" (EB 4,531,1). Compare the disputed questions *De anima* a.9 ad 10 (EB 3,380,2-381,1).

22. See the introduction to the Leonine edition, EL 43, p. 6, col. 1.

23. From the introduction to the Leonine edition: "on se defend mal contre l'impression que l'opuscule thomiste entend précisément rectifier et

depasser le chapitre d'Alvredus *De specie motu cordis*, cité plus haut [scil. c. 9]'' (EL 43, p. 96, col.1).

24. See the edition of Alfred's work by Clemens Baeumker, p. 1, fn.4.

25. *Quaestiones de animalibus* III, q.5, *Opera omnia* XII pp. 126-27.

26. See EL lines 24-27 and 151-52; 43-45; 59; and 209-210, respectively.

27. *Super De Trin.* q.5, a.1 ad 9 & ad 10 (EB 4,533,1). Compare *Super Librum de causis*, lect.1 (EB 4,507,1-3; ed. Pera #18), and *Sent. Ethic.* VI, lect 7 n.17 (EB 4,197,1).

28. *Rabi Mossei Aegypti Dux seu director dubitantium aut perplexorum*, f. 2r. On the peculiarities of this Latin version, which reproduces that used by Thomas, see Wolfgang Kluxen, ''Literargeschichtliches zum lateinischen Moses Maimonides'' and ''Die Geschichte des Maimonides im lateinischen Abendland.''

NOTES FOR SECTION 3.2

1. *Sent. De caelo* I, lect.22, n.8 (EB 4,17,3); *Super meteora* I, lect.1, nn.7 & 9 (EB 4,312,2).

2. For example, *Super Meta.* IV, lect.1, n.5: ''ista scientia, quae prae manibus habetur'' (EB 4,418,2). *Super de anima* I, lect.1, n.2: ''in tractatu autem de anima, quem habemus prae manibus'' (EB 6,5,1). *Super Meteor.* I, lect.1, n.4: ''reliqua pars 'huius methodi', idest scientiae naturalis, quam prae manibus habemus'' (EB 4,312,1). The commentary on Book I of *De anima* is given in the early catalogues as a *reportatio* made by Reginald of Piperno; Fr. Busa's edition thus prints it apart from the rest of the commentary. R. A. Gauthier has argued in the recently published Leonine edition, however, that Book I is not a *reportatio* but a work written by Thomas; see EL 45, pp. 279*-281*.

3. On the sources for the commentary on the *Physics* see Callus, ''Les sources,'' pp. 115-117.

4. Averroes follows a variation of the standard scheme: ''Intentionem libri, Utilitatem, Ordinem, Divisionem, Proportionem, Viam doctrinae, Nomen libri, Nomen authoris'' (Proemium, p. 1B). See R. W. Hunt, ''The Introductions to the 'Artes' in the Twelfth Century.''

5. Averroes, *In Physica*, 3C-G.

6. The first level is that ''quorum esse dependet a materia, nec sine materia definiri possunt.'' The second comprises the intelligibles, ''licet esse non possint nisi in materia sensibili, in eorum tamen definitione materia sensibilis non cadit.'' The third group is the highest: ''quaedam vero sunt quae non dependent a materia nec secundum esse nec secundum rationem'' *(Super Phys.* I,lect.1, n.2 [EB 4,59,1]).

7. *Super Phys.* I, lect.1, n.3 (EB 4,59,1).

8. *Super Phys.* I, lect.1, n.4 (EB 4,59,1).

9. *Super Phys.* I, lect.1, n.4 (EB 4,59,1).

10. Averroes, *In Physica*, lib.1, c. 1, f. 6E.

11. *Super Phys.* I, lect.1, n.7, (EB 4,59,2): ''illa quae sunt magis nota secundum naturam, sunt minus nota secundum nos.''

12. One might compare this to the structure of Ptolemy's *Almagest*, where the treatment of earlier Books is made simple by the omission of certain anomalies, these being introduced only when it is time to modify the abstract neatness of the first account.

13. *Sent. De caelo* Proem. n.2 (EB 4,1,1).
14. *Sent. De caelo* Proem. n.2 (EB 4,1,1).
15. *Sent. De caelo* Proem. n.3 (EB 4,1,1).
16. *Sent. De caelo* Proem. n.3 (EB 4,1,1).
17. *Sent. De caelo* Proem. n.4 (EB 4,1,2).
18. *Sent. De caelo* Proem. n.5 (EB 4,1,2).
19. *Super De gen*. Proem. n.1 (EB 4,49,1).
20. *Super De gen*. Proem. n.1 (EB 4,49,1): "in solis inferioribus."
21. *Super De gen*. Proem. n.2 (EB 4,49,1).
22. *Super Meteor*. I, lect.1, n.1 (EB 4,311,3).
23. *Super Meteor*. I, lect.1, n.3 (EB 4,312,1).
24. *Super Meteor*. I, lect.1, n.3 (EB 4,312,1).
25. *Super Meteor*. I, lect.1, n.3 (EB 4,312,1).
26. *Super Meteor*. I, lect.1, nn.5-8 (EB 4,312,1-2), of the four respectively.
27. *Super Meteor*. I, lect.1, n.9 (Eb 4,312,2).

NOTES FOR SECTION 3.3

1. *Super Phys*. I, lect.12, n.1: "hic incipit determinare veritatem" (EB 4,65,2).
2. *Super Phys*. I, lect.12, n.2, (EB 4,65,2-3).
3. *Super Phys*. I, lect.12, n.4: "in quolibet fieri aliud *dicatur* fieri ex alio ... vel alterum ex altero ... propter hoc quod omnis mutatio habet duos terminos; dupliciter contingit hoc *dicere*, eo quod termini alicuius factionis vel mutationis possunt *accipi* ut simplices vel compositi" (EB 4,65,3), emphases added against the rhythm of the sentence.).
4. *Super Phys*. I, lect.12, n.4: "Significatur fieri ut simplex," "significatur fieri ut compositum" (EB 4,65,3).
5. *Super Phys*. I, lect.12, n.4: "ultimur duplici modo loquendi" (EB 4,65,3).
6. *Super Phys*. I, lect.12, n.7: "cum enim attribuitur homini quod fiat musicus, homo quidem est unum subiecto, sed duo ratione" (EB 4,65,3).
7. *Super Phys*. I, lect.12, n.9: "hoc contingit quia nomine aeris intelligimus infiguratum" (EB 4,65,3).
8. *Super Phys*. I, lect.12, n.9 (EB 4,66,1).
9. *Super Phys*. I, lect.14, nn.4-8, (EB 4,67,1-2).
10. Wallace, *Causality and Scientific Explanation*, I, pp. 72-76; and Wallace, "Aquinas on Temporal Relations between Cause and Effect," particularly pp. 572-574, 580. By leaving aside the role of the causes in demonstration, I must also neglect the distinction between demonstration *quia* and demonstration *propter quid*, one of the most important discoveries of the Latin readers of the *Posterior Analytics* (especially I,13 and II,1). See the remarks by Thomas *ad loc*., particularly *Super Post. An*. I, lect.23, nn.3-4

(EB 4,284,3), and II, lect.1, nn.5-6 (EB 4,299,3). More general remarks can be found in Wallace, *Causality and Scientific Explanation*, I, pp. 33-46, 67.

11. Wallace, "Temporal Relations," p.574.

12. *Super Post. An.* II, lect.10-12 (EB 4,305,3-307,1). See also the discussions by Wallace cited in fn. 10, above.

13. *Super Post. An.* II, lect.11, n.4: "accipi potest quomodo causa, quae accipitur ut medium in demonstratione, se habeat consequenter ei quod est in fieri vel generari: quia etiam in his demonstrationibus, quae syllogizant de his quae sunt in fieri, necesse est accipere aliquod medium et primum quae sint immediata" (EB 4,306,2-3).

14. *Super Phys.* II, lect.5, n.1, (EB 4,70,3).

15. *Super Phys.* II, lect.5, n.2, (EB 4,70,3).

16. *Super Meta.* V, lect.3, n.7, (EB 4,430,2).

17. E.g., *Super Phys.* II, lect.5, nn.6,8.

18. *Super Phys.* II, lect.4, n.10, (EB 4,70,2-3).

19. Avicenna recognizes that the metaphysician extends the physical notion of moving cause in order to admit non-moving causes, such as the divine creation of the world. See his *Liber de philosophia prima*, ed. S. Van Riet, p.292, lines 20-22: "divini philosophi non intelligunt per agentum principium motionis tantum, sicut intelligunt naturales, sed principium essendi et datorem eius, sicut creator mundi." This is not an Aristotelian view, of course, and would not be endorsed by Thomas as it stands.

20. Respectively, *Super Phys.* II, lect.5, nn.3-5, (EB 4,70,3); and *Super Meta.* V, lect.2, n.1, (EB 4,429,2).

21. For example, *Super Phys.* II, lect.5, n.6 (EB 4,71,1) and lect.4, nn.5,10 (EB 4,70,1,3); *Super Meta.* V, lect.2, n.9 (EB 4,429,3) and lect.3, n.12 (EB 4,430,2-3).

22. *Super Phys.* II, lect.5, n.5, (EB 4,71,1). The position is attributed to Avicenna at *Super Meta.* V, lect.2, n.4 (EB 4,429,3). The citation seems to be to the *Sufficientia* of Avicenna, lib1, c.10, in *Opera philosophica*. Compare the mention of causes "adiutrices" and "praeparatrices" in his *Liber de philosophia prima* tract.6, c. 2, ed. Van Riet, p.301, line 19, and 302, line 29.

23. *Super Phys.* II, lect.5, n.8 (EB 4,71,1-2).

24. *Super Phys.* II, lect.5, n.9 (EB 4,71,2).

25. Avicenna, *Liber de philosophia prima* tract.6, c. 4, ed. Van Riet, p.321, lines 46-50.

26. *Super Phys.* II, lect.5, n.10 (EB 4,71,2).

27. Compare *Super Meta.* V, lect.3, n.2 (EB 4,430,1).

28. *Super Phys.* II, lect.5, n.2 (EB 4,70,3).

29. *Super Meta.* V, lect.2, n.11 (EB 4,430,1).

30. *Super Phys.* II, lect.5, n.7 (EB 4,71,1); compare *Super Meta.* V, lect.2, n.12 (EB 4,430,1).

31. *Super Phys.* II, lect.5, n.7 (EB 4,71,1); compare *Super Meta.* V, lect.2, n.14, (EB 4,430,1).

32. *Super Phys.* II, lect.5, nn.9-10 (EB 4,71,2).

33. *Super Phys.* II, lect.5, n.11, where the locution "causa causarum" appears twice (EB 4,71,2).

34. Avicenna, *Liber de philosophia prima* tract.6, c. 5, ed. Van Riet, p.337, lines 90-91, and 338, lines 12-13.

35. *Super Meta.* V, lect.3, n.6 (EB 4,430,2). On the distinction between an order of causes and an order of causality, see also Avicenna, *Liber de philosophia prima* tract.6, c. 5, ed. Van Riet, from p. 336, line 84, to 339, line 32.

36. *Super Meta.* V, lect.3, n.7 (EB 4,430,2).

37. *Super Phys.* II, lect.6, nn.2-5,7 (EB 4,71,2-3).

38. *Super Phys.* II, lect.6, n.8 (EB 4,71,3).

39. *Super Meta.* V, lect.3, nn.8-10 (EB 4,430,2).

40. *Super Meta.* V, lect.3, nn.11-13 (EB 4,430,2-3).

41. *Super Meta.* V, lect.3, n.18 (EB 4,430,3).

42. *Super Phys.* II, lect.6, n.9 (EB 4,71,3-72,1).

43. *Super Phys.* II, lect.6, n.10 (EB 4,72,1).

44. *Super Phys.* II, lect.6, n.11 (EB 4,72,1).

45. Aristotle, *Peri hermeneias* I,9; *Physics* II, 4-9; *Metaphysics* IX, 4. One finds certain passages which seem to count in the opposite sense, especially *Metaphysics* VI,3. See Sorabji, *Necessity, Cause, and Blame*, pp.51-56.

46. For the history of the doctrine, see J. A. Weisheipl, "The Principle 'Omne quod movetur ab alio movetur' in Mediaeval Physics" and *Quidquid Movetur ab Alio Movetur: A Reply*. In denying the Averroistic *motor conjunctus*, Thomas is also denying causal singularity in any literal sense; rather, the entire principle is shifted into the realm of forms or natures. See also Weisheipl, "The Spect(er) of *Motor Coniunctus* in Medieval Physics," and "The Principle," pp. 41, 47.

47. Raymond Laverdière, *Le principe de causalité: Recherches thomistes récentes.*

NOTES FOR SECTION 3.4

1. Cornelio Fabro, *Participation et causalité selon S. Thomas d'Aquin*, pp. 461-468.

2. *Summa theol.* Ia, q.115, art.1 (EB 2,348,2); the reference is to the *Fons Vitae* II,10. There the *magister* tells his student that no body would move if there were no spiritual force: "Nisi esset vis spiritualis agens, penetrabilis per haec corpora, nec moverentur nec agerent" (ed. C. Baeumker, p. 42, lines 1-2).

3. *Summa theol.* Ia, q.115, art.1: "secundum enim quod participatur aliquid, secundum hoc est necessarium quod participetur id quod est proprium ei ... agere autem, quod nihil est aliud quam facere aliquid actu, est per se proprium actus, inquantum actus, unde et omne agens agit sibi simile" (EB 2,348,2).

4. *Super Phys.* II, lect.11, n.2: "et hoc praecipue in agentibus univocis, in quibus agens facit sibi simile secundum speciem ... in his enim forma generantis, quae est principium generationis, est idem specie cum forma generati,

quae est generationis finis'' (EB 4,74,2).

5. *Super Phys.* II, lect.11, n.2: "participant aliquam similitudinem eius secundum quod possunt" (EB 4,74,2).

6. Here one approaches the metaphysical foundations of causality. So much was clear in the argument of *Summa theol.* Ia, q.115, a.1, cited above, fn. 3. It also becomes clear in the *Super Phys.*, e.g., III, lect.4, n.6: "Omne agens moveat secundum formam. Omne enim agens agit inquantum est actu" (EB 4,78,3).

7. *Super Phys.* II, lect.10, n.15: "omne agens agit quod est sibi conveniens" (EB 4,74,1).

8. *Q.D. De verit.* q.11, a.1 sed contra 5 (EB 3,73,1).

9. E.g., *Super De anima* III, lect.6, n.4 (EB 4,361,3). It appears also as a sign of the order in nature at III, lect.14, n.17 (EB 4,368,1) and II, lect.7, n.9 (EB 4,346, 1-2).

10. E.g., *Super Sent.* I, d.2, q.1, a.1 obj.2 (EB 1,7,1); II, d.14, q.1, a.2 ad 3 (EB 1,64,1); III, d.3, q.1, a.2 (EB 1,268,3-270,3); IV, d.24, q.1, a.1 (EB 1,570,2-571,2).

11. E.g., *Contra gent.* I, c.37; II, c.88; III, c.52; IV, c.24.

12. E.g., *Summa theol.* Ia, q.33, a.2 ad 4; I-IIae, q.54, a.2; IIIa, q.31, a.6.

13. *Resp. art. 108*, a.9: "secundum quod consuevit dici quod omne agens facit simile sibi" (EB 3,638,3).

14. The Aristotelian contribution ought not to be forgotten; see *Metaphysics* II,1, 993b24-27.

15. This insistence figures in three different treatments: Bernard Lonergan, *Grace and Freedom*, Chapter 4, particularly pp. 69, 71, 72-76; *Collection*, pp. 54-67; *Verbum*, pp. 87-140.

16. Weisheipl, *Friar Thomas*, 383, #51.

17. *Super De causis*, Proemium (EB 4,507,1; ed. C. Pera, sect. #9).

18. *Super De causis*, Proemium: "Sicut Philosophus dicit in X Ethicorum ... ut patet per Philosophum in II Metaphysicae ... ut patet per Philosophum in I De partibus animalium ..." (EB 4,507,1; Pera ##1,3-5).

19. *Super De causis* Proemium: "oportet igitur quod ultima felicitas homini quae in hac vita haberi potest, consistat in consideratione primarum causarum, 'quia illud modicum quod de eis sciri potest, est magis amabile et nobilius omnibus his quae de rebus inferioribus cognosci possunt'" (EB 4,507,1; Pera #5).

20. *Super De causis* lect. 1: "verificatur hoc exemplum in ipso rerum ordine" (EB 4,507,2; Pera #21).

21. *Super De causis* lect. 1: "Proclus autem expressius hoc sic probat," "hoc autem uno medio Proclus sic probat" (EB 4,507,2; Pera ##24,29).

22. *Super De causis* lect. 1 (EB 4,507,2-3).

23. *Super De causis* lect. 1: "in causis igitur per se ordinatis haec propositio habet veritatem ... in causis autem ordinatis per accidens est e converso" (EB 4,507,3; Pera ##41-42).

24. *Super De causis* lect. 6: "et, quia a cognitione processit ad narrationem, ostendit consequenter quod causa prima, cum sit supra cognitionem, oportet quod sit supra narrationem" (EB 4,511,1; Pera #170).

25. *Super De causis* lect.3: "effectus autem omnis participat aliquid de vir-

tute suae causae" (EB 4,508,3; Pera #78).

26. *Super De causis* lect.9: "virtus causati dependet ex virtute causae et non ex converso" (EB 4,512,2; Pera #219).

27. *Super De causis* lect.12: "Causa autem agit in effectum per modum ipsius causae" (EB 4,514,2; Pera #282).

28. *Super De causis* lect.18: "in unoquoque genere est causa illud quod est primum in genere illo, a quo omnia quae sunt illius generis in illo genere constituuntur" (EB 4,516,2; Pera #340).

29. *Super De causis* Proemium: "causa secundum sui naturam est magis intelligibilis quam effectus" (EB 4,507,1; Pera #2).

30. *Super De causis* lect.9: "semper causa est melior causato" (EB 4,512,1; Pera #210).

31. *Super De causis* lect.6: "causa autem excedens effectum non sufficienter cognosci potest per suum effectum" (EB 4,511,2; Pera #177).

32. *Super De causis* lect.12: "effectus sit in causa per modum causae" (EB 4,514,2; Pera #282).

33. *Super De causis* lect.18 (EB 4,516,2; Pera ##340-342).

34. *Super De causis* lect.9 (EB 4,512,2; Pera #229).

35. *Super De causis* lect.6: "res enim consueverunt narrari per suas causas" (EB 4,511,1; Pera #169).

NOTES FOR SECTION 3.5

1. For example, *Super Phys.* II, lect.3, n.6. See also Robert J. Henle, *Saint Thomas and Platonism*, especially pp. 333-340 and the passages cited there.

2. For example, *Super Phys.* I, lect.2, nn.2-3, and lect.8, nn.2-4; II, lect.12, n.1; VIII, lect.12, n.5.

3. For a discussion of Thomas's remarks on astronomical hypotheses, see Wallace, *Causality and Scientific Explanation*, I, pp. 86-88. Charles Lohr interprets these same remarks as an attempt to dissolve objections against a theological use of Aristotelian astronomy; see his "The Medieval Interpretation of Aristotle," especially pp. 93-94. Lohr's suggestion seems to reduce what distinguishes the discussion of astronomical hypotheses from other versions of the 'conflict' between theology and philosophy.

4. For example, *Sent. De caelo* II, lect.17, nn.4-5 (EB 4,36,2-3).

5. *Sent. De caelo* II, lect.17, n.2-5 (EB 4,36,1-3).

6. *Sent. De caelo* II, lect.17, n.2 (EB 4,36,2).

7. *Sent. De caelo* II, lect.17, n.8 (EB 4,37,1); compare the remarks on the expression "a longe" in II, lect.4, n.3 (EB 4,25,3-4,26,1).

8. For both citations, *Sent. De caelo* II, lect.4, n.3 (EB 4,25,3).

NOTES FOR THE PROLOGUE TO CHAPTER 4

1. Thus, most studies of Thomas's remarks on mathematics are confined to describing the intelligible status of mathematical objects. See, for example, John F. Whittaker, "The Position of Mathematics in the Hierarchy of Speculative Science"; Vincent E. Smith, *St. Thomas and the Object of*

Geometry; Armand A. Maurer, "A Neglected Thomistic Text on the Foundations of Mathematics"; Thomas C. Anderson, "Intelligible Matter and the Objects of Mathematics in Aquinas."

2. *Sent. Ethic.* VI, lect.7, n.17 (EB 4,197,1). Thomas had referred to this text in the *Ethics* much earlier in his exposition of Boethius' *De Trinitate*, at q.5, a.1 obj.10: "Praeterea, mathematica prius occurrit addiscenda quam naturalis, eo quod mathematicam facile possunt addiscere pueri, non autem naturalem nisi provecti, ut dicitur in VI Ethicorum. Unde et apud antiquos hic ordo scientiis addiscendis fuisse dicitur observatus, ut primo logica, deinde mathematica, post quam naturalis et post hanc moralis, et tandem divinae scientiae homines studerent" (EB 4,532,2). Thomas concedes the curricular point in his reply, q.5, a.1 ad 10 (EB 4,533,1); see also q.5, a.1 ad 2 (EB 4,532,3), and the discussion in Section 2.P above concerning the relation of the liberal arts to philosophy.

3. *Super De causis* Proemium (EB 4,507,1; Pera #8).

4. Thomas's list seems to combine the Aristotelian and Stoic hierarchies of learning as mediated by various of his predecessors. For a comparison of some of these schemata, see J. A. Weisheipl, "Classifications of the Sciences in Medieval Thought," especially pp. 57-68.

5. *Sent. Ethic.* VI, lect.7, n.17 (EB 4,197,1).

6. *Sent. Ethic.* VI, lect.7, n.17 (EB 4,197,1).

7. See Jordan, "The Protreptic Structure of the *'Summa contra Gentiles.'*" Chenu used to stress, with good textual support, that the *Summa theologiae* represented in its structure a neo-Platonic *exitus* and *reditus*; cf. his *Introduction*, pp. 258-265. Whether justly or not, Thomas reads this structure into Peter Lombard's *Sentences*. See *Super Sent.* I, Proem. (EB 1,1,1-3); cf. Weisheipl, *Friar Thomas*, pp. 212-21.

9. See Boyle, p. 23 and n.36; cf. Weisheipl, *Friar Thomas*, pp. 360-361, #3.

10. I am not referring to the Stoic ordering of Aristotle's treatises so much as to the progression of his inquiry. The works on living beings contain amplifications and illustrations of principles learned in physics, but they also introduce a different realm of activity and operation which prepares for the crucial metaphysical insight into pure act.

11. E.g., *Contra gent.* II, c.68, n.6 (EB 2,45,2). The reference is to the *Liber de causis*, prop. II, for which see also Thomas's commentary *ad loc.*, (EB 4,507,3-508,2; Pera #61).

12. Indeed, for writers in the Augustinian tradition, the discourse about soul is characterized as having a lucidity like the mathematical.

NOTES FOR SECTION 4.1

1. For the history of treatments of soul in Thomas's predecessors see Odon Lottin, *Psychologie et Morale*, I, pp. 427-502. Unfortunately, Lottin's topical approach does not preserve the shapes of the various texts he uses. The same is true of more recent works such as Richard Heinzmann, *Die Unsterblichkeit der Seele*.

2. I do not mean, of course, that their sequence is the same: the discussion

of angels precedes the discussion of men in the *Summa*, but follows it in the *Contra gentiles*. I do mean that the nature of created intellect is clarified fundamentally in the case of angels and not of men.

3. *Super De trin.* 9.6, a.1 (EB 4,536,1-537,2); cf. Section 2.6, above.

4. *Q.D. De virt. comm.* q.5, a.2 ad 6 (EB 3,435,2); cf. *Super Heb.* c.11, lect.1 (EB 6,544,3-545,1).

5. *Super Phys.* II, lect.14, n.8 (EB 4,76,1).

6. *Contra Gent.* III, c.154, n. 11 (EB 2,111,2); cf. *Summa theol.* II-IIae, q.171, a.5 (EB 2,733,1).

7. *Super Sent.* III, d.26, a.1, a.4 (EB 1,355,3); *Sent. Ethic.* III, lect.6, n.7 (EB 4,176,2).

8. *Super Sent.* III, d.26, q.2, a.4 (EB 1,357,3); *Summa theol.* II-IIae, q.4, a.8 ad 3 and q.18, a.4.

9. *Q.D. De verit.* q.14, a.1 (EB 3,91,1); *Summa theol.* II-IIae, q.1; *Super Sent.* III, d.23, qq.2-3 (EB 1,342,1-347,2) We lack a disputed question on the virtue of faith.

10. *Q.D. De verit.* q.14, a.1 (EB 3,91,3).

11. *Summa theol.* II-IIae, q.1, a.4 (EB 2,524,2).

12. *Summa theol.* II-IIae, q.1, a.4 ad 3 (EB 2,524,3).

13. *Summa theol.* II-IIae, q.14, a.8 (EB 2,531,3).

14. *Summa theol.* II-IIae, q.18, a.4 (EB 2,547,1).

15. *Summa theol.* Ia, q.23, a.1 ad 4.

16. Joseph Kleutgen, *La philosophie scholastique exposée et defendue*, I, 224.

17. Désiré Mercier, Notes from a course in epistemology (1878-1879), recorded by F. Olmen, as quoted in Georges Van Riet, *Thomistic Epistemology*, I, p. 127, and fn. 9.

18. Joseph Maréchal, *Le point de départ de la métaphysique, Cahier 5: Le thomisme devant la philosophie critique*, pp. 373-374.

19. Charles Boyer, "Le sens d'un texte de Saint Thomas: 'De Veritate, q.1 a.9,' " pp. 424-443. See the response by Desmond Cornell, "St. Thomas on Reflection and Judgment," pp. 234-247, especially with regard to the alleged parallels to *Q.D. De verit.* q.1, a.9.

20. P. Hoenen, *La théorie du jugement d'aprés St. Thomas d'Aquin*, pp. 176-189.

21. Bernard Lonergan, *Verbum*, pp. 74-75, 84, 86-87.

22. *Q.D. De verit.* q.1, a.2 (EB 3,2,1); cf. q.1, a.5 ad 2 (EB 3,4,2): "ex virtute eiusdem speciei nata est sibi intellectum nostrum adaequare, in quantum, per similitudinem sui receptam in anima, cognitionem de se facit."

23. The following refers to *Q.D. De verit.* q.1, a.9 (EB 3,6,2-3), until otherwise noted.

24. J. Wébert has gathered 78 texts from Thomas that mention '*reflexio*' in his " 'Reflexio'. Etude sur les opérations réflexives," pp. 287-307, with commentary pp. 307-324. See the discussion of *Summa theol.* Ia, q.87, a.2 in Section 4.2, below.

25. Cf. J. H. Walgrave, "Zelfkennis en innerlijke Ervaring bij St. Thomas," pp. 61-62.

NOTES FOR SECTION 4.2

1. *Q.D. De anima* art.16 (EB 3,389,1; Robb ed., p. 218).

2. *Q.D. De anima* art.16 (EB 3,390,1; Robb ed., p. 224): "anima intellectiva humana ex unione ad corpus habet aspectum inclinatum ad phantasmata; unde non informatur ad intelligendum aliquid nisi per species phantasmatibus acceptas."

3. *Q.D. De anima* art.16 (EB 3,390,1; Robb ed., p. 224).

4. *Q.D. De anima* art.16 (EB 3,389,1; Robb ed., p. 219).

5. *Q.D. De anima* art.16 (EB 3,390,1-2; Robb ed., p. 226).

6. *Q.D. De anima* art.16 (EB 3,389,7; Robb ed., p. 219).

7. These texts have been the occasion of much dispute for the last sixty years. In 1923, Blaise Romeyer published his "Notre science de l'esprit humain," which argued that an intuitive self-knowledge could secure a philosophical psychology. Simonne Leuret replied instantly in the *Revue thomiste*, defending the reading in favor of an indirect self-knowledge. After a balanced summary of Romeyer's exegeses, Leuret writes: "Par réflexion sur son acte l'âme ne s'atteint pas dans son essence mais dans son existence seulement. Pourtant même dans cette connaissance et dans le plan psychologique, on trouve une note d'intimité qui n'est pas à negliger" (p. 385). A. Gardeil's "La perception expérimentale de l'âme," published in the same year, seemed to give credence to the view. Gardeil wrote, "L'âme, par elle-même, se saisit elle-même, non toute entière, mais elle-même. Elle se perçoit directement à la source de ces actes intellectuels ..." (p. 236). Romeyer amplified his claims in a 1925 essay on truth and his arguments in 1928 with his small monograph, "Saint Thomas et notre connaissance de l'Esprit humain." Reginald Garrigou-Lagrange answered with a disputed question, "Utrum mens seipsam per essentiam cognoscat an per aliquam speciem." He concluded, in part: "*mens cum corpore unita non seipsam cognoscit actualiter per suam essentiam*, sed in actibus suis et cum conversione ad phantasmata per species a sensibilibus abstractas" (p. 54, with italics in original). Gardeil himself reviewed Romeyer's second piece and distanced himself from it in "A propos d'un cahier du R. P. Romeyer" (1929). But the controversy was aflame. M.-D. Roland-Gosselin, who had already reviewed the first essay negatively, attacked Romeyer's monograph in a 1929 review for the *Bulletin thomiste*. The piece was, he wrote, distinctly Suarezian (p. 474). Gardeil reconsidered matters in a contritely entitled "Examen de conscience" (1928-1929). But Roland-Gosselin was not to be put off and attacked again in "Peut-on parler d'intuition intellectuelle dans la philosophie thomiste?" (1930). The answer to the title's rhetorical question was negative and Roland-Gosselin drew its corollary for psychology: "La réflexion, ou conscience psychologique, est une intuition de nos actes, mais determinée premièrement par leur objet" (p. 730). Meanwhile E. Peillabue had attacked Romeyer in the *Revue de philosophie* (1929) as presuming a neo-Platonic or Cartesian view of the soul-body union (p. 245). In subsequent issues, Romeyer replied and Peillaube sharpened the substantive disagreement. As if in an odd appendix, the *Revue*

published in 1933 an eirenic review by Régis Jolivet of the second edition of Romeyer's monograph (1932) in which Romeyer appears as a Thomist with an odd terminology. The controversy's sum is drawn out by J. H. Walgrave in "Zelfkennis en innerlijke Ervaring bij St Thomas" (1947), though one can find a late echo of Romeyer in John P. Ruane, "Self-Knowledge and Spirituality of the Soul in St Thomas" (1958). My own reading convinces me that Roland-Gosselin was right, if perhaps too tenacious.

8. *Q.D. De verit.* q.10, aa.8-9.

9. Thus the entire discussion of qq.75-87 is controlled by the order of discussion enunciated in the prologue to q.47 — the threefold order, namely, of the distinction of things in general, the distinction of good and evil, and the distinction of spiritual and corporeal creatures. The order of considering the distinction is recalled in the prologue to q.75.

10. *Summa theol.* Ia, q.87, a.1 (EB 2,314,1).

11. *Summa theol.* Ia, q.76, a.1 (EB 2,291,3).

12. *Summa theol.* Ia, q.14, a.2 (EB 2,206,2).

13. *Q.D. De verit.* q.10, a.8 (EB 3,66,3-68,2).

14. *Summa theol.* Ia, q.87, a.1 (EB 2,314,1), until otherwise noted.

15. *Summa theol.* Ia, q.84, a.5 (EB 2,308,3): "Et sic necesse est dicere quod anima humana omnia cognoscat in rationibus aeternis, per quarum participationem omnia cognoscimus. Ipsum enim lumen intellectuale, quod est in nobis, nihil est aliud quam quaedam participata similitudo luminis increati, in quo continentur rationes aeternae."

16. Compare Augustine, *De Trinitate*, XIV, esp. vi-viii, *De libero arbitrio*, II,vi,13-14; *De diversis quaestionibus 83*, q.15.

17. Compare Wébert: "La réflexion 'scientifique' est le fondement de la psychologie, car elle est une connaissance universelle. Elle s'oppose à la réflexion-reploiement qui est une perception singulière, bien que spirituelle ... [I]l fait reconnaître qu'il doit y avoir passage de la réflexion-reploiement à la réflexion-considération pour qu'on puisse constituer une science" (" 'Reflexio,' " p. 324). But Wébert then speaks of an inference from the one reflection to another (p. 325). A more exact formulation would be that of Ernst Ruppel in his *Unbekanntes Erkennen* (p. 1): "Die Selbsterkenntnis ... ist nicht das metaphysische Wissen um den Menschen, das in der spekulativen Psychologie zur Darstellung kommt. Hier handelt es sich um jenes unmittelbare Erkennen, das alle sinnlichen und geistigen Erkenntnis- und Strebensakte begleitet. Es ist allgemeine, sondern eine Einzelerkenntis ..."

18. *Q.D. De verit.* q.10, a.8 (EB 3,67,2).

19. *Q.D. De verit.* q.10, a.8 (EB 3,67,2).

20. The question is entitled "Queritur utrum anima coniuncta cognoscat seipsam per essentiam." It has been edited by L. A. Kennedy as "The Soul's Knowledge of Itself: An unpublished Work attributed to St. Thomas Aquinas." On its authenticity, see F. Pelster, "Eine ungedruckte Quaestio des hl. Thomas von Aquin über die Erkenntnis der Wesenheit der Seele"; Weisheipl, *Friar Thomas*, pp. 361-363, but cf. p. 479; and Kennedy, pp. 31-32.

21. Ed. Kennedy, line 7: "sicut patet in Summa."

22. Ed. Kennedy, line 19: "Circa veritatem huius questionis sunt due sollemnes opiniones."

23. Ed. Kennedy, lines 28-59.

24. Ed. Kennedy, lines 75-78.

25. Ed. Kennedy, lines 79-80.

26. Ed. Kennedy, lines 100 and 92-95, respectively. The species abstracted is that of the soul generally; see the ad 21, lines 323-327.

27. Ed. Kennedy, lines 111-112. He says in the reply to the third objection: "per reflexionem et representacionem proporcionis" (line 178). But Thomas resists any appeals to literal likeness or proportionality; see the critique of reasoning by similtude in the ad 8 and ad 19, lines 215-225 and 309-310, and the distinction of proportions in the ad 18, lines 301-302.

28. Ed. Kennedy, 1, 132, and ad 14, lines 278-279.

29. *Summa theol.* Ia, q.87, a.2 (EB 2,314,2).

30. *Summa theol.* Ia, q.87, a.2 (EB 2,314,2), until otherwise noted.

31. *Summa theol.* Ia, q.87, a.2 ad 2 (EB 2,314,2).

32. *Summa theol.* Ia, q.87, a.2 ad 3 (EB 2,314,2).

33. *Q.D. De verit.* q.10, a.9 (EB 3,68,3).

34. *Q.D. De verit.* q.10, a.9 (EB 3,68,3).

35. *Summa theol.* Ia, q. 87, a.3 (EB 2,314,3).

36. *Summa theol.* Ia, q. 87, a.3 ad 1 (EB 2,314,3).

37. *Summa theol.* Ia, q. 87, a.3 ad 2 (EB 2,314,3).

38. *Summa theol.* Ia, q. 87, a.3 ad 3 (EB 2,314,3).

39. *Summa theol.* Ia, q. 87, a.4 (EB 2,314,3-315,1).

40. *Summa theol.* Ia, q. 87, a.4 ad 3 (EB 2,315,1).

NOTES FOR SECTION 4.3

1. Jacques Leclercq writes: "Saint Thomas dit: l'homme agit en vue d'une fin et, comme il est libre, il doit choisir. La morale est la science des actes proprement humains. On la definit aussi 'science du bien et du mal'; mais le bien est l'être en tant que fin, nous l'avons vu. On tourne donc constamment autour de la notion de fin." See his *La philosophie morale de saint Thomas*, p. 380 and pp. 211-226 generally.

2. *Summa theol.* I-IIae, q.90, a.1 ad 2 (EB 2,474,3) for the first appearance. The parallel is drawn again, e.g., at q.91, a.3 (EB 2,476,1), q.92, a.2 (EB 2,477,2), q.94, a.1 (EB 2,479,1). It is discussed below in respect to the content of natural law.

3. *Summa theol.* I-IIae, q.91, a.2 (EB 2,475,3).

4. *Summa theol.* Ia, q.87, a.1 (EB 2,314,1); see Section 4.2, above.

5. *Summa theol.* I-IIae, q.91, a.1 ad 3 (EB 2,475,3).

6. On the historical and political character of human law in Thomas's moral thought, see Bénézet Bujo, *Moralautonomie und Normenfindung bei Thomas von Aquin*, pp. 287-306. Bujo provides a summary of natural law doctrine as it appears in Thomas's scriptural commentaries, on pp. 232-283.

7. *Summa theol.* I-IIae, q.91, a.3 ad 1 (EB 2,476,1).

8. *Summa theol.* I-IIae, q.91, a.4 ad 1 (EB 2,476,2); cf. a.5 ad 3 (EB 2,476,3).

9. This does not mean that the natural law is opposed to the other laws. On the contrary, the three laws are caught up in that divine providence which orders the cosmos. See Oscar J. Brown, *Natural Rectitude and Divine Law in Aquinas*, especially pp. 74-84.

10. *Summa theol.* Ia, q.2, a.1 (EB 2,187,1-2). One source for the distinction is the first axiom of Boethius's letter *De hebdomadibus*.

11. R. A. Armstrong paraphrases the criterion of self-evidence in this way: "St. Thomas shows that he is prepared to describe as self-evident, all those propositions whose truth could be immediately grasped as soon as the terms were understood" (*Primary and Secondary Precepts*, pp. 37-38). But this criterion cannot be applied to God, for whom understanding is not terministic. Armstrong considers the problem of self-evidence generally on pp. 24-55.

12. *Summa theol.* I-IIae, q.94, a.2 (EB 2,479,2).

13. *Summa theol.* I-IIae, q.94 a.2 (EB 2,479,2).

14. *Summa theol.* I-IIae, q.94, a.2 (EB 2,479,2). As Crowe says, this triplet "cuts across" the older distinction between primary and secondary precepts which had been adopted by Thomas in commenting on the *Sentences*. See M. B. Crowe, *The Changing Profile of the Natural Law*, p. 179, and pp. 174-184 generally. R. A. Armstrong finds the distinction made most strongly within the *Summa* at q.100 of the *prima secundae*, in connection with a discussion of the precepts of the Old Law; see his *Primary and Secondary Precepts*, p. 86-114.

15. *Summa theol.* I-IIae, q.94, a.2 (EB 2,479,2).

16. *Summa theol.* I-IIae, q.94, a,3 (EB 2,479,3).

17. *Summa theol.* I-IIae, q.94, a.3 (EB 2,479,3): "Multa enim secundum virtutem fiunt, ad quae natura non primo inclinat; sed per rationis inquisitionem ea homines adinvenerent, quasi utilia ad bene vivendum."

18. See Crowe, *Changing Profile*, pp. 187-191, for similar arguments. Crowe concludes: "St. Thomas is, indeed, driven to say more than once in this connection: *Natura humana mutabilis est*. The phrase may epitomize his views on human nature and morality" (p. 190). The opposite view is represented by Gallus Manser, *Das Naturrecht in thomistischer Beleuchtung*, pp. 51-61 ("Das Unveranderlichkeit des Naturrechts").

19. *Summa theol.* I-IIae, q.94, a.4 (EB 2,480,1).

20. *Summa theol.* I-IIae, q.94, a.4 (EB 2,480,1).

21. On the short space given this doctrine in the *Summa*, see Crowe, "*Synderesis* and the Notion of Law in St. Thomas" and *The Changing Profile*, pp. 136-141. For the long debate over the history of the word 'synderesis', see Oscar Brown, *Natural Rectitude and Divine Law*, pp. 175-177. Crowe suggests that Thomas no longer needed the doctrine of *synderesis* once he had become familiar enough with Aristotle's *Nicomachean Ethics*, especially with the practical syllogism (*Profile*, p. 140).

This "evolution" shows a rejection of "neo-Platonizing moral philosophy" and an emphasis on "the central importance of the reasoning process in matters of natural law" (p. 141).

22. There is also a treatment of *synderesis* in the *Sentences* commentary, *Super Sent.* II, d.24, q.2, a.3 (EB 1,195,1-196,1).

23. *Q.D. De verit.* q.16, a.1 (EB 3,105,2-3).

24. *Q.D. De verit.* q.17, a.1 ad 15 (EB 3,105,3); compare q.17, a.2 on error in conscience.

25. *Q.D. De verit.* q.16, a.2 (EB 3,106,1); compare q.17, a.2.

26. *Q.D. De verit.* q.16, a.2 ad 1 & ad 2 (EB 3,106,1-2); compare W. A. Wallace, *Role of Demonstration*, pp. 117-142, especially pp. 128-132.

27. *Q.D. De verit.* q.16, a.3 (EB 3,106,2-3).

NOTES FOR SECTION 4.4

1. *Super De anima* I, lect.1, n.6 (EB 6,5,2).

2. *Super De anima* III, lect.9, n.5 (EB 4,364,2); cf. fn.6.

3. *Super De anima* III, lect.9, n.5 (EB 4,364,2).

4. *Super De anima* III, lect.9, n.5 (EB 4,364,2).

5. *Super De anima* III, lect.9, n.5 (EB 4,364,2).

6. *Super De anima* III, lect.7, nn.7-13 (EB 4,362,2-3).

7. *Super De anima* II, lect.3, n.1 (EB 4,342,3).

8. *Super De anima* II, lect.3, nn.11-14 (EB 4,343,1-2).

9. *Super De anima* II, lect.3, n.12 (EB 4,343,2).

10. *Contra gent.* II, c. 60, n.5 (EB 2,43,1).

11. *Contra gent.* II, c. 61, nn.2,4 (EB 2,43,3). Boethius's version is compared with that of Moerbeke; the latter is cited as is it were the Greek original.

12. *Contra gent.* II, c. 66, n.3 (EB 2,44,1).

13. *Contra gent.* II, c. 59, n.9 (EB 2,42,2).

14. *Summa theol.* Ia, q.76, a.1 (EB 2,291,2-292,1).

15. *Summa theol.* Ia, q.76, a.1 (EB 2,291,3). Compare the other locutions: "oportet quod inveniat modum quo ista actio quae est intelligere sit huius hominis actio"; "[c]um igitur dicimus Socratem aut Platonem intelligere"; "intellectus quo Socrates intelligit est aliqua pars Socratis ita quod intellectus aliquomodo corpori Socratis unitur," and so on.

16. *Sent. Ethic.* I, lect.3 (EB 4,145,2).

17. *Sent. Ethic.* I, lect.3 (EB 4, 145,3).

18. *Sent. Ethic.* I, lect.3 (EB 4,145,3).

19. *Sent. Ethic.* I, lect.3 (EB 4,145,3).

20. See the description of the office of the *sapiens* in *Contra gent.* I, cap.1, and of the *doctor* in the Paris *principium*.

NOTES FOR SECTION 5.1

1. For a history of this dispute as it reaches the Latins, see Albert Zimmermann, *Ontologie oder Metaphysik?*, pp. 108-117. Zimmermann provides an exact survey of the views on metaphysics from Roger Bacon to John Buridan. His remarks on Aquinas will be considered below.

2. Avicenna, *Metaphysica*, I,2, ed. Van Riet, I, p. 12, lines 30-31. Compare the suggestion at the end of the *reductio* of the first Chapter: "oportebit tunc ut ens, inquantum est ens, sit subiectum, quod est convenientius" (ed. Van Riet, I, p. 8, lines 51-52).

3. These are the counter-positions considered by Avicenna in I,1. Compare the paraphrase by Verbeke in Van Riet ed., pp. 13*-20*.

4. Averroes, *In Phys*. I, com. 83.

5. See E. Gilson, "L'objet de la métaphysique selon Duns Scot," especially pp. 67-69.

6. Dominicus Gundissalinus, *De divisione philosophiae*, ed. Baur, pp. 36-37.

7. Robert Kilwardby, *De ortu scientiarum*, c. 26, ed. Judy, sect. 217, p. 83, lines 28-30.

8. Albert, *Metaphysica*, I, tract.1, c.2. Geyer opines that the work was written "non multo post annum 1262-1263" (ed. Geyer, p. viii). This would place it after Thomas's Boethius exposition but before his commentary on Aristotle's *Metaphysics*.

9. Albert, *Metaphysica* I, tract.1, c.2, ed. Geyer, p. 4, lines 52-54.

10. Albert, *Metaphysica* I, tract.1, c.2, ed. Geyer, p. 5, lines 34-58. Doig thinks that Aquinas's views are like those attacked by Albert; see Doig, *Aquinas on Metaphysics*, pp. 81-84.

11. See the discussion in Section 2.6, above.

12. *Super De Trin*. q.5, a.4. Reference will be had to this passage until otherwise noted.

13. *Super De Trin*. q.5, a.4 (EB 4,535,2).

14. *Super De Trin*. q.5, a.4 (EB 4,535,2).

15. *Super De Trin*. q.5, a.4 (EB 4,535,3).

16. Avicenna, *Metaphysica* I,1, ed. Van Riet, I, p. 5, lines 76-79. On Aquinas's relation to Avicenna here, see Doig, *Aquinas on Metaphysics* pp. 85-87.

17. Avicenna, *Metaphysica* I,1, ed. Van Riet, I, p. 5, line 88, to p. 6, line 96.

18. For the definition of metaphysics here, see Doig, *Aquinas on Metaphysics*, pp. 55-64.

19. *Super Meta*. proem. (EB 4,390,3-391,2).

20. *Super Meta*. proem. (EB 4,391,1).

21. *Super Meta*. proem. (EB 4,391,1).

22. *Super Meta*. proem. (EB 4,391,1). For an attempt at harmonizing Thomas's various explanations of the name 'first philosophy', see John Wippel, "The Title 'First Philosophy,' " especially pp. 599-600.

23. *Super Meta*. proem. (EB 4,391,1).

24. *Super Meta*. I, lect.2, nn.1-7 (EB 4,393,1).

25. *Super Meta*. I, lect.2, nn.8-14 (EB 4,393,2-3).

26. *Super Meta*. IV, lect.1, n.1 (EB 4,418,1-2).

27. *Super Meta*. IV, lect.1, n.2 (EB 4,418,2).

28. *Super Meta*. IV, lect.1, n.4 (EB 4,418,2).

29. *Super Meta*. IV, lect.1, n.5 (EB 4,418,2), with emphases added.

30. *Super Meta*. IV, lect.1, n.7 (EB 4,418,3).

31. *Super Meta*. IV, lect.1, n.7 (EB 4,418,3).

32. *Super Meta*. IV, lect.1, n.8 (EB 4,418,3).

33. *Super Meta*. IV, lect.1, n.11 (EB 4,418,3).

34. *Super Meta*. IV, lect.1, n.12 (EB 4,418,3), with the whole list in nn.12-15.

35. *Super Meta*. XII, lect.1, nn.2-8 (EB 4,497,1-2).

36. *Super Meta*. XII, lect.2, nn.1-3 (EB 4,497,2).

37. *Super Meta*. XII, lect.2, n.4 (EB 4,497,2).

38. *Super Meta*. XII, lect.2, n.2 (EB 4,497,2).

39. *Super Meta*. XII, lect.4, nn.30-32 (EB 4,499,3), and throughout the *lectio*.

40. *Super Meta*. XII, lect.5, nn.2-8 (EB 4,500,1-2).

41. For example, *Super Meta*. XII, lect.7, n.17 (EB 4,502,1).

42. *Super Meta*. XI, lect.7 generally.

43. *Super Meta*. XI, lect.7, nn.13-21 (EB 4,491,2-3).

44. *Super Meta*. XI, lect.7, n.13 (EB 4,491,2); compare lect.7, n.17.

45. *Super Meta*. XI, lect.7, n.19 (EB 4,491,2-3).

46. *Super Meta*. XI, lect.7, n.21 (EB 4,491,3).

47. Zimmermann, *Ontologie oder Metaphysik?*, pp. 179-180. Zimmermann finds that the separate substances are treated as part of being in general, while God is clearly not. Doig writes, more generally: "In leading his students from an examination of predication to the existence of Pure *Esse*, Aquinas would have pushed them to the limits of human understanding.... In other words, Aquinas would have impressed on them the recognition of the impossibility of understanding God, apart from a supernatural vision. Thus, he would have explained the working of first philosophy — the systematic attempt to discover the words, the sign posts, which can truly be used to refer to the unique perfection of God" (*Aquinas on Metaphysics*, pp. 385-386).

NOTES FOR SECTION 5.2

1. In the *De Trinitate* exposition itself, Thomas uses *'separatio'* to explain abstraction: "in abstrahendo significaretur esse separatio secundum ipsum esse rei" *Super De Trin*. q.5, a.3 (EB 4,534,1-3). Sample passages from other works would be *Summa theol*. Ia, q.85, a.2 ad 2 (EB 2,310,1-2), *Super Phys*. II, lect.3 (EB 4,69,3), *Super De anima* III, lect.12 (EB 4,366,2).

2. Paul Wyser's edition of Questions 5 and 6 appeared in *Divus Thomas*

(Fribourg) during 1947 and 1948. Bruno Decker's edition of the complete work was published in 1955.

3. See Louis B. Geiger, "Abstraction et séparation d'après S. Thomas" (1947), p. 5, fn. (1). Geiger summarizes the stages of redaction, pp. 15-20. But Geiger had already stressed the importance of the distinction between *abstractio* and *separatio* in his *La participation* (1942), pp. 318-321.

4. Geiger, "Abstraction et séparation," p. 21.

5. Representative articles would include the following: Philip Merlan, "Abstraction and Metaphysics in St. Thomas's *Summa*" (1953); Robert W. Schmidt, "L'emploi de la séparataion en métaphysique" (1960); Lorenzo Vicente, "De modis abstractionis iuxta sanctum Thomam" (1963-1964); Joseph Owens, "Metaphysical Separation in Aquinas" (1972); John Wippel, "Metaphysics and *Separatio* according to Thomas Aquinas" (1978). Schmidt provides a bibliographical survey to 1960 on pp. 373-376.

6. M. V. Leroy, " 'Abstractio' et 'separatio' d'après un texte controversé."

7. Gustavo Eloy Ponferrada, "Nota sobre los 'grados de abstracción.' "

8. C. Vansteenkiste, review of Wippel, "Metaphysics and *Separatio*."

9. Ponferrada, "Nota," p. 279.

10. Ponferrada, "Nota," pp. 283-284.

11. See the Appendix to Bruno Decker's edition of the *Expositio*, p. 231, line 15, to p. 233, line 26, for the deleted sections. Thomas struck out sections in which abstraction was used as the general term to cover all three sciences: e.g., "diversos modos abstractionis, intellectus abstrahere dicitur" (ed. Decker, p. 232, lines 32-33, and p. 233, lines 17-18), "triplex est abstractio" (ed. Decker, p. 233, line 20).

12. It is the combination of these two conditions which helps to explain Cajetan's notorious views on the demonstrability of the soul's immortality. See Carlo Giacon, *La seconda Scolastica*, I, pp. 53-72.

13. See Section 2.6, above.

14. *Super De Trin.* q.5, a.3 (EB 4,534,2).

15. *Super De Trin.* q.5, a.3 (EB 4,534,1).

16. *Super De Trin.* q.5, a.3 (EB 4,534,2).

17. *Super De Trin.* q.5, a.3 (EB 4,534,3).

18. *Super De Trin.* q.5, a.3 (EB 4,534,3). On the abandonment of other modes of reasoning in metaphysics, see Louis-M. Régis, "Analyse et synthèse," pp. 319-320; to the contrary, Schmidt, "L'emploi de la séparation," pp. 388-389.

19. *Super De Trin.* q.5, a.4 (EB 4,535,3).

20. *Super De Trin.* q.5, a.4 (EB 4,535,3).

21. *Super De Trin.* q.5, a.4 (EB 4,535,3).

22. *Super De Trin.* q.5, a.4 (EB 4,535,3).

23. Aristotle, *Physics* VII-VIII; *Metaphysics*, XII,6. Geiger also thinks that the existence of immaterials is established in *De Anima* III,5 ("Abstraction et séparation," p. 24). This leads him to trace a 'psychological' argument from the soul's reflection on its own immateriality. See Geiger, "Abstraction et séparation," pp. 25-26; compare Schmidt, "L'emploi de la séparation," pp.

384-385; and Edouard Wéber, "La négativité méthodique," p. 749, where one reads of "la découverte, en l'intellect, d'une nature dotée du privilège de transcender le mode matériel d'être." It is true that Thomas invokes the *De Anima* on the existence of immaterial beings, e.g., *Super Meta*. I, lect.12 (EB 4,400,3). It is not clear that Thomas regards the *De Anima* as a work built on reflection. See Sections 4.P and 4.1, above.

24. E.g., *Metaphysics* XII,7,9,10.

25. E.g., *Contra gent*. I, cc.16-27; II, cc.50-54.

26. Wippel, "Metaphysics and *Separatio*," pp. 446-468.

27. Wippel, p. 455.

28. Wippel, p. 462.

29. Wippel, p. 462-467.

30. Wippel, p. 469.

31. Wippel, pp. 469, 435 respectively.

32. I will return to the pedagogical issue when discussing the hierarchy of sciences in Section 5.4, below.

33. E.g., Geiger, "Abstraction et séparation," pp. 14, 24, 26; Schmidt, "L'emploi de la séparation," p. 383; J. D. Robert, "La métaphysique, science distincte," p. 218.

34. *Super Meta*. IV, lect.5 (EB 4,421,1-2). On these few lines as representing the negative judgment, see Geiger, "Abstraction et séparation," p. 24; Weber, "La négativité méthodique," p. 750. Similar formulations are given by Schmidt, "L'emploi de la séparation," p. 383. Compare *Super Meta*. I, lect.12 (EB 4,400,3): "in rebus non solum sunt corporea, sed etiam quaedam incorporea, ut patet ex libro *de Anima*."

35. *Super De Trin*. q.5, a.4 ad 5 (EB 4,536,1).

36. Schmidt, "L'emploi de la séparation," pp. 385-386.

37. *Super De Trin*. q.5, a.3 (EB 4,534,1).

38. *Super Sent*. I, d.24, q.1, a.3 (EB 1,66,1-3), where the first objector's phrases "secundum remotionem tantum" and "per remotionem" are taken up by Thomas into the more general vocabulary of "negatio." See also *Super Sent*. I, d.28, q.1, a.1 ad 1 (EB 1,76,2), with regard to the logical parsing of *'ingenitus'*: "illud cuius ratio consistit in remotione, optime per negationem certificatur." The mention of *'remotio'* in *Super De Trin*. q.6, a.2 will be discussed just below.

39. *Super De Trin*. q.6, a.2 (EB 4,537,3).

40. *Super De Trin*. q.6, a.2 (EB 4,537,3).

41. *Super De Trin*. q.6, a.2 (EB 4,537,3).

42. *Super De Trin*. q.6, a.2 (EB 4,537,3).

43. *Super De Trin*. q.6, a.2 ad 5: "Patet enim quod non possumus intelligere Deum esse causam corporum sive supra omnia corpora sive absque corporeitate, nisi imaginemur corpora, non tamen iudicium divinorum secundum imaginationem formatur" (EB 4,538,1).

44. *Super De Trin*. q.6, a.4, (EB 4,539,1), as for the following.

45. *Super De Trin*. q.6, a.4.

46. *Super De Trin*. q.6, a.4 ad 2.

47. *Super De Trin.* q.6, a.4 ad 3.
48. *Super De Trin.* q.6, a.4 ad 5.

NOTES FOR SECTION 5.3

1. For the ancient and medieval history of the treatment of the names, see Jordan, "Names of God," pp. 169-175, and the bibliographical notes there.
2. Thomas treats the divine names *ex professo* in the *Sentences*-commentary (I, d.22, qu. unica), in the *Contra Gent.* (I, c.30-36), in *Q.D. De potentia Dei* (q.7, aa.3-6), and the *Summa theologiae* (I, q.13), as well as in the commentary on Ps-Dionysius's *Divine Names.* I will follow the treatment in the *De potentia* here becaue it is fully technical and mature, being contemporary with the composition of the parallel text in the *prima pars.*
3. *Q.D. De pot..* q.7, aa.3-7, within the frame of aa.1-2 and 8-11.
4. *Q.D. De pot.* q.7, a.1 (EB 3,240,2), where the reference is to the *Physics.*
5. *Q.D. De pot.* q.7, a.5 (EB 3,243,2-3).
6. *Q.D. De pot.* q.7, a.5 (EB 3,243,2).
7. *Q.D. De pot.* q.7, a.5 (EB 3,243.3).
8. *Q.D. De pot.* q.7, a.5 (EB 3,243,3). Compare Section 3.4, above.
9. *Q.D. De pot.* q.7, a.5 ad 2 (EB 3,244,1).
10. *Q.D. De pot.* q.7, a.5 ad 2 (EB 3,244,1); compare the ad 5.
11. *Summa theol.* Ia, q.13, a.1 (EB 2,202,1).
12. *Summa theol.* Ia, q.13, a.1 (EB 2,202,1).
13. *Summa theol.* Ia, q.13, a.2 (EB 2,202,3).
14. *Summa theol.* Ia, q.13, a.11 (EB 2,205,2-3).

NOTES FOR SECTION 5.4

1. For expositions of the divided line as a pedagogical ascent, see Jacob Klein, *A Commentary on Plato's Meno*, pp. 112-125.
2. See Aristotle, *Metaphysics* VI, 1026a6-19, and XI, 1064b1-3; *Physics* II, 193b22-36. On Aristotle's relation to the Platonic division, see Augustin Mansion, *Introduction à la physique aristotélicienne*, pp. 127-142.
3. For example, Dominicus Gundissalinus, *De divisione philosophiae*, ed. Baur, p. 42, lines 4-17; Robert Kilwardby, *De ortu scientiarum*, cc.28-29, ed. Judy, pp. 86-88. For brief surveys of the divisions of the sciences, see James A. Weisheipl, "Classifications of the Sciences"; Leo Elders, *Faith and Science*, pp. 85-91; Malgorzata Frankowska-Terlecka, *L'unité du savoir aux XIIe et XIIIe siècles*, pp. 20-41.
4. For example, Dominicus Gundissalinus, *De divisione philosophiae*, ed. Baur, p. 38, lines 7-24 (to which compare the fourth fragment from Michael Scot, ed. Baur, p. 400); Robert Kilwardby, *De ortu scientiarum*, c.26, ed. Judy, p. 84, sect. 218 (compare c.5, p. 14, lines 19-29).
5. *Super De Trin.* q.5, a.1 ad 9 (EB 4,533,1).
6. These two readings are analyzed by Wippel in his "Commentary on Boethius's *De Trinitate*," pp. 142-148. Wippel prefers the second reading in

part because it "allows for a certain autonomy of the particular theoretical sciences. Granted that they do receive principles from metaphysics, in some way they can also discover their own starting points or first principles by grounding them in what is self-evident" (p. 146). I will argue that the dichotomy of the views is misleading.

7. *Super De Trin*. q.5, a.1 (EB 4,532,2), ed. Decker, p. 166, lines 4-6: "Dicitur etiam philosophia prima, in quantum alia omnes scientiae ab ea sua principia accipientes eam consequuntur." See the discussion of metaphysics as first philosophy in Section 5.1, above.

8. *Super De Trin*. ed. Decker, pp. 172-173, source apparatus.

9. Wippel, "Commentary on Boethius's *De Trinitate*," pp. 136-142.

10. Avicenna, *Metaphysica* I,3, ed. Van Riet, I, p. 18, line 41, to p. 19, line 43.

11. Avicenna, *Metaphysica* I, 3, ed. Van Riet, I, p. 20, lines 71-72.

12. Avicenna, *Metaphysica* I, 3, ed. Van Riet, I, p. 23, lines 33-34.

13. Avicenna, *Metaphysica* I, 3, ed. Van Riet, I, p. 24, lines 38-41.

14. *Summa theol*. Ia, q.108, a.1 (EB 2,338,3).

15. *Summa theol*. Ia, q.108, a.1 (EB 2,338,3).

16. *Summa theol*. Ia, q.108, a.1 ad 1.

17. *Super Sent*. II, d.9, q.unica, a.1 (EB 1,148,2-149,1); *Contra gent*. II, cap.95, n.4 (EB 2,59,1).

18. Cf. *Summa theol*. Ia, q.62, a.6.

19. See Section 3.4, above, on the dialectic of likeness and difference in causal hierarchies.

20. *Super De Trin*. q.6, a.4 ad 3 (EB 4,539,1).

21. There are certainly qualifications to be made in the question of desire for beatitude, and I do not mean to commit myself to the sort of position argued by De Lubac in *Surnaturel*.

NOTES FOR THE PROLOGUE TO CHAPTER 6

1. See Maimonides, *Guide of the Perplexed*, tr. Shlomo Pines, I, 6-10.

2. Thus, the center of Book VI of the *Republic* is replaced by Averroes with an Aristotelian treatment of the virtues and sciences (tr. Lerner, pp. 79-94).

3. Compare the *Collationes in Ave Maria*, art.2 (EB 6,25,3-26,1; ed. Spiazzi and 1120), with *Summa theol*. IIIa, q.27, a.2, (EB 2,809,3). See the remarks by Weisheipl, *Friar Thomas*, p. 402, #88; and Appendix II by Thomas Hill in volume 55 in the Blackfriars' edition of the *Summa*.

4. Plato, *Phaedrus*, 274c-278b.

5. See Maimonides, *Guide*, 6, 8-9.

6. Isidore, *Etymologiae*, II,xxiv,9, ed. Lindsay, lines 24-26.

NOTES FOR SECTION 6.1

1. See the discussion of Abelard in Section 2.4, above.

2. *Summa theol*. I-IIae, q.97, a.1 (EB 2,483,2). But compare the distinction

between the stability of laws and the mutability of arts in q.97, a.2 (EB 2,483,3).

3. Much was written against Aristotle's historiography in the wake of Harold Cherniss's *Aristotle's Criticism of Pre-Socratic Philosophy*. A moderate corrective is provided by W. K. C. Guthrie in his "Aristotle as a Historian of Philosophy: Some Preliminaries." Even Guthrie may concede too much to the prejudices of recent historical 'method'.

4. Though the tradition of medieval Latin doxography is complicated, a study of the sources of Thomas's Aristotelian commentaries, for example, will show his great dependence on Aristotle's historical summaries. See Section 1.P, above.

5. *Super Meta*. II, lect.1, n.16 (EB 4,406,2).

6. A small confirmation of this is that Thomas does not call Aristotle 'Philosophus' when he is revising him. See the passages in nn. 20 and 21, below, and the texts collated by Simon-Pierre East, "Remarques sur la double appellation du Stagirite."

7. Van Steenberghen says it neatly: "... l'option de S. Thomas en faveur d'Aristote n'est ni absolue, ni exclusive; elle va de pair avec une surprenante faculté d'accueil pour toute verité, d'où elle vienne, et avec une souveraine indépendance à l'égard du Philosophe" ("L'avenir du thomisme," rptd. in *Introduction à l'étude de la philosophie médiévale*, p. 244).

8. *De subst. sep.* (EB 3, 516, 1; Lescoe #11).

9. *De subst. sep.* (EB 3, 516, 1-2; Lescoe ##11-13).

10. See the discussion of the received etymologies and various senses for 'auctoritas' in M.-D. Chenu, *La théologie au XIIe siècle*, pp. 353-357. Compare the remarks on techniques for using authority, especially the principles *exponere reverenter*, in Chenu, pp. 360-365. Chenu traces these points through Thomas in his *Introduction a l'étude*.

11. Here I disagree with Michel Riquet, who writes: "Thomas ne demande à des citations scientifiquement choisies et interpretées qu'une *confirmation* et plus souvent un simple *illustration* des thèses philosophiques dont la démonstration rationelle, corroborée par l'expérience, fournit la seule preuve véritable ("S. Thomas d'Aquin et les 'Auctoritates,' " p. 124). Again, "pour notre saint Docteur, l'argument d'autorité humaine, *en philosophie*, ne vaut rien ou presque rien" (p. 292, with reference to *Summa theol.* Ia, q.1, a.8 ad 2, *Q.D. De verit.* q.11, a.1, and *Super Phys.* VIII, lect.3). It is true that demonstration remains the pedagogical ideal in Thomas, but the reality of the composition of the texts qualifies that ideal by a dependence on philosophical traditions. Moreover, the ideal of demonstration itself depends on an inherited philosophical language in its premises and first principles as in the construction of each of its subordinate premises.

12. Riquet emphasizes the importance of direct experience as a source superior in authority to Aristotle (p. 135). But the passages which he mentions in *Summa theol* Ia, q.88, a.1 may be seen to fall under that shared 'introspection' which I considered above in regard to the claims for the human being's knowledge of itself (see Section 4.2, above). A shared description of

experience is one dependent to some extent on the received technical language — which, for Thomas, is chiefly a version of the Aristotelian.

13. An extended comparison between Descartes and Aquinas as philosophical 'revolutionaries' was attempted by Jean Rimaud in his *Thomisme et méthode*, pp. 57-102. The comparison fails, both because Rimaud is not careful enough with texts and because he imagines that Thomas adopted Aristotelianism because it was new. He makes Thomas out as a teacher who sought innovation for the sake of vitality (see, e.g., p. 101).

14. Riquet provides samples of Thomas's exegetical criticisms on pp. 269-276.

15. For texts contrasting the authority of revelation with that of philosophy, *Super Sent*. II, d.14, q.1, a.2 sol and ad 1 (EB 1,164,1); *Super Phys*. VIII, lect.3, n.1 (EB 4,127,2-3); *Resp. art. 42* proemium (EB 3,640,2), art. 33 (EB 3,641,3) and art. 39 (EB 3,642,1).

16. Even so, Thomas is scrupulous in applying exegetical analysis to theological texts. A fine example is the *Contra errores graecorum*, which is prefaced with remarks on the problem of interpretation (EB 3,501,2-3).

17. On Thomas's great care as an exegete, see the first two essays by A. Gardeil under the general heading, "La réforme de la théologie catholique" (1903). Gardeil, in defending Thomas from unthinking attack by modern critics, is perhaps too anxious to find that Thomas's "documentation" is, "dans l'ensemble, indentique à la documentation fondamentale de la Théologie contemporaine" (p. 215, in the first essay). Surely the relation to the tradition is very different in the two cases. On Thomas's teaching about the role of tradition in theology, see Etienne Menard, *La tradition*, especially the discussion of the lexical connections between *'tradere'* and *'docere'* or *'doctrina'* (pp. 13-46).

18. *Topics*, 100b21-22.

19. *Topics*, 101a37.

20. *Topics*, 101b3-4.

21. *Super Peri*. I, lect.14, nn.8-9 (EB 4,338,1).

22. *Super Phys*. VIII, lect.2, nn. 16-20, (EB 4,127,1).

NOTES FOR SECTION 6.2

1. *Super Meta*. I, lect.3, n.17 (EB 4,394,3), lect.4 n.4 (EB 4,394,3); *Sent. Pol*. I, lect.1, n.8 (EB 4,248,3).

2. *Super De anima* I, lect.1, n.4 (EB 6,5,1).

3. *Super De anima* I, lect.1, n.9 (EB 6,5,2-3).

4. *Super Meta*. I, lect.1, n.29 (EB 4,392,3).

5. *Super Meta*. I, lect.1, nn.23-30 (EB 4,392,2-3).

6. *Super Meta*. I, lect.1, n.32 (EB 4,392,3).

7. *Super Meta*. I, lect.1, n.34 (EB 4,392,3-393,1).

8. *Super Meta*. I, lect.1, n.34 (EB 4,392,3-393,1). The definition of *'ars'* as "recta ratio factibilium" is based on Aristotle's *Ethics* VI, 4, 1140a3-5. Thomas repeats the definition more than a dozen times from early works to

late. See, for example, *Super Sent*. III, d.23, q.1, a.4 sol.2 ad 3 (EB 1,341,3); d.33, q.1, a.1 qc.2 obj.3 (EB 1,379,2); *Contra gent*. II, c.24, n.5 (EB 2,30,1); *Summa theol*. I-IIae, q.57, a.4 (EB 2,426,3), q.57, a.5 ad 1 (EB 2,427,1), q.58, a.2 ad 1 (EB 2,428,1); *Summa theol*. II-IIae Prologue (EB 2,523,3) and q.134, a.1 obj.4 (EB 2,690,2); *Sent. Ethic*. I, lect.1, n.8 (EB 4,144,2), II, lect.4, n.3 (EB 4,157,1), VII, lect.7, n. 14 (EB 4,208,3); *Resp. art. 36* a.9 (EB 3,638,3); *Super Post. An*. II, lect.20, n.11 (EB 4,311,2). Thomas discusses the Aristotelian reference explicitly in *Sent. Ethic*. VI, lect.3 (EB 4,194,1-195,2).

9. Recall the discussion of this principle in Section 3.4, above.

10. See, for example, *Super Post. An*. II, lect.20, nn.11-15 (EB 4,311,1-3); *Sent. Ethic*. VI, lect. 5-6 (EB 4,195,1-196,2).

11. I call the question Augustinian only because it reaches Thomas most pointedly in the *De Magistro*. Augustine also discusses it in the Prologue to *De Doctrina Christiana*.

12. The only earlier remarks would be *Super Sent*. II, d.9 q.1, a.2 ad 4 (EB 1,149,2) and d.28, q.1, a.5 ad 3 (EB 1,209,1).

13. *Q.D. De verit*. q.11, a.1 (EB 3,73,3, and EL p. 352, lines 357-358).

14. *Q.D. De verit*. a.11, a.1 ad 8 (EB 3,73,3).

15. *Q.D. De verit*. q.11, a.3 (EB 3,75,1-2, and EL p. 359, lines 249-260).

16. *Q.D. De verit*. q.11, a.4 (EB 3,76,1, and EL p. 362, lines 60-73).

17. The articles on teaching fall under the tripartite discussion of the activity of angels (aa.110-114), of bodies (qq.115-116), and of men (q.117).

18. *Summa theol*. Ia q.117, a.1 (EB 2,351,1-2).

19. *Summa theol*. Ia, q.117, a.1.

20. *Summa theol*. Ia, q.117, a.2.

21. Compare the context in *Contra gent*. II, c.75.

22. See Josef Pieper, *Hinführung zu Thomas von Aquin*, pp. 127-144, which is based on his 1949 lecture, "Thomas von Aquin als Lehrer." With Pieper, I think that the desire for teaching explains Thomas's understanding of composition even as it characterizes his life. Thomas is "vor allem eines: Lehrer" not only in his work but in the substance and mode of his thinking (compare *Hinführung*, p. 127).

23. Thomas says this about the teaching of theology: "Quaedam vero disputatio est magistralis in scholis non ad removendum errorem, sed ad instruendum auditores ut inducantur ad intellectum veritatis quam intendit: et tunc oportet rationibus inniti invetigantibus veritatis radicem, et facientibus scire quomodo sit verum quod dicitur ..." *Quodl*. IV, q.9, a.3 (EB 3,461,2). The 'root of truth' is found in the student's appropriation, the student's *inventio*. Theological teaching which does not aim at the student's good, which seeks rather its own glory, merits damnation (*Quodl*. V, q.12, a.1 (EB 3,470,1-2), where the teacher's culpability in lesser cases is also discussed).

NOTES FOR SECTION 6.3

1. *Contra gent*. I, c.3, n.2 (EB 2,1,2).

2. *Contra gent*. I, c.3, n.2 (EB 2,1,2).

3. *Contra gent.* I, c.5, nn.3-4 (EB 2,2,1).

4. *Contra gent.* I, c.9, n.2 (EB 2,2,3).

5. *Summa theol.* Ia, q.1, a.3 (EB 2,185,2). Of the enormous number of pieces written over the years on the first Question of the *Summa*, Gerald Van Ackeren's *Sacra Doctrina* is useful as providing a comparison of Tridentine and modern readings; Chenu's *Introduction* as fixing the medieval context; and Michel Corbin's *Le chemin de la théologie*, pp. 681-903, for reading the text itself dialectically. Van Ackeren seems mistaken in imagining that the *Summa* has the artificially exact terminology and the syllogistic manner of later scholasticism (see especially his pp. 118-119). Corbin is mistaken, I believe, in holding that the *Summa* records Thomas's discovery of something like the *loci theologici* of Melchior Cano (see especially Corbin, *Le chemin de la théologie*, pp. 850-852).

6. *Summa theol.* Ia, q.1, a.3 ad 2 (EB 2,185,2).

7. *Contra gent.* II, c.4 (EB 2,26,1).

8. See the texts in nn. 1-4, above.

9. Perhaps it is also the case that the intention of theological instruction, being always pastoral in some sense, forces a very different manner of teaching. Recall here Boyle's arguments for the context of the composition of the *Summa*.

10. Recall the arguments in *Contra gent.* I, c.5.

11. Chenu has shown that the typical thirteenth-century contrast between *philosophi* and *sancti* was not a contrast between two methods or two sets of propositions, but between two ways of life. See his "Les 'Philosophes' dans la philosophie chrétienne médiévale," especially pp. 28-29.

12. *Super Credo* prologus, nn.1-4 (EB 6,15,3-16,1).

13. *Super Credo* prologus (EB 6,15,3).

14. *Super Credo* art.1 (EB 6,16,1).

15. *Super Credo* art.1 (EB 6,16,1-2).

16. *Super Credo* prologus (EB 6,15,3).

17. *Summa theol.* Ia, q.1, a.2 (EB 2,185,1).

18. The pedagogy of Scripture is well presented in Andre Guindon's *La pédagogie de la crainte*, in which Thomas is seen replacing the *lex timoris/lex amoris* couplet with a richer understanding of the pedagogy of law. For Thomas's doctrine on the Church as pedagogical, see Max Seckler, *Das Heil in der Geschichte*, especially Chapter 8. Victor White understands the *Summa* itself as a book for teachers who must teach in the manner of Christian wisdom; see his *Holy Teaching*, especially pp. 6-7.

19. For example, *Super De Trin.* q.6, a.4 (EB 4,538,1-539,1).

20. *Super De Trin.* q.6, a.4 (EB 4,538,1-539,1).

21. *Super De Trin.* q.6, a.4 (EB 4,538,1-539,1).

22. There is a technical exception made by Thomas for the case of rapture, as in *Summa theol.* II-IIae, q.175, a.3. But the exception is sufficiently qualified — and sufficiently rare — to leave the principle untouched.

23. *Summa theol.* II-IIae, q.175, a.3 (EB 2,739,1).

BIBLIOGRAPHY
LOCI THOMISTICI
INDEX OF NAMES AND TOPICS

BIBLIOGRAPHY

The works listed here are only those to which reference has been made in the notes. More complete bibliographies can be found in many of these works and in the bibliographic tools cited in the first note to the Introduction. The following abbreviations have been used in this list and in the notes:

AL: *Aristoteles Latinus*
Atti: *Atti del Congresso Internazionale...1974*
BGPh[Th]M: *Beiträge für die Geschichte des Philosophie [und Theologie] des Mittelalters*
BT: *Bibliothèque Thomiste*
CCL: *Corpus Christianorum Latinorum*
CHLMP: Kretzmann *et al.*, eds., *Cambridge History of Later Medieval Philosophy*
CLCAG: *Corpus Latinum Commentariorum in Aristotelem Graecorum*
GL: Keil *et al.*, eds., *Grammatici Latini*
PG: J.-P. Migne, ed., *Patrologia Graeca*
PL: J.-P. Migne, ed., *Patrologia Latina*
SE: Beckmann *et al.*, eds., *Sprache und Erkenntnis*
Full bibliographic information for each of these works can be found at the appropriate place below.

I. Ancient and Medieval Authors

Adam of Balsham 'Parvipontanus'. *Ars disserendi*. Edited by Lorenzo Minio-Paluello. In *Twelfth-Century Logic: Texts and Studies*, vol. 1. Rome: Ed. Storia e letteratura, 1956.
Adelard of Bath. *De eodem et diverso*. Edited by Hans Wilner. BGPhM, vol. 4/1. Munster: Aschendorff, 1903.
Albert the Great. *Commentarii in librum...de coelesti hierarchia*. Edited by Auguste Borgnet. In *Opera omnia*, vol. 14. Paris: Vivès, 1892.
——— *De caelo et mundo*. Edited by Paul Hossfeld. In *Opera omnia*, vol. 5/1. Munster: Aschendorff, 1971.
——— *Metaphysica*, Books 1-5. Edited by Bernhard Geyer. In *Opera omnia*, vol. 16/1. Munster: Aschendorff, 1960.
——— *Quaestiones de animalibus*. Edited by Ephrem

Filthaut. In *Opera omnia*, vol. 12. Munster: Aschendorff, 1955.

Alcuin. *De dialectica*. PL 101:951-976.

Alexander Neckham. *De naturis rerum*. Edited by Thomas Wright. Rerum Britannicarum Medii Aevi Scriptores, vol. 34. London: Longman, Green, 1863.

Alexander of Villa-Dei. *Doctrinale*. Edited by Dietrich Reichling. Berlin: A. Hofmann, 1893.

Alfred of Sareshel. *Des Alfred von Sareshel (Alfredus Anglicus) Schrift De motu cordis*. Edited by Clemens Baeumker. BGPhM, vol. 23/1-2. Munster: Aschendorff, 1923.

Ammonius. *Commentaire sur le Peri Hermeneias d'Aristote*. Edited by Gerhard Verbeke. CLCAG, vol. 2. Leiden: E. J. Brill, 1961.

Anselm of Canterbury. *De grammatico*. In *Opera omnia*, ed. F. S. Schmitt, vol. 1, pp. 141-168. Edinburgh: Thomas Nelson, 1946.

———— *De veritate*. In *Opera omnia*, ed. F. S. Schmitt, vol. 1, pp. 169-199. Edinburgh: Thomas Nelson, 1946.

Aristotle. *Categoriae et liber de interpretatione*. Edited by Lorenzo Minio-Paluello. Oxford: Clarendon Press, 1949.

———— *Ethica Nicomachea*. Edited by I. Bywater. Oxford: Clarendon Press, 1890.

———— *De interpretatione vel Periermenias: Translatio Boethii...*. Edited by Lorenzo Minio-Paluello. AL, vol. 2/1-2. Leiden: E. J. Brill, 1965.

———— *Metaphysics*. Edited by W. D. Ross. Oxford: Clarendon Press, 1924.

———— *Physica*. Edited by W. D. Ross. Oxford: Clarendon Press, 1950.

———— *Topica*. In *Organon Graece*, edited by Theodor Weitz, vol. 2. Leipzig, 1846; reprinted Aalen: Scientia, 1965.

Augustine. *De doctrina christiana*. Edited by Joseph Martin. CCL, vol. 32. Turnhout: Brepols, 1972.

———— *De magistro* and *De ordine*. Edited by W. M. Green. CCL, vol. 29. Turnhout: Brepols, 1970.

———— *De Trinitate*. Edited by W. J. Mountain with F. Glorie. CCL, vols. 50-50A. Turnhout: Brepols, 1968.

———— *In Iohannis evangelium tractatus CXXIV*. Edited by Radbod Willems. CCL, vol. 36. Turnhout: Brepols, 1954.

———— *Sermo* 119. PL 38:673-676.

Augustine?. *De dialectica*. Text edited by Jan Pinborg, translated by B. Darrell Jackson. Dordrecht and Boston: D. Reidel, 1975.

Averroes. *Commentarium medium in Aristotelis De generatione et corruptione*. Edited by F. H. Fobes with S. Kurland. Cambridge, Mass.: Mediaeval Academy of America, 1956.

——— *Commentarium in libros de coelo*. In *Aristotelis opera cum Averrois commentariis*, vol. 5. Venice, 1562; rptd. Frankfurt a. M.: Minerva, 1962.

——— *Commentarium magnum in libros de physico audito*. In *Aristotelis opera cum Averrois commentariis*, vol. 4. Venice, 1562; rptd. Frankfurt a. M.: Minerva, 1962.

Avicebron. *Fons vitae ex Arabico in Latinum translatus ab Iohanne Hispano et Dominico Gundissalino*. Edited by Clemens Baeumker. BGPhM, vol. 1/2. Munster: Aschendorff, 1892.

Avicenna. *Logica*. In *Opera philosophica*. Venice, 1508; rptd. Louvain: Eds. de la bibliothèque S. J., 1961.

——— *Liber de philosophia prima*. Edited by S. Van Riet. 3 vols. Louvain: E. Peeters, and Leiden: E. J. Brill, 1977-83.

Bernard Silvestris. *De mundi universitate*. Edited by Carl Sigmund Barach and Johann Wrobel. Bibliotheca philosophorum medii aevi, vol. 1. Innsbruck: Wagner'sche Universitätsverlag, 1876.

Boethius. *De differentiis topicis*. PL 64:1173-1218.

——— *In Categorias Aristotelis*. PL 64:159-294.

——— *In librum Aristotelis de interpretatione, maiora commentaria*. PL 64:393-638.

——— *In librum Aristotelis de interpretatione, minora commentaria*. PL 64:293-392.

Bonaventure. *Commentaria in IV libros Sententiarum*. In *Opera omnia*, vols. 1-4. Quaracchi: Collegium S. Bonaventurae, 1882-1889.

Cassiodorus. *Institutiones*. Edited by R. A. B. Mynors. Oxford: Clarendon Press, 1937.

——— *Variae*. Edited by Ake J. Fridh. CCL, vol. 96. Turnhout: Brepols, 1973.

'Cicero'. *Ad C. Herennium*. Edited by C. F. W. Müller. Leipzig: Teubner, 1890.

Cicero. *Ad M. Brutum orator*. Edited A. E. Douglas. Oxford:

Clarendon Press, 1966.

—— *De inventione*. Edited by C. F. W. Müller. Leipzig: Teubner, 1890.

Conrad of Hirsau. *Dialogus super auctores*. Edited by J. C. B. Huygens.

Diogenes Laertius. *Vitae philosophorum*. Edited by H. S. Long. Oxford: Clarendon Press, 1964.

Dominicus Gundissalinus. *De divisione philosophiae*. Edited by Ludwig Baur. BGPhM, vol. 4/2-3. Munster: Aschendorff, 1903.

Donatus. *Ars grammatica*. In GL, vol. 4.

(Ebbesen, Sten, ed.) *Incertorum auctorum Questiones super Sophisticos Elenchos*. Corpus philosophorum Danicorum medii aevi, vol. 7. Copenhagen: Almqvist & Wiksell, 1977.

Gregory the Great. *Moralia in Job*. Edited by Marc Adriaen. CCL, vols. 143-143A. Turnhout: Brepols, 1979.

Gregory of Nyssa. *De anima*. PG 45:187-222.

Hugh of Saint-Victor. *De grammatica*. In *Opera propaedeutica*. University of Notre Dame, Publications in Medieval Studies, vol. 20. Edited by Roger Baron. Notre Dame: University of Notre Dame Press, 1966.

—— *De scriptoris et scriptoribus sacris*. PL 175:9-28.

—— *Didascalicon de studio legendi*. Edited by C. H. Buttimer. Studies in Medieval and Renaissance Latin, vol. 10. Washington: Catholic University of America Press, 1939.

Isidore. *Etymologiae*. Edited by W. M. Lindsay. Oxford: Clarendon Press, 1911.

Jerome. *Epistula* 53. PL 22:540-549.

John Chrysostom. *Homiliae in Genesim*. PG 53:21-384.

John Damascene. *De fide orthodoxa*. Edited by E. M. Buytaert. Franciscan Institute Publications, Text Series, vol. 18. St. Bonaventure, NY: Franciscan Institute Press, 1955.

John of Salisbury. *Metalogicon*. Edited by C. C. I. Webb. Oxford: Clarendon Press, 1929.

John Scotus Eriugena. *Annotationes in Marcianum*. Edited by Cora E. Lutz. Mediaeval Academy of America, Publication no. 34. Cambridge, Mass.: Mediaeval Academy of America, 1939.

Jordanus, magister. *Notulae super Priscianum minorum*. Edited by Mary Sirridge. Cahiers, 36. Copenhagen: Institut du moyen-âge grec et latin, University of Copenhagen, 1980.

(Keil, Heinrich, ed.) *Grammatici Latini*. 7 vols. Leipzig: Teubner, 1857-1890.

Marius Victorinus. *Ars grammatica*. Edited by Italo Mariotti. Biblioteca nazionale, Serie dei classici greci e latini: Testi con commenti filologice, vol. 6. Florence: F. Le Monnier, 1967.

Martianus Capella. *De nuptiis Philologiae et Mercurii*. Edited by A. Dick. Leipzig: Teubner, 1925.

Moses Maimonides. *Dux seu Director dubitantium aut perplexorum*. Edited by Joseph de Voisin. Paris, 1520.

——— *Guide of the Perplexed*. Translated by Shlomo Pines. Chicago: University of Chicago Press, 1963.

Peter Abelard. *Dialectica*. Edited by L. M. De Rijk. 2d rev. ed. Assen: Van Gorcum, 1970.

——— *Editio super Aristotelem De interpretatione*. In *Scritti di logica*, edited by Mario Dal Pra. 2d ed. Pubblicazioni della Facoltà di lettere e filosifia dell'Università di Milano, vol. 34; Sezio a cura dell'Instituto di storia della filosofia, vol. 3. Florence: La Nuova Italia, 1969.

——— *Logica Ingredientibus*. Edited by Bernhard Geyer. In *Peter Abaelards philosophischen Schriften*. BGPhThM, vol. 21. Munster: Aschendorff, 1919.

——— *Sic et Non*. Edited by Blanche Boyer and Richard McKeon. Chicago: University of Chicago Press, 1977.

Peter Helias. *The Summa of Petrus Helias on Priscianus Minor*. Edited by James E. Tolson. Cahiers, 27-28. Copenhagen: Institut du moyen-âge grec et latin, University of Copenhagen, 1978.

Peter of Ireland. Commentary on Aristotle's *Peri hermeneias*. Edited by Karen Elisabeth Dalgaard. In Cahiers, vol. 43, pp. 3-44. Cophenhagen: Institut du moyen-âge grec et latin, University of Copenhagen, 1982.

——— Disputation *Dubitavit rex Manfredus...* Edited by Clemens Baeumker. In *Petrus de Hibernia, der Jugendlehrer des Thomas von Aquino und seine Disputation vor König Manfred*. SB Bayerische Akademie (1920), Abhandlung 8.

Peter of Spain. *Tractatus, called afterwards Summule logicales*. Edited by L. M. de Rijk. Assen: Van Gorcum, 1972.

Plato. *Phaedo*. Edited by John Burnet. Oxford: Clarendon Press, 1911.

Porphyry. *In Categorias commentarium*. Edited by A. Busse. Commentaria in Aristotelem Graeca, vol. 4/1. Berlin: G. Reimer, 1887.

Priscian. *Institutiones grammaticae*. In GL, vols. 2-3.

Rabanus Maurus. *De institutione clericorum*. PL 107:293-420.

Radulphus Brito. *Quaestiones super Priscianum minorem*. Edited by Heinz W. Enders and Jan Pinborg. Grammatica Speculativa, vol. 3. Stuttgart — Bad Canstatt; Frommann — Holzboog, 1980.

(de Rijk, Lambertus M., ed.) *Logica Modernorum: A Contribution to the History of Early Terminist Logic*. Wijsgerige teksten en studies, vol. 6. Assen: Van Gorcum, 1962.

Robert Kilwardy. *The Commentary on 'Priscianus major' ascribed to Robert Kilwardy*. Text edited by K. M. Fredborg, N. J. Green-Pedersen, Lauge Nielsen, and Jan Pinborg. Cahiers, vol. 15. Copenhagen: Institut du moyen-âge grec et latin, University of Copenhagen, 1975.

——— *De ortu scientiarum*. Edited by Albert G. Judy. Auctores Britannici medii aevi, vol. 4. London: British Academy, 1976.

Thomas Aquinas. See the "Note on Citations to Aquinas" for the main editions of his *Opera omnia*.

——— *Expositio super librum Boethii de Trinitate*. Edited by Bruno Decker. Studien und Texte, vol. 44. Leiden: E. J. Brill, 1955.

——— *Expositio super librum Boethii de Trinitate*, questions 5 and 6. Edited by Paul Wyser. In "Die wissenschaftstheoretischen Quaest. V u. VI in Boethium de Trinitate des hl. Thomas von Aquinas." *Divus Thomas* [Fribourg] 25 (1947): 437-485, and 26 (1948): 74-98.

——— *In librum De causis expositio*. Edited by Ceslao Pera. Turin: Marietti, 1955.

——— *Scriptum super libros Sententiarum...*. Edited by Pierre Mandonnet and Maria Fabianus Moos. 4 vols. Paris: P. Lethielleux, 1929-1933.

——— *Quaestio de anima*. Edited by Leonard A. Kennedy. In "The Soul's Knowledge of Itself: An Unpublished Work Attributed to St. Thomas Aquinas." *Vivarium* 15 (1977):31-35.

(Thurot, Charles, ed.) *Notices et extraits de divers manuscrits Latins pour servir à l'histoire de doctrines grammaticales au moyen âge.* Notices et extraits des manuscrits de la Bibliothèque Impériale et autres bibliothèques, vol. 22/2. Paris: Imprimerie Impériale, 1869.

Urso of Salerno. *De commixtionibus elementorum.* Edited by Wolfgang Stürner. Stuttgarter Beiträge zur Geschichte und Politik, vol. 7. Stuttgart: Klett, 1976.

William of Conches. *Glosae super Platonem.* Edited by Edouard Jeauneau. Textes philosophiques du moyen âge, vol. 13. Paris: J. Vrin, 1965.

———— *Philosophia mundi*, 1. Edited by Gregor Maurach. Pretoria: University of South Africa, 1974.

William of Shyreswood (or Sherwood). *William of Sherwood's Introduction to Logic.* Edited and translated by Norman O. Kretzmann.

II. Modern Authors

Aarsleff, Hans. *From Locke to Saussure: Essays on the Study of Language and Intellectual History.* Minneapolis: University of Minnesota Press, 1982.

Abelson, Paul. *The Seven Liberal Arts: A Study in Mediaeval Culture.* New York: Teachers College, Columbia University, 1906.

Allard, Guy-H. "Arts libéraux et langage chez saint Augustin." In ALPMA, pp. 481-492.

———— "Le 'Contra Gentiles' et le modèle rhétorique." *Laval Théologique Philosophique* 30 (1974):237-250.

Alonso Alonso, Manuel. "Las fuentes literarias del Liber de causis." In *Temas filosóficos medievales: Ibn Dawud y Gundisalvo*, pp. 103-151. Publicacciones anejas a Miscelánea Comillas, Série filosófica, vol. 10. Comillas: Pontificia Universitas Comillensis, 1959.

Anderson, Thomas C. "Intelligible Matter and the Objects of Mathematics in Aquinas." *New Scholasticism* 43 (1969):555-576.

Armstrong, Ross A. *Primary and Secondary Precepts in Thomistic Natural Law Teaching.* The Hague: Martinus Nijhoff, 1966.

Ashworth, E. J. *The Tradition of Medieval Logic and Speculative Grammar*. Subsidia Mediaevalia, vol. 9. Toronto: P. I. M. S., 1978.

Atti del Congresso Internazionale (Roma-Napoli — 17/24 Aprile 1974): Tommaso d'Aquino nel suo settimo centenario. 9 volumes. Naples: Edizioni Dominicane Italiane, 1975-1978.

Bazan, Bernardo Carlos. "Le dialogue philosophique entre Siger de Brabant et Thomas d'Aquin. A propos d'un ouvrage récent de E. H. Wéber, OP." *Revue philosophique de Louvain* 72 (1974):53-155.

Béa, Augustin. "*Deus auctor Sacrae Scripturae*. Herkunft und Bedeutung der Formel." *Angelicum* 20 (1943):16-31.

Beckmann, Jan P.; Honnefelder, Ludger; Jüssen, Gabriel; Münxelhaus, Barbara; Schrimpf, Gangolf; Wieland, Georg; under the direction of Kluxen, Wolfgang, eds. *Sprache und Erkenntnis im Mittelalter: Akten des VI. Internationalen Kongresses für mittelalterliche Philosophie des SIEPM...* Berlin and New York: Walter de Gruyter, 1981.

Beonio-Brocchieri Fumagalli, Maria Teresa. *La logica di Abelardo*. Pubblicazioni dell'Istituto di storia della filosofia dell'Università degli Studi di Milano, vol. 6. Florence: Nuova Italia, 1964.

Bertola, Ermenegildo. "I precedenti storici del metodo del 'Sic et Non' di Abelardo." *Rivista di filosofia neo-scolastica* 53 (1961):253-280.

Blanche, F. Albert. "Le sens littéral des Ecritures d'après saint Thomas d'Aquin: Contribution à l'histoire de l'exégèse catholique au moyen âge." *Revue thomiste* 14 (1906):192-212.

Bloch, Herbert. "Monte Cassino, Byzantium, and the West in the Earlier Middle Ages." *Dumbarton Oaks Papers* 3 (1946):163-224.

Bonner, Stanley F. *Education in Ancient Rome*. Berkeley and Los Angeles: University of California Press, 1977.

Bourke, Vernon J., comp. *Thomistic Bibliography, 1920-1940*. Supplement to *Modern Schoolman*, vol. 21. St. Louis: B. Herder, 1945.

Boyer, Charles. "Le sens d'un texte de saint Thomas: *De veritate*, Q.1, A.9." *Gregorianum* 5 (1924):424-443. Reprinted without alteration in *Doctor Communis* 31 (1978):3-19.

Boyle, Leonard E. *The Setting of the Summa theologiae of Saint Thomas*. Etienne Gilson Series, vol. 5. Toronto: P. I. M. S., 1982.

Braza Diez, Mariano. "Tomás de Aquino y el analisis lingüistico." *Studium* [Madrid] 16 (1976):463-493.

Brown, Oscar J. *Natural Rectitude and Divine Law in Aquinas: An Approach to an Integral Interpretation of the Thomistic Doctrine of Law*. Studies and Texts, vol. 55. Toronto: P. I. M. S., 1981.

Bujo, Bénézet. *Moralautonomie und Normenfindung bei Thomas von Aquin. Unter Einbeziehung der neutestamentlichen Kommentare*. Paderborn: Ferdinand Schöningh, 1979.

Burrell, David B. *Aquinas: God and Action*. Notre Dame: University of Notre Dame Press, 1979.

Bursill-Hall, Geoffrey L. *A Census of Medieval latin Grammatical Manuscripts*. Grammatica speculativa, vol. 4. Stuttgart — Bad Canstatt: Frommann — Holzboog, 1981.

———— Introduction to R. W. Hunt, *Collected Papers*, q.v., pp. xxvii— xxxvi.

———— *Speculative Grammars of the Middle Ages*. The Hague and Paris: Mouton, 1971.

———— "Teaching Grammars of the Middle Ages: Notes on the Manuscript Tradition." *Historiographia Linguistica* 4 (1977):1-29.

Busa, Roberto, ed. *Index Thomisticus*. Stuttgart—Bad Canstatt: Frommann— Holzboog, 1974-1980.

Callus, D. A. "Les Sources de Saint Thomas: Etat de la question." In *Aristote et Saint Thomas*, ed. L. de Raeymaeker, pp. 93-174. Louvain: Publications universitaires, and Paris: Béatrice-Nauwelaerts, 1957.

Caplan, Harry. "Classical Rhetoric and the Medieval Theory of Preaching." *Classical Philology* 28 (1933):73-96. Reprinted with revisions in *Of Eloquence*, q.v., pp. 105-134.

———— *Of Eloquence: Studies in Ancient and Mediaeval Rhetoric*. Edited by Anne King and Helen North. Ithaca and London: Cornell University Press, 1970.

Cardoletti, Pietro. *L'analisi del linguaggio come metodo dell'indagine metafisica in S. Tommaso d'Aquino, dal De ente et essentia e dal in V. Metaphysicorum.* Varese: Gallarete, 1960. Excerpted from a dissertation in the Philosophical Faculty "Aloisianum." Reprinted from the same plates as "Analisi logico del linguaggio e construzione metafisica nel *De ente et essentia* di San Tommaso d'Aquino." In *Miscellanea Adriano Gazzano*, vol. 2, pp. 51-112. Archivum philosophicum Aloisianum, series 2, number 10. Milan: C. Marzorati, 1960.

Chadwick, Henry. *Boethius: The Consolations of Music, Logic, Theology, and Philosophy.* Oxford: Clarendon Press, 1981.

Chenu, Marie-Dominique. *Introduction à l'étude de Saint Thomas d'Aquin.* Publications de l'Institut d'études médiévales, vol. 11. 3rd ed., Montreal: Institut d'études médiévales, and Paris: J. Vrin, 1974.

―――― "Les *Philosophes* dans la Philosophie chrétienne médiévale." *Revue des sciences philosophiques et théologiques* 26 (1937):27-40.

―――― *La Théologie au XIIe siècle.* 3d ed. Etudes de philosophie médiévale, vol. 45. Paris: J. Vrin, 1976.

Cherniss, Harold F. *Aristotle's Criticism of Presocratic Philosophy.* Baltimore: Johns Hopkins Press, 1935.

Colish, Marcia L. *The Mirror of Language: A Study in the Medieval Theory of Knowledge.* Yale Historical Publications, Miscellany, vol. 88. New Haven: Yale University Press, 1968. Revised edition, Lincoln: University of Nebraska Press, 1983.

Corbin, Michel. *Le chemin de la théologie chez Thomas d'Aquin.* Bibliothèque des Archives de Philosophie, NS vol. 16. Paris: Beauchesne, 1974.

Cornell, Desmond. "St. Thomas on Reflection and Judgment." *Irish Theological Quarterly* 45 (1978):234-247.

Cowdrey, H. E. J. *The Age of Abbot Desiderius: Montecassino, the Papacy, and the Normans in the Eleventh and Early Twelfth Centuries.* Oxford: Clarendon Press, 1983.

Cranz, F. Edward. "The Publishing History of the Aristotle Commentaries of Thomas Aquinas." *Traditio* 34 (1978):157-192.

Crowe, Michael Bertram. *The Changing Profile of the Natural Law.* The Hague: Martinus Nijhoff, 1977.

―――― "On Re-Writing the Biography of Aquinas." *Irish*

Theological Quarterly 46 (1974):255-273.

——— "*Synderesis* and the Notion of Law in St. Thomas." In *L'Homme et son destin, d'après les penseurs du moyen âge: Actes du Premier Congrès international de philosophie médiévale...* Louvain: Nauwelaerts, 1960.

Curtius, Ernst Robert. *European Literature and the Latin Middle Ages*. Translated by Willard R. Trask. Bollingen Series, vol. 36. Princeton: Princeton University Press, 1953.

Delhaye, Philippe. "*Grammatica* et *ethica* au XIIe siècle." *Recherches de théologie ancienne et médiévale* 25 (1958):59-110.

Denifle, Heinrich, and Chatelain, Emile. *Chartularium Universitatis Parisiensis*. 4 vols. Paris: Frères Delalain, 1889-1891.

De Renzi, Salvatore, ed. and comp. *Collectio Salernitana*. 5 vols. Naples: Filiatre-Sebezio, 1852-1859.

De Wulf, Maurice. *An Introduction to Scholastic Philosophy, Medieval and Modern*. Translated by P. Coffey. New York: Dover, 1956. A translation of *Introduction à la philosophie néo-Scholastique*.

Dod, Bernard G. "*Aristoteles latinus*." In CHLMP, pp. 45-79.

Doig, James C. *Aquinas on Metaphysics: A Historico-Doctrinal Study of the Commentary on the Metaphysics*. The Hague: Martinus Nijhoff, 1972.

Dondaine, H. F., and Shooner, H. V.. *Codices manuscripti operum Thomae de Aquino*, vol. 1. Editores operum Sancti Thomae de Aquino, vol. 2. Rome: Comissio Leonina, 1967.

Dronke, Peter. "New Approaches to the School of Chartres." *Anuario de estudios medievales* 6 (1969):117-140.

Duhem, Pierre. *Le Système du Monde*. Volume 5: *La crue de l'aristotélisme (suite)*. Paris: A. Hermann, 1917.

East, Simon-Pierre. "Remarques sur la double appellation du Stagirite *Aristoteles* et *Philosophus* par Thomas d'Aquin." In *Atti*, vol. 1, pp. 186-202.

Ebbesen, Sten. "Ancient Scholastic Logic as the Source of Medieval Scholastic Logic." In CHLMP, pp. 101-127.

Elders, Leo. *Faith and Science: An Introduction to St. Thomas' Expositio in Boethii de Trinitate*. Studia Universitatis S. Thomae in Urbe, vol. 3. Rome: Herder, 1974.

———— "Structure et fonction de l'argument *Sed contra* dans le Somme Théologique de Saint Thomas." *Divus Thomas* [Piacenza] 80 (1977):245-260.

Evans, Gillian R. *Anselm and Talking about God*. Oxford: Clarendon Press, 1978.

Fabro, Cornelio. *Participation et causalité selon Saint Thomas d'Aquin*. Chaire Cardinale Mercier, Institut supérieur de philosophie, vol. 2. Louvain: Publications universitaires, and Paris: Béatrice-Nauwelaerts, 1961.

Faulhaber, Charles B. "The *Summa dictaminis* of Guido Faba." In *Medieval Eloquence*, edited by James Murphy, pp. 85-111. Berkeley, etc.: University of California Press, 1978.

Frankowska-Terlecka, Malgorzata. *L'unité du savoir aux XIIe et XIIIe siècles*. Translated by Hanna Sitkowska. Wroclaw, etc.: Ossolineum, Polish Academy of Sciences, 1980.

Frati, C. Review of Mandonnet-Destrez, *Bibliographie Thomiste*. *La Bibliofilia* 26 (1924-25):23-26.

Frede, Michael. "The Original Notion of Cause." In *Doubt and Dogmatism*, edited by Jonathan Barnes, pp. 217-249. Oxford: Clarendon Press, 1980.

Gardeil, A. "A propos d'un cahier du R. P. Romeyer." *Revue thomiste* NS 12 (1929):520-532.

———— "Examen de conscience." *Revue thomiste* NS 11 (1928):156-180; NS 12 (1929):70-84.

———— "La perception expérimentale de l'âme par elle-même d'après saint Thomas." In *Mélanges Mandonnet*, q.v., pp. 219-236.

———— "La réforme de la théologie catholique." *Revue thomiste* 11 (1903):197-215 and 428-457.

Garrigou-Lagrange, Réginald. "Utrum mens seipsam per essentiam cognoscat an per aliquam speciem." *Angelicum* 5 (1928):37-54.

Geiger, Louis-B. "Abstraction et séparation d'après S. Thomas. *In De Trinitate*, q. 5, a. 3." *Revue des sciences philosophiques et théologiques* 31 (1947):3-40.

———— *La participation dans la philosophie de S. Thomas d'Aquin*. 2d ed. Paris: J. Vrin, 1953.

de Ghellinck, Joseph. *Le mouvement théologique du XIIe siècle....* Museum Lessianum, Section historique, vol. 10. 2d rev. ed. Bruges: De Tempel, 1948.

Giacon, Carlo. *La seconda scolastica. I grandi commentatori di San Tommaso*. 2 volumes. Archivum philosophicum Aloisianum, series 2, vol. 3. Milan: Fratelli Bocca, 1943-1946.

———— "Sussidi lessicali e bibliografici per lo studio di S. Tommasso." *Seminarium* 29 (1977):918-993.

Gilson, Etienne. *History of Christian Philosophy in the Middle Ages*. New York: Random House, 1955.

———— "L'objet de la métaphysique selon Duns Scot." *Mediaeval Studies* 10 (1948):21-92.

———— "Pourquoi saint Thoms a critiqué saint Augustin." *Archives d'histoire doctrinale et littéraire du moyen âge* 1 (1926):5-127.

Glorieux, Palémon. *La faculté des arts et ses maîtres au XIIIe siècle*. Etudes de philosophie médiévale, vol. 59. Paris: J. Vrin, 1971.

———— "Le quodlibet et ses procédés rédactionnels." *Divus Thomas* [Piacenza] 42 (1939):61-93.

Grabmann, Martin. "Eine für Examinazwecke abgefasste Questionensammlung der Pariser Artistenfakultät aus der ersten Hälfte des 13. Jahrhunderts." *Revue néo-scolastique* 30 (1934):211-229. Reprinted in his *Mittelalterliches Geistesleben*, vol. 2, pp. 183-199. Munich: Max Hueber, 1936.

———— "Kaiser Friedrich II. und sein Verhältnis zur aristotelischen und arabischen Philosophie." In his *Mittelalterliches Geistesleben*, vol. 2, pp. 103-137. Munich: Max Hueber, 1936.

Guindon, André. *La pédagogie de la crainte dans l'histoire du salut selon Thomas d'Aquin*. Recherches, vol. 15. Montreal: Bellarmin, and Paris—Tournai: Desclée, 1975.

Guthrie, W. K. C. "Aristotle as a Historian of Philosophy: Some Preliminaries." *Journal of Hellenic Studies* 77 (1957):35-41.

Heinzmann, Richard. *Die Unsterblichkeit der Seele und die Auferstehung des Leibes: Eine problemgeschichtliche Untersuchung der frühscholastischen Sentenzen- und Summenliteratur von Anselm von Laon bis Wilhelm von Auxerre*. BGPhThM, vol. 40/3. Munster: Aschendorff, 1965.

Henry, Desmond Paul. *Commentary on De Grammatico: The Historical-Logical Dimensions of a Dialogue of St. Anselm's*. Dordrecht and Boston: D. Reidel, 1974.

Hoenen, P. *La théorie du jugement d'après Saint Thomas d'Aquin*. Analecta Gregoriana, vol. 39. Rome: Pont. Univ. Gregoriana, 1946.

Howell, Wilber Samuel, translator and editor. *The Rhetoric of Alcuin and Charlemagne*. Princeton Studies in English, vol. 23. Princeton: Princeton University Press, and London: Humphrey Milford/Oxford University Press, 1941.

Hunt, R. W. *Collected Papers on the History of Grammar in the Middle Ages*. Edited by G. L. Bursill-Hall. Amsterdam Studies in the Theory and History of Linguistic Science, series 3: Studies in the History of Linguistics, vol. 5. Amsterdam: John Benjamins, 1980.

——— "Introduction to the Artes." In *Studia Mediaevalia...R. J. Martin*, q.v., pp. 85-112.

Isaac, Jean. "La notion de dialectique chez Saint Thomas." *Revue des sciences philosophiques et théologiques* 34 (1950):481-506.

——— *Le Peri hermeneias en Occident de Boèce à Saint Thomas: Histoire littéraire d'un traité d'Aristote*. BT, vol. 29. Paris: J. Vrin, 1953.

——— "Saint Thomas interprète des oeuvres d'Aristote." In *Scholastica ratione historica-critica instauranda: Acta Congressus scholastici internationalis Romae anno sancto 1950 celebrati*, pp. 353-363. Rome: Pontificium Athenaeum Antonianum, 1951.

Jackson, B. Darrell. "The Theory of Signs in St. Augustine's *De doctrina Christiana*." *Revue des études augustiniennes* 15 (1969):9-49.

Jolivet, Jean. *Arts de langage et théologie chez Abélard*. Etudes de philosophie médiévale, vol. 57. Paris: J. Vrin, 1969.

——— "Comparaison des théories du langage chez Abélard et chez les Nominalistes du XIVe siècle." In *Peter Abelard*, edited by E. M. Buytaert, pp. 163-178. Leuven: Leuven University Press, 1974.

Jolivet, Régis. "Etude critique: Saint Thomas et notre connaissance de l'esprit humain." *Revue de philosophie* NS 4 (1933):295-311.

Jordan, Mark D. "The Names of God and the Being of Names." In *The Existence and Nature of God*, edited by Alfred

J. Freddoso, pp. 161-190. University of Notre Dame Studies in the Philosophy of Religion, vol. 3. Notre Dame and London: University of Notre Dame Press, 1983.

——— "The Protreptic Structure of the '*Summa contra Gentiles*'." *The Thomist* 50 (1986): 173-209.

Keller, Albert. "Arbeiten zur Sprachphilosophie Thomas von Aquins." *Theologie und Philosophie* 49 (1974):464-476.

Klein, Jacob. *A Commentary on Plato's Meno*. Chapel Hill: University of North Carolina Press, 1965.

Kleutgen, Joseph. *La philosophie scholastique expliquée et defendue*. Paris: Gaume Frères and J. Duprey, 1868-1870.

Kluxen, Wolfgang. "Die Geschichte des Maimonides in lateinishcen Abendland." In *Judentum im Mittelalter*, edited by Paul Wilpert, pp. 146-166. Miscellanea Mediaevalia, vol. 4. Berlin: W. de Gruyter, 1966.

——— "Literargeschichtliches zum lateinishcen Moses Maimonides." *Recherches de théologie ancienne et médiévale* 21 (1954):32-50.

Koch, Joseph, ed. *Artes liberales von der antiken Bildung zur Wissenschaft des Mittelalters*. Leiden: E. J. Brill, 1959.

Kretzmann, Norman; Kenny, Anthony; and Pinborg, Jan, eds. *The Cambridge History of Later Medieval Philosophy*. Cambridge: Cambridge University Press, 1982.

Kristeller, Paul Oskar. "Bartholomaeus, Musandinus, and Maurus of Salerno and Other Early Commentators of the *Articella....*" *Italia medioevale e umanistica* 19 (1976):57-87.

——— "Beitrag der Schule der Salerno zur Entwicklung der scholastischen Wissenschaft im 12. Jahrhundert." In *Artes liberales*, edited by Joseph Koch, q. v., pp. 84-90.

——— "Philosophy and Medicine in Medieval and Renaissance Italy." In *Organism, Medicine, and Metaphysics*, edited by S. F. Spicker, pp. 29-40. Dordrecht: D. Reidel, 1978.

——— "School of Salerno." *Bulletin of the History of Medicine* 17 (1945):133-194. Reprinted in his *Studies in Renaissance Thought and Letters*, pp. 495-551. 2d ed. Rome: Storia et letteratura, 1969.

——— *La scuola medica di Salerno secondo ricerche e scoperte recenti*. Quaderni CSDMS, vol. 5. Salerno: Centro studi e documentazione della Scuola medica Salernitana, 1980.

Lachance, L. "Saint Thomas dans l'histoire de la logique." In

Etudes d'histoire littéraire et doctrinale du XIIIe siècle, series 1, pp. 61-103. Paris: J. Vrin, and Ottawa: Institut d'études médiévales, 1932.

Laverdière, Raymond. *Le principe de causalité: Recherches thomistes récentes*. BT, vol. 39 . Paris: J. Vrin, 1969.

Lawn, Brian. *I quesiti Salernitani....* Translated by Alessandro Spagnuolo. [n.p.]: Di Mauro, 1969. A revised version of *The Salernitan Questions*. Oxford: Clarendon Press, 1963.

Leccisotti, Tommaso S. *Tommaso d'Aquino e Montecassino*. Montecassino: Abbey of Montecassino, 1965.

Leclercq, Jacques. *La philosophie morale de saint Thomas devant la pensée contemporaine*. Bibliothèque philosophique de Louvain, vol. 15. Louvain: Publications universitaires, and Paris: J. Vrin, 1955.

Leroy, M.-V. "*Abstractio* et *separatio* d'après un texte controversé." *Revue thomiste* 48 (1948):328-339.

Leuret, Simonne. "Saint Thomas et *Notre science de l'esprit humain*." *Revue thomiste* NS 6 (1923):368-386.

Lewry, Osmund. "Boethian Logic in the Medieval West." In *Boethius: His Life, Thought, and Influence*, edited by Margaret Gibson, pp. 90-134. Oxford: Basil Blackwell, 1981.

————— "Thirteenth Century Examination Compendia from the Faculty of Arts." In *Les genres littéraires dans les sources théologiques et philosophiques médiévales*, , pp. 101-106. Louvain: Institut d'études médiévales, Université catholique de Louvain, 1982.

Lohr, Charles. "Medieval Latin Aristotle Commentaries, Authors: Narcissus— Richardus." *Traditio* 28 (1972):281-396.

————— "Medieval Latin Aristotle Commentaries, Authors: Robertus-Wilgelmus." *Traditio* 29 (1973):93-197.

Lonergan, Bernard J. F. *Collection*. Edited by F. E. Crowe. New York: Herder and Herder, 1967.

————— *Grace and Freedom: Operative Grace in the Thought of St. Thomas Aquinas*. Edited by J. Patout Burns. London: Darton, Longman, & Todd, and New York: Herder and Herder, 1971.

————— *Verbum: Word and Idea in Aquinas*. Edited by David B. Burrell. Notre Dame: University of Notre Dame Press, 1967.

Lottin, Odon. *Psychologie et morale aux XIIe et XIIIe siècles*. Volume 1: *Problèmes de psychologie*. Louvain: Abbey of Mont César, and Gembloux: J. Duculot, 1942.

de Lubac, Henri. *Exégèse médiévale: Les quatre sens de l'Ecriture*. 2 volumes in 4. Etudes Lyon-Fourvière, Théologie, volumes 41, 42, and 59. Paris: Aubier, 1959-1964.

————— *Surnaturel: Etudes historiques*. Etudes Lyon-Fourvière, Théologie, vol. 8. Paris: Aubier, 1946.

Lutz, Cora E. "Martianus Capella." In *Catalogus Translationum et Commentariorum*, vol. 2, edited by P. O. Kristeller and F. Edward Cranz, pp. 267-381. Washington: Catholic University of America Press, 1971.

Maier, Anneliese. *An der Grenze von Scholastik und Wissenschaft*. 2d ed. Storia e letteratura, vol. 41. Rome Ed. Storia e letteratura, 1952.

Mailhiot, M.-D. "La pensée de saint Thomas sur le sens spirituel." *Revue thomiste* 59 (1959):613-663.

Mandonnet, Pierre. "Les opuscules de Saint Thomas d'Aquin." *Revue thomiste* NS 10 (1927): 121-157.

————— and Destrez, J., comp. *Bibliographie Thomiste*. BT, 1. Paris: J. Vrin, 1923. Revised edition with addenda by M.-D. Chenu. Paris: J. Vrin, 1960.

Manser, Gallus. *Das Naturrecht in thomistischer Beleuchtung*. Thomistische Studien, vol. 2. Fribourg: Paulusdruckerei, 1944.

Mansion, Augustin. "Dates de quelques commentaires de saint Thomas sur Aristote (*De Interpretatione*, *De Anima*, *Metaphysica*)." In *Studia Mediaevalia...R. J. Martin*, q.v., 271-287.

————— *Introduction à la physique aristotélicienne*. 2d ed. Louvain: Institut supérieur de philosophie, and Paris: J. Vrin, 1946.

Manthey, Franz. *Die Sprachphilosophie des hl. Thomas von Aquin und ihre Anwendung auf Probleme der Theologie*. Paderborn: Ferdinand Schöningh, 1937.

Maréchal, Joseph. *Le Point de départ de la métaphysique, Cahier 5: Le Thomisme devant la philosophie critique*. Museum Lessianum, Section philosophique, vol. 7. 2d ed. Brussells: Edition universelle, and Paris: Desclée de Brouwer, 1949.

Marenbon, John. *From the Circle of Alcuin to the School of Auxerre: Logic, Theology, and Philosophy in the Early Middle Ages*. Cambridge Studies in Medieval Thought and Life, 3rd series, vol. 15. Cambridge: Cambridge University Press, 1981.

Mariétan, Joseph. *Problème de la classification des sciences d'Aristotle à Saint Thomas*. St-Maurice (Switzerland): St-Augustin, and Paris: Félix Alcan, 1901.

Markus, R. A. "St. Augustine on Signs." *Phronesis* 2 (1957):60-83.

Maurer, Armand A. "A Neglected Thomistic Text on the Foundations of Mathematics." *Mediaeval Studies* 21 (1959):185-192.

McInerny, Ralph M. *The Logic of Analogy: An Introduction to St. Thomas*. The Hague: Martinus Nijhoff, 1961.

McKeon, Richard P. "Philosophy and Theology, History and Science in Bonaventure and Thomas Aquinas." *Journal of Religion* Supplement to 58 (1978):S24-S51.

———— "Rhetoric in the Middle Ages." *Speculum* 17 (1942):25-32.

Mélanges Mandonnet: Etudes d'histoire littéraire et doctrinale du moyen âge. BT, vols. 13-14. Paris: J. Vrin, 1930.

Mélanges Thomistes publiés par les Dominicains de la Province de France à l'occasion du VIème centenaire de la canonisation de saint Thomas (18 juillet 1323). BT, vol. 3. Kain (Belgium): Le Saulchoir/*Revue des sciences philosophiques et théologiques,* 1923.

Ménard, Etienne. *La tradition: Révélation, Ecriture, Eglise selon saint Thomas d'Aquin*. Studia, 18. Bruges and Paris: Desclée de Brouwer, 1964.

Merlan, Philip. "Abstraction and Metaphysics in St. Thomas' *Summa*." *Journal of the History of Ideas* 14 (1953):284-291. Reprinted in his *Kleine philosophische Schriften*, edited by Franciszka Merlan, pp. 488-497. Collectanea, vol. 20. Hildesheim: G. Olms, 1976..

Miethe, Terry L., and Bourke, Vernon L., comps. *Thomistic Bibliography, 1940-1978*. Westport, Conn.: Greenwood Press, 1980.

Minio-Paluello, Lorenzo. "Les traductions et les commentaires de Aristote de Boèce." *Texte und Untersuchungen zur*

Geschichte der altchristlichen Literatur 64 [= *Studia Patristicia*] (1957):358-365. Reprinted in his *Opuscula: The Latin Aristotle*. Amsterdam: Hakkert, 1972.

Mondin, Battista. "La logica di S. Tommaso d'Aquino." *Rivista di filosofia neo-scolastica* 60 (1968):261-271.

Moody, Ernest A. *Studies in Medieval Philosophy, Science, and Logic*. Berkeley: University of California Press, 1975.

Murphy, James. *Rhetoric in the Middle Ages: A History of Rhetorical Theory from St. Augustine to the Renaissance*. Berkeley: University of California Press, 1974.

Neumann, Siegfried. *Gegentstand und Methode der theoretischen Wissenschaften nach Thomas von Aquin auf Grund der Expositio super librum Boethii De Trinitate*. BGPhThM, vol. 41/2. Munster: Aschendorff: 1965.

Owens, Joseph. "Aquinas as Aristotelian Commentator." In *St. Thomas Aquinas, 1274-1974: Commemorative Studies*, vol. 1, pp. 218-238. Toronto: P. I. M. S., 1974.

———— "Metaphysical Separation in Aquinas." *Mediaeval Studies* 34 (1972):287-306.

Paetow, Louis J. *The Arts Course at Medieval Universities with Special Reference to Grammar and Rhetoric....* Champaign, Illinois, 1910. Reprinted from University Studies of the University of Illinois, vol. 3, no. 7.

Peghaire, Julien. *Intellectus et Ratio selon saint Thomas d'Aquin*. Publications de l'Institut d'études médiévales d'Ottawa, vol. 6. Paris: J. Vrin, and Ottawa: I. é. m., 1936.

Peillaube, E. "Avons-nous l'expérience du spirituel? [I and II]." *Revue de philosophie* 36 (1929):245-267 and 660-685.

Pelster, F. "Die älteren Biographen des hl. Thomas v. Aquin: Eine kritische Studie." *Zeitschrift für katholische Theologie* 44 (1920):244-274 and 366-397.

———— "Eine ungedruckte Quaestio des hl. Thomas von Aquin über die Erkenntnis der Wesenheit der Seele." *Gregorianum* 36 (1955):618-625.

Pieper, Josef. *Hinführung zu Thomas von Aquin: Zwölf Vorlesungen*. Munich: Kösel, 1958.

———— "Thomas von Aquin als Lehrer." In his *Weistum, Dichtung, Sakrament: Aufsätze und Notizien*, pp. 138-155. Munich: Kösel, 1954.

Pinborg, Jan. *Die Entwicklung der Sprachtheorie im Mittelalter*. BGPhThM, vol. 42/2. Munster: Aschendorff, and Copenhagen: Arne Frost-Hansen, 1967.

—— *Logik und Semantik im Mittelalter: Ein Uberblick*. Problemata, vol. 10. Stuttgart—Bad Cannstatt: Frommann-Holzboog, 1972.

Ponferrada, Gustavo Eloy. "Nota sobre los grados de abstracción." *Sapientia* [Buenos Aires] año 33/numero 130 (1978):267-284.

Pouchet, Robert. *La rectitudo chez Saint Anselme: Un itinéraire augustinien de l'âme à Dieu*. Paris: Etudes augustiniennes, 1964.

Prümmer, D., and Laurent, M.-H., eds. *Fontes Vitae Sancti Thomae Aquinatis*. Toulouse: [*Revue thomiste,* c1934]. A compilation of material originally published as supplements to the *Revue thomiste*, 1912-1934.

Rand, E. K. *Cicero in the Courtroom of St. Thomas Aquinas*. Aquinas Lecture, 1945. Milwaukee: Marquette University Press, 1946.

—— "The Classics in the Thirteenth Century." *Speculum* 4 (1929): 249-269.

Rashdall, Hastings. *The Universities of Europe in the Middle Ages*. Edited by F. M. Powicke and A. B. Emden. 3 vols. Oxford: Clarendon Press, 1936.

Régis, Louis-M. "Analyse et synthèse dans l'oeuvre de saint Thomas." In *Studia Mediaevalia...R. J. Martin*, q.v., pp. 304-330.

van Riet, Georges. *Thomistic Epistemology*. Translated by Gabriel Franks. St. Louis: B. Herder, 1963. Translation of *L'épistémologie thomiste: Recherches sur le problème de la connaissance dans l'école thomiste contemporaine*. Bibliothèque philosophique de Louvain, vol. 3. Louvain: Editions de l'Institut supérieur de philosophie, 1946.

de Rijk, Lambertus M. "Abelard's Semantic View in the Light of Later Developments." In *English Logic and Semantics from the End of the Twelfth Century...*, edited by H. A. G. Braakhuis, C. H. Kneepkens, and L. M. de Rijk, pp. 1-58. Artistarium Supplementa, vol. 1. Nijmegen: Ingenium, 1981.

Rimaud, Jean. *Thomisme et méthode: Que devrait être un discours de la méthode* pour avoir le droit de se dire thomiste?

Paris: Gabriel Beauchesne, 1925.

Riquet, Michel. "S. Thomas et les *auctoritates* en philosophie." *Archives de philosophie* 3 (1925):117-155.

Robert, J. D. "La métaphysique, science distincte de toute autre discipline philosophique, selon saint Thomas d'Aquin." *Divus Thomas* [Piacenza] 50 (1947):206-222.

Roland-Gosselin, M.-D. "Peut-on parler d'intuition intellectuelle dans la philosophie thomiste?" In *Philosophia Perennis: Abhandlungen zu ihrer Vergangenheit und Gegenwart* [Festgabe Josef Geyser], ed. Fritz-Joachim von Rintelen, vol. 2, pp. 709-730. Regensburg: Josef Habbel, 1930.

———— Review of Romeyer (1923). *Bulletin thomiste* 1/4 (1924):113-115.

———— Review of Romeyer (1926). *Bulletin thomiste* 6/2 (1929):469-474.

Romeyer, Blaise. "A propos de *Saint Thomas et notre connaissance de l'esprit humain.*" *Revue de philosophie* 36 (1929):551-573.

———— "La doctrine de Saint Thomas sur la vérité: Esquisse d'une synthèse." *Archives de philosophie* 3 (1925):[145]-[198] in the continuous pagination.

———— "Notre science de l'esprit humain d'après saint Thomas d'Aquin." *Archives de philosophie* 1 (1923):32-55.

———— "Saint Thomas et notre connaissance de l'esprit humain." *Archives de philosophie* 6 (1928):1-114. A revised edition was published under the same title and journal number in 1932, with pagination 1-114***.

Roos, Heinrich. *Die Modi Significandi des Martinus de Dacia.* BGPhThM, vol. 37/2. Munster: Aschendorff, and Copenhagen: Arne Frost-hansen, 1952.

———— "Die Stellung der Grammatik im Lehrbetrieb des 13. Jahrhunderts." In *Artes Liberales*, ed. Joseph Koch, q.v., pp. 94-106.

Ruane, John P. "Self Knowledge and the Spirituality of the Soul in St. Thomas." *The New Scholasticism* 32 (1958):425-442.

Rüppel, Ernst. *Unbekanntes Erkennen: Das Erfassen der Wirklichkeit nach dem hl. Thomas von Aquin.* Wurzburg: Konrad Triltsch, 1971.

Schipperges, Heinrich. *Die Assimilation der arabischen*

Medizin durch das lateinische Mittelalter. Sudhoffs Archiv, Beihefte, vol. 3. Wiesbaden: Franz Steiner, 1964.

Schmidt, Robert W. *The Domain of Logic according to St. Thomas Aquinas.* The Hague: M. Nijhoff, 1966.

―――― "L'emploi de la séparation en métaphysique." *Revue philosophique de Louvain* 58 (1968):373-393.

Seckler, Max. *Das Heil in der Geschichte: Geschichtstheologisches Denken bei Thomas von Aquin.* Munich: Kösel, 1964.

Silverstein, Theodore. "*Elementatum*: Its Appearance among Twelfth-Century Cosmologists." *Mediaeval Studies* 16 (1954):156-162.

―――― "Guillaume de Conches and the Elements: *Homoiomera* and *Organica.*" *Mediaeval Studies* 26 (1964):163-167.

Siraisi, Nancy G. *Arts and Sciences at Padua: The Studium of Padua before 1350.* Toronto: P. I. M. S., 1973.

Skarica Zuñiga, Mirko. "La *disputatio* en Tomás de Aquino, su validez para la *scientia.*" *Philosophica* 1 (1978):155-171.

Smalley, Beryl E. *The Gospels in the Schools c1100-c1280.* London and Ronceverte: Hambledon Press, 1985.

―――― *The Study of the Bible in the Middle Ages.* 2d ed. Oxford: Basil Blackwell, 1952.

Smith, Vincent Edward. *St. Thomas and the Object of Geometry.* Aquinas Lecture, 1953. Milwaukee: Marquette University Press, 1953.

Sorabji, Richard. *Necessity, Cause, and Blame: Perspectives on Aristotle's Theory.* Ithaca, New York: Cornell University Press, 1979.

Southern, R. W. "Lanfranc of Bec and Berengar of Tours." In *Studies presented to Frederick Maurice Powicke*, edited by R. W. Hunt, W. A. Patin, and R. W. Southern, pp. 27-48. Oxford: Clarendon Press, 1948.

Spicq, Ceslao. *Esquisse d'une histoire de l'exégèse latine au moyen âge.* BT, vol. 26. Paris: J. Vrin, 1944.

van Steenberghen, Fernand. "L'avenir du thomisme." *Revue philosophique de Louvain* 54 (1956):201-218. Reprinted in his *Introduction à l'étude de la philosophie médiévale*, pp. 240-256. Philosophes médiévaux, vol. 18. Louvain: Publications universitaires, and Paris: Béatrice—Nauwelaerts, 1966.

———— Letter. *Bulletin de philosophie médiévale* 24 (1982):76-77.

———— *Maître Siger de Brabant*. Louvain: Publications universitaires, and Paris: Vander-Oyez, 1977.

———— *La philosophie aux XIIIe siècle*. Louvain: Publications universitaires, and Paris: Béatrice-Nauwelaerts, 1966.

———— *Thomas Aquinas and Radical Aristotelianism*. Washington: Catholic University of America Press, 1980.

Studia Mediaevalia in honorem admodum Reverendi Patris Raymundi Josephi Martin, Ordinis Praedicatorum s. theologiae magistri LXXum natalem diem agentis. Bruges: De Tempel, 1948.

Synave, Paul. "La doctrine de saint Thomas d'Aquin sur le sens littéral des Ecritures." *Revue biblique*, January 1926, 40-65.

———— Review of articles by Ceuppens, Zarb, Breton, and De Ambroggi. *Bulletin thomiste* 10/1 (1933):711-718.

Thorndike, Lynn, and Kibre, Pearl, comps. *A Catalogue of Incipits of Medieval Scientific Writings in Latin*. Rev. ed. Mediaeval Academy of America Publications, no. 29. London: Mediaeval Academy of America, 1963.

Toccafondi, Eugenio Teodolfo. "Il pensiero di San Tommaso sulle arti liberali." In ALPMA, pp. 639-651.

Ullmann, Manfred. *Die Medizin im Islam*. Handbuch der Orientalistik 1/6/1. Leiden: E. J. Brill, 1970.

Van Ackeren, Gerald. *Sacra Doctrina: The Subject of the First Question of the Summa theologica of St. Thomas Aquinas*. Rome: Catholic Book Agency, 1952.

Vansteenkiste, Clemens. "Cicerone nell'opera di s. Tommaso." *Angelicum* 36 (1959):343-382.

———— Review of Wippel, "Metaphysics and *Separatio*." *Rassegna di letteratura tomistica* 14 (1981):127-128, no. 444.

Vicente, Lorenzo. "De modis abstractionis iuxta sanctum Thomam." *Divus Thomas* [Piacenza] 66 (1963):33-65 and 189-218; 67 (1964):278-299.

Vlastos, Gregory. "Reasons and Causes in the *Phaedo*." In *Plato*, edited by Vlastos, vol. 1, pp. 132-166. Garden City, New York: Doubleday, 1971.

Walgrave, J. H. "Zelfkennis en innerlijke Ervaring bij St Thomas." *Tijdschrift voor Philosophie* 9 (1947):3-62.

Wallace, William A. "Aquinas on the Temporal Relation between Cause." *Review of Metaphysics* 27 (1974):569-584.

——— Appendix 4 in *Summa theologiae*, vol. 10. London: Blackfriars, with Eyre & Spottiswoode, and New York: McGraw Hill, 1967.

——— *Causality and Scientific Explanation*. 2 vols. Ann Arbor: University of Michigan Press, 1972-1974.

——— *The Role of Demonstration in Moral Theology: A Study of Methodology in St. Thomas Aquinas*. Thomist Press Text and Studies, vol. 2. Washington: Thomist Press, 1963.

Walsh, J. "St. Thomas on Preaching." *Dominicana* 5 (1921): 6-14.

Walz, Angelus. *Saint Thomas d'Aquin*. Edited and translated by Paul Novarina. Louvain: Publications universitaires, and Paris: Béatrice— Nauwelaerts, 1962.

——— *San Tommaso d'Aquino: Studi biografici*. Rome: Edizioni Liturgiche, 1945.

Warnach, Viktor. "Das äussere Sprechen und seine Funktionen nach der Lehre des hl. Thomas von Aquin." *Divus Thomas* [Fribourg] 16 (1938):393-419.

Wéber, Edouard-H. *La controverse de 1270 à l'université de Paris et son retentissement sur la pensée de S. Thomas d'Aquin*. BT, vol. 40. Paris: J. Vrin, 1970.

——— "La négativité méthodique comme moment critique de l'épistémologie et du langage chez Albert le Grant et Thomas d'Aquin." In *Sprache und Erkenntnis*, ed. Beckmann *et al.*, q. v., vol. 2, pp. 746-752.

Wébert, J. "*Reflexio*: Etude sur les opérations réflexives dans la psychologie de saint Thomas d'Aquin." In *Mélanges Mandonnet*, q.v., vol. 1, pp. 287-325.

Weisheipl, James A. "Albert's Disclaimers in the Aristotelian Paraphrases." *Proceedings of the PMR Conference* 5 (1980): 1-27.

——— "Albert's Works on Natural Science (*libri naturales* in Probable Chronological Order." In *Albertus Magnus and the Sciences...*, edited by Weisheipl, Appendix 1, pp. 564-577. Toronto: P. I. M. S., 1980.

———— "Classifications of the Sciences in Mediaeval Thought." *Mediaeval Studies* 27 (1965):54-90.

———— "Curriculum of the Faculty of Arts at Oxford in the early Fourteenth Century." *Mediaeval Studies* 26 (1964):143-185.

———— *Friar Thomas d'Aquino: His Life, Thought, and Works.* Garden City, N.Y.: Doubleday, 1974. Reprinted with corrigenda and addenda, Washington: Catholic University of America Press, 1983.

———— "The Life and Works of St. Albert the Great." In *Albertus Magnus and the Sciences...*, edited by Weisheipl, pp. 13-51. Toronto: P. I. M. S., 1980.

———— "The Principle *Omne quod movetur ab alio movetur* in Medieval Physics." *Isis* 58 (1965):26-45.

———— "The Spect[er] of *Motor Coniunctus .*" In *Studi sul XIV secolo in memoria di Anneliese Maier*, edited by A. Maierù and A. Paravicini Bagliani, pp. 81-104. Storia e letteratura, vol. 151. Rome: Ed. Storia e letteratura, 1981.

———— *Thomas d'Aquino and Albert His Teacher.* Etienne Gilson Series, vol. 2. Toronto: P. I. M. S., 1980.

White, Victor. *Holy Teaching: The Idea of Theology according to St. Thomas Aquinas.* Aquinas Society of London, Aquinas Paper no. 33. London: Blackfriars, 1958.

Whittaker, John F. "The Position of Mathematics in the Hierarchy of Speculative Science." *The Thomist* 3 (1941):467-506.

Wieruszowski, Hélène. "Rhetoric and the Classics in Italian Education of the Thirteenth Century." *Studia Gratiana* 11 (1967):169-207.

Wilder, Alfred. "St. Albert and St. Thomas on Aristotle's *De intepretatione*: A Comparative Study." *Angelicum* 57 (1980):496-532.

Wippel, John F. "Commentary on Boethius's *De Trinitate*: Thomas Aquinas and Avicenna on the Relationship between First Philosophy and the Other Theoretical Sciences: A Note on Thomas's *Commentary on Boethius's De Trinitate*, q.5., a.1, ad 9m." *The Thomist* 37 (1973):133-154.

———— "Metaphysics and *Separatio* according to Thomas Aquinas." *Review of Metaphysics* 31 (1978):431-470.

———— "The Title *First Philosophy* according to Thomas

Aquinas and his Different Justifications for the Same." *Review of Metaphysics* 27 (1974):585-600.

Zimmermann, Albert. *Ontologie oder Metaphysik? Die Diskussion über den Gegenstand der Metaphysik im 13. und 14. Jahrhundert.* Studien und Texte, vol. 8. Leiden and Cologne: E. J. Brill, 1965.

LOCI THOMISTICI

The entries given here are for citations to Thomas's works in the notes (pp. 205-258 above). Each cited locus is followed by references to the pages and note numbers in which it is cited. Page numbers appear after the colon; they are joined to note numbers, which appear in parentheses. Thus '*a(b)*' means that the locus is cited on page *a* within note number *b*. An asterisk beside the note number—as in *b**—indicates that the reader should be careful to notice that there is more than one note with that number on the page. Thomas's works are listed in the alphabetical order of the established abbreviations.

Catena
for *John* c.1 n.1: 216(12)

Contra err.
proem: 254(16)

Contra gent.
I c.3 n.2: 255(1)(2)
I c.5: 256(10)
I c.5 nn.3-4: 256(3)
I c.9 n.2: 256(4)
I cc.16-27: 250(4)
I c.30: 223 (19)(20)
I c.30 n.3: 223(21)
I cc.30-32: 223(19)(20)
I cc.30-36: 223(20)
I c.32: 223(19)(20)(22)
I c.32 nn.2-3: 223(23)
I c.32 n.7: 223(23)
I c.37: 238(11)
I cc.37-102: 223(20), 251(2)
II c.4: 256(7)
II c.24 n.5: 254(8)
II cc.50-54: 250(25)
II c.59 n.9: 246(13)
II cc.63-64: 232(7)
II c.66 n.3: 246(12)
II c.68: 232(7)
II c.68 n.6: 240(11)
II c.75: 255(21)
II c.88: 238(11)
II c.95 n.4: 252(17)
III c.52: 238(11)
III cc.84-86: 232(19)
III c.90: 232(8)
III c.154 n.11: 241(6)
IV c.11: 217(28)

IV c.12: 217(28)
IV c.12 n.5: 217(29)
IV c.24: 238(11)
IV c.70 n.2: 221(38)

Contra impugn.
c.5 obj.4: 224(3)
c.5 resp: 224(4)(5)(11)
c.5 ad 3, ad 4: 224(11)

De ente
c.3 n.31: 223(10)
c.3 n.36: 223(10)
c.3 nn.43-44: 223(10)
c.3 n.48: 223(10)
c.4 nn.54-65: 223(15)

De fall.
prol: 229(47)
n.3: 222(61), 224(11)

De mixt.
223(13)(14)

De motu
234(26)

De regno
I c.1: 212(32)

De subst. sep.
253(8)(9)

In Job
c.6: 227(26)
c.7: 227(24)
c.9: 227(23)

c.13: 227(25)(27)
c.21: 227(29)
c.22: 227(30)
c.23: 227(30)
c.33: 227(31)
c.34: 227(28)
c.39: 227(32)

Post. Isaiam
prol: 225(37)

Post. Jeremiam
prol: 225(37)

Post. Threnos
prol: 225(37)
c.1 n.1: 224(11)

Quaeritur utrum anima
  coniuncta...
(ed. L. Kennedy)
240(20), 244(21)-(28)

Q.D. De anima
a.9 ad 10: 233(21)
a.16: 242(1)-(6)

Q.D. De malo
q.1 a.5: 222(60)
q.3 a.1: 221(38)
q.3 a.6: 221(39)

Q.D. De pot.
q.4 a.1: 215(41)(43)
q.7: 251(2*)(3*)
q.7 a.1: 251(4*)
q.7 a.5: 251(5*)-(8*)
q.7 a.5 ad 2: 251(9*)(10*)
q.7 a.5 ad 5: 251(10*)
q.7 a.10 ad 8: 222(63)

Q.D. De verit.
q.1 a.2: 241(22)
q.1 a.5: 223(18)
q.1 a.5 ad 5: 241(22)
q.1 a.9: 241(19)(23)

q.4 a.1: 217(21)(22)
q.4 a.1 ad 5: 217(23)
q.4 a.3: 217(24)
q.9 a.4: 214(20)(21)(24), 217(24)
q.9 a.4 obj.4-5: 214(16)
q.10 a.8: 243(8)(13)(18)(19)
q.10 a.9: 243(9), 244(33)(34)
q.11 a.1: 253(11), 255(13)
q.11 a.1 sc: 238(8)
q.11 a.1 ad 8: 255(14)
q.11 a.3: 255(15)
q.11 a.4: 255(16)
q.14 a.1: 229(38), 241(9)(10)
q.16 a.1: 246(23)
q.16 a.2: 246(25)
q.16 a.2 ad 1, ad 2: 246(26)
q.16 a.3: 246(27)
q.17 a.1 ad 15: 246(24)
q.17 a.2: 246(24)(25)
q.24 a.6: 221(36)

Q.D. De virt. comm.
q.1 a.7 ad 5: 222(60)
q.5 a.2 ad 6: 241(4)

Quodl.
I q.6 a.1: 217(26)
IV q.9 a.2: 223(17)
IV q.9 a.3: 226(19)(20)
VII q.6 a.1: 215(46), 217(25)
VII q.6 a.1 ad 5: 215(42)
VII q.6 a.2: 215(37)

Report. Inedit. Leon. (as in EB)
n.2 c.6 vs.9: 224(16)
n.3 c.13 vs.1: 217(27)

Resp. art. 36
a.9: 254(8)

Resp. art. 42
prol: 254(15)
a.33: 254(15)
a.39: 254(15)

Resp. art. 108
a.9: 238(19)

Sent. De caelo
proem n.2: 235(13)(14)
proem n.3: 235(15)(16)
proem n.4: 235(17)
proem n.5: 235(18)
I lect.22 n.8: 234(1)
II lect.4 n.3: 239(7)(8)
II lect.17 nn.2-5: 239(5)(6)
II lect.17 n.8: 239(7)

Sent. Ethic.
I lect.1 n.8: 254(8)
I lect.3 n.5: 224(9), 225(26), 246(16)-(19)
I lect.16 n.10: 224(15)
I lect.18 n.10: 224(14)
II lect.4 n.2: 221(39)
II lect.4 n.3: 254(8)
II lect.6 n.11: 221(38)
VI lect.3: 254(8)
VI lect.5-6: 255(10)
VI lect.7 n.17: 222(62), 234(27), 240(2*)(5)(6)
VII lect.7 n.14: 254(8)

Sent Pol.
I lect.1 n.8: 254(1)
I lect.1 n.24: 212(33)

Summa theol.
I q.1 a.2: 230(5), 256(17)
I q.1 a.3: 256(5)
I q.1 a.3 ad 2: 256(6)
I q.1 a.8 ad 2: 253(11)
I q.1 a.10: 215(33)-(35), (46)
I q.1 a.10 ad 3: 216(49)(50)
I q.2 a.1: 245(10)
I q.13 a.1: 251(11*)(12*)
I q.13 a.2: 251(13)
I q.13 a.5: 223(19)
I q.13 a.11: 251(14)
I q.14 a.2: 243(12)
I q.23 a.1 ad 4: 241(15)

I q.33 a.2 ad 4: 238(12)
I q.34 a.1: 216(1)
I q.39 a.8 ad 1: 222(63)
I q.41 a.1 ad 3: 222(63)
I q.62 a.6: 252(18)
I q.70 a.1 ad 3: 232(9)
I q.76 a.1: 243(11), 246(14)(15)
I q.83 a.1: 224(24)
I q.84 a.5: 243(15)
I q.85 a.2 ad 2: 248(1)
I q.87 a.1: 243(10)(14), 244(4)
I q.87 a.2: 241(24), 244(29)(30)
I q.87 a.2 ad 2: 244(31)
I q.87 a.2 ad 3: 244(32)
I q.87 a.3: 244(35)
I q.87 a.3 ad 1: 244(36)
I q.87 a.3 ad 2: 244(37)
I q.87 a.3 ad 3: 244(38)
I q.87 a.4: 244(39)
I q.87 a.4 ad 3: 244(40)
I q.88 a.1: 253(12)
I q.107 a.1: 214(22)
I q.107 a.1 ad 2: 214(23)
I q.108 a.1: 252(14)(15)
I q.108 a.1 ad 1: 252(16)
I q.115 a.1: 237(2)(3), 238(6)
I q.117 a.1: 255(18)(19)
I q.117 a.2: 255(20)
I-II q.7 a.2 obj.3: 224(20)
I-II q.7 a.3 ad 2: 224(21)
I-II q.9 a.5: 232(19)
I-II q.54 a.2: 238(12)
I-II q.56 a.3: 221(37), 222(60)
I-II q.57 a.3 ad 3: 229(46)
I-II q.57 a.4: 254(8)
I-II q.57 a.5 ad 1: 254(8)
I-II q.58 a.2 ad 1: 254(8)
I-II q.59 a.2: 232(6)
I-II q.90 a.1 ad 3: 244(2)
I-II q.91 a.1 ad 3: 244(5)
I-II q.91 a.2: 244(3)
I-II q.91 a.3: 244(2)
I-II q.91 a.3 ad 1: 245(7)
I-II q.91 a.4 ad 1: 245(8)
I-II q.91 a.5 ad 3: 245(8)
I-II q.92 a.2: 244(2)

I-II q.93 a.1 ad 2: 217(33)
I-II q.94 a.1: 221(39), 244(2)
I-II q.94 a.2: 245(12)-(15)
I-II q.94 a.3: 245(16)(17)
I-II q.94 a.4: 245(19)(20)
I-II q.97 a.1: 252(2)
I-II q.97 a.2: 252(2)
II-II prol: 254(8)
II-II q.1 a.4: 241(11)
II-II q.1 a.4 ad 3: 241(12)
II-II q.1 a.6: 224(19), 241(9)
II-II q.4 a.8 ad 2: 241(8)
II-II q.14 a.8: 241(13)
II-II q.18 a.4: 241(8)(14)
II-II q.48 a.uni: 224(6), 225(29)
II-II q.49 a.4 obj.3: 224(7)
II-II q.49 a.4 ad 3: 224(8)
II-II q.55 a.4 ad 2: 213(2)
II-II q.72 a.1: 213(2)
II-II q.76 a.1: 217(32)
II-II q.91 a.1: 217(31)
II-II q.134 a.1 obj.4: 254(8)
II-II q.171 a.5: 241(6)
II-II q.175 a.3: 256(22)(23)
II-II q.177 a.1 obj.1: 224(12)
II-II q.177 a.1 ad 1: 224(13)
III q.12 a.3 ad 2: 217(30)
III q.27 a.2: 252(3*)
III q.30 a.4: 224(18)
III q.31 a.6: 238(12)
III q.60 a.1 ad 1: 214(31)
III q.60 a.2: 214(29)(30)
III q.60 a.5: 214(27)
III q.60 a.5 ad 1: 214(28)
III q.60 a.6: 214(26)
III q.60 a.6 ad 1: 213(1)
III q.60 a.7: 214(27)
Suppl. q.65 a.3: 232(10)
Suppl. q.86 a.3 ad 3: 232(7)

Super Ave
a.2: 252(3*)

Super Coloss.
c.2 n.1: 224(2)

Super Credo
prol: 256(12)(13)(16)
a.1: 245(14)(15)

Super De anima
I lect.1 n.2: 225(31), 234(2)
I lect.1 n.4: 254(2)
I lect.1 n.6: 246(1)
I lect.1 n.9: 254(3)
I lect. 1 n.15: 225(28)
II lect.3 n.1: 246(7)
II lect.3 n.11: 246(8)
II lect.3 n.12: 246(8)(9)
II lect.3 nn.13-14: 246(8)
II lect.7 n.9: 238(9)
II lect.11 n.4: 222(57)
III lect.6 n.4: 238(9)
III lect.7 nn.7-13: 246(6)
III lect.9 n.5: 246(2)-(5)
III lect.11 nn.4-6: 223(18)
III lect.12: 248(1)
III lect.14 n.17: 238(9)

Super De caus.
proem (Pera 1, 3-4): 238(18)
proem (P 2):239(29)
proem (P 5): 238(18)(19)
proem (P 8): 222(62), 240(3)
proem (P 9): 238(17)
lect.1 (P 18): 234(27)
lect.1 (P 21): 238(20)
lect.1 (P 24): 238(21)
lect.1 (P 29): 238(21)
lect.1 (P 41-42): 238(23)
lect.2 (P 61): 241(11)
lect.3 (P 78): 238(25)
lect.6 (P 169): 239(35)
lect.6 (P 170): 238(24)
lect.6 (P 177): 239(31)
lect.9 (P 210): 239(30)
lect.9 (P 219): 239(26)
lect.9 (P 229): 239(34)
lect.12 (P 282): 239(27)(32)
lect.18 (P 340): 239(28)(33)
lect.18 (P 341-342): 239(33)

Super De gen.
proem n.1: 235(19)(20)
proem n.2: 235(21)

Super De hebd.
lect.2 n.22: 223(12)(13)
lect.2 n.23: 223(14)
lect.5 n.2: 222(56)

Super De Trin.
q.4 a.3 ad 6: 233(21)
q.5 a.1 obj.3: 217(3), 218(4)(6)(8)
q.5 a.1 obj.10: 240(2*)
q.5 a.1 corp: 230(1), 252(7)
q.5 a.1 ad 2: 240(2)
q.5 a.1 ad 4: 230(3)
q.5 a.1 ad 5: 230(3)(4)
q.5 a.1 ad 6: 230(2)
q.5 a.1 ad 9: 234(27), 251(5*)
q.5 a.1 ad 10: 240(2*)
q.5 a.3: 230(8)-(10), 248(1),
    249(14)-(18), 250(37)
q.5 a.4: 247(12)-(15), 249(19)-(22)
q.5 a.4 ad 5: 250(35)
q.6 a.1: 241(3)
q.6 a.1 qc.1: 230(11), 231(12)
q.6 a.1 qc.2: 231(15)
q.6 a.1 qc.3: 231(17)(19)
q.6 a.2: 250(38)-(42)
q.6 a.2 ad 5: 250(43)
q.6 a.4: 250(44)(45), 256(19)-(21)
q.6 a.4 ad 2: 250(46)
q.6 a.4 ad 3: 251(47), 252(20)
q.6 a.4 ad 5: 251(48)

Super Galat.
c.4 lect.7: 215(46)
c.4 lect.7 n.8: 215(38)

Super Hebreos
c.1 lect.1: 217(27)
c.11 lect.1: 241(4)

Super I Cor.
c.1 lect.1 n.3: 224(11)
c.2 lect.1: 225(26)

c.13 lect.1 n.1: 217(27)

Super II Tim.
c.2 lect.1: 224(16)
c.2 lect.2: (224(15)

Super Joh.
c.1 lect.1: 216(12)

Super Matt.
c.6 lect.3: 224(16)
c.11 lect.3: 217(27)

Super Meta.
proem: 247(19)-(22), 248(23)
I lect.1 nn.23-30: 254(5)
I lect.1 n.29: 254(4)
I lect.1 n.32: 254(6)
I lect.1 n.33: 218(11)
I lect.1 n.34: 254(7)(8)
I lect.2 nn.1-7: 248(24)
I lect.2 nn.8-14: 248(25)
I lect.3 n.17: 254(1)
I lect.4 n.4: 254(1)
II lect.1 n.16: 253(5)
III lect.2 n.8: 225(27)(28)
IV lect.1 n.1: 248(26)
IV lect.1 n.2: 248(27)
IV lect.1 n.4: 248(28)
IV lect.1 n.5: 234(2)
IV lect.1 n.7: 248(30)(31)
IV lect.1 n.8: 248(32)
IV lect.1 n.11: 248(33)
IV lect.1 n.12: 248(34)
IV lect.1 nn.12-15: 248(34)
IV lect.1 n.19: 22(59), 248(29)
IV lect.2 n.16: 218(7)
IV lect.3 n.1: 221(39)
IV lect.4 nn.3-4: 225(27)
V lect.2 n.1: 236(20)
V lect.2 n.4: 236(22)
V lect.2 n.9: 236(21)
V lect.2 n.11: 236(29)
V lect.2 n.12: 236(30)
V lect.2 n.14: 236(31)
V lect.3 n.2: 236(27)
V lect.3 n.6: 236(35)

II lect.5 n.1: 236(14)
II lect.5 n.2:236(15)(28)
II lect.5 nn.3-5: 236(20)
II lect.5 n.5: 236(22)
II lect.5 n.6: 236(17)(21)
II lect.5 n.7: 236(30)(31)
II lect.5 n.8: 236(17)(23)
II lect.5 n.9: 236(24)(32)
II lect.5 n.10: 236(26)(32)
II lect.6 nn.2-7: 237(37)
II lect.6 n.8: 237(38)
II lect.6 n.9: 237(42)
II lect.6 n.10: 237(43)
II lect.6 n.11: 237(44)
II lect.10 n.15: 238(7)
II lect.11 n.2: 237(4), 238(5)
II lect.12 n.1: 239(2)
II lect.14 n.2: 221(38)
II lect.14 n.8: 241(5)
III lect.4 n.6: 238(6)
III lect.8 n.1: 225(28)
VIII lect.2 nn.16-20: 254(22)
VIII lect.3: 253(11)
VIII lect.3 n.1: 254(15)
VIII lect.5 n.3: 224(23), 225(28)
VIII lect.12 n.5: 239(2)

Super Post An.
proem n.1: 229(33)
proem n.4: 229(35)
proem n.5: 229(36)
proem n.6: 229(39)(40)
I lect.1 nn.2-3: 227(1)
I lect.1 n.6: 225(29)
I lect.1 n.9: 224(25)
I lect.1 n.12: 224(15)
I lect.4: 222(58)
I lect.4 nn.2-3: 230(52)
I lect.4 nn.4-5: 230(51)
I lect.4 nn.10-16: 230(53)
I lect.6 n.5: 206(8)
I lect.7 n.6: 230(54)
I lect.7 n.8: 230(55)(56)
I lect.10-12: 236(12)
I lect.11 n.14: 236(13)
I lect.13 n.1: 229(41)

I lect.13 n.7: 225(30)
I lect.20 n.5: 229(43)
I lect.20 n.6: 225(29)
I lect.20 n.11: 230(58), 254(8)
I lect.20 nn.11-15: 255(10)
I lect.20 n.12: 230(59)

Super Sent.
prol: 240(7)
prol q.1 a.5: 215(37)
I d.2 q.1 a.1 obj.2: 238(10)
I d.4 q.1 a.2 ad 1: 222(63)
I d.9 q.1 a.1 obj.1: 217(2), 220(25)
I d.17 q.2 a.3 ad 4: 225(28)
I d.22 q.uni: 251(2*)
I d.22 q.uni a.2: 223(19)
I d.24 q.1 a.3: 250(38)
I d.27 q.2 a.1 obj.1: 217(2), 219(9)
I d.27 q.2 a.1 sc: 216(10)
I d.27 q.2 a.1 sol: 216(11), 217(15)
I d.28 q.1 a.1 ad 1: 250(38)
II d.9 q.uni a.1: 252(17)
II d.9 q.uni a.2 ad 4: 255(12)
II d.11 q.2 a.3 sol: 217(17)(18)
II d.14 q.1 a.2 sol: 254(15)
II d.14 q.1 a.2 ad 1: 254(15)
II d.14 q.1 a.2 ad 3: 238(10)
II d.15 q.2 a.2 ad 1: 232(7)
II d.17 q.2 a.2: 232(8)
II d.23 q.2 a.1 ad 3: 217(2), 220(28)
II d.24 q.2 a.3: 246(22)
II d.25 q.1 a.2 ad 5: 232(9)
II d.28 q.1 a.5 ad 3: 255(12)
II d.38 q.1 a.2 ad 6: 232(10)
III d.13 q.1 a.2: 238(10)
III d.23 q.1 sol.2 ad 3: 254(8)
III d.23 qq.2-3: 241(8)
III d.26 q.2 a.4: 241(8)
III d.33 q.1 a.1 qc.2 obj.3: 254(8)
III d.33 q.2 a.4 obj.3: 222(60)
III d.33 q.3 a.1 qc.4: 224(10)
IV d.15 q.3 a.1 qc.2 ad 3: 232(7)
IV d.15 q.4 a.3: 224(16)
IV d.15 q.4 a.3 ad 2: 224(16)
IV d

INDEX

The entries for proper names given here refer only to those mentioned in the body of the text. No entries are given for names appearing in the notes. Names of Latin authors have been put into English; names of Arabic authors are given in an English form derived from the Latin. The only entries given for Thomas Aquinas concern biographical details. Discussions of his doctrines can be found under the appropriate topic; citations of his works are listed above in the table of *loci Thomistici*.

Abelard. *See* Peter Abelard
Abstraction: and knowledge of self, 126-128, 130; and *separatio*, 79-80, 156-163. *See also* Metaphysics; Psychology
Accessus, 10, 60, 93
Adam Balsamiensis Parvipontanus, 68-69
Adelard of Bath, 88
Albert the Great, 8, 90, 149-150
Albumasar, 89
Alcuin, 62
Alexander of Aphrodisias, 95, 144
Alexander of Villa-Dei, 49
Alfarabi, 48, 70
Alfred of Sareshel, 90-91
Algazel, 89
Allard, Guy, 60-61
Ambrose, 56
Ammonius, 9-10, 14, 18, 20
Anaxagoras, 142
Andronicus of Rhodes, 9
Angels: speech of, 22-24
Anselm of Canterbury, 52, 122-123
Aristotle, xiii, 3, 4-9, 22, 42-43, 48, 58-61, 63, 77-79, 88-90, 93-94, 104-106, 115, 117, 128-130, 149-150, 159, 164, 170-172, 184, 186-194, 197; *Analytica posteriora*, 68, 70-77, 100, 104; *Analytica priora*, 11, 72-73; *Categoriae*, 11, 68, 71; *De anima*, 9, 14, 60, 90, 94, 116, 142-144, 191; *De caelo*, 93-97, 112; *De generatione*, 93, 96-97; *Ethica Nicomachaea*, 9, 74, 115, 146, 192; *Metaphysica*, 99-103, 151-154, 160, 186, 190, 191-194; *Meteorologica*, 93,

96-97, 107; *Peri hermeneias*, 9-15, 18-20, 51-53, 68, 71, 167, 190; *Physica*, 90, 92-100, 103-104, 106-107, 110, 140, 149, 190; *Poetica*, 9, 70; *Politica*, 9, 16; *Rhetorica*, 9, 60, 70; *Sophistici elenchi*, 68, 70, 73; *Topica*, 68, 70, 72, 74, 189
Ars, 191-192
Astronomy: hypotheses in, 111-113
Augustine, 20-21, 23, 28, 32-34, 47, 89, 122-123, 125, 127, 129-130, 133, 142; *De doctrina Christiana*, 21-22, 24-25, 28, 29
Aulus Gellius, 88-89
Authorship: in philosophy, 183-185
Averroes, 8, 42, 90, 93-94, 144, 149, 183-184
Avicebron, 106
Avicenna, 6, 102, 122, 144, 149-150, 173-174

Blanche, Albert, 28
Boethius, 5-6, 8-10, 12-13, 17, 19, 68, 70, 137, 148; *De Trinitate*, 42, 77, 79-80, 91, 115, 150, 156, 171, 177
Boethius of Dacia, 52, 184
Boyer, Charles, 121
Bursill-Hall, Geoffrey L., 45

Callus, D. A., 89
Cajetan, Thomas de Vio Cardinal, 157
Caplan, Harry, 62
Cassiodorus, 47
Causes: division of, 100-104; final,

293